MANUAL OF THERAPEUTICS FOR ADDICTIONS

MANUAL OF THERAPEUTICS FOR ADDICTIONS

Edited by

NORMAN S. MILLER
MARK S. GOLD
and
DAVID E. SMITH

 **WILEY-LISS**

A JOHN WILEY & SONS, INC., PUBLICATION

New York Chichester Weinheim Brisbane Singapore Toronto

MT

Address All Inquiries to the Publisher
Wiley-Liss, Inc., 605 Third Ave, New York, NY 10158-0012

Copyright © 1997 Wiley-Liss, Inc.

Printed in the United States of America

While the authors, editors, and publisher believe that drug selection and dosage and the specifications and usage of equipment and devices, as set forth in this book, are in accord with current recommendations and practice at the time of publication, they accept no legal responsibility for any errors or omissions, and make no warranty, express or implied, with repect to material contained herein. In view of ongoing research, equipment modifications, changes in governmental regulations and the constant flow of information relating to drug therapy, drug reactions and the use of equipment and devices, the reader is urged to review and evaluate the information provided in the package insert or instructions for each drug, piece of equipment or device for, among other things, any changes in the instructions or indications of dosage or usage and for added warnings and precautions.

Library of Congress Cataloging-in-Publication Data

Manual of therapeutics for addictions / [edited by] Norman S. Miller.
     p.   cm.
     Includes index.
     ISBN 0-471-56176-2 (paper : alk. paper)
     1. Substance abuse—Treatment.   I. Miller, Norman S.
     [DNLM: 1. Substance Dependence—therapy.   2. Behavior, Addictive
—therapy.   WM 270 M2939 1997]
     RC564.M27   1997
     616.86'06—dc20
     DNLM/DLC
     for Library of Congress   96-30946

The text of this book is printed on acid-free paper.

10   9   8   7   6   5   4   3

4|3|06

CONTENTS

PART II
Pharmacologic Treatment of Intoxication and Withdrawal

PART ▌▌▌
Treatment in Specific Populations

PART **IV**
Treatment Practices

PART **V**
Special Topics

CHAPTER 24 Forensic and Ethical Issues   **325**
Amin N. Daghestani, M.D.

Index   **337**

PREFACE

We have created this *Manual* to assist the clinician in the diagnosis and treatment of the addictive disorders. We have attempted to provide the principles common to the practice of Addiction Medicine in a concise and useful format. The emphasis is on the clinical presentations of addictive disease and on effective treatment. We have targeted the *Manual* for the physician who sees vast numbers of addicted patients in a variety of clinical settings. However, other professionals responsible for the care of the addicted patient can benefit from chapters in the *Manual*.

Manual of Therapeutics for Addictions is divided into Sections for easy reference to specific clinical problems.

Section I: Assessment and Diagnosis of Intoxication and Withdrawal in Addictive Disorders. Alcohol, Marijuana, Cocaine, etc.

Section II: Pharmacological Treatment of Intoxication and Withdrawal. Alcohol, Opiates, etc.

Section III: Treatment in Specific Populations. Medical, Psychiatric, Surgical, etc.

Section IV: Treatment Practices. General Principles, Treatment Efficacy, etc.

Section V: Special Topics. Managed Care, Forensic Issues, etc.

We hope that house officers and busy clinicians will use the *Manual* to look up common ways to solve common clinical cases, and specialists to investigate solutions to difficult clinical problems. Most clinicians cannot avoid being confronted with addicted patients. As many as 50% of general medicine populations and 75% of general psychiatric populations contain patients with addictive disorders. Enthusiasm for treating addictive disorders can result from developing and possessing knowledge and skill in their diagnosis and treatment, especially when patients are followed into their recovery.

The diagnosis and treatment of addictive disorders have become standard components of medical practice. The *Manual* can be an important aid in meeting standards in primary care and specialized practices by physicians and other addiction and mental health care specialists. We dedicate this book to those who have labored away and formed the bedrock of Addiction Medicine.

NORMAN S. MILLER, M.D.
MARK S. GOLD, M.D.
DAVID E. SMITH, M.D.

PART I

ASSESSMENT AND DIAGNOSIS OF INTOXICATION AND WITHDRAWAL IN ADDICTIVE DISORDERS

CHAPTER 1

ASSESSMENT AND DIAGNOSIS IN ADDICTIVE DISORDERS

Norman S. Miller, M.D.,
University of Illinois at Chicago, Chicago, Illinois

Mark S. Gold, M.D.,
University of Florida Brain Institute, Gainesville, Florida

David E. Smith, M.D.
Haight Ashbury Free Clinics, San Francisco, California

I. INTRODUCTION: GENERAL PRINCIPLES OF DIAGNOSIS

A. Prevalence. The prevalence rate for alcoholism in the general population in the United States is 16% (28% in males and 8% in females) and for drug addiction, it is 8% (19% in males and 5% in females). The addictive use of alcohol in combination with other drugs such as cannabis, cocaine, and opiates is common (30–84%). Careful assessment of the patient and collateral sources through history, physical, and psychiatric examinations is standard practice for evaluation of alcohol and drug disorders in patients from most clinical settings. Drug testing on urine and blood and use of a Breathalyzer have become routine as a standard of practice, and as important methods to correctly identify the role of alcohol and drugs in clinical practice.

B. Diagnosis. More people are using alcohol and illicit drugs in recent decades than previously. The medical and psychosocial consequences associated with drug and alcohol use have become larger and more pervasive. The age range of those affected has widened as drug and alcohol problems associated with children and the elderly, in addition to middle-aged people, has become increasingly common.

Social strata, ethnicity, and occupational and financial status provide no barriers to the onset and complications from drug and alcohol addiction. Some studies indicate that 25–50% of patients in a typical primary-care setting will have significant medical and psychosocial consequences from alcohol use. These consequences are increased if additional and other drug problems are included. It is imperative that physicians and other professionals be skilled at the diagnosis and treatment of the conditions that are associated with drug and alcohol use, as well as the diagnosis and treatment of the drug and alcohol addictive illness itself.

The diagnosis of an addiction to alcohol should be suspected if the presence of a medical or major life problem related to alcohol or drug use is detected. The diagnosis can be confirmed by identifying the essential features

Manual of Therapeutics for Addictions, Edited by Norman S. Miller, Mark S. Gold, and David E. Smith.
ISBN 0471-56176-2 © 1997 John Wiley & Sons, Inc.

of addictive use. The behaviors of addiction are a reliable and consistent means of diagnosis of drug and alcohol addiction: (1) a preoccupation with the acquisition, (2) a compulsive use, and (3) relapse to alcohol and drug use. Addictive behaviors are the most sensitive indicators that alcohol and drugs are a persistent problem of central importance.

C. Treatment. Clinical practice and outcome studies confirm that effective treatment for alcohol and drug addiction is available. With proper diagnosis, intervention, and treatment, abstinence rates of 50–90% can be achieved on a long-term basis in recovery from drug and alcohol addiction. A biopsychosocial approach to addiction treatment including various modalities of treatment is indicated for the types and severity of drug and alcohol addiction. The treatment methods include detoxification, cognitive-behavior techniques, group and individual therapies, attendance in 12-step programs such as Alcoholics Anonymous, and treatment of medical, surgical, and psychiatric comorbidities.

II. GENERAL APPROACH TO DIAGNOSIS

A. DSM-IV (*Diagnostic and Statistical Manual of Mental Disorders*)

1. Addiction, tolerance, and dependence. The criteria for substance-related disorders in *DSM-IV* represent the manifestations of addictive use of alcohol / drugs (behavioral criteria 3–7) in addition to tolerance and dependence (pharmacologic criteria 1 and 2). (See *DSM-IV*.)

a. Definition of addiction

1. Preoccupation with acquiring alcohol and drugs.
2. Compulsive use (continued use despite adverse consequences from alcohol and drugs).
3. A pattern of relapse to alcohol and drugs over time despite the reinstitution of adverse consequences.

b. Definition of pharmacologic tolerance

1. Adaptation or loss of an effect with repeated use or the need to increase the dose to achieve the same effects.

c. Definition of pharmacological dependence

1. Deadaptation or the onset of predictable signs and symptoms of withdrawal on cessation of use or decreasing dose. The withdrawal syndrome is aborted or suppressed with resumption of adequate doses of the drug.

Addiction is drug seeking and can occur independently of tolerance and dependence, such as return to use of alcohol or drugs after a period of abstinence beyond the withdrawal period. Tolerance and dependence can occur without clinically observable signs of addiction, including medications to which tolerance of pharmacologic effects develops, and the onset of withdrawal without a return or relapse to the use of the medication ensues following discontinuation.

It is important to differentiate drug seeking in addictive use (biological drive) from the distress of withdrawal (physiological deadaptation); whereas the former is the active pursuit of specific drug effects, the latter is the desire for relief of withdrawal symptoms. Drug or alcohol withdrawal is often short-lived (hours to days) and successfully treated with short-term substitution drug therapy or none at all. Treatment of addiction requires specific interventions to suppress the continual desire for drug effects (beyond the withdrawal period) that results in loss of control and endures indefinitely over the life of the alcohol- or drug-addicted individual.

2. Abuse and dependence. The terms *abuse* and *dependence* as used in *DSM-IV* are misleading and nonmedical. *Abuse* is a pejorative term that implies voluntary unethical conduct and does not connote a disease state as in addictive diseases. *Dependence* is a pharmacologic term that describes withdrawal, is not specific for addiction, and is also a pejorative term that implies characterologic or moralistic reliance on drugs. The term *addictive* is the proper term that reflects a behavioral state of *loss of control* over the use of alcohol or drugs that is generated by biological drives set up by alcohol and drugs. Nonetheless, it is suggested that the terms *abuse* and *dependence* be used when compliance with *DSM-IV* nomenclature is indicated, until they are replaced by more medically exacting terminology.

B. Clinical Diagnosis

1. Historical considerations. The diagnostic features of alcohol addiction have many parallels to the diagnosis of syphilis in the prepenicillin era. Before penicillin prevented the secondary and tertiary stages, syphilis was considered the great masquerader because it mimicked many other diseases. Manifestations of the spectrum of the disease of syphilis were confused with a variety of other medical and psychiatric disorders. The diagnosis often was overlooked if the suspicion of syphilis was not adequately high or avoided because of its moral implications. The long course, the wide systemic and neurologic involvement, inadequate serologic testing, and social stigmata associated with syphilis obscured and distracted its accurate diagnosis. Fortunately, because of early detection and adequate treatment, the many masks of syphilis are no longer seen as often.

Drug or alcohol addiction provides many and varied expressions of medical and psychiatric consequences, as well as moral implications. If the presence of drug and alcohol use and their significance are not recognized, the diagnosis and treatment of addiction will be obscured and the addictive disease will continue unabated.

2. Denial. Denial (minimization and rationalization) is important to the propagation of the drug and alcohol addiction. The denial is present not only in the addict (toward self and others) but also in those associated with the addict. Inherent in addictive illness is the resistance by the addict and those affected by the addict to consider that drugs and alcohol can be problematic for the individual. Treatment of the alcohol or drug addiction often provides a solution to the related medical and personal adverse consequences produced by their addictive use.

C. Diagnostic Screens

1. MAST and DAST. The Michigan Alcohol Screening Test (MAST) is a validated and widely used screening instrument to assess for alcohol and drug use and a presumptive diagnosis of alcoholism. The Drug Abuse Screening Test (DAST) was validated as a screening instrument to assess drug use and a presumptive diagnosis of drug addiction. Both MAST and DAST can be self-administered by the patient and are available in standard-length, short, and brief forms.

2. CAGE ("cut down–annoyed–guilty–eye-opener" strategy) and DAGE. These brief screening instruments are also self-administered by the patients, and are widely used to objectively assess alcohol and drug disorders.

3. Others. The SCID is a structured interview for a *DSM-IV* diagnosis, and is not commonly used in clinical practice; rather, it is used as a research instrument.

D. Other Drugs and Medications. Studies indicate that 80% of alcoholics under the age of 30 years use at least one other drug regularly and addictively. The propensity to freely exchange one drug for another, or to use them simultaneously in an addictive way, is common. The use of alcohol by the drug addict is also common as 50–75% of heroin addicts, 80% of cocaine addicts, and 40% of cannabis addicts are addicted to alcohol.

In obtaining a history of alcohol intake and related consequences, a careful screen for other drugs is mandatory or vice versa, alcohol use in a history of drug intake. The vulnerability for abuse and addiction to alcohol and drugs appears to extend to a significant number of other drugs, suggesting a generalized susceptibility to addiction of chemicals possessed by alcoholics and drug addicts.

Because drug-seeking behavior appears to be common in alcoholics and drug addicts, careful, judicious, and sparing use of any medications should be exercised. Drug-seeking behavior for any drug or medication should be met with scrutiny, and may require confrontation of the motivations behind medication requests and demands. Common illicit drugs and prescription medications used regularly by alcoholics include marijuana, cocaine, opiates, phencyclidine, hallucinogens, benzodiazepines, barbiturates, and anticholinergics.

E. Medical Comorbidity

1. Medical populations. Addictive disorders are commonly found among those patients with medical disorders. Addictive disorders also commonly lead to acute and chronic medical complications. Proper diagnosis and treatment of medical comorbidities are fundamental to the overall approach to addictive disorders. Studies indicated that 25–50% of patients (and higher in selected medical populations) who see a physician for a medical reason have an alcohol and/or drug diagnosis. Assessment and diagnosis of addictive illness are essential to proper management of the associated medical complications and other medical disorders. Specific medical treatments, interventions, and referral for addiction treatment are important in reducing medical morbidity and mortality associated with addictive illnesses.

2. Selected medical comorbidities

a. Gastrointestinal symptoms. Gastrointestinal disturbances occur commonly in alcohol use. The diagnosis of esophagitis (heartburn) and peptic ulcer disease are suggestive of regular alcohol consumption. Also, vague abdominal discomfort, diarrhea, constipation, positive guaiac stools, and gastric cancer are associated with acute and chronic alcohol use.

b. Hypertension. Hypertension and tachycardia are common sequelae of alcohol ingestion (withdrawal state). The hypertension and tachycardia are normal physiological responses by the sympathetic nervous system to the alcohol withdrawal that can follow a single episode of consumption or dose of alcohol. An individual who consumes alcohol (1 oz) will have elevated blood pressure over baseline in the acute withdrawal period. An elevation in the first 24–72 h of 20–30 mmHg in systolic blood pressure and 10–20 mmHg in diastolic blood pressure over that of baseline is typical for mild to moderate alcohol withdrawal. The blood pressure often reverts to normal or lower in abstinent state without specific therapy in the initial withdrawal period. The elevation in blood pressure may be sustained for weeks after chronic alcohol use. Individuals with hypertension should be screened for alcohol use before one makes the diagnosis of essential hypertension and prescribes potentially unnecessary antihypertensive drug therapy.

c. Heart disease. Alcohol-induced cardiomyopathy, atrial fibrillation, and other cardiac arrythmias can follow chronic alcohol use. Accurate alcohol histories obtained from individuals with cardiomyopathy indicate that alcohol is frequently the etiology.

Congestive heart failure from any etiology may be precipitated or aggravated by a combination of the toxic effects of alcohol on the heart and the hypertension and tachycardia induced by stimulation of the sympathetic nervous system in response to alcohol ingestion (withdrawal).

d. Liver disease. Laënnec's cirrhosis of the liver occurs in about 5–10% of all alcoholics. Because of its relatively uncommon occurrence, cirrhosis is not a particularly useful diagnostic finding. Transient elevations of liver enzymes such as alkaline phosphatase, SGOT (serum glutamic–oxaloacetic transaminase), and GGTP (gamma-glutamyl transpeptidase) can be useful, if present, to indicate recent alcohol use. These enzyme markers usually return to normal within days to weeks after cessation of alcohol consumption.

e. Hematological manifestations. An elevated mean corpuscular volume (MCV) of the peripheral blood erythrocytes often indicates regular alcohol use or a folate or vitamin B_{12}-deficient state that is commonly found in alcoholics. Also, alcohol use can lead to suppression of bone marrow to produce a pancytopenia, including a thrombocytopenia. These hematologic deficiencies frequently revert to normal over weeks to months after cessation of alcohol use.

f. Endocrine disease. Other medical conditions that are caused, or significantly aggravated, by regular alcohol use include glucose intolerance or diabetes mellitus. Management of diet and weight control is made difficult because of chronic alcohol use in which there is poor compliance with diet. Ethanol is used for an energy source in preference to other food sources. The direct toxic effects of alcohol may produce chronic pancreatitis with insulin deficiency and subsequent glucose intolerance.

g. Cancer. Cancers, including carcinomas of the oral pharynx and gastrointestinal tract (esophagus, stomach, and liver) have been associated with chronic alcohol use. Because alcoholics frequently smoke cigarettes (80%), lung cancer also is common among alcoholics (27% of smokers are alcoholics).

h. Respiratory disease. Alcoholics frequently have chronic pulmonary problems because of associated cigarette smoking and suppression by alcohol of the immune system. Chronic obstructive pulmonary disease, such as chronic bronchitis and emphysema occur commonly in alcoholics who use cigarettes. Regular drinkers who smoke often have a productive, irritative, sometimes nauseating cough in the morning. Pneumonia, particularly *Streptococcus pneumoniae* and *Klebsiella pneumoniae,* and tuberculosis show a predilection for alcoholics.

i. Skin manifestations. An array of skin abnormalities may be present on the physical examination of the alcoholic. These may include cigarette burns, decrease in hair, gynecomastia, increased flushing or vascularity of the face, livedo reticularis (reddish-blue mottling), multiple contusions, abrasions and cuts in various stages of healing, nicotine stains in fingers, palmar erythema, rhinophyma, poor personal hygiene, spider angiomas, and unexplained edema.

3. Selected neurologic comorbidities. Neurologic complications such as dementia syndrome, amnestic state (blackouts), Wienicke's encephalopathy, seizures, hallucinosis, and peripheral neuropathy are relatively common in chronic alcohol consumption. Cognitive impairment, as indicated by a reduction in intellectual function in areas of concentration, memory, and abstraction abilities, is a frequent accompaniment of regular alcohol use. As little as 2 oz per day of 80-proof whiskey can result in measurable cognitive deficits that often are reversible with complete abstinence from alcohol. Depressed IQ scores in the areas of concentration, memory, and abstractions measured in alcoholics continue to show improvement as long as 2 years following cessation of alcohol consumption and maintenance of abstinence.

F. Surgical Comorbidity

1. Surgical populations. Addictive disorders are commonly found among patients with surgical disorders. Addictive disorders also lead to surgical complications and aggravate surgical problems. Traumatic injury and other surgical complications that are particularly prevalent in addicted surgical patients can be prevented.

2. Selected surgical comorbidities

a. Trauma. Trauma frequently is associated with alcohol use. Visible evidence of trauma such as bruises, new and old wounds, and fractures seen on examination are indications of intoxication. The intoxicated state that affects mental judgment and motor coordination lends itself to vulnerability to accidental trauma. Also, a toxic effect of alcohol suppresses certain clotting factors, thus increasing susceptibility to bruising and bleeding. Accidents are a leading cause of death at any age. Alcohol and drugs often play a prominent role in accidents. At least 50% of all highway fatalities are related to alcohol use, and accidents are a leading cause of death among adolescents.

G. Psychiatric Comorbidity

1. Psychiatric populations. Addictive disorders are commonly found among populations of other psychiatric disorders (50% prevalence rates). Psychiatric disorders that commonly coexist with addictive disorders are schizophrenia (80%), personality disorders (80%), and bipolar (manic–depressive) disorders (30%). On the other hand, the prevalence rates for comorbid psychiatric disorders among populations of addictive disorders are not particularly elevated above those rates found in the general population.

2. Alcohol/drug-induced psychiatric comorbidities

a. Exclusionary criteria. Exclusionary criteria are prominent among the psychiatric diagnoses in *DSM-IV*. These criteria require exclusion of the psychiatric symptoms induced by alcohol or drugs before an independent psychiatric diagnosis can be made; for instance, a drug-induced depression will resolve with abstinence. Many psychiatric diagnoses include exclusionary criteria, such as depressive, anxiety, and psychotic disorders. (See *DSM-IV*.)

3. Selected psychiatric complications. Alcohol and drugs produce subtle and overt psychiatric symptoms. If alcohol or drug use is not detected by a medical history, psychiatric examination, or laboratory investigation, the psychiatric symptoms can be attributed to causes other than alcohol and drugs. The manifestations of psychiatric symptoms induced by alcohol and drugs can be indistinguishable from and identical to those produced by nonalcohol/drug etiologies.

a. Depression. A common symptom induced by drugs and alcohol is depression. Depression that is secondarily induced by alcohol can be severe and associated with high suicide rates. The full spectrum of disturbances in mood, affect, cognition, and neurovegetative signs can be attributed to drug and alcohol use. Alcoholism and drug addiction represent the second most important risk factor in suicide, next to age.

Depression induced by alcohol and drugs includes the same subjective symptoms and objective signs as those required for the diagnosis of a major depression (affective disorder). Subjective complaints include sadness, dysphoria, profound hopelessness, a sense of worthlessness, and self-blame that, at times, can be of delusional proportions. Use of alcohol and drugs tends to induce poor control of emotions, tearfulness, crying spells, lethargy, poor initiative, lack of energy, and general mental and spiritual demoralization similar to the syndromes of diffuse brain disturbance from any etiology. Objective signs include a depressed affect, psychomotor retardation, and disturbance in appetite and sleep. The initial treatment of depression induced by alcohol and drugs is removal of and abstention from the primary etiologic agents: alcohol and drugs.

No studies actually support the popularly held notion that alcohol or drug use occurs *because* of the symptom of depression. Initially depressed individuals tend to consume less alcohol or do not show a consistent pattern of drinking in the presence of depression. An alcoholic continues to drink despite the alcohol-induced depression for reasons attributable to addictive drinking. The exclusionary criteria in *DSM-IV* require consideration of an alcohol- or drug-induced depression before a diagnosis of depression from another course can be made.

b. Anxiety. Anxiety and agitation are clinically useful indicators of frequent or excessive alcohol use and withdrawal. Anxiety and agitation are produced by the discharge of the autonomic nervous system (largely through the contribution of the sympathetic discharge) that is excited during alcohol withdrawal. Anxiety symptoms include apprehension, tension, diaphoresis, tremors, overreactivity to internal and external stimuli, and excessive responses to stress. Anxiety may range from a subtle, mild, and pervasive to a strikingly agitated state, as in delirium tremens, which is an extreme manifestation of anxiety in alcohol withdrawal. A decline in the blood alcohol level triggers the firing of the sympathetic nervous system to produce the onset of withdrawal symptoms. The blood alcohol level cannot be practically maintained at a steady state beyond hours, especially in the presence of the development of tolerance to alcohol.

c. Sexual problems. Sexual dysfunction and various forms of impotency are commonly associated with alcohol and drug use. Complaints in the area of sexual performance require the physician to investigate the history for alcohol and drug use. Decreased desire (libido) regularly occurs in men and women who frequently consume alcohol and drugs. Paradoxically, alcohol can also induce uninhibited, aggressive sexual behavior that may be offensive and even dangerous. More subtly, alcohol use may dull the emotions and impair the ability to experience the intimacy required for mutual satisfaction in sexual performance.

Excessive sympathetic discharge during alcohol withdrawal may lead to failure to maintain an erection and/or premature ejaculation in men. Alcohol intoxication produces difficulty in achieving and maintaining an erection and experiencing ejaculation in men and absence of orgasm in women. In males, chronic, persistent alcohol intake may result in testicular atrophy and subsequent feminization by unopposed estrogen effects.

d. Personality. Personality disturbances that result from alcohol and drug addiction are common. Hysterical, narcissistic, asocial, and antisocial attitudes and behaviors often are evident in those addicted individuals who might not ordinarily manifest them in an abstinent or treated state. Alcoholics and drug addicts become attention-seeking, self-seeking, demanding, aggressive, emotionally labile, and immature. They blame others for their problems. The defense mechanisms of denial and projection that are operative in addiction extend to other facets of the addict's life. A refusal to admit and accept responsibility for one's actions and the attribution of one's faults to others are consistent characteristics of the addict.

A large variety of personalities are represented among alcoholics and drug addicts before the onset of addiction. No specific type of personality appears to predispose to the development of drug and alcohol addiction.

III. GENERAL OBJECTIVES IN TREATMENT

A. Interventions. Treatment interventions begin with proper assessment, diagnosis, and referral to specific addiction treatment strategies. Physicians have an opportunity to intervene at all stages in the course of addictive illness. Patients with addictive illness can present to physicians early, mid, and late stages of complications from addictive diseases. Each stage can be characterized by severity of the addictive illness and by types and severity of medical and psychiatric comorbidities.

B. Detoxification. Pharmacologic therapies are indicated to increase compliance and retention with other forms of addiction treatment and prevent life-threatening withdrawal complications from addictive disorders such as seizures and delirium tremens. While detoxification is an essential process in the initial stages of engagement in treatment, many alcoholics and drug addicts experience a medically benign course of withdrawal. Detoxification without pharmacologic therapies is possible in a large number of cases of patients in alcohol and drug withdrawal. Social detoxification is behavioral support and monitoring of withdrawal without pharmacologic interventions unless medically indicated.

C. Treatment. The hallmark of addictive disorders is that they readily respond to effective treatment interventions. Abstinence is the goal in treatment and recovery. Short- and long-term abstinence can be achieved with the use of proper treatment methods. Standard treatment practices have indicated that abstinence-based treatment methods are effective in inducing and maintaining abstinence from alcohol and drugs. The abstinence-based method is used to treat the disease of alcohol or drug addiction and utilizes cognitive behavioral techniques, and referral to 12-step recovery programs, such as Alcoholics Anonymous (AA) and Narcotics Anonymous (NA).

D. Effectiveness. Abstinence rates of 60% at one year can be achieved following an inpatient or outpatient abstinence-based treatment program. One year abstinence rates can be increased to 80% with active participation (weekly attendance) in a 12-step recovery program, such as the Alcoholics Anonymous program, or participation in continuing care (weekly attendance) in a treatment program.

According to survey results (1992) conducted by Alcoholics Anonymous, recovery rates achieved in the AA fellowship were

1. Of those sober in AA less than a year, 41% will remain in the AA fellowship another year.
2. Of those sober more than 1 year and less than 5 years, 83% will remain in the AA fellowship another year.
3. Of those sober 5 years or more, 91% will remain in the AA fellowship another year.

Attendance in an abstinence-based treatment program can increase the recovery rates in AA, for example, 80% from 41% with referral to AA following the treatment program.

IV. CONCLUSIONS REGARDING ALCOHOL AND DRUG DISORDERS (ADDICTION)

1. A chronic disorder of exacerbations and remissions that follows a progressive course over years.
2. The cardinal manifestation of an addictive disorder is loss of control over alcohol and drug use that results in adverse consequences.
3. A medical, psychiatric, psychological, or spiritual disorder that responds to specific addiction treatment; the more specific the treatment, the greater the treatment outcome, particularly in the long view.

SELECTED READINGS

Adams RP, Victor M: *Principles of Neurology*, 3rd ed. New York: McGraw-Hill, 1985.

Clark LT, Friedman HS: Hypertension associated with alcohol withdrawal: assessment of mechanisms and complications of alcoholism. *Clin Exp Res* 9:125–132, 1985.

Galizio M, Maisto SA: *Determinants of Substance Abuse.* New York: Plenum Press, 1985.

Gold MS, Dackis CA: Role of the laboratory in the evaluation of suspected drug abuse. *J Clin Psychiatry* 47:17–23, 1986.

Goodwin DW: *Anxiety.* London: Oxford University Press, 1986.

Goodwin DW, Guze SB: *Psychiatric Diagnosis*, 3rd ed. London: Oxford University Press, 1984.

Harrison's Principles of Internal Medicine, 10th ed. New York: McGraw-Hill, 1983.

Holden C: Alcoholism and the medical cost crunch. *Science* 235:1132, 1987.

Jaffe JH: Drug and addiction abuse. In AG Gilman, LS Goodman, TW Rall, F Murad (eds): *The Pharmacological Bases of Therapeutics*, 7th ed. New York: Macmillan, 1985, pp 532–581.

Kannel WB, Sorlie P: Hypertension in Framingham. In O Paul (ed): *Epidemiology and Control of Hypertension.* New York: Station Incontinental Medical Book Corp., 1974.

Katchadourian HA, Lunde DT: *Fundamentals of Human Sexuality*, 3rd ed. New York: Holt, Rinehart and Winston, 1975.

Klatsky AL, Friedman GD, Siegelaum AB, Gerad MJ: Alcohol consumption and blood pressure. *N Engl J Med* 296:1194–1200, 1977.

Lieber CS: *Medical Disorders of Alcoholism*. Philadelphia: Saunders, 1982.

Litman RE, Farberow NJ, Wold CI, Brown TR: Prediction models of suicidal behavior. In AT Beck, HLP Resnick, DJ Lettieri (eds): *The Prediction of Suicide*. Bowie, MD: Charles Press, 1974, p 141.

Martin RL, Cloninger CR, Guze SB, Clayton PJ: Mortality in a follow-up of 500 psychiatric outpatients. *Arch Gen Psychiatry* 42:47–66, 1985.

Mayfield DG: Alcohol and affect: experimental studies. In DW Goodwin and CK Erickson (eds): *Alcoholism and Affective Disorders*. New York: SP Medical and Scientific Books, 1979, pp 99–107.

Mendelson JH, Mello NK: *The Diagnosis and Treatment of Alcoholism*, 2nd ed. New York: McGraw-Hill, 1985.

Milam J: *The Emergent Concept of Alcoholism*. Kirkland, WA: Alcoholism Center Associates Press, 1978.

Milam J, Ketcham, K: *Under the Influence*. New York: Madrona Publishers, 1981.

Miller NS: *Treatment of the Addictions: Applications of Outcome Research for Clinical Management*. New York: Haworth Press, 1995.

Miller NS, Gold MS: The diagnosis and treatment of alcohol dependence. *New Jersey Med* 84(12):873–879, 1987.

Parsons OA, Leber WR: The relationship between cognitive dysfunction and brain damage in alcoholics: Causal or epiphenomena. *Clin Exp Res* 5:326–343, 1981.

Schuckit MA: The history of psychiatric symptoms in alcoholics. *J Clin Psychiatry* 43:53–57, 1982.

Schuckit MA: The disease alcoholism. *Postgrad Med* 64:78–84, 1978.

Schuckit MA: Alcoholism and affective disorder: diagnostic confusion: In DW Goodwin and CK Erickson (eds): *Alcoholism and Affective Disorders*. New York: SP Medical and Scientific Books, 1979, pp 9–19.

Schuckit MA: Alcohol patients with secondary depression. *Am J Psychiatry* 140:711–714, 1983.

Schuckit MA: Alcoholism and other psychiatric disorders. *Hosp Commun Psychiatry* 34:1022–1027, 1983.

CHAPTER 2

INTOXICATION AND WITHDRAWAL FROM ALCOHOL

Mark S. Gold, M.D.
University of Florida Brain Institute, Gainesville, Florida

Norman S. Miller, M.D.
University of Illinois at Chicago, Chicago, Illinois

I. ALCOHOL

The behavioral criteria describe the loss of control over alcohol that leads to the adverse consequences and disruption in interpersonal relationships. The manifestations of a pathologic attachment to alcohol is the disruption in interpersonal relationships and in marital, legal, employment, and other areas of the alcoholic's life.

A. Epidemiology of Use, Abuse, and Dependence. Alcohol intoxication and dependence and abuse are among the most prevalent mental disorders in the general population (see Fig. 2.1). A community study conducted in the United States from 1980 to 1985 using *DSM-III* criteria found that about 8% of the adult population had alcohol dependence and about 5% had alcohol abuse at some time in their lives. Approximately 6% had alcohol dependence or abuse during the preceding year. From data collected prospectively, about 7.5% had symptoms that met criteria for an alcohol-related disorder during a 1–year period. A United States national probability sample of noninstitutionalized adults (ages 15–54 years) conducted in 1990/91 using *DSM-III-R* criteria reported that around 14% had alcohol dependence at some time in their lives, with approximately 7% having had dependence in the past year.

Alcohol consumption among high-school seniors and tenth-grade and eighth-grade students has been reported by the University of Michigan as part of the Monitoring for the Future study (see Figs. 2.2–2.3).

B. Where Do We Find the Alcoholic? According to most studies and clinical experience, the typical alcoholic is white, black, or other; has a job; is married; and has achieved any level of education. It is important here to remember the age ranges for half (50%) of all alcoholics: over 22 years old for men and over 25 years old for women. The racial breakdown indicates that alcohol knows no racial barriers—the lifetime rates of alcoholism are about the same for whites, blacks, and others. Age, educational status, and annual income are poor predictors of alcohol abuse, chronic heavy drinking, or alcohol dependence. The locations where alcoholics can be found are well known but useful to summarize. The household contains an alcoholism rate of 14%. This means that 1 out

Manual of Therapeutics for Addictions, Edited by Norman S. Miller, Mark S. Gold, and David E. Smith.
ISBN 0471-56176-2 © 1997 John Wiley & Sons, Inc.

- Alcohol is the number one drug of abuse in the USA
- At least 15.4 million adults have serious alcohol-related problems
- At least 4.6 million adolescents have serious alcohol-related problems
- More years are lost to alcohol-related causes than to heart disease—the nation's number 1 killer
- Alcohol-related years lost in the United States are second only to cancer
- NIAAA estimated the costs to US society from alcoholism and alcohol related problems at approximately $116.0 billion in 1990
- Alcohol abuse is the number 1 cause of preventable mental retardation

FIGURE 2.1. Alcohol dependence. (*Source:* NIAAA.)

of 6 people living in households will suffer from alcoholism at one point in their lives, most likely early in their lives. Among men, 1 out of 4 will suffer from alcoholism, and among women, 1 out of 12 will suffer from alcoholism. The prevalence of alcoholic patients seen in clinical practice is common, especially in view of the fact that alcoholics are overrepresented among patients seen in clinical practice. Approximately 25% of patients in a general medical practice is composed of alcoholics (see Figs. 2.4–2.6).

C. Occupations. The rate of alcoholism among occupations does tend to be more common among the less skilled, but this may represent a phenomenon of "downward drift" in which the alcoholism retards the acquisition of education and skills. As described above, the prevalence of alcoholism according to levels of education does not confirm higher rates of alcoholism among the less educated. Because the onset of the first symptom of alcoholism is commonly between the ages of 15 and 19 years, it is not surprising that job development is impaired in the critical formative years when decisions are made and performances that have far-reaching consequences are judged. Even so, the rate of alcoholism is 16.3% for alcoholics completing somewhere between elementary grades 0 and 7, 11.1% for those completing grade 8, 18.3% for those completing 9–11/GED (general equivalency diploma), 12.8% for high-school graduates, 13.8% for college level, and 10% for college graduates. The majority of alcoholics have at least a high-school education or a GED.

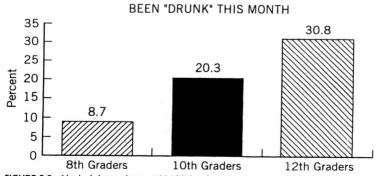

FIGURE 2.2. Alcohol dependence: 1994 high-school senior survey for 1-month period.

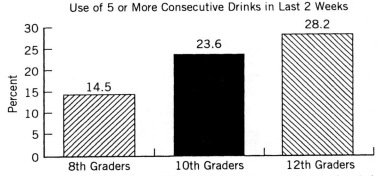

FIGURE 2.3. Alcohol dependence: 1994 high-school senior survey for 2-week period.

D. Marital Status. Alcoholics are most likely to marry or cohabitate. Although 8.9% have a stable marriage, 29.2% cohabitate. Only 15% never married, and 40.4% have had at least one divorce or separation. The major consequence of alcoholism is a disruption in the interpersonal relationships; therefore, it is easy to see why so many alcoholics have problems in their marriages.

E. Gender and Race. The prevalence of alcoholism is equal for whites and blacks at 14% lifetime prevalence and 17% for Hispanics. A further analysis reveals that white and black women are also equal at 5%. Hispanic men have a higher rate of alcoholism at 30% and Hispanic women, lower at 4%. When heavy or problem drinkers are considered as a group, the number of men who fulfill criteria for alcoholism is 50%, or an additional 23% of men drink heavily but do not meet criteria for alcohol dependence. The proportion of women who are alcoholic among heavy drinkers is 35%. Clearly, drinking is a common event, and problem drinkers are also common.

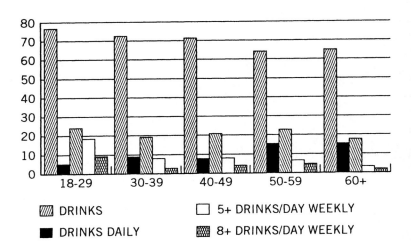

FIGURE 2.4. Who drinks how much and how often, by age. (*Source: Fortune Magazine,* 1995.)

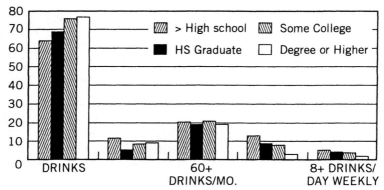

FIGURE 2.5. Who drinks how much and how often, by education. (*Source: Fortune Magazine*, 1995.)

F. Geography. Not all areas in the United States have the same prevalence of alcoholism. Northern Florida appears to have more alcohol dependence and more nicotine dependence than does southern Florida. The rates of alcoholism are higher among the urban dwellers than among rural or suburban dwellers as a lifetime prevalence rate of 15% is found in Baltimore, St. Louis, and Los Angeles and 11% in Durham (NC) and New Haven (CT).

G. Age. The age groups that predominate in prevalence of alcoholism are 18–29 years in white men and women, whereas 45–64 years is the range for black men and 30–44 for Hispanic men. For women, both whites and Hispanics

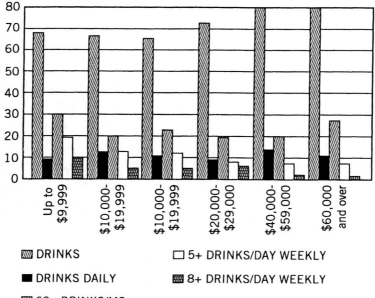

FIGURE 2.6. Who drinks how much and how often, by family income. (*Source: Fortune Magazine*, 1995.)

peak at 18–29 years, and black women like black men peak at 45–64 years. Any discussion of the younger alcoholic of today is remiss if the prevalence of other drug use along with alcohol is not considered. The alcoholic under the age of 30 years old, which constitutes the majority of the alcoholics today, is addicted to at least one other drug in addition to alcohol. The most common drug is marijuana, followed by cocaine, sedative/hypnotics, hallucinogens, and others.

1. Reversing the index drug. Of those who are addicted to marijuana, 36% are alcoholics; of those who are addicted to barbiturates, 71% are alcoholics; of those who are addicted to cocaine, 84% are alcoholics; of those who are addicted to opioids, 67% are alcoholics. The contemporary alcoholic is a multiple drug addict who combines and substitutes one drug for another. Carefully planned detoxification schedules are based on accurate histories and diagnoses. Just as LSD (lysergic acid diethylamide) history is useful before starting a SSRI (selective serotonin reuptake inhibitor), alcohol and other drug dependence suggests caution since these individuals become easily addicted to a wide variety of drugs, presumably because of generalized vulnerability to drug and alcohol addiction.

H. Duration. The duration of alcoholism is relatively predictable. Alcoholism tends to be a progressive illness overall, with a steady deterioration in personality and health over time. Progression is longer than for cocaine. According to the studies, the mean duration of alcoholism is 9 years for those who eventually experience a remission of 1 year or more. Because the mean age of alcoholism is in the early and middle 20s, the typical duration of alcoholism is between 1 and 5 years, followed by 6–10 years in duration. This is in contradistinction to the popular conception that the typical alcoholic is old and a long-time drinker. What is very interesting is that alcoholism can and does develop within a year as 17% of those in remission from alcoholism for more than a year were alcoholic within 1 year from the onset of the drinking histories. The importance of the physician in making an early diagnosis and initiating treatment is clearly suggested by the data. The majority of the alcoholics are diagnosable and treatable by 5 years after the onset of drinking. This is so because the distribution of the duration of alcoholism is skewed toward the shorter duration of alcoholism. A small but significant number report a duration of > 10 years with a large range between 10 and > 50 years. The mode or most frequent duration is 1–5 years, and almost 50% of those who report a remission of alcoholism for greater than a year experienced a duration of alcoholism 5 years or less.

I. Diagnosis. The diagnosis of alcoholism can be made earlier in the natural history of the disease than most have suspected. Effective treatment for alcoholism does exist so that earlier intervention is desirable. Many of the medical complications that are usually relied on for the diagnosis occur later in onset; although they are reliable indicators of adverse consequences of alcoholism, medical complications are not particularly sensitive earlier in the course of alcoholism. Broken bones, accidents, DUIs ("driving under the influence" convictions), marital problems, divorce, abuse, violent fights, and other behavioral markers occur (see Fig. 2.7). We will describe alcohol's effects on various physiological systems since these are frequently used by practitioners to intensify their questioning and to actively rule out alcoholism or alcohol abuse. However, early diagnosis requires an active clinician asking all patients about their relationship to and with alcohol—not merely the amount of alcohol they consume but their attachment to drinking and alcohol per se. In the CAGE

C	Have you ever felt that you ought to CUT DOWN on your drinking?
A	Have people ANNOYED you by criticizing your drinking?
G	Have you ever felt bad or GUILTY about your drinking?
E	Have you ever had a drink first thing in the morning (EYE OPENER) to steady your nerves or get rid of a hangover?

No false-positive if all four questions are answered positively. With two or more positive answers, sensitivity is >72% and specificity >77%.

(*Source:* Ewing, JA. Detecting alcoholism: the CAGE questionnaire. *JAMA* 252:1905–1907, 1984.)

FIGURE 2.7. CAGE questionnaire.

questions, the C is particularly useful in primary-care settings since it gives the clinician a barometer of the person's worst fears and concerns regarding the use of alcohol.

J. General Medicine. Because a general medical practice is devoted to a large number of chronic-care patients, it is not surprising that the proportion of alcoholics in such a practice is so high. The prevalence of alcoholism is 14.4% among chronic-care patients, defined as chronic illnesses. Some of the chronic illnesses are a consequence of alcoholism; others are not. Certainly, alcoholism aggravates or contributes to the severity, course, and prognosis of the chronic illness. The primary practitioner identifying a problem or problems (see Fig. 2.8) asks the patient CAGE questions, and can follow up that person's diagnosis with the MAST or other instruments and interviews with friends and family.

K. Psychiatric Patients. A not-too-surprising figure is that the prevalence of alcoholism among the psychiatric population is as high as 50%. Alcoholism itself produces psychiatric symptoms, so that many of these patients have alcoholism as the primary problem. The diagnosis and treatment of alcoholism in many instances will resolve the psychiatric symptoms. However, the correct diagnosis of alcoholism must be made before proper treatment can be instituted.

L. Criminal Justice. The prevalence of alcoholism among the incarcerated is alarmingly high. Fifty-seven percent of those incarcerated qualify for the diagnosis of alcoholism. Approximately half of them have had active alcoholism in the past year. Other well-known statistics are that over 80% of murders involve someone who was intoxicated with alcohol at the time of the murder. Eighty percent of domestic violence involves someone who was intoxicated at the time of the violence. More than 50% of automobile deaths involve someone who was drinking.

M. Summary. The conclusions that can be derived from the epidemiologic data confirm what clinicians have suspected and researchers have documented for some time. Alcoholism is the most common psychiatric disorder in the United States. Over their lifetimes, nearly 16% of adults have diagnosable alcoholism, and half of these have been in the active stage in the past year. Men are about 5 times as likely as women to suffer from alcoholism, but the gap between the two is closing. For both men and women, the onset of alcoholism is in the early and middle 20s. If a general medical practice is defined as consisting of the typical household, in any class population, with no predominance of a particular illness, then as-reported substance abuse and alcoholism are the major

- Morning retching, nausea, vomiting, anorexia
- History of gastritis or nonspecific acid-peptic distress
- Symptoms of gastroesophageal reflux
- Esophageal peristalsis
- Recurrent diarrhea
- Peristaltic waves without affecting propulsive movement
- Palpitations
- Sleep disturbance, anxiety, depression
- Multiple, nonspecific symptoms
- Sexual dysfunction

FIGURE 2.8. Problems and complaints associated with alcoholism.

unrecognized and undertreated diseases in general practice. The consequences of the alcoholism are commonly hypertension, gastrointestinal problems, upper respiratory illness, cardiac complaints, trauma, and other abnormalities.

II. DEPENDENCE: GENERAL ISSUES

A. Primary Disease. Alcoholism is not a reaction to something else; rather, it is a basic primary drive as powerful as sex or hunger itself that has been tapped by and associated with the chemical alcohol. The alcoholic continues to drink *in spite of* the developing consequences of the addictive drinking. From this compulsion arises a preoccupation with the acquisition of alcohol that is conscious or unconscious, often the latter. Frequently the alcoholic chooses or wills not to drink but does so anyway in spite of the most fervent decision not to drink. What appears to be a loss of will is really an overpowering of the will to drink that is at the basis of the addiction to alcohol. It is not a lack of will any more than the drive to have sex or eat is eradicated by willpower or personal resolve. Will or self-control can and does moderate the pursuit and intake of alcohol to some extent, and a measure of at least partial control over eating and sexual behavior is possible.

B. Pharmacologic Dependence. Pharmacologic dependence or biological neuroadaptation are not a good criterion by which to diagnose alcoholism because physiological dependence is denied, not recognized, and not necessary for a diagnosis of substance or alcohol dependence. Fewer people appear pharmacologically dependent early on, and a preoccupation with pharmacologic dependence renders an early diagnosis of abuse or dependence less likely. The duration of alcoholism is, on the average, 9 years, and almost 50% of the alcoholics have the onset of alcoholism before 5 years of alcohol consumption. The pathologic attachment to alcohol, the preoccupation with acquiring alcohol and using it compulsively in spite of adverse consequences, and the tendency to relapse or be unable to reduce or eliminate the drinking in spite of the adverse consequences are the essential features of an addiction to alcohol. The pervasive force behind preoccupation, compulsivity, and relapse is loss of control or the inability to overcome the drive to drink. The addiction has a life of its own and is generated by the underlying drive to consume alcohol. It does not require other conditions or states to trigger or sustain it. The drive state to drink sets up a tension to drink that is relieved by alcohol in the same way as other drive states to eat or have sex are relieved by food or a sexual act.

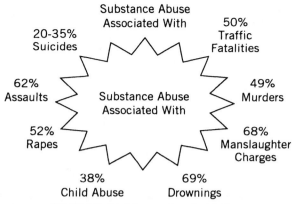

FIGURE 2.9. Possible sequelae of addiction.

C. Prevention Is Needed. Alcohol abuse requires early detection and prompt intervention once self-control prevention has failed. Dependence or alcoholism is an illness or disease that requires the earliest possible medical diagnosis and treatment. Alcoholism is not a moral problem; rather, moral problems result from alcoholism. Most of what appears to be alcoholism are actually the consequences of untreated alcoholism. Failure to prevent and subsequent failure to diagnose and treat have made untreated alcoholism a major public health problem in the United States. According to a recent Robert Wood Johnson (RWJ) healthcare report prepared by the Institute for Health Policy, Brandeis University, substance abuse is the nation's number one health problem:

> The costs of substance abuse will frustrate any attempt to curb health care costs. . . . Of the $238 billion the nation spends each year on substance abuse, $34 billion is spent on unnecessary health care. A heavy smoker will stay 25% longer when hospitalized than a nonsmoker, a problem drinker four times as long as a non drinker. . . . Without a reduction in substance abuse, health care costs cannot be curtailed effectively.

Each year, there are more deaths and disabilities due to substance abuse than to any other preventable cause. Of the two million U.S. deaths each year, one in four is attributable to alcohol, illicit drug, or tobacco use—100,000 people die as a result of alcohol; 19,000, of illicit-drug use and AIDS-related deaths; and 400,000, of tobacco-related deaths. Various crimes and other traumatic events have been attributed to substance abuse, as shown in Figure 2.9.

III. ALCOHOL INTOXICATION

A. Definition. *Alcohol intoxication* is defined by the presence of important maladaptive behavioral or psychological changes that can be related to alcohol. A variety of out-of-character behaviors are considered in this definition. Inappropriate sexual or aggressive behavior, evidence of mood lability, impaired judgment, and impaired social or occupational functioning should be readily related in time to the ingestion of alcohol. Behavioral changes occurring during or immediately after intoxication can be related to the intoxication on the basis of history or with blood alcohol or Breathalyzer data. Clinicians, as do the sobriety-checkpoint or driving impairment police or state Highway Patrol officers, look for presence of slurred speech, lack of coordination, unsteady gait, nystagmus, and impairment in attention or memory span related to blood alcohol. Stupor or coma can follow these signs if a sufficiently high dose of alcohol is consumed. To meet the criteria for alcohol intoxication, symptoms must not be due to a general medical condition or other mental disorder.

B. Similar Intoxication States. The clinical syndrome observed in alcohol intoxication is similar—in mechanism and clinical features—to what is observed during benzodiazepine or barbiturate intoxication. The combination of benzodiazepine and alcohol or barbiturate plus alcohol is a more lethal intoxication state than either state alone.

C. Common Presentation. Alcohol intoxication is a common presentation to the campus infirmary, campus police, city police, county sheriff, and workplace. The patient shows evidence of motor impairment, and the smell of alcohol is detectable or a person or persons gives a history of multiple drinks in a discrete period of time. With alcohol consumption, benzodiazepine use, barbiturate use, or combinations of these, motor disabilities interfere with driving abilities and with performing routine activities to the point of causing accidents. Judgment is negatively affected as well, putting the person at further risk. "I'm not impaired; give me the keys and shut up," said one patient before a traffic collision. Evidence of alcohol use can be obtained by smelling alcohol on the individual's breath, eliciting a history from the individual or another observer, and—when available—having the individual undertake breath, blood, or urine toxicology analyses.

D. Alcohol Intoxication: Individual Differences. Specific behavior changes or symptoms that are difficult to generalize are applicable for every patient. The particular host or patient factors at low blood levels are important determinants of the intoxication state. At very high blood alcohol levels (> 200 mg/dL), a nontolerant individual is likely to fall asleep and enter a first stage of anesthesia. High blood levels can and do cause death in naive and even regular users. Blood alcohol levels in excess of 300–400 mg/dL can cause inhibition of respiration and pulse and death in nontolerant individuals.

E. The *DSM-IV* Diagnostic Criteria for 303.00 Alcohol Intoxication. The duration of intoxication depends on how much alcohol was consumed over what period of time. In general, the body is able to metabolize approximately one drink per hour, so that the blood alcohol level generally decreases at a rate of 15–20 mg/dL per hour. Signs and symptoms of intoxication are likely to be more intense when the blood alcohol level is rising than when it is falling.

   A. Recent ingestion of alcohol.
   B. Clinically significant maladaptive behavioral or psychological changes (e.g., inappropriate sexual or aggressive behavior, mood lability, impaired judgment, impaired social or occupational functioning) that developed during, or shortly after, alcohol ingestion.
   C. One (or more) of the following signs, developing during, or shortly after, alcohol use:

   Slurred speech
   Lack of coordination
   Unsteady gait

Nystagmus
Impairment in attention or memory
Stupor or coma

D. The symptoms are not due to a general medical condition and are not better accounted for by another mental disorder.

F. Progression. The first episode of alcohol intoxication is likely to occur in the middle-school years with drinking 5 or more drinks in one sitting increasing dramatically in the 8th and 12th grades and then doubling in college-age young people. Alcohol dependence peaks in the 20s to mid-30s. The large majority of those who develop alcohol-related disorders do so by their late 20s or 30s. The first evidence of withdrawal is not likely to appear until after many other aspects of dependence have developed. Alcohol abuse and dependence have a variable course that is frequently characterized by periods of remission and relapse. A decision to stop drinking, often in response to a crisis, is likely to be followed by weeks or more of abstinence, which is often followed by limited periods of controlled or nonproblematic drinking. However, once alcohol intake resumes, it is highly likely that consumption will rapidly escalate and that severe problems will once again develop. While alcohol abuse generally precedes alcohol dependence in years, both addicts and abusers frequently come to medical attention after an accident or another untoward event. Efforts to increase physician detection are continuing. Decrements in school or job performance can be a cause of detection of both the abuser or the addict. Both can suffer from a change in motivation and effort or the direct aftereffects of drinking or from actual intoxication on the job or at school. Abuser- or addict-mothers may come to medical attention by state agency referrals. Any person may use alcohol too close in time to driving a car or boat or when required to perform a dangerous task around the home or at work.

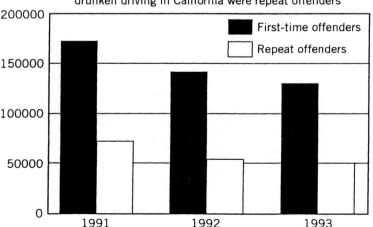

Repeat offenders

In each of three years, 31% of those convicted of drunken driving in California were repeat offenders

FIGURE 2.10. Incidence of DUI recidivism in California. (*Source:* California Department of Motor Vehicles, reported in *USA Today,* June 21, 1995.)

G. Repeat Offenders. Law-enforcement authorities and clinicians have noted that some alcohol abusers resist treatment and repeatedly consume alcohol. These individuals may even be identified as repeat offenders (see Fig. 2.10) by the police and forfeit driving privileges. Alcohol abusers may continue to consume alcohol even though they recognize its role in family and work problems, fights, arguments, and physical and mental abuse. Insight and behavior changes do not occur in many patients, and abuse-related problems that are accompanied by evidence of tolerance, withdrawal, or compulsive behavior should be evaluated for a diagnosis of alcohol dependence, rather than abuse.

IV. ALCOHOL WITHDRAWAL

A. Phenomenology of Alcohol Withdrawal. By definition, alcoholics continue to use alcohol despite evidence of adverse psychological or physical consequences—even extreme consequences such as loss of self-esteem, depression, blackouts, liver disease, or other sequelae. In alcoholics or in those who engage in chronic drinking, the alcohol withdrawal syndrome follows abrupt discontinuation or attempts to cut down. Withdrawal symptoms begin 12 h or so after the reduction or abrupt discontinuation. Once a pattern of compulsive use develops, addicted individuals devote substantial periods of time to thinking about drinking, maintaining access, and obtaining and consuming alcoholic beverages. If Happy Hour starts at 5:00 p.m. after work, they think about it at 4:00 and then at 3:00 and then after a few drinks at lunch. Just knowing that they will be able to drink without becoming discovered as an alcohol abuser or alcoholic produces a sense of anticipation. Early signs of alcohol withdrawal can be recognized by some patients as cues to start drinking. The dependent patient may give a history of periods of early withdrawal reversed by consumption, often to feel "normal." Naturally, drinking produces reinforcement directly through the effects of alcohol on the brain and also when it removes the adverse or negative state that is associated with abstinence. Withdrawal can be a life-threatening event but most often is benign. Only 5% of individuals with alcohol dependence ever experience severe complications of withdrawal such as delirium tremens or grand mal seizures.

B. Withdrawal Timeline. The alcohol withdrawal syndrome, even in acute form, is usually transient, lasting only a few days (see Figs. 2.11 and 2.12).

C. Alcohol Withdrawal. The essential feature of alcohol withdrawal is the presence of a characteristic withdrawal syndrome that develops after the cessation of (or reduction in) heavy and prolonged alcohol use. The withdrawal syndrome includes two or more of the following symptoms: autonomic hyperactivity (e.g., sweating or pulse rate > 100); increased hand tremor; insomnia; nausea or vomiting; transient visual, tactile, or auditory hallucinations or illusions; psychomotor agitation; anxiety; and grand mal seizures. The symptoms cause clinically significant distress or impairment in social, occupational, or other important areas of functioning. The symptoms must not be due to a general medical condition and are not better accounted for by another mental disorder (e.g., sedative, hypnotic, or anxiolytic withdrawal or generalized anxiety disorder). It is generally useful and important to note that alcohol withdrawal resembles benzodiazepine withdrawal, sedative/hypnotic withdrawal, and naturally occurring generalized anxiety disorder.

Alcohol Withdrawal Syndrome . . .

- Is usually transient (lasting 3-7 days) and marked by tremulousness that may be accompanied by hallucinations and grand mal seizures
- Can be treated with benzodiazepines, B vitamins, IV fluids
- Is not caused by drinking, but caused by not drinking
- Occasionally accompanied by delirium tremens (DTs), marked by disorientation, memory disturbance, and hallucinations

---

FIGURE 2.11. Causes, characteristics, and treatment of alcohol withdrawal syndrome.

D. Reversal by Alcohol. Symptoms are relieved by administering alcohol, a benzodiazepine, clonidine, or any other brain depressant. The withdrawal symptoms typically begin when blood concentrations of alcohol decline sharply (i.e., within 4–12 h) after alcohol use has been stopped or reduced. Because of the short half-life of alcohol, symptoms of alcohol withdrawal usually peak in intensity during the second day of abstinence and are likely to improve markedly by the fourth or fifth day. Following acute withdrawal, however, symptoms of anxiety, insomnia, and autonomic dysfunction, referred to as "white knuckles," "dry drunks," so on, may persist for up to 3–6 months.

E. Progression to DTs. Fewer than 5% of individuals who develop alcohol withdrawal develop dramatic alcohol withdrawal delirium with disturbances in consciousness and cognition and visual, tactile, or auditory hallucinations (delirium tremens). Grand mal seizures occur in fewer than 5% of individuals. When alcohol withdrawal delirium develops, it is likely that a clinically relevant general medical condition such as liver failure, pneumonia, gastrointestinal bleeding, sequelae of head trauma, hypoglycemia, or an electrolyte imbalance may also be present. Delirium tremens (DTs) generally occur within the first 96 hours and can include disorientation, confusion, auditory and / or visual hallucinations, confusion, and psychomotor hyperactivity. Alcohol withdrawal is associated with decreased levels of the inhibitory neurotransmitter γ-aminobutyric acid (GABA), supersensitivity of N-methyl-D-aspartate (NMDA) receptors, hyperactivity of the hypothalamic–pituitary–adrenal axis, and increased noradrenergic and therefore sympathetic nervous system activ-

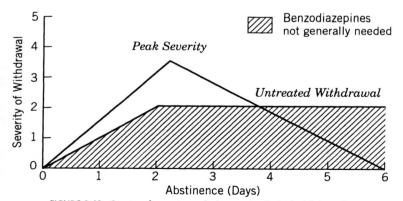

FIGURE 2.12. Course of symptoms during acute alcohol withdrawal.

ity. Pharmacologic management of acute alcohol withdrawal generally involves the use of benzodiazepines (BZs). BZs reduce ethanol–withdrawal-related anxiety, restlessness, insomnia, tremors, DTs, and withdrawal seizures by enhancing the functional activity of the GABA / BZ receptor.

F.   *DSM-IV* Diagnostic Criteria for 291.8 Alcohol Withdrawal

 A. Cessation of (or reduction in) alcohol use that has been heavy and prolonged.

 B. Two (or more) of the following, developing within several hours to a few days after criterion A:

   Autonomic hyperactivity (e.g., sweating or pulse rate > 100)
   Increased hand tremor
   Insomnia
   Nausea or vomiting
   Transient visual, tactile, or auditory hallucinations or illusions
   Psychomotor agitation
   Anxiety
   Grand mal seizures

 C. The symptoms in criterion B cause clinically significant distress or impairment in social, occupational, or other important areas of functioning.

 D. The symptoms are not due to a general medical condition and are not better accounted for by another mental disorder.

G. Withdrawal Similarities. Abrupt discontinuation or even cutting down on the amount of drinking by individuals who are physiologically dependent produces a characteristic withdrawal syndrome with sweating, tachycardia, hypertension, tremors, anorexia, insomnia, agitation, anxiety, nausea, and vomiting. However, the descriptive criteria themselves do not reliably separate patients. Misdiagnosis is common, and since multiple-substance abuse and dependence is so common, even when one smells of alcohol and manifests the signs and symptoms commonly associated with alcohol withdrawal, one may have another diagnosis or diagnoses as well. Alcohol withdrawal resembles opiate withdrawal, nicotine withdrawal, and barbiturate and benzodiazepine withdrawal. All have been treated with the antihypertensive clonidine, supporting a common noradrenergic rebound hyperactivity. Where alcohol withdrawal is strikingly different from opiate withdrawal is that some alcoholics progress from the autonomic hyperactivity common to many withdrawal states to seizures. History of withdrawal seizures, autonomic reactivity, and instability is a useful albeit not foolproof marker for patients who will have difficulties during withdrawal.

H. Pharmacologic Reversal. While pharmacologic treatment of withdrawal is not necessary for all patients, patients with significant symptoms are generally treated with BZs such as 10 mg of diazepam or 25 mg of chlordiazepoxide PO (orally) every 4–6 h (Q4–6h) until withdrawal subsides. Such a treatment response supports the diagnosis of alcohol withdrawal. More severe withdrawal or the history of more severe withdrawal is generally treated with 20 mg of diazepam or 100 mg of chlordiazepoxide every hour or Q2h. Other protocols have been proposed, especially for patients with cirrhosis, using the shorter-acting and easier-to-titrate BZs such as lorazepam or oxazepam given Q8h for the first day and then tapered to 20–25% per day. Non-BZs are also in widespread worldwide use for the treatment of acute ethanol withdrawal. For example, clonidine and similar agents have been used to reduce autonomic withdrawal symptoms. Although it appears that these treatments are equal in efficacy to the BZs, it is still unclear whether they provide as much protection against seizures and delirium. Interestingly, anticonvulsants like phenytoin are ineffective in overcoming withdrawal seizures except in patients with preexisting epilepsy. Carbamazepine 200 mg QID for 2 days TID for 2 days BID for 2 days QD for 2 days has recently been used during alcohol detoxification providing symptomatic and seizure protection without BZ abuse risk during outpatient detoxification. Since neuroscientific research has suggested that NMDA (*N*-methyl-D-aspartate) receptors are quite critical to the development of withdrawal seizures, a new medication class may be found to eliminate the major life-threatening problems associated with alcohol withdrawal.

V. ALCOHOL DEPENDENCE

A. Introduction to Diagnosis. The diagnosis of alcoholism advanced greatly when alcoholism was given the antecedent position instead of the consequent position. Jellinek introduced the notion that alcoholism caused a variety of manifestations that are consequent to loss of control over the use of alcohol. Useful schemes for diagnosing alcoholism were developed that emphasized the consequences of alcoholism. The National Council on Alcoholism and other authoritative groups developed criteria for alcoholism that required identification of psychological, physical, and sociologic impairments from abnormal alcohol use. Although these criteria are useful and do identify a substantial number of alcoholics, the consequences do not describe the essential features of alcoholism. Problems also arise from disagreement as to what is a consequence and what is its relevance. For instance, physicians tend to rely heavily on medical consequences that are not present in the majority of alcoholics. Furthermore, the consequences are frequently denied by the alcoholic, so that ascertainment of the consequences is often elusive and difficult. Also, consequences may result from alcohol use in those who are not alcoholic; that is, younger drinkers tend to drink heavily and with some consequences but are not always alcoholic. Finally, the consequences of alcoholism are attributed to other conditions, or, sometimes, back to the consequences. An alcoholic may have marital or employment problems because of the alcoholism, but the reverse is sometimes asserted, that the bad marriage or boring job are causing the alcoholism, which does not happen.

B. The Concept of Addiction. The concepts of the behaviors that underlie and generate alcoholism are embodied in the concept of addiction. *Addiction* is a behavioral term that describes the behaviors that define the specific nature of the loss of control in regard to alcoholism; this term comprises only the bare minimum of alcoholism but is useful in identifying alcoholism and distinguishing it from other disorders.

Alcohol Dependence

1. *Stereotypic set of signs and symptoms or cessation of use of drug.*
2. *Drug will abort its withdrawal symptoms.*
3. *Addiction.* Addiction is defined by three principal behaviors: preoccupation, compulsivity, and relapse. Addiction to alcohol is characterized by the preoccupation with the acquisition of alcohol and the compulsive use and relapse to alcohol in spite of adverse consequences.

Criteria for Abuse, Addiction, and Tolerance

Abuse	Addiction	Tolerance
Use outside the accepted norm	Preoccupation with acquisition of alcohol or drugs	Need to increase dose of drug to achieve same effect
Abnormal use	Compulsive use in spite of adverse consequensces	Loss of effect from drug at a particular dose
Not addiction	Recurrent pattern of use or relapse	

Preoccupation with alcohol is demonstrated in the acquisition of alcohol. The alcoholic is obsessed with alcohol. Alcohol has a high priority in the alcoholic's life to the exclusion of other important and vital needs. Alcoholics often neglect their own basic needs such as self-care, health, and interpersonal relationships among family, employment, and other arenas of their lives and may provide countless reasons why they are drinking, but the addiction to alcohol is major and preeminent. The alcoholic continues to be preoccupied with alcohol when sanity would forget it. The compulsive use of alcohol is demonstrated by the continued use of alcohol in spite of adverse consequences. The use of alcohol may or may not be regular. Compulsivity is marked by relentless and persistent use when common sense would dictate stopping and desisting from the use of alcohol. The consequences may be trivial or enormous—often the latter, without significant effect on curbing or eliminating the use of alcohol. The order of the cause and effect is critical. The cause of the adverse consequences is alcoholism, and not vice versa, that the adverse consequences lead to alcoholism. Relapse is the sine qua non of alcoholism. Occasionally preoccupation with acquisition is, for some other reason than alcohol addiction, transient. Moreover, compulsive use may be temporary and precipitated by some event or condition. However, the pattern or recurrent use of alcohol in spite of adverse consequences is confirmatory of an addiction. The repeated return to the use of alcohol when common sense dictates moderation or abstinence is explained only by an addiction to alcohol. Relapse may be frequent and only after a few days of abstinence or after a prolonged period of years. An inability to cut back or reduce the alcohol intake is also considered relapse as it is indicative of loss of control over alcohol use.

4. *Loss of control.*   Loss of control is pervasive to the three criteria of addiction. Behind preoccupation with acquisition, compulsive use, and relapse is loss of control due to alcohol dependence. Loss of control is relative and rarely (if even possible) absolute. Alcoholics can and do exert some control over alcohol use, but always identifiable is a significant degree of loss of control. The loss of control is manifested differently for each alcoholic as drinking patterns vary, and consequences vary from individual to individual. The consequences of the addiction

to alcohol are what arouses suspicion of the diagnosis of alcoholism initially. The major life areas are the most easily detected and the most commonly affected, although any aspect of the individual may be affected by the alcohol addiction. The fundamental defect in alcoholism is a disturbance in interpersonal relationships between the alcoholic and others. This disturbance is manifested in interpersonal relationships with spouses, friends, employees and employers, the laws, and society.

5. *Impairment.* A multitude of impairments are possible in any facet of the alcoholic's life. Just as with loss of control, the impairments are relative and difficult to detect. Also, rationalizations and minimization of the consequences as well as misattribution are obstacles to the correct assessment of alcoholism as being responsible. Marital difficulties arise for a variety of reasons, of which alcoholism is one, albeit common, cause. Job performance may be significantly affected before impairment is noticed. Employment is not a sensitive indicator of alcoholism, as noticeable impairment of work performance is a late occurrence. Denial by the alcoholic and others frequently inhibits an accurate assessment of the consequences of alcoholism. The tendency is to look for excuses other than the drinking to explain the problems. The defenses are always working to distract the focus away from the alcoholism as the primary instigator.

6. *Standard criteria.* Valid criteria available are contained in the *Diagnostic and Statistical Manual of Mental Disorders* published by the American Psychiatric Association. The manual is updated periodically, and the current version is available as *DSM-IV*. The *DSM-IV* is an attempt to formulate the essentials of alcoholism for clinical use. The criteria are operational so that they can be applied to clinical conditions. The criteria have been validated in field trials and have been shown to be reliable indicators of an addiction to alcoholism.

VI. *DSM-IV* ALCOHOL DEPENDENCE

As the prototypical, substance-dependence syndrome, alcohol dependence will be viewed as the model for all of the *DSM-IV* dependence syndromes. The essential feature of alcohol or substance dependence is a cluster of cognitive, behavioral, and physiological symptoms indicating that the individual continues use of the substance despite significant substance-related problems. There is a pattern of repeated self-administration that usually results in tolerance, withdrawal, and compulsive self-administration. Using the *DSM-IV* approach, a diagnosis of substance dependence can be applied to every class of substance except caffeine. Although not specifically listed as a criterion item, "craving" is likely to be experienced by most individuals with alcoholism or other substance dependence. *Dependence* is defined as a cluster of three or more of the following symptoms occurring at any time in the same 12-month period:

"Tolerance" (criterion 1) is the need for greatly increased amounts of the substance to achieve intoxication (or the desired effect) or a markedly diminished effect with continued use of the same amount of the substance. Alcohol tolerance can also be pronounced, but is usually much less extreme than for amphetamine tolerance.

"Withdrawal" (criterion 2a) is a maladaptive behavioral change, with physiological and cognitive concomitants, that occurs when blood or tissue concentrations of a substance decline in an individual who had maintained prolonged heavy use of the substance.

After developing unpleasant withdrawal symptoms, the person is likely to take the substance to relieve or to avoid those symptoms (criterion 2b), typically using the substance throughout the day beginning soon after awakening.

Neither tolerance nor withdrawal is necessary or sufficient for a diagnosis of substance dependence. The specifics *with physiological dependence* and *without physiological dependence* are provided to indicate the presence or absence of tolerance or withdrawal.

The following items describe the pattern of compulsive substance use that is characteristic of dependence:

The individual may take the substance in larger amounts or over a longer period than was originally intended (e.g., continuing to drink until severely intoxicated despite having set a limit of only one drink) (criterion 3).

The individual may express a persistent desire to cut down or regulate substance use. Often, there have been many unsuccessful efforts to decrease or discontinue use (criterion 4).

The individual may spend a great deal of time obtaining the substance, using the substance, or recovering from its effects (criterion 5).

In some instances of substance dependence, virtually all of the person's daily activities revolve around the substance. Important social, occupational, or recreational activities may be given up or reduced because of substance use (criterion 6).

The individual may withdraw from family activities and hobbies in order to use the substance in private or to spend more time with alcohol-using friends. Despite recognizing the contributing role of the substance to a psychological or physical problem , the person continues to use the substance (criterion 7). The key issue in evaluating this criterion is not the existence of the problem, but rather the individual's failure to abstain from using the substance despite having evidence of the difficulty it is causing.

What about tolerance and dependence? Tolerance and dependence are misleading clinical criteria to use in clinical practice. The relationship between tolerance and dependence is not direct as it is considered to be and is not bilateral as many think. Furthermore, tolerance and dependence are not specific to addiction. Although tolerance and dependence occur frequently in addiction, their low threshold for detection make them unreliable in clinical practice. Obtaining a history of tolerance and dependence in alcoholism where denial is an inherent part of the disease is formidable. Moreover, the development of tolerance and dependence is seldom clinically significant in younger alcoholics who do not have a long history of chronic alcohol consumption. Only a minority of alcoholics demonstrate dramatic escalation in tolerance and withdrawal syndromes that include tremor, seizures, and delirium. The degree of tolerance and dependence to alcohol is mild compared to opiates, so that the criteria used for withdrawal are important determinants of whether dependence actually exists. The diagnosis of alcoholism can be made simply and effectively. Alcoholism is an insidious disorder that is cunning, baffling, and powerful to those who have it and those who must diagnose it. Alcoholism should be suspected when a major life problem or psychological or physical health condition exists in the setting of drinking. The diagnosis of an addiction to alcohol is confirmed by identifying a preoccupation with the acquisition of alcohol, compulsive use of alcohol, and a pattern of relapse or inability to reduce the use of alcohol in spite of adverse consequences.

VII. MEDICAL FINDINGS

A. General. Some of the frequent psychological consequences of alcoholism are anxiety, depression, phobias, and suicidal thinking and less frequent, delusions, hallucinations, and suicidal actions. These psychological manifestations are usually transient in the acute phase but persist less intensely over a protracted period of months. These effects are secondary to the pharmacologic properties of alcohol and the emotional changes that occur without the presence of alcohol.

In general, physiological findings and serious medical complications are not particularly common in the modern, youthful alcoholic, although they are present in a substantial minority. The majority of the somatic complaints are minor. These tend to cluster in the cardiovascular, gastrointestinal, pulmonary, endocrinologic, and traumatic complications. Examples are transient, mild hypertension and tachycardia; esophagitis or heartburn; chronic, productive cough; menstrual and weight abnormalities; and bruises (contusions). It is imperative that the physician look beyond the "physical aspect" of the alcoholism at some of the psychological manifestations.

Denial and rationalization are nearly always obstacles to obtaining an accurate history on which to base the diagnosis. Corroborative sources for history are often needed to obtain the necessary information to make the diagnosis. Family, employers, and others are potential sources of historical data. A high index of suspicion is necessary to make the diagnosis of alcoholism. Alcoholism is a common disorder that warrants the vigilance of the physician. Alcoholism masquerades as many other conditions, so the "atypical" cases of anything should prompt consideration of alcoholism.

Finally, alcoholism is a medical disease or disorder that is the responsibility of the physician and the medical profession. Physicians see more alcoholics than any other single group of people than perhaps do legal professionals. Early diagnosis is critical to eliminating or reducing the specter of morbidity and mortality in alcoholism. Early diagnosis and intervention are possible and desirable. Making the diagnosis of alcoholism is not an intrusion into the life of the alcoholic but a saving of one's life. Making the diagnosis of alcoholism is a major and necessary step in solving health problems. Without a proper diagnosis, specific treatment for alcoholism cannot be instituted. The natural history of alcoholism is a chronic progression from occasional intoxication or euphoria-like "high" states to more frequent, compulsive use of alcohol to total addiction to alcohol.

B. Biological Markers. Alcohol is easily absorbed into the body, widely distributed, and associated with changes in many systems. State markers for heavy drinking are generally considered "routine" chemistry evaluations that evaluate liver function by measuring changes in enzymes (e.g., γ-glutamyl transferase), bone marrow, and other effects as seen in the CBC (complete blood count) characterization of red blood cell (RBC) mean corpuscular volume and alterations in hemoglobin, and in tests that relate to lipids, kidneys, and other general functioning.

These abnormalities are often the reason given by primary clinicians for asking additional questions of the past and family regarding the role that alcohol might play in the symptoms described. These state changes are temporary and generally return toward normal within a few weeks of abstinence. There is no evidence that these same chemical findings serve as markers of a predisposition toward alcohol dependence.

C. Cardiovascular Findings. A common complication from acute and chronic alcohol consumption is an elevation of blood pressure and pulse. After acute administration of alcohol, the physiological response to the elimination of ethanol is a discharge of the sympathetic nervous system with a concomitant rise in blood pressure and pulse. The development of sustained hypertension and tachycardia are common sequelae of regular and chronic alcohol consumption.

An elevation can be detected during the intoxicated state and especially in the early abstinent state while the blood alcohol level is either dropping or was recently zero. The absolute values for blood pressure and pulse may or may not be in the abnormal range, depending on the individual reaction to alcohol withdrawal. Those who are young and without existing hypertension are less likely to have an elevation than those who are older and predisposed to some degree of hypertension.

A vast majority of those alcoholics with an elevation in blood pressure and pulse will turn out to be normotensive. The remainder who continue to have some degree of hypertension will require less medications while in the alcohol abstinent state. Elevated blood pressures, often in the hypertension range, occur with a high prevalence. Any patient with hypertension and tachycardia should be assessed for alcohol intake and alcoholism.

Alcoholic cardiomyopathy is probably more common than currently considered because of underdiagnosis of alcoholism in general, particularly in medical populations. A significant proportion of the "idiopathic cardiomyopathy" heretofore attributed to a viral ideology almost certainly have an alcohol-induced basis.

What is generally known about patients with cardiomyopathy (underdiagnosis notwithstanding) is that a chronic drinking history of at least 10 years, especially with heavy intake, is noted. The signs and symptoms of cardiac insufficiency from cardiomyopathy are generally gradual in onset, although precipitous occurrences have been reported. Patients present most often with heart failure, manifested by breathlessness, fatigability, palpitations, anorexia, and dependent edema as in any syndrome of congestive heart failure. Symptoms of angina pectoris are generally absent, although chest pain of an ischemic type does occur in some patients. The blood pressure may be normal or low, or even elevated in some patients.

The physical findings are similar to those found in other forms of dilated cardiomyopathy, lateral displacement of the apical pulse, an S3 and S4 heart sound, systolic murmurs, elevated venous pressure, hepatomegaly, and edema. The EKG findings are also nonspecific, with atrial and ventricular arrhythmia, intraventricular conduction abnormalities, pathologic Q waves, and decreased QRS voltage as common findings. The chest x-ray generally shows a symmetrical cardiomegaly, and cardiac catheterization reveals reduced output, high diastolic pressures, and pulmonary hypertension. The histologic features are varied and nonspecific; myocardial fiber hypertrophy and fibrosis as well as lipid or glycogen vacuolization are also found.

Alcoholic cardiomyopathy is not an inevitably fatal condition, and improvement frequently follows abstinence from alcohol, particularly in those patients in whom cardiac symptoms are of recent onset. It is likely that many of the cases of cardiomyopathy that receive heart transplantation have an alcoholic basis. This is important to note because continued drinking may contribute to a poor-outcome posttransplantation. All cases of cardiomyopathy should be evaluated for possible alcoholism.

D. Gastrointestinal System Findings. Disturbances attributable to the gastrointestinal tract occur commonly following alcohol use, particularly in higher-dose and chronic administration. Any complaint arising from the gastrointestinal system deserves an evaluation of alcohol use and possible alcoholism. Alcohol produces irritation and inflammation of the mucosa lining the gastrointestinal tract. Frank ulceration may occur with chronic alcohol use.

The well-known "heartburn" is due to the esophageal reflux with esophagitis that commonly occurs with irritation and inflammation of the gastroesophageal junction by alcohol. Severe vomiting may result in mucosal tears at this junction, with hematemesis as in the Mallory–Weiss syndrome. Esophageal varices are an expression of portal hypertension from liver disease, also often induced by alcohol. These varices are engorged, dilated capillaries that represent a collateral circulation. Significant and sometimes fatal hemorrhage may occur from these varices.

The stomach and duodenum are sites vulnerable to the corrosive effects of alcohol. Short- and long-term alcohol ingestion is associated with general gastritis, erosive gastritis, gastric ulceration, atrophic gastritis, and gastric hemorrhage. Furthermore, duodenitis and duodenal ulceration are a direct result of chronic alcohol irritation and inflammation. Scarring and obstruction may result from chronic ulceration.

Chronic administration of alcohol may result in chronic pancreatitis. However, acute ingestion of alcohol is associated with an alteration in the secretion of pancreatic enzymes and abnormalities in intestinal absorption in acute and chronic alcohol use. Abdominal pain and vomiting are common during acute pancreatitis. The pain is poorly localized to the upper abdomen, radiating to the back. Other signs may be lacking in mild cases, and in more severe cases, hypoactive bowel sounds and rebound tenderness suggestive of peritonitis may be present. In cases of high fever, a pancreatic abscess may be suspected, also an abdominal mass, a pseudocyst, and shifting dullness, and ascites may be encountered. Helpful diagnostic features are serum amylase, ultrasonography, and CT or MRI (computerized tomography or magnetic resonance imaging) scannings.

Diabetes mellitus or hyperglycemia is a complication resulting from the eventual destruction of the islet cells in the pancreas from persistent, alcohol-induced, chronic pancreatitis. Often insulin is necessary to compensate for the lost insulin production in the fibrosed, contracted pancreas. At times, replacement therapy of pancreatic enzymes for pancreatic insufficiency may be necessary.

Malabsorption and diarrhea are common in alcoholics and are a result of a number of interactive factors. These include alterations in gastric motility, mucosal erosions, and impaired transport of glucose, amino acids, and vitamins, particularly thiamine and vitamin B_{12} and the minerals calcium and magnesium.

The liver is a particularly vulnerable organ in alcohol consumption, in part because it is where alcohol is metabolized and broken down for reuse and elimination from the body. The most common manifestation is fatty metamorphosis or "fatty liver." For some alcoholics, a fatty liver may precede the onset of alcoholic cirrhosis. However, a large number of those who consume alcohol will develop fat in the liver but not cirrhosis. In fact, evidence in animals suggests that fatty metamorphosis occurs regularly with acute ingestion of alcohol. Transient, mild elevations of liver enzymes, particularly ALT and AST, will occur. These return to normal within a few weeks.

Alcoholic hepatitis is a severe condition that is characterized by jaundice, fever, anorexia, and right-upper-quadrant pain. The liver histologically shows parenchymal and portal infiltration with polymorphonuclear leukocytes, steatosis, cholestasis, and sometimes hyaline bodies. The serum levels of ALT (alanine transferase), AST (aspartate transaminase), and LDH (lactic dehydrogenase) are elevated, at times, at high levels. Prolongation of the prothrombin time and ascites may occur.

Alcoholic cirrhosis is not a particularly common condition among alcoholics as a total population. However, its prevalence increases in older and more chronic populations of alcoholics. The overall prevalence rate for cirrhosis is 5–10% of all alcoholics. The most common signs of uncomplicated cirrhosis are weight loss, weakness, and anorexia. In more severe cases, the signs may include jaundice, a small or large liver, splenomegaly, ascites, asterixis, testicular atrophy, edema, spontaneous peritonitis, gynecomastia, spider angiomata, palmar erythema, and Dupuytren's contracture. Laboratory findings are hypoalbuminemia and hyperglobinemia with or without elevation of liver enzymes. *Cirrhosis* is scarring of the liver from alcohol with a microscopic picture of fibrosis of portal and central zones and an overall distortion of the architecture of the liver, which may be small and shrunken.

1. Complications of cirrhosis. Serious complications from cirrhosis are ascites, esophageal varices, hepatorenal syndrome (renal failure) and hepatic encephalopathy, coma, and death. Once cirrhosis has developed, the life expectancy is around 50% if abstinence is maintained and significantly less if alcohol is continued to be ingested. It is not known why and which individuals will develop cirrhosis except that it tends to occur in chronic, older drinkers—although there are many exceptions to this rule.

E. Nutritional Complications. Alcohol and nutritional status are interrelated. Alcohol intake may interfere with the absorption, digestion, metabolism, and utilization of nutrients, particularly vitamins. The use of alcohol as a source of calories to the exclusion of other food sources, including nutrients, may also lead to a nutrient deficiency.

Alcohol disrupts absorption of nutrients in the various ways outlined in previous sections by acting on the intestinal wall such as the small intestine and damaging organs such as the pancreas that are responsible for digestion. The effect of alcoholism on metabolism is to alter the inactivation and activation of the nutrients. For instance, alcohol decreases the net synthesis of pyridoxal phosphate from pyridoxine. These effects have been linked to the oxidation of ethanol.

These nutritional effects of alcohol are more than an academic interest. Admission to hospitals for malnutrition with alcoholism remains a significant portion of admissions for malnutrition alone. Alcoholism is suggested as the most common cause of vitamin and trace-element deficiency in adults in the United States. And malnutrition remains a significant cause of admissions to general hospitals.

The regular consumption of alcohol itself contributes to the poor intake of other foodstuffs containing proper nutrients. Alcohol contains calories, supplying 7.1 kcal/g (of body weight). Thus consumers of 600 mL of 86-proof distilled spirits derive 1500 kcal or more than 50% of their daily caloric needs. The calories derived from alcohol are called "empty" calories because of the small amounts of vitamins, minerals, essential amino acids, or essential fatty acids contained in most alcoholic beverages. Primary malnutrition resulting from a decrease in the actual ingestion of nutrients is frequently associated with regular and heavy alcohol use.

1. Folic acid deficiency. Megaloblastic anemia is common in malnourished alcoholics and most often is due to folate deficiency. Thrombocytopenia and granulocytopenia may accompany the megaloblastic changes, especially if the folate level is severely low. The deficiency results from poor intake and disruption of absorption in the small bowel. The hematologic manifestations of the folate deficiency are rapidly reversible despite persistently low serum levels.

2. Pyridoxine deficiency. Pyridoxine deficiency has been implicated in the development of sideroblastic anemia in the alcoholic. The sideroblastic changes induced by ethanol and a diet low in pyridoxine is reversed by the intake of the vitamin in spite of continued alcohol ingestion.

3. Thiamine deficiency. The thiamine deficiency in the alcoholic may result from malabsorption and perhaps defective activation of thiamine. Thiamine deficiency is the cause of Wernicke–Korsakoff syndrome. It is certain that latent or subclinical thiamine deficiency is common in the alcoholic, and the administration of parental glucose without thiamine may precipitate Wernicke's encephalopathy in such patients.

4. Iron deficiency. Iron deficiency is usually present only when other factors related to iron deficiency are present, such as gastrointestinal bleeding and infection. Iron overload or excess is more likely than deficiency because of increased iron absorption from a pancreatic insufficiency. Because an anemia from another cause may be present, iron may be given incorrectly.

5. Zinc deficiency. Zinc deficiency may be associated with the pathogenesis of nightblindness seen in alcoholics because of its role as a cofactor of vitamin A dehydrogenate, the enzyme responsible for the conversion of retinol to retinal.

F. Fat Soluble Vitamin Deficiency

1. Vitamin A. A deficiency in vitamin A may result from a decreased uptake from malabsorption (steatorrhea), impaired storage, increased degradation, and diminished activation. Chronic consumption of ethanol decreases hepatic vitamin A levels. Clinically, vitamin A deficiency is related to abnormal dark adaptation and hypogonadism. Repletion of vitamin A and zinc may reverse these conditions but should be done cautiously because alcohol increases the hepatotoxicity of even moderate doses of vitamin A.

2. Vitamin D. Vitamin D deficiency may result from decreased dietary intake, decreased absorption, and altered metabolism. Vitamin D depletion and impairment of calcium transport may lead to a decrease in bone density and increased susceptibility to fractures and aseptic necrosis.

3. Vitamin K. Steatorrhea, decreased intake, and altered colonic microflora may combine to produce vitamin K deficiency. In patients with liver damage, further vitamin K deficiency may result in a depression of an already marginal synthesis of clotting factors and result in bleeding.

G. Endocrinologic Effects. Alcohol affects the endocrine system in a variety of ways by interacting at all levels of the endocrine axis. The levels at which alteration from alcohol may occur are the hypothalamus and the pituitary, adrenal, thyroid, and gonadal glands. Furthermore, liver injury from alcohol disturbs the peripheral metabolism of hormones by changes in hepatic blood flow, protein binding, enzymes, cofactors, or receptors.

1. Adrenocortical function. Chronic alcohol consumption results in increased plasma cortisol levels. Occasionally, alcohol use is associated with Cushingoid changes such as increased plasma-cortisol levels (more consistently), an abnormal response to dexamethasone, and evidence of pituitary dysfunction. Alcohol activates the hypothalamic–pituitary–adrenal axis to promote ACTH (adrenocorticotropic hormone) release and cortisol secretion.

2. Adrenomedullary function. Alcohol consumption results in stimulation of adrenal medullary secretion of catecholemines. The peripheral metabolism of catecholemines shifts from an oxidative (3-methoxy-4-hydroxymandelic acid) to a reductive pathway (3-methoxy-4-hydroxyphenylglycol), a change that reflects an increase in the NADH / NAD ratio or acetaldehyde production. This ratio change may be important in the generation of condensation products in the formation of the tetrahydroisoguinolines. Chronic alcohol consumption also leads to the stimulation of the secretion of catecholemines from the sympathetic portion of the autonomic nervous system. Alcohol withdrawal is characterized by alterations in vital signs and arousal state that are indicative of a massive release of catecholemines.

3. Thyroid function. Alcohol administration increases the liver to plasma ratios of thyroid hormone that may lead to a hepatic "hyperthyroidism." This state is responsible for increased oxygen consumption, local anoxia, and possibly liver injury.

4. Gonadal function. Alcohol consumption decreases plasma testosterone, an effect that results from a decrease in production and increased metabolic clearance of the hormone. Alcoholic cirrhosis is known to lead to primary hypogonadism with subsequent feminization. The pathologic basis is multifactorial—destruction of the testosterone-producing cells in the testes, elevated estradiol and estrogen levels, and increased conversion of testosterone and androstenedione to estrogen because of decreased breakdown by the liver. The clinical manifestations are loss of male secondary sex characteristics and a feminization, including decreased libido, hair, and muscle mass; gynecomastia; and smooth, feminine skin. These changes may or may not be reversible, depending on the degree of permanent damage.

5. Pituitary function. The release of the gonadotropin from the hypothalamic–pituitary axis is defective. Also, the release of the antidiuretic hormone in the posterior pituitary gland is inhibited by alcohol. The end result is a diuretic action of alcohol and subsequent dehydration from a lack of action of the antidiuretic hormone on the reabsorption of free water in the tubules in the kidney.

6. Alcoholic hypoglycemia. This is due to an inhibition by alcohol of gluconeogenesis in the liver. Gluconeogenesis is the major source of glucose during chronic alcohol consumption, particularly when other dietary sources of glucose are not available to the liver. The symptoms of hypoglycemia may be severe, with fatigue, tremors, seizures, and other manifestations of low blood sugar.

7. Alcoholic ketosis. This condition usually follows regular consumption of alcohol, anorexia, and hyperemesis. The level of β-hydroxybutyrates are higher than that of acetoacetate.

8. Neurologic complications. Neurologic complications from chronic alcohol consumption are numerous and occur in most chronic drinkers. The type and number of neurologic complications depend on the severity of the alcohol use, nutritional status, and individual susceptibility to alcohol.

The most common abnormality is a decrease in intellectual functioning or dementia syndrome with a subsequent decrease in recent memory, abstractions, calculations, general knowledge, and other aspects of cognitive functions. Studies show that a reduction in IQ may result from as little as 2 oz of alcohol consumed on a regular basis over a prolonged period of months. Studies of alcoholics show that the depression in IQ may be reversible, improving over a period of months and years from the time of cessation of alcohol use.

Furthermore, MRI, CT, and other scans of the brain have confirmed that cerebral atrophy occurs in alcoholics frequently at any age but is more common and pronounced at older ages. The changes seen in the CT scans are representative of a decrease in brain mass with a concomitant increase in ventricular size. The changes are diffuse and widespread, indicative of a generalized effect of alcohol in the brain. The cerebral atrophy correlates with impairments in the intellect. With abstinence, atrophy as well as the reduction in IQ is noted to reverse with subsequent CT scanning of the brain and resetting of the IQ.

The underlying mechanism is a direct toxicity by alcohol on the neurons and their processes, the axons, and dendrites as well as the supporting cells, the astroglia. These neuropathologic changes have been noted in animal and human studies, when nutritional factors have been controlled for.

Interestingly, the most classic neurologic syndrome from chronic alcohol consumption may not be due to the direct toxic effects of alcohol. *Wernicke–Korsakoff syndrome* is the result of a thiamine deficiency but does not play a role in the direct toxicity on nerve cells. The neuropathologic changes are due to alterations in the cerebellum, brain stem, and diencephalon. These changes are often small hemorrhages and infarct in the structures. The clinical manifestations are predictable for Wernicke's syndrome and include a delirium with a clouded sensorium and confusion, ophthalmoplegia, nystagmus, and ataxia. Peripheral neuropathies are commonly associated with the syndrome. All as aspects of the syndrome will improve with the administration of thiamine, although not always completely. Many of the patients with Wernicke's syndrome will develop the Korsakoff syndrome, although a few will return to their premorbid state. The Korsakoff syndrome is characterized by a profound loss in recent memory out of proportion to the other cognitive deficits. In other words, the Korsakoff patient may not remember dates and names but can calculate and abstract reasonably well in an intact personality.

Alcoholic peripheral neuropathy is characterized by diminished sensitivity to touch, pinprick, and vibration (objectively), and paraesthesias (subjectively). These symptoms appear bilateral and symmetrical, most prominent in the distal portions of the extremities, in greater frequency and severity in the lower extremities. Both sensory and motor nerves are affected.

The alcoholic myopathy can be acute, subacute, and chronic in onset. Muscle weakness and atrophy may be present. More often an elevated CPK (creatinine phosphokinase) occurs in association with the symptoms of muscle cramps, weakness, and occasional dark urine (myoglobinuria). In severe cases, the rhabdomyolysis produces significant myoglobinuria with renal failure that may be fatal. Most likely, the etiology of the muscle damage is the direct toxic effect of ethanol on muscle. In most cases, discontinuation of alcohol consumption leads to improvement of the myopathy.

H. Oncology. Heavy drinking increases the risk of cancer in the tongue, mouth, oropharynx, hypopharynx, esophagus, larynx, and liver. In the United

States, these sites represent approximately 10% of all cancers in the white population and 12% in the black population.

1. Buccal cavity, pharynx, and larynx. Cancers of the mouth, pharynx, and larynx appear to be related to heavy drinking. Tobacco is the leading risk factor for the development of these cancers, but alcohol carries an additional, increased risk to the development of cancer. Of course, cigarette smoking commonly occurs among alcoholics. One study showed that 93% of men and 91% of women in a group of alcoholic outpatients were smokers, proportions far above the prevalence for smoking in the general population. A study, however, separated out the individual risk for cancer of the mouth and concluded that "heavy drinkers" had a tenfold greater risk of having cancer of the mouth than did minimal drinkers. As the amount of alcohol consumed is increased, the relative risk of cancer of the mouth, extrinsic larynx, and esophagus was also increased, much more so with whiskey than beer and wine.

2. Esophagus. Two-thirds of patients with cancer of the esophagus also have a history of heavy alcohol use. Investigators have shown a relationship between heavy drinking, especially of whiskey or other spirits, and esophageal cancer, after corrections for age and tobacco were made. Smoking has been reported to be less important than alcohol in the absence of heavy drinking.

3. Large intestine and rectum. Studies have revealed a strong association between rectal and colonic cancer and alcohol, particularly beer.

4. Liver, primary. Worldwide, almost 90% of all liver-cell cancer arises in cirrhotic organs. The typical person in whom a primary cancer of the liver (hepatoma) occurs is an alcoholic with cirrhosis. However, hepatoma may occur in alcoholics who do not have cirrhosis. The hepatoma seems to occur 2–8 years after the onset of cirrhosis.

5. Pancreas. There may be an association between alcohol consumption and pancreatic malignancy, particularly if pancreatitis exists before the onset of the pancreatic malignancy.

I. The Alcoholic and Infectious Disease. Pneumonia is a frequent cause of illness and death for alcoholics. In some studies, as many as 50% of all patients admitted with pneumonia were alcoholics. Also, tuberculosis appears to be prevalent among alcoholics. Other infectious diseases that are overrepresented among alcoholics are bacterial meningitis, peritonitis, and ascending cholangitis. Less serious infections are chronic sinusitis, pharyngitis, and other minor infections.

The basis for an increased risk for infection among alcoholics is a depressed immune system by alcohol at the various sites of the immune defense in the reticuloendothial system. Studies have demonstrated decreased white-cell production and response in active drinkers, in addition to impaired antibody production.

HIV and AIDS have been reported in alcoholic populations, and alcohol abuse is associated with increases in unsafe sex among high-school and college-age populations.

VIII. FAMILY HISTORY AND RISK

A. General. Alcohol dependence often has an important genetic or familial pattern. The most impressive data come from the Goodwin et al. (1979) classic evaluation of sons and daughters of alcoholic persons who were adopted away early in life and usually raised without knowledge of their biological parents' problems. These and other studies carried out since 1950 have demonstrated a twofold to fourfold increased risk for alcohol dependence in these children, with no commensurate increased risk for severe alcohol problems in adopted-away children of nonalcoholic persons. It does not appear that being raised by an alcoholic person increases the risk for future alcohol dependence beyond the level predicted by an alcoholic biological parent alone. The risk for alcohol dependence is 3–4 times higher in close relatives of people with alcohol dependence. Higher risk is associated with a greater number of affected relatives, closer genetic relationships, and the severity of the alcohol-related problems in the affected relative. Most studies have found a significantly higher risk for alcohol dependence in the monozygotic twin than in the dizygotic twin of a person with alcohol dependence. Adoption studies have revealed a three- to fourfold increase in risk for alcohol dependence in the children of individuals with alcohol dependence when these children were adopted away at birth and raised by adoptive parents who did not have this disorder.

B. Children of Alcoholics. Over a decade ago, Schuckit (1994) began to study the effects of alcohol in sons of alcoholic men compared with subjects without a family history of alcoholism using 454 male staff at the University of California, San Diego. Individuals who were relatively insensitive to a moderate alcohol dose in subjective response and body sway were significantly more likely to be abusing alcohol or dependent at long-term follow-up. A low level of response to alcohol at age 20 was associated with a fourfold greater likelihood of future alcoholism in both the sons of alcoholics and the comparison subjects. Of the sons of alcoholics with the lesser alcohol response, 56% developed alcoholism during the subsequent decade. Schuckit clearly separated the risk for development of alcoholism from the risk of development of other psychiatric disorders with this paradigm of sensitivity to the intoxicating effects of alcohol. Insensitivity was highly significant for young men with a positive family history for alcoholism. The basic science literature is quite supportive of these data. For example, rats bred for alcohol preference appear to be less sensitive to the effects of alcohol than do other rats. A number of family, adoption, and twin studies have identified important genetic influences on the risk for the development of alcoholism.

C. Other Markers. There are a number of possible biological markers of the alcoholism risk. These include a diminished response to an ethanol challenge, the absence of the low-K_m form of ALDH, electrophysiological measures such as a diminished P3 amplitude, and several promising protein markers including MAO (monoamine oxidase), adenylate cyclase, and cyclic adenosine monophosphate activity levels.

IX. CONCLUSION

Most Americans drink alcohol. Reliable surveys indicate that 90% of adult Americans have had a drink of alcohol at some point in their lives. According to the most rigorous study, about 16% of the population suffers from alcoholism. However, 80% or more of the alcohol consumed in the United States is consumed by the alcoholic. In other words, only 16% of the alcohol consumed in the United States is done so by 80% of the population. Alcoholics are a devoted and dedicated lot when it comes to consuming alcohol.

The target population for early detection and prompt intervention can be further characterized by recognizing that the onset of alcoholism in the United States is 22 years for males and 25 years for females. Interestingly, this age gap is narrowing as more women are becoming alcoholic and doing so at a younger age. These findings suggest that alcoholism is a disorder of the young and not the old, as is the popular myth. The image of the elderly skid-row drinker is a distorted fantasy that exists in a fraction of reality. Skid-row alcoholics represent only 3% of the alcoholics in the United States, and many of them are younger than is commonly recognized.

Focusing on the attachment for alcohol and the distorted importance that alcohol has in a person's life has the capacity to increase the physician's ability to diagnose and treat alcohol abuse and dependence. Treatment is not merely reversal of abstinence but rather a complex process of relearning and development of alternative attachments and skills. Once diagnosis is made, the physician must work with the patient and family to maximize the success of treatment and by focusing on recovery, to reduce relapse.

REFERENCES

Cloninger CR: Neurogenetic adaptive mechanisms in alcoholism. *Science* 236:410–416, 1987.

Dackis CA, Gold MS, Estroff TW: Inpatient treatment of addiction. In TB Karasu (ed): *Treatments of Psychiatric Disorders*. Washington, DC: A Task Force Report of the American Psychiatric Association, APPI, 1989, vol 2, pp 1359 1379.

DSM-IV. Washington, DC: APA Press, 1994.

Gold MS: Neurobiology of addiction and recovery: the brain, the drive for the drug and the 12-Step Fellowship. *J Substance Abuse Treatment* 11(2):93–97, 1994.

Gold MS: Overview: Role of the physician, prevention of addictive disorders, section III, chapter 1, *ASAM Manual*, 1995.

Gold MS, Miller NS: The neurobiology of drug and alcohol addictions. In NS Miller, MS Gold (eds): *Pharmacological Therapies for Drug and Alcohol Addictions*. New York: Marcel Dekker, 1995, pp 11–28.

Gold MS, Miller NS: Seeking drugs/alcohol and avoiding withdrawal: the neuroanatomy of drive states and withdrawal. *Psychiatric Ann* 22:430–435, 1992.

Goldstein A: *Addiction: from Biology to Drug Policy.* New York: Freeman, 1994.

Goodwin DW: Alcoholism and heredity. *Arch Gen Psychiatry* 36:57–61, 1979.

Institute for Health Policy, Brandeis University: *Substance Abuse: The Nation's Number One Health Problem; Key Indicators for Policy.* Princeton, NJ: Robert Wood Johnson Foundation, October 1993.

Kessler RC, McGonagle KA, Zhao S, et al: Lifetime and 12 month prevalence of DSMIII-R psychiatric disorders in the United States: results from the National Co-morbidity Survey. *Arch Gen Psychiatry* 51:8–19, 1994.

Litten RZ, Allen JP: Pharmacological therapies of alcohol addiction. In NS Miller, MS Gold (eds): *Pharmacological Therapies for Drug and Alcohol Addictions*. New York: Marcel Dekker, 1995, pp 127–142.

Meyer RM: What for, alcohol research. *Am J Psychiatry* 151:165–167, 1994.

Miller NS: *Addiction Psychiatry: Current Diagnosis and Treatment.* New York: Wiley, 1995.

Miller NS, Gold MS: *Drugs of Abuse: A Comprehensive Series for Clinicians.* Vol. II: *Alcohol.* New York: Plenum Medical Book Company, 1991.

Miller NS, Dackis CA, Gold MS: The relationship of addiction, tolerance and dependence: a neurochemical approach. *J Substance Abuse Treatment* 4:197–207, 1987.

Rigmaiden RS, Pistorello J, Johnson J, Mar D, Veach TL: Addiction medicine in ambulatory care: prevalence patterns in internal medicine. *Substance Abuse* 16:49–57, 1995.

Schuckit MA: Low level of response to alcohol as a predictor of future alcoholism. *Am J Psychiatry* 151:184–189, 1994.

Vaillant GE: *The Natural History of Alcoholism.* Cambridge, MA: Harvard University Press, 1983.

CHAPTER 3

INTOXICATION AND WITHDRAWAL FROM MARIJUANA, LSD, AND MDMA

Mark S. Gold, M.D.
University of Florida Brain Institute, Gainesville, Florida

Norman S. Miller, M.D.
University of Illinois at Chicago, Chicago, Illinois

I. MARIJUANA

A. General. Marijuana is one of the major drugs of abuse. Regular use of marijuana has been reported to be increasing as the principal psychoactive component of marijuana is increasing in commercially available marijuana. Cannabinoids, especially cannabis, are also the most widely used illicit psychoactive substances in the United States, even though lifetime prevalence figures had slowly decreased from the figures obtained by surveys in the 1980s. Use is currently increasing again, especially in adolescents. A community survey conducted in the United States in 1991 reported that about one-third of the population had used marijuana one or more times in their lifetime; 10% had used it in the last year; and 5% had used it in the last month. A community study conducted in the United States from 1980 to 1985 that used the more narrowly defined *DSM-III* criteria found that about 4% of the adult population had cannabis dependence or abuse at some time in their lives. In excess of 2% of high-school seniors use marijuana every day (see Fig. 3.1).

B. Description. The upper leaves, tops, and stems of the cannabis plant are cut, dried, and rolled into cigarettes; the product is called *marijuana*. Marijuana is the most commonly available and used cannabinoid. Hashish and hashish oil are also used. Cannabinoids are usually smoked, but may be taken orally, and sometimes marijuana is even mixed with food or drunk in tea. The cannabinoid that has been identified as primarily responsible for the centrally reinforcing effects, mood, and behavior changes of cannabis is Δ^9-tetrahydrocannabinol (THC, or Δ^9-THC). Animal self-administration and daily human use are linked to THC.

C. Epidemiology: 6th–12th-Grade Students. National Household Survey data reported for 1985 found 18,000,000 users of marijuana. By 1992 this survey reported 9,000,000 marijuana users for a 50% decrease from 1985 to 1992. Annual high-school-senior data reported decreases in marijuana use in the past year from 1977 and 1978 to 1989 and 1990. We reported that annual and

Manual of Therapeutics for Addictions, Edited by Norman S. Miller, Mark S. Gold, and David E. Smith.
ISBN 0471-56176-2 © 1997 John Wiley & Sons, Inc.

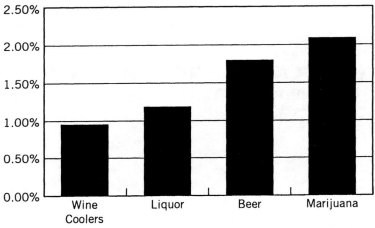

FIGURE 3.1. Daily marijuana use surpasses daily alcohol use in 12th-graders. (*Source:* 1992/93 PRIDE survey of 26,438 12th-graders.)

monthly use of marijuana increased significantly in all grades surveyed. Among senior high-school students, marijuana use rates increased each year since 1991:

Marijuana rates (%)

Grade	1991/92	1992/93	1993/94
6th-8th	4.8	5.8	8.2
9th-12th	16.4	19	24.6
12th	21.9	25	28.9

Monthly Use of Marijuana

Grade	1992/93	1993/94
6th-9th	3.3	4.9
9th-12th	11.3	15.6
12th	14.6	18

Annual PRIDE survey data demonstrate that student marijuana use is accelerating. Most alarming is that marijuana use is increasing in popularity among the youngest students in our survey and among African-American students in grades 6, 7, and 9 marijuana use tripled in the past 2 years from 3.2 to 10.1%.

D. Why Increased Marijuana Intoxication Today? Previous reports of increased student perception of extreme danger associated with marijuana use have now been replaced by questions of danger, a renewal of interest in promarijuana singing groups, shirts and hats that feature the marijuana leaf as a logo, and debate about legalization. We reported PRIDE data where 77% of students said marijuana was very harmful; however, this year only 73% said the marijuana use was very harmful. Marijuana smoking, while most common among young people, persists in ≥35-year-old adults (Fig. 3.2).

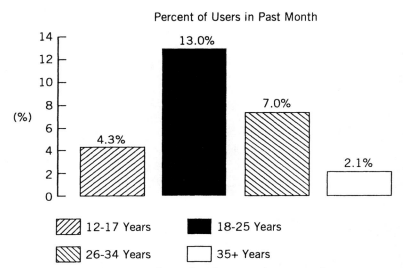

FIGURE 3.2. Prevalence of marijuana use. (*Source:* RWJ.)

E. Tobacco or Marijuana Gateway. Recent surveys report increases in smoking nicotine and also marijuana cigarettes. A recent study examined whether a sample of drug abusers in New York City follows the same developmental pathways as observed in the general population. The results suggest that alcohol is no longer a prerequisite for use of marijuana, but that marijuana use nearly always precedes use of cocaine, crack, and heroin. With the growing prevalence of marijuana use, the importance of alcohol as a gateway to marijuana appears to have declined and marijuana's role as a gateway to drug use and addiction appears to have increased. In another study in which detailed marijuana and tobacco smoking histories were obtained from 467 adult regular smokers of marijuana and/or tobacco, 49% began smoking tobacco before marijuana, while 33% began smoking marijuana first; 85% of marijuana smokers who quit tobacco smoking did so after beginning regular marijuana smoking. Before these studies, we had believed that early onset of tobacco smoking is associated with more frequent progression to marijuana smoking, as well as the use of other illicit drugs. In people with a single smoking habit of either tobacco or marijuana who began smoking the other substance, the amount of the first substance smoked decreased in approximately one-third of subjects, while the amount did not change in slightly more than half of the subjects. Initiation of a new smoking habit can lead to concurrent use of both marijuana and tobacco or reduced smoking of the other substance regardless of which substance was smoked first. Of all smokers of both tobacco and marijuana, one-half began smoking tobacco before marijuana, while one-third began smoking marijuana first. The finding that so many subjects began smoking marijuana before smoking tobacco is at odds with the generally held belief that cigarette smoking almost always precedes marijuana smoking in young people. Marijuana is perceived as less dangerous than tobacco (see Fig. 3.3) and is increasingly the gateway drug.

F. THC

1. Pharmacology. Tetrahydrocannabinol (THC) is the principal psychoactive ingredient in marijuana and is self-administered in animals and humans.

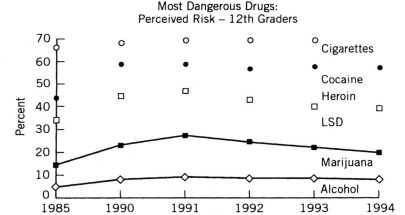

FIGURE 3.3. Relative changes in potency for marijuana and LSD from 1985 to 1994. (*Source:* National Narcotics Intelligence Consumers Committee report; NIDA/UM 1994.)

THC content of the marijuana that is generally available varies greatly. The THC content of illicit marijuana has increased significantly since the late 1960s from an average of approximately 1% to as much as 15%. Synthetic Δ^9-THC has been used on occasion for nausea and vomiting caused by chemotherapy, for anorexia, and even for weight loss in individuals with acquired immunodeficiency syndrome (AIDS).

2. THC dose–response curve. The higher the THC content, the more users prefer and choose it over less THC marijuana. Recent street reports of selling marijuana as "blunts" or "KGB" or "Kryptonite," a.k.a. "Krippie" by THC content, is of great concern. Daily marijuana use has increased to the point that it exceeds daily alcohol use in some surveys of high-school seniors. With higher THC potency marijuana available, analogies of Woodstock I versus Woodstock II marijuana to cocaine-leaf chewing versus crack may not be too far off.

3. THC receptors. Endogenous THC receptors have been identified in brain and on white blood cells. At present, anandamide is the only endogenous candidate ligand for the recently identified cannabinoid receptor. While peripheral receptors are found on white blood cells, THC receptors are found in hippocampus, periaqueductal gray dorsal raphe, and other brain areas. The recent cloning of the peripheral cannabinoid receptor has a number of important implications. The identification of the cannabinoid receptors in brain and the periphery and a candidate ligand suggests that we may soon understand the basis for the seemingly diverse cannabinoid effects, in a manner similar to the understanding of the diverse opiate effects in humans that have followed the discovery of endorphins and opioid receptors. The discovery of a G-protein-coupled cannabinoid receptor together with the identification of the putative endogenous cannabinoid ligand anandamide and the partial purification of other putative ligands for the cannabinoid receptor provide a strong argument for the existence an endogenous cannabinoid neural system. The following lines of evidence suggest that one function of this novel system is to modulate pain sensitivity:

    a. Cannabinoids produce analgesia with nearly the same potency and efficacy as morphine in rodents.

    b. The inactivity of the enantiomers of cannabinoids, the development of tolerance, and the strong correlation between cannabinoid receptor binding affinity and behavioral potency indicate that this effect is mediated by cannabinoid receptors.

    c. The analgesic effects of cannabinoids are centrally mediated and have both spinal and supraspinal substrates.

    d. Cannabinoids inhibit nociceptive responses in wide-dynamic-range-neurons in the spinal cord and the thalamus, thus illustrating that cannabinoid effects on behavioral measures of pain are due at least in part to the inhibition of neurotransmission within spinothalamic nociceptive pathways. These findings suggest that endogenous cannabinoids may serve naturally to inhibit the processing of painful inputs.

G. Marijuana Intoxication. Intoxication begins with a "high" feeling followed by symptoms that include euphoria with inappropriate laughter and grandiosity, sedation, lethargy, impairment in short-term memory, difficulty carrying out complex mental processes, impaired judgment, distorted sensory perceptions, impaired motor performance, and the sensation that time is passing slowly. Occasionally, users complain of excessive fearfulness, anxiety, depression, and social isolation. Anxiety (which can be severe), dysphoria, or social withdrawal may occur. These psychoactive effects are accompanied by two or more of the following signs, developing within 2 h of cannabis use: conjunctival injection, increased appetite, dry mouth, and tachycardia (criterion C). The symptoms must not be due to a general medical condition and are not better accounted for by another mental disorder (criterion D).

Intoxication develops within minutes if the cannabis is smoked, but may take a few hours to develop if ingested orally. The effects usually last 3–4 h; the duration is somewhat longer when the substance is ingested orally. The magnitude of the behavioral and physiological changes depends on the dose, the method of administration, and the individual characteristics of the person using the substance, such as rate of absorption, tolerance, and sensitivity to the effects of the substance. Motor performance, concentration, and alertness may be affected for hours to days. Because most cannabinoids, including Δ^9-THC, are fat-soluble, the effects of cannabis or hashish may occasionally persist or reoccur for 12–24 h as the result of a slow release of psychoactive substances from fatty tissue or to enterohepatic circulation.

H. Diagnostic Criteria for 292.89 Cannabis Intoxication

    1. Recent use of cannabis.

    2. Clinically significant maladaptive behavioral or psychological changes (e.g., impaired motor coordination, euphoria, anxiety, sensation of slowed time, impaired judgment, social withdrawal) that developed during, or shortly after, cannabis use.

    3. Two (or more) of the following signs, developing within 2 hours of cannabis use:

        a. Conjunctival injection

        b. Increased appetite

        c. Dry mouth

        d. Tachycardia

    4. The symptoms are not due to a general medical condition and are not better accounted for by another mental disorder.

I. Other Unintended Intoxication Events. Cannabinoids have psychoactive effects that can be similar to those of hallucinogens [e.g., lysergic acid diethylamide (LSD)], and individuals who use cannabinoids can experience adverse mental effects that resemble hallucinogen-induced "bad trips." There may also be frank delusions and hallucinations. Fatal traffic accidents have been found to occur more often in individuals who test positive for cannabinoids than in the general population. Driving under the influence of intoxicating drugs other than alcohol may be an important cause of traffic injuries. Using a rapid urine test to identify reckless drivers who were under the influence of cocaine or marijuana, of 150 subjects stopped for reckless driving and providing a urine sample, 59% tested positive. Intoxicated drivers were difficult to characterize with many differences in driving, behavior, and appearance. Toxicologic screening at the scene is a practical means of identifying drivers under the influence of drugs and as an adjunct to standard roadside sobriety testing.

J. Urine Documentation of Use, Blood Intoxication, and Other Testing. Urine testing reliably identifies cannabinoid metabolites, and blood testing can identify THC. Because THC and other cannabinoids are fat-soluble, they persist and can be detected in urine and other bodily fluids for extended periods of time. Urine cannabinoid testing of regular or heavy users can remain positive for up to 4 weeks.

K. Dependence. Individuals with cannabis dependence, like all other addictions, have compulsive use. Regular administration of potent marijuana is associated with dependence. Users report selling everything from furniture to football tickets for the most expensive and potent marijuana. Tolerance to most of the effects of cannabis has also been reported in individuals who use cannabis chronically. Clinicians report increasing numbers of clients reporting for treatment of marijuana dependence. Clinicians have also been reporting patient complaints of withdrawal discomfort. Individuals with cannabis dependence show striking preoccupation with their marijuana and a pathologic attachment to their plants, supplies, and use. They may spend several hours a day preparing, processing, growing, acquiring, and using the substance. They may demonstrate striking anticipation of their next use. Marijuana dependence often interferes with their ability to function at levels that they had previously. School and rigorous athletic programs suffer, as do relationships with family and friends. Recreation is generally tied to use, and even considering going to a concert or social event without marijuana may be perceived as painful. Marijuana acquisition and use becomes primary, and school, work, or recreational activities secondary. Individuals with cannabis dependence persist in their use despite knowledge of physical, social, motivational, attentional, and other problems.

L. Chronic Cannabis Use Syndrome. Over the last 10 years Lundqvist (1995) studied approximately 400 patients with chronic cannabis use (use from six months through 25 years). The symptoms associated with this use occur with remarkable regularity among clients and contribute to a new pattern of thinking that can be considered a cannabis-state-dependent set of cognitive processes. These mental and behavioral changes are unique to cannabis use. Clinical observations show that the use of cannabis more often than about every 6 weeks (elimination time of THC) for approximately 2 years, leads to changes in cognitive functioning. These changes create a new state of consciousness that can be described as a "cannabis-state-dependent" effect. The users show weaknesses an analytic and synthetic skills and have difficulty sorting out information, synthesizing from part to whole (e.g., classifying information correctly), and understanding subtle shades of meaning (poor comprehension). They have weaknesses in psychospatial skills, including difficulties differentiating time and space. In addition, they have poor mental representations of the environment and poor routines of daily life. On the basis of the present findings, it is suggested that the cannabis-induced thought pattern is a result of temporary prefrontal dysfunction, since the symptom pattern that has been described is very similar to the prefrontal syndrome. This hypothesis is also supported by the fact that cannabinoid receptors are more dense in the forebrain than in the hindbrain.

M. Periodic Marijuana Use. Periodic cannabis use and intoxication can interfere with performance at work or school and may be physically hazardous in situations such as operating heavy machinery, or even driving a car. Legal problems may occur as a consequence of arrests for cannabis growing, sale, or possession. There may be arguments with spouses or parents over the excessive spending on cannabis, possession of cannabis in the home, or default of other activities and obligations. Cannabis smoke is highly irritating to the nasopharynx and bronchial lining and thus increases the risk for chronic cough and other signs and symptoms of nasopharyngeal pathology. Chronic cannabis use is sometimes associated with weight gain, probably resulting from overeating and reduced physical activity. Sinusitis, pharyngitis, bronchitis with persistent cough, emphysema, and pulmonary dysplasia may occur with chronic, heavy use. Marijuana smoke contains many of the same toxins and irritants as tobacco smoke and other chemicals (e.g., cannabinoids) not found in tobacco. Bronchoalveolar lavage (BAL) and peripheral blood samples were taken from 14 nonsmokers, 14 tobacco smokers, 19 heavy habitual marijuana smokers, and 9 marijuana-and-tobacco smokers. Marijuana use was associated with significantly higher alveolar macrophage concentration as well as higher bronchoalveolar lymphocyte and neutrophil concentration. Both tobacco and marijuana use are associated with the accumulation of inflammatory cells in the lower respiratory tract. However, marijuana and tobacco have different effects on circulating T-lymphocyte subpopulations. Pulmonary effects of tobacco smoke, marijuana smoke, and the combination of tobacco and marijuana smoke require additional epidemiologic data on malignancy and infection. Marijuana smoke contains even larger amounts of known carcinogens than tobacco, and heavy use may increase the risk of developing malignant disease.

N. Withdrawal. Reminiscent of the cocaine epidemic, withdrawal or abstinence symptoms are debated by experts. In our experience, symptoms of cannabis withdrawal include irritability, aggressive behavior, anxiety, depression, boredom, loss of appetite, sleep and concentration problems, anhedonia, tremor, perspiration, and nausea. At present, the diagnosis of cannabis withdrawal is not included in the *DSM-IV*.

II. LSD

A. Epidemiology: The LSD Resurgence. Data from the Annual National High School Senior Survey (1993) suggest that many young people believe that nicotine or cocaine is more dangerous than LSD; only 42.3% of high-school seniors report that there is "great risk" associated with LSD experimentation compared to 56.8% for cocaine. NIDA's high-school-senior survey also indicates an increased acceptance of LSD use among seniors: disapproval of LSD "experimentation" fell from 91.6% in 1987 to 88% in 1992. In our survey, young students appear to believe that LSD is "spiritually uplifting" and 55%

of high-school seniors believed that trying LSD a few times is not harmful. Perception of danger, integral to successful cocaine education and decreased cocaine use, does not appear to have been applied to LSD (see Fig. 3.4). The significance of antidrug attitudes (e.g., see Fig. 3.5) can be seen in the dramatic decline in cocaine use by high-school seniors in the United States from 1985 to 1991. In 1985, The National High School Survey revealed that 13.1% of 12th-graders had used cocaine within the last year, and that by 1992 this number had declined to 3.1%. During the same period, the percentage of students disapproving of adults even trying cocaine increased from 79.3 to 93%.

B. Dose. Data from the Drug Enforcement Administration (DEA) (see Fig. 3.6) suggest that LSD appears to have been reformulated at a lower dose, 20–80 μg per dose today compared with 100–200 μg in the 1960s. This 560% decrease in dosage strength coincides with an increase of 160% in the THC potency of marijuana. Apparently, LSD has been reformulated in order to make the drug more appealing to younger and first-timer users (see Fig. 3.3). Reformulation may decrease the incidence of naive user, single-dose-related "bad trips" or emergency-room visits. However, total LSD dose may be *increasing* as students report taking enough LSD to become "bombed": 83% of hallucinogen users reported most often getting "very high" or "bombed or stoned" when they used LSD as compared to 24% of beer drinkers. Also, data from animals suggest that LSD is exceptionally potent with low doses producing longlasting effects on important neuronal systems. Already, emergency-room visits for LSD are increasing in the United States.

C. Hallucinogens. Lysergic acid diethylamide is considered the prototypical hallucinogen or psychotomimetic because of its ability to produce perceptual distortions, hallucinations, and delusions that are naturally occurring in psychotic states such as schizophrenia. It is generally considered in the nitrogen or alkaloid group of empirically detected plant-derivative hallucinogens that

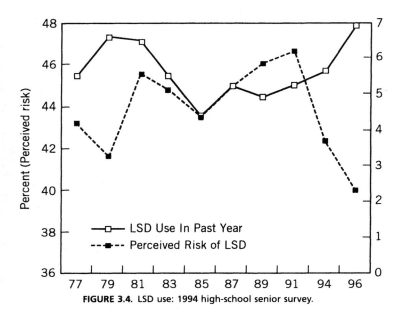

FIGURE 3.4. LSD use: 1994 high-school senior survey.

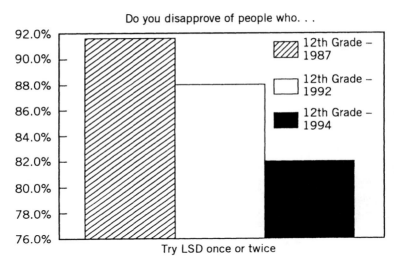

FIGURE 3.5. Attitudes (among 12th-graders surveyed in 1987, 1992, and 1994) toward LSD users.

contain peyote, mescaline, psilocybine, and harmine as well as the synthetic hallucinogens, the veterinary tranquilizer PCP, and methoxylated amphetamine derivatives STP and MDA.

While nearly 750,000 plant species are known in the world, approximately 50 have been found by humans through what is believed to be an extensive process of trial and error to be hallucinogens (see Table 3.1). LSD is synthesized from lysergic acid and diethylamine with the lysergic acid found in the ergot fungus *Claviceps purpura*. LSD is only psychoactive in the *d*-LSD isomer. Its precursor lysergic acid occurs naturally as an ergot alkaloid in grains parasitized by a fungus *C. purpura* or in the morning seed. LSD is colorless and odorless and is generally sold impregnated on a blotting paper, stamp, or cube.

D. LSD Pharmacology. LSD is well-absorbed orally from the gastrointestinal tract and other mucous membranes with peak LSD levels occurring within 60 min after ingestion. LSD is slowly eliminated in the urine, and detection of metabolites may be possible for 3 or 4 days. However, the very small dose necessary to produce psychosis-like effects makes detection quite difficult. A dose of 50 μg produces LSD-related psychotomimetic effects mainly through specific interactions with serotonergic systems in the brain. Effects in humans

---

- In 1990, LSD-induced seizures ranked third among all seizures caused by dangerous-drug use.
- Over 500,000 LSD dosage units were confiscated in 1990 by the DEA.
- LSD potency decreased from 150–300 μg in the 1960s to 20–80 μg in the 1990s.

FIGURE 3.6. LSD use in the United States. (*Source:* National Narcotics Intelligence Consumers Committee report, June 1991.)

TABLE 3.1. Hallucinogenic Plants and Their Major Psychoactive Compounds

Major Hallucinogenic Plants	Major Psychoactive Component
Amanita muscaria	Pantherine, ibotenic acid
Banistereopsis species	Harmaline, harmine
Cannabis sativa	Δ^9-THC
Datura species	Scopolamine
Ipomoea violacea	*d*-Lysergic acid amide
Mimosa species	*d*-Isolysergic acid amide tryptamines
Psilocybe mexicana	Psilocybine
Lophophora williamsii	Mescaline
Tabernanthe iboga	Ibogaine

can be reported with 1 µg within one hour of ingestion lasting for up to 6 h. Sympathetic stimulation with increased heart rate and respiration and some cholinergic effects with lacrimation, salivation, and nausea have been reported. The user reported marked alterations in visual perceptions. LSD's interaction with the 5-HT2 receptors is highly correlated with hallucinogenicity. However, LSD has marked effects on the so-called 5-HT1a or presynaptic autoreceptors in the raphe nucleus and elsewhere. Delusions of persecution and grandiosity with hallucinations, alteration of body image, changes in hearing, synesthesia (seeing smells, hearing colors), magnification of touch, and distortion of time have been reported. LSD flashbacks, recalling parts of the previous LSD experience, may be quite problematic and occurs in many exusers. These flashbacks may be triggered by marijuana or other drug use.

Emotions and emotional responses become intensified, labile, and difficult to control. Responses to LSD may be described as positive or extremely negative. While the lethal dose of LSD is not known, acute psychotic states with hallucinations and paranoia, judgment and perceptual problems, mood lability, and depression may be associated with unusual and dangerous behaviors.

III. HALLUCINOGEN INTOXICATION

This diverse group of substances includes ergot and related compounds (LSD, morning-glory seeds), phenylalkylamines [mescaline, "STP" (2,5-dimethoxy-4-methylamphetamine)], MDMA (3,4-methylenedioxymethamphetamine; also marketed under the tradename "Ecstasy"), and indole alkaloids [psilocybin, DMT (dimethyltryptamine)], and miscellaneous other compounds (292.89 Hallucinogen Intoxication).

The essential features of hallucinogen intoxication are the presence of marked anxiety or depression, ideas of reference, fear of losing one's mind, paranoid ideation, impaired judgment, or impaired social or occupational functioning developing during, or shortly after, hallucinogen use. Perceptual changes develop during or shortly after hallucinogen use and occur in a state of full wakefulness and alertness. These changes include subjective intensification of perceptions, depersonalization, derealization, illusions, hallucinations, and synesthesias. In addition, the clinical diagnosis requires that two of the following physiological signs also be present: pupillary dilation, tachycardia, sweating, palpitations, blurring of vision, tremors, and incoordination. Blood levels should be detectable by GC/MS (gas chromatography/mass spectrometry) at this time. Hallucinogen intoxication usually begins with restlessness and autonomic activation, and slight nausea may occur.

A. Acute Effects. Mood swings or lability with feelings of euphoria rapidly being replaced with crying, depression, or anxiety have been reported. Initial visual illusions or enhanced sensory experience may give way to hallucinations. At higher doses, the perceptual changes do not include hallucinations, synesthesias (a blending of senses), and hallucinations. The hallucinations are usually visual, often of geometric forms or figures, sometimes of persons and objects. The user may believe that these images are real and act on this belief. More rarely, auditory or tactile hallucinations are experienced. However, in most cases, reality testing is preserved (i.e., the individual knows that the effects are substance-induced).

B. *DSM-IV* **Criteria for Hallucinogen Intoxication**

1. Recent use of a hallucinogen.
2. Clinically significant maladaptive behavioral or psychological changes (e.g., marked anxiety or depression, ideas of reference, fear of losing one's mind, paranoid ideation, impaired judgment, or impaired social or occupational functioning) that developed during, or shortly after, hallucinogen use.
3. Perceptual changes occurring in a state of full wakefulness and alertness (e.g., subjective intensification of perceptions, depersonalization, derealization, illusions, hallucinations, synesthesias) that developed during, or shortly after, hallucinogen use.
4. Two (or more) of the following signs, developing during, or shortly after, hallucinogen use:
   a. Pupillary dilation
   b. Tachycardia
   c. Sweating
   d. Palpitations
   e. Blurring of vision
   f. Tremors
   g. Incoordination
5. The symptoms are not due to a general medical condition and are not better accounted for by another mental disorder.

IV. FLASHBACKS

Rather than withdrawal, the user may complain of LSD-like experiences long after use. The flashback is the transient recurrence of disturbances in perception that are reminiscent of those experienced during a hallucinogen intoxication. This reexperiencing of perceptual symptoms can cause clinically significant distress or impairment in social, occupational, or other important areas of functioning. Most often the perceptual disturbances may include geometric forms, peripheral-field images, flashes of color, intensified colors, trailing images, perceptions of entire objects, afterimages, halos around objects, macropsia, and micropsia. The abnormal perceptions that are associated with hallucinogen persisting-perception disorder occur episodically and may be self-induced merely by thinking about them or triggered by entry into a dark environment, various drugs, anxiety or fatigue, or other stressors.

V. ECSTASY

A. Epidemiology. MDMA (3,4-methylenedioxymethamphetamine)(tradenames Ecstasy, X, Adam) use appears confined to suburban youth, well-educated at present, and homosexual youth on both coasts. In the United States accurate estimates of usage are difficult to determine; however, some estimate that 100,000 doses a month are sold. Ecstasy and LSD are sold openly at communal all-night dances or "RAVES" characterized by costumes, "techno" music, pulsating bright lights, plus an open-air drug market. Drugs are sold and taken in the open with lots of dealers walking around selling LSD, Ecstasy, and marijuana. With Ecstasy selling at $25 per dose, switching to the cheaper methamphetamine increases dealers' profits.

B. Neurotoxicity. Mechanism of action is very much like amphetamine, although the compound is more of a hybrid mescaline plus amphetamine. MDMA causes the release of serotonin and also blocks reuptake—like a more specific amphetamine targeted to the 5-HT system. One problem in MDMA research is that the neurochemical effects are greater for monkeys than rodents—in fact, many of the neurochemical findings became clear only in monkeys and humans. At the highest doses studied, MDMA can reduce brain 5HT by 90% with long-lasting decreases for 1 or even $1\frac{1}{2}$ years in hippocampus and cortex—time needed to regrow axons. Street lore, attempting to achieve maximum euphoria while reducing toxicity and harm, suggests that when MDMA is concerned "less is more" or "save it for a special occasion." MDMA toxicity in humans is predicted by studies in animals. Studies using doses in monkeys similar to doses taken by humans, clearly are neurotoxic. Clear deficits and major neurotoxicity appear to be related to total exposure or dose and be cumulative. MDMA produces a 30–35% drop in 5HT metabolism in humans (decreased 5HIAA). MDMA effects in women are much greater than those observed for men with a 50% decrease in 5HT in women users, although less body weight and more frequent use may be the explanation for these remarkable sex differences. MDMA produces marked sleep-stage changes and changes in sleep—total sleep and stage 2 sleep decrease, although users are unaware of these changes and say that they are sleeping well. Personality changes were also clear and remarkable—increased conformity and decreased impulsivity, more sense of belonging to a group or cult.

C. Intoxication. MDMA is associated with 5HT long-lasting neurotoxicity and silver stains in animals and scans in humans show loss of 5HT organization and cortical 5HT. The methamphetamine derivatives are frequently sold as MDMA since they all produce an intense euphoria. Ecstasy replaced MDA in the 1970s and 1980s, but MDA use still persists. Acute MDMA problems include jitteriness, anxiety, jaw clenching, and fear and occurs at any dose. At high doses visual distortions such as viewing an object that appears to be shimmering, shiny, or moving and shaking have been reported (see Fig. 3.7). Ideas of reference and suspicion, and even frank paranoid reactions can occur. Some people report that they at first desire to be alone and then are concerned that people are noticing their odd behavior. With higher doses or more vulnerability they can have panic with tachycardia, psychosis, paranoia, and violence. While these effects are not commonly reported now, it is likely that

Subjective Effects of MDMA	Adverse Effects of the Use of MDMA	Short-Term MDMA Effects
Altered time perception	Decreased desire to perform mental or physical tasks	Decreased sleep
Increased social interactions	Decreased appetite	Decreased appetite
Decreased defensiveness	Trismus	Increased sensitivity to emotions
Changes in visual perception	Bruxism	Decreased ability to perform mental or physical tasks
Increased awareness of emotions	Decreased libido	Decreased desire to perform mental or physical tasks
Decreased aggression	Inability to complete the sexual response cycle	Increased ability to interact with or be open with others
Speech changes	Increased restlessness	Fatigue
Decreased obsessiveness	Increased anxiety	Decreased aggression
Decreased impulsivity	Decreased ability to perform mental or physical tasks	Decreased fear
	Depressed mood	Depressed mood
	Nystagmus	Decreased obsessiveness
	Motor tics	Altered perception of time
	Headaches	Decreased anxiety
		Decreased libido

FIGURE 3.7. General effects of MDMA–Ecstasy use. (*Source:* Gold MS, Gleaton TJ: Paper presented at 49th Annual Society of Biological Psychiatry, Philadelphia, May 20, 1994.)

this will be seen more in the future. Treatment is symptomatic with panic and/or anxiety treated with reassurance and/or minor tranquilizers and psychosis or psychotic symptoms treated with haloperidol.

D. Chronic Use. Effects of prolonged use of Ecstasy and/or LSD are now coming to attention with users reporting that use for a week or two can lead to confusion, loss of interest in hygiene, fatigue, memory impairment, and sleep dysfunction. Other psychological symptoms include bizarre and poorly formed geometric patterns, and complex visual images, especially with closed eyes, similar to other hallucinogens. Physical symptoms are common and include jawclenching, bruxism (teeth grinding), sweating, ataxia, nausea, and dizziness in addition to the sympathomimetic effects of tachycardia, hypertension, hyperreflexia, and tremor. Other adverse effects include residual withdrawal effects that can last for weeks, including exhaustion, depression, fatigue, nausea, and numbness. Because of the sympathomimetic effects, certain medical conditions may be aggravated by MDMA, MDA, and other hallucinogens. These include diabetes mellitus, liver disease, seizure disorders, glaucoma, cardiovascular disease, hypertension, hypoglycemia, hyperthyroidism, and pregnancy.

Other toxic manifestations include ataxia, nystagmus, emotional lability, vomiting, and paresthesias. Overdose reactions include tachycardia, palpitations, hypertension, hypotension, hyperthermia, renal failure, disseminated intravascular coagulation, and rhabdomyolyses.

The adverse psychological reactions are similar to those of classic hallucinogens, and include panic dissociative and psychotic reactions, insomnia, rage reactions, and delusions. Suicidal actions are prominent, particularly with methamphetamine use. The expression "speed kills" is an outgrowth of the intense feelings of depression with despair, hopelessness, helplessness, and paranoid delusions that may accompany chronic use of these drugs.

REFERENCES

Annual National High School Senior Survey. Rockville, MD: National Institute on Drug Abuse, April 13, 1993.

Brookoff D, Cook CS, Williams C, Mann, CS: Testing reckless drivers for cocaine and marijuana, *N Engl J Med* 331:518–522, 1994.

Devane WA: New dawn of cannabinoid pharmacology. *Trends Pharmacol Sci* 15:40–41, 1994.

Garratt JC, Alreja M, Aghajanian GK: LSD has high efficacy relative to serotonin in enhancing the cationic current Ih: intracellular studies in rat facial motoneurons. *Synapse* 13:123–134, 1993.

Gold MS: Prevention, education and drug therapy in cocaine abuse and dependence. *Biol Psychiatry* 2:60–62, 1991.

Gold MS: *Cocaine. Drugs of Abuse: A Comprehensive Series for Clinicians,* vol 3. New York: Plenum Publishing, 1993.

Golub A, Johnson BD: The shifting importance of alcohol and marijuana as gateway substances among serious drug abusers. *J Stud Alcohol* 55:607–614, 1994.

Kelly TH, Foltin RW, Emurian CS, Fischman MW: Effects of delta-9-THC on marijuana smoking, drug choice, and verbal reports of drug liking. *J Exp Anal Behav* 61:203–211, 1994.

Lundqvist T: Specific thought patterns in chronic cannabis smokers observed during treatment. *Life Sci* 56:2141–2144, 1995.

Martin WJ, Patrick SL, Coffin PO, Tsou D, Walker MJ: An examination of the central sites of action of cannabinoid-induced antinocoception in the rat. *Life Sci* 56:2103–2109, 1995.

National Drug Control Strategy. Washington, DC: The White House, January 1992.

Simmons MS, Tashkin DP: The relationship of tobacco and marijuana smoking characteristics. *Life Sci* 56:2185–2191, 1995.

Wallace JM, Oishi JS, Barbers RG, Simmons MS, Tashkin DP: Lymphocytic subpopulation profiles in bronchovalveolar lavage fluid and peripheral blood from tobacco and marijuana smokers. *Chest* 105:847–852, 1994.

CHAPTER 4

INTOXICATION AND WITHDRAWAL FROM NICOTINE, COCAINE, AND AMPHETAMINES

Mark S. Gold, M.D.
University of Florida Brain Institute, Gainesville, Florida

Norman S. Miller, M.D.
University of Illinois at Chicago, Chicago, Illinois

A major focus for our work and these chapters is prevention and, when that fails, identification of nicotine, alcohol, and marijuana intoxication, abuse, and dependence. Naturally, as the principal drugs of abuse and dependence, we devote the most time to them.

I. NICOTINE

A. Epidemiology

1. Introduction. After considerable public education, prevention, and treatment, tobacco use rates decreased in the late 1980s, along with use of other drugs. In the United States, approximately 45% of the general population have never smoked, and 25% are former smokers (see Fig. 4.1). Of the current users, 30% currently smoke cigarettes, 4% use pipes or cigars, and 3% use smokeless tobacco. In the United States, the prevalence of smoking has been decreasing approximately 0.7–1.0% per year. Less than two decades ago, cigarette smoking was hardly an antisocial act. It was, in fact, part of the definition of sophistication and savoir faire. No one was treated by a mental health professional for "cigarette addiction." Quite the contrary; heroes smoked cigarettes—James Bond, for example, seduced opposing spies over a martini and French cigarettes.

B. Nicotine Use Increasing Again. The lifetime prevalence of nicotine dependence in the general population is now estimated to be 20%. However, most recently nicotine use has initially leveled off and then increased, especially among women and teenagers. On the basis of the 20th national survey of high school seniors and the fourth national survey of 8th- and 10th-grade students on July 20, 1995, cigarette smoking is rising among young Americans. According to Lloyd Johnston, "We are now in a period of clear and continuing increase in cigarette smoking. . . . The proportional increase in smoking is greatest among the eighth graders. . . . Their rate of current smoking rose by 30% between 1991 and 1994 from 14.3 to 18.6 percent." Tenth-grade current

Manual of Therapeutics for Addictions, Edited by Norman S. Miller, Mark S. Gold, and David E. Smith.
ISBN 0471-56176-2 © 1997 John Wiley & Sons, Inc.

	1985	**1992**	**% Change**
Alcohol	113,000,000	98,200,000	−13%
Cigarettes	60,000,000	54,000,000	−10%
Marijuana	18,000,000	9,000,000	−50%
Cocaine	6,000,000	1,300,000	−79%

Current use (within previous 30 days) of drugs in United States, 1985–1992.

FIGURE 4.1. Use of alcohol and drugs in the United States, 1985 to present.

smoking increased to 25.4%, and that of high-school seniors rose to 31.2%. Teens appear to minimize the risks associated with smoking since only half of all 8th-graders believe that smokers run a great risk of harm by smoking a pack or more daily. According to Johnston, "Before they finish high school a majority (56%) of the half-pack a day smokers say they tried to quit smoking and found they could not. Many of them have quit on multiple occasions." Increased smoking was found in all demographic and ethnic groups (males, females, whites, African-Americans, college-bound individuals, etc.). The investigators attribute these increases to ready availability, low cost, low peer disapproval, decreases in perceived danger, media images, and the resurgence of marijuana smoking:

> Cigarette smoking and marijuana smoking are very highly correlated, with cigarette smoking usually coming first . . . in order to smoke marijuana, youngsters must learn to take smoke into their lungs, which is not a normal behavior for any species. Cigarette smoking provides excellent training for that . . . cigarettes will kill far more of today's children than all other drugs combined, including alcohol.

C. Special Groups. In the United States, 50–80% of individuals who currently smoke have nicotine dependence. Lifetime prevalence of nicotine withdrawal among persons who smoke appears to be about 50%. Nicotine dependence is more common among individuals with other mental disorders. Depending on the population studied, 55–90% of individuals with other mental disorders smoke, compared to 30% in the general population. Tobacco-related illnesses are the primary cause of death among alcoholics. Mood, anxiety, and other substance-related disorders may be more common in individuals who smoke. Prospectively, it is estimated that about 50% of those with comorbid psychiatric disorders, especially depression, who quit smoking on their own may reduce the likelihood of successful detoxification and abstinence.

II. PHARMACOLOGY OF ABUSE

A. General. Nicotine is a naturally occuring alkaloid, a weak base found only in tobacco plants. While considerable variation exists, the half-life of nicotine is approximately 100 min. General effects in the dopaminergic reward areas of the brain and on gross measures of central nervous system (CNS) activation are similar to those seen with other stimulants. Nicotine produces activation, alertness, and increased performance on a variety of continuous performance tests related, at least, to decreased boredom. Nicotine is readily absorbed

cigarette contains approximately 10 mg of nicotine, but the smoke contains up to 4000 other chemicals, including benzene, radon, and carbon monoxide (see Table 4.1). Toxicity effects in naive users include nausea, tachycardia, coronary vasospasm, anxiety, and hypertension. Early in the natural history of use, tolerance is reported with increasing amounts of nicotine necessary to produce the same effect. Nicotine must be separated from other inhaled compounds in tobacco smoke, but it appears that nicotine suppresses appetite, reduces weight, and improves mood and energy. Still, nicotine dependence has been difficult to study in animals since it is most commonly used after combustion and inhalation of tobacco smoke.

B. Self-Administration. Useful animal models should utilize the route of administration common in humans when studying and demonstrating self-administration. The procedure for studying self-administration of smoked drugs by rhesus monkeys involves reinforcement of sucking air from a pipe or smoking with sweetened water. Even after extensive training, only 10% of monkeys will voluntarily suck on a pipe attached to a burning cigarette. Smoking in the monkey is very difficult to study since (1) the behavioral activity of smoking and inhaling is more complicated than lever pressing for an intravenous infusion and (2) the smoke itself is aversive. Most studies of research animals' self-administration of nicotine have involved intravenous nicotine delivery. Nicotine differs from other drugs in that the range of environmental conditions under which it serves as a reinforcer appears to be restricted. Most drugs that show an extreme ability to stimulate their own use or maintain high rates of self-stimulation have a wide range of doses where this effect can be demonstrated. For nicotine the range of doses is limited by toxicity. Nicotine self-administration by humans and animals clearly supports the role of nicotine in maintaining human tobacco cigarette smoking. Nicotine use is also powerfully influenced by both environmental and social variables. Nicotine may be more reinforcing and reach peak brain levels with the shortest latency from initiation of the drug event, when it is smoked. Smoking is a powerful delivery system, status symbol of the past, and secondary reinforcer.

C. Gum and Patch. Nicotine gum and the nicotine patch are in widespread use as pharmacologic adjuncts for withdrawal amelioration as part of smoking cessation. Nicotine gum is available to the public without a prescription. These new treatments have also allowed researchers to study the effects of nicotine in humans. In the United States, approximately 45% of the general population have never smoked, and 25% are ex-smokers. Of the current users, 30% currently smoke cigarettes, 4% use pipes or cigars, and 3% use smokeless tobacco. In the United States, the prevalence of smoking has been decreasing by approximately 0.7–1.0% per year. Subjects who had never smoked cigarettes do not like them or self-administer 2-mg nicotine gum. However, 10% of the ex-smokers and 22% of the current smokers chose nicotine above placebo. Low rates of self-administration indicate that nicotine gum alone has low abuse liability but is influenced by host factors, including previous dependence and abuse. Human nicotine self-administration is particularly sensitive to environmental manipulations and individual family history, personality, and other factors. History of tobacco and drug use interacts with current environmental conditions to determine drug self-administration.

D. User Experiences. Clinicians have noted that nicotine self-administration is not inconsistent with work and other productive activities. In other words, the

TABLE 4.1. Marijuana and Tobacco Reference Cigarette Analysis of Mainstream Smoke

	Measurements	Marijuana Cigarette	Tobacco Cigarette
Cigarettes			
	Average weight (mg)	1,115	1,110
	Moisture (%)	10.3	11.1
	Pressure drop (cm)	14.7	7.2
	Static burning rate (mg/s)	0.88	0.80
	Puff number	10.7	11.1
Mainstream smoke	Carbon monoxide (vol%)	3.9	4.58
Gas phase	mg	17.6	20.2
	Carbon dioxide	8.27	9.38
	(vol% mg)	57.3	65.0
	Ammonia (μg)	228	199
	HCN (μg)	532	498
	Cyanogen $(CN)^2$ (μg)	19	20
	Isoprene (μg)	83	310
	Acetaldehyde (μg)	1,200	980
	Acetone (μg)	443	578
	Acrolein (μg)	92	85
	Acetonitrile (μg)	132	123
	Benzene (μg)	76	67
	Toluene (μg)	112	108
	Vinyl chloride (ng)	5.4	12.4
	Dimethylnitrosamine (ng)	75	84
	Methylethynitrosamine (ng)	27	30
	pH		
	Third puff	6.56	6.14
	Fifth puff	6.57	6.15
	Seventh puff	6.58	6.14
	Ninth puff	6.56	6.10
	Tenth puff	6.58	6.02
Particulate phase	Total particulate matter, dry, mg	22.7	39.0
	Phenol (μg)	76.8	138.5
	o-Cresol (μg)	17.9	24
	m-, p-Cresol (μg)	54.4	65
	Dimethylphenol (μg)	6.8	14.4

TABLE 4.1. (Continued)

Measurements	Marijuana Cigarette	Tobacco Cigarette
Catechol (μg)	188	328
Δ⁹-Tetrahydro-cannabinol (μg)	820	—
Cannabinol (μg)	190	—
Cannabidiol (μg)	190	—
Nicotine (μg)	—	2,850
N-Nitrosoornicotine (ng)	—	390
Naphthalene (μg)	3.0	1.2
1-Methylnaphthalene (μg)	6.1	3.65
2-Methylnaphthalene (μg)	3.6	1.4
Benz(_)anthracene (ng)	75	43
Benzo(_)pyrene (ng)	31	21.1

[a]Indicates known carcinogens
Source: Marihuana and Health, National Academy of Sciences, Institute of Medicine Report, Washington DC, 1982, p 16.

intoxication state, especially in the tolerant person, is difficult to detect. Nicotine and its metabolite cotinine are readily measured in urine and this is an integral part of life insurance applications and examinations when it is important to have an accurate appraisal of current nicotine use. The basic effect of nicotine seems to be, at first, intoxication. But many people deny that intoxication exists. Generally, they fail to remember the dizziness and nausea they felt when they started smoking. Eventually this goes away and is replaced by a biological tolerance, meaning the smoker needs more and more nicotine to feel the same effect felt at a lower dose. Most smokers, when asked why they smoke, will, however, describe both feeling and physiological changes associated with intoxication. There is some debate regarding the mechanism of the addiction, but not the fact that smoking tobacco *is addictive*. By any definition, use causes repeated use in the face of clear, specific evidence that it will harm you. Tolerance is recognized by asking about the absence of nausea, dizziness, and other characteristic intoxication symptoms despite the use of substantial amounts of nicotine. Other patients will describe some effects or a diminished nicotine effect with chronic use of the same amount of nicotine-containing products. Withdrawal appears to play an important part of the nicotine self-administration cycle. Some patients describe rushing out of bed in the morning and smoking before they brush their teeth, others smoke within the first 30 min, and still others report awakening in the middle of the night to smoke. Switching the patient to placebo nicotine cigarettes or administering an antagonist can provoke abstinence symptoms. While the positive aspects of the drug predominate, any positive reinforcement can result from the relief of early nicotine withdrawal.

Symptoms of withdrawal reflective of neuroadaptive change can be elicited from patients by asking about symptomatology in restricted-access environments. Smokers may be able to take a break and self-administer nicotine at work, but it is difficult on transatlantic smoke-free flights without nicotine gum or a patch. Individuals who smoke and other individuals who use nicotine are likely to find that they may try to cut down, count their cigarettes, or not buy them, but somehow they use up their supply of cigarettes or other nicotine-containing products faster than originally intended. Although over 80% of individuals who smoke express a desire to stop smoking and 35% try to stop each year, less than 5% are successful in unaided attempts to quit. Smokers think about smoking and pay attention to the time of their next smoking break. They also can spend a great deal of time chain-smoking or have many cigarettes in a row to "get going." Continued use despite knowledge of medical problems related to smoking is a particularly important health problem and the essential feature and definition of dependence. Many individuals continue to smoke with heart disease, bronchitis, or even lung cancer. As mentioned before, nicotine may be dependence-producing but all delivery forms are not equal. One reason why nicotine gum and patches seem to have a beneficial effect is that their delivery systems release less nicotine and have a "slower onset of action," thus mitigating the level of dependence.

E. Nicotine Cravings? There is no question that cigarette smokers have the same sort of cravings that cocaine addicts experience. Cravings occur more frequently in heavy smokers and can be reversed somewhat by the patch. The smoker seeks reward from nicotine and from the release of dopamine. Cravings are often "learned." Cigarettes are used in situations such as meetings, studying, after dinner or sex, or as a way of preoccupying oneself when under stress. Teen and college students use cigarettes as a stress-reduction mechanism. Craving occurs more frequently in heavy smokers, is dose-related, and thus may result from depletion of dopamine. Smokers experience cravings because they actually perceive benefits from smoking—it helps them cope or concentrate.

F. General Health Consequences. Smoking is an addiction, in part, because of the data linking smoking, with a variety of consequences. Continued use despite severe, life-threatening consequences is a compelling intervention strategy and clearly supports dependence. What are the consequences? Smoking is linked to most major healthcare problems. According to the U.S. Department of Health and Human Services, smoking

1. Is associated with 80–90% of chronic, obstructive pulmonary disease.
2. Causes increased incidences of respiratory cough, infections, asthma, ephysema, lung cancer, and hardening of the arteries.
3. Decreases lung function.
4. Increases lung infections among children whose parents smoke.
5. Is linked to 30% of chronic heart disease deaths.
6. Is linked to 21% of deaths due to other cardiovascular disease.
7. Increases risk of sudden death and cerebrovascular disease.
8. Increases risk of coronary artery disease.
9. Causes a "synergistic interaction with hypertension and high cholesterol to greatly increase coronary heart disease risk."
10. Increases risk of coronary heart disease and other health problems in women using oral contraceptives.
11. Increases risk of miscarriage, stillbirth, and low birth weight.
12. Increases incidence of peptic ulcer.

13. Has been linked to increase in cancer in the throat, larynx, esophagus, kidneys, bladder, and pancreas.
14. Can change the results of many clinical tests such as blood counts and creatinine levels.
15. Can change the effectiveness of many prescription and over-the-counter (OTC) medications, which, in turn, leads to increase in illness.

Although most of these problems appear to be caused by the carcinogens and carbon monoxide in tobacco smoke rather than by nicotine itself, nicotine may increase the risk for cardiovascular events.

III. NICOTINE DEPENDENCE

A. Animal Models. Basic science has made considerable progress in understanding dependence through neuroscientific study. Clearly the core of these studies is animal drug self-administration. These paradigms have been extended to humans. The classic studies with animals self-administering cocaine to the point of inducing epileptic seizure, regaining consciousness, and starting again are similar to those studies of other drugs in which animals were fitted with chronic indwelling venous catheters. Animals are provided with a response device that administers the drugs. Drug self-administration studies indicate that drugs that are self-administered by nonhuman subjects are self-administered by humans. These studies have helped to identify neurochemical and pharmacologic treatments and mechanisms that underly drug dependence. While elegant and almost universally relevant, drug self-administration models have been less salient in nicotine dependence, a drug that is almost exclusively abused by inhalation.

B. Human Experience. Other clues to drug-seeking behavior in smokers—intense brand loyalty, denial, defiance, and recovery rates from nicotine dependence—are similar to those of other drug dependencies. Nicotine dependence has at least five components, including addiction to the drug nicotine, satisfaction from smoking behavior, identification with the image of a smoker, ritualized behaviors associated with smoking, and conditioned responses.

IV. WITHDRAWAL

A. General. Most individuals who smoke have numerous failures before they succeed. In the United States, about 45% of those who have ever smoked eventually stop smoking. Withdrawal symptoms can begin within a few hours of cessation, typically peak in 1–4 days, and last for 3–4 weeks. Depressive symptoms postcessation may be associated with a particularly high relapse to smoking. Whether other nicotine withdrawal symptoms play a major role in relapse to smoking is debatable. Withdrawal itself is successfully treated with nicotine replacement, but relapse is the rule rather than the exception. Mild symptoms of withdrawal may occur after cutting down or switching to low-tar/nicotine cigarettes. Withdrawal symptoms can be reported after stopping the use of smokeless tobacco, nicotine gum, or nicotine patches.

B. *DSM-IV* **Diagnostic Criteria for 292.0 Nicotine Withdrawal**

1. Daily use of nicotine for at least several weeks.
2. Abrupt cessation of nicotine use, or reduction in the amount of nicotine used, followed within 24 h by four (or more) of the following signs:

   a. Dysphoric or depressed mood
   b. Insomnia
   c. Irritability, frustration, or anger
   d. Anxiety
   e. Difficulty concentrating
   f. Restlessness
   g. Decreased heart rate
   h. Increased appetite or weight gain
3. The symptoms in criterion 2 cause clinically significant distress or impairment in social, occupational, or other important areas of functioning.
4. The symptoms are not due to a general medical condition and are not better accounted for by another mental disorder.

Craving for nicotine, loss of organization of the day, nothing to do with hands, weight gain, anxiety, stressful job or home, problems concentrating, and depression are commonly reported by patients during abstinence. Increased hunger and weight gain often persist for at least 6 months. Relaspe is common. Six months postcessation, 50% of individuals who have quit smoking report having had a desire for a cigarette in the last 24 hs.

V. COCAINE, AMPHETAMINES, AND OTHER STIMULANTS

A. Cocaine

1. Epidemiology. Cocaine use increased dramatically through the late 1970s and early 1980s. Use peaked in 1985 and has dropped thereafter. Since use has decreased from its epidemic levels, many have mistakenly concluded that cocaine problems would disappear. To the contrary, intoxication and abstinence problems remain. Coca-leaf chewing or sucking never caught on in the United States. Rather, regular high-dose intranasal use, freebasing, and then crack and intravenous use have become the dominant delivery systems.

Cocaine when inhaled as a vapor produces rapid and almost instant increases in peak blood and brain levels with resultant reports of euphoria. Tremendous euphoria is rapidly replaced by dysphoria, and the vicious cycle of continuous or binge use until supply has dissipated is supported. Although cocaine use is significantly reduced from peak levels in 1985 (see Fig. 4.2), 8th-, 10th-, and 12th-grade use data reported in the most recent Monitoring for the Future survey suggest the continuation of use among a sizable minority of youth. In addition, the number of continuous or current cocaine users has remained stable during the 1990s, suggesting that the number of occasional or experimental users may have decreased since 1985 but addictive use has remained unchecked. Cocaine and crack use are widespread and linked to a variety of violent crimes.

2. Pharmacology. Unfortunately, even when large-scale reports of human cocaine addiction surfaced in the mid-1980s, addiction to the drug was seen as exaggerated or dismissed as "psychological" and not addiction. One reason was the place that cocaine occupied in the hearts of the users and experts, but another was that cocaine was such a unique drug that it didn't fit the standard profile of a drug with high addiction liability. While animal studies showed extremely high rates of self-administration, many experts dismissed these reports, focusing instead on abstinence. It had been thought that anyone who became addicted or who showed signs of drug dependence did so primarily as a result of attempts to avoid the pain and discomfort associated with with-

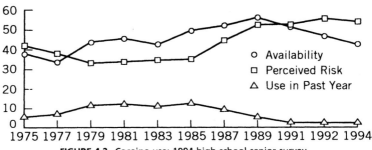

FIGURE 4.2. Cocaine use: 1994 high-school senior survey.

drawal. Since abstinence was rarely observed in the 1970s and 1980s, when cocaine was expensive, inaccessible, and sniffed rather than injected or smoked, numerous errors in expert judgment were made and confirmed by other experts.

3. Abuse and Dependence. Cocaine has become a—or should we say *the*—lesson that abuse liability: (1) can be predicted in animal self-administration experiments, (2) is dependent on dose, (3) is dependent on route, (4) is dependent on price and chemical formulation, and (5) is dependent on stigma, prohibition, or perception of danger. Cocaine was ipso facto declared safe on the basis of wishes and the axiom that drugs of abuse are safe until proven dangerous rather than the converse. Presumption of safety provided a necessary precondition for massive experimentation. Once safe and chic, cocaine in this field trial could do what it does best: stimulate its own taking. Animal and human self-administration studies have demonstrated the most striking example of dependence in the shortest periods of time with the least evidence of physical abstinence symptoms. Cocaine, once and hopefully forever more, has allowed clinicians and researchers to understand that drugs are taken for their positive, brain-reinforcing effects (see Fig. 4.3). Abstinence symptoms are not necessary for dependence to occur and for dependence to remain active and resistent to treatment. Cocaine hydrochloride is well absorbed across any moist mucous membrane but traditionally inhaled. While slower in onset and peak than inhalation of cocaine vapors, as in crack or freebase smoking or intravenous administration, all are quite apt to produce a dependence syndrome. From the time that the warm pipe touches the user's lips, self-reported euphoria can be documented.

a. Compulsive self-administration leading to death. This has been reported in animals and humans. Acute cocaine deaths have been widely reported among celebrities and covered widely in the media. Pathologic attachment, drug reinforcement-related reprioritization of acquisition and use, and powerful goal-directed behavior toward cocaine occur. Family, financial, employment, health, and other consequences occur and are minimized or denied during the run. Cocaine has helped the public understand dependence as choosing a drug over a multi-million-dollar-per-year sports contract.

B. Cocaine and Dopamine. While cocaine's effect on brain stimulation reward is complex, many studies have documented cocaine's ability to acutely enhance dopamine release and levels at the synapse corresponding to the production of positive effects (see Fig. 4.4). Research indicates that these dopaminergic neural systems play an important part in rewarding effects

---

All drugs of abuse and addiction

- Are voluntarily self-administered by animals
- Acutely enhance brain reward mechanisms
- Produce a "rush" or "high"
- Affect brain-reinforcement circuits through basal neuronal firing and/or basal neurotransmitter discharge
- Have their reinforcement properties significantly attenuated by blockades of the brain-reinforcement system (either through lesions or pharmacologic methods)
- Appear capable of increasing (directly or indirectly) dopamine release in nucleus accumbens *and* also producing sizeable increases as the animal waits or anticipates opportunity to self-administer the drug

---

FIGURE 4.3. Common characteristics and effects of abused drugs.

associated with feeding, male sexual motivation, self-stimulation, drug use, and place-preference conditioning. This endogenous positive reward system is accessed *now* by exogenous self-administration of cocaine. The user is in control of the brain and its reward hierarchy. Such a profound change from hard work for small reward is replaced by drug self-administration, providing users with an experience that their brain equates with profoundly important events such as eating, drinking, and sex. Cocaine use soon becomes an acquired drive state that permeates all aspects of human life, potentially to the point where this new "drug drive" supersedes even basic survival drives. Withdrawal symptoms from cocaine may actually not be "symptoms" per se, but anhedonia and reequilibration of the work reward equation. The user in the cocaine binge is exquisitely sensitive to the absence of the cocaine effect and feels slow, dull, boring, or the opposite of the effects that cocaine produces.

C. Intoxication

1. The acute effects of cocaine. The acute effects of a low to average dose of cocaine (approximately 20–30 mg when sniffed) are as follows:

1. Euphoria, seldom dysphoria
2. Increased sense of energy
3. Enhanced mental acuity
4. Increased sensory awareness (sexual, auditory, tactile, visual)
5. Decreased appetite (anorexia)

- Several studies of chronic cocaine abusers have demonstrated substantially elevated prolactin levels.
- Elevated prolactin levels persist for at least 1 month after stopping cocaine.
- Positron emission tomography (PET) studies found marked decrease D_2 receptor density persisting for at least 2 weeks after stopping cocaine.
- Athletes and others coplain of parkinsonian-like symptoms.
- Clinical efficacy of bromocriptine and other dopamine agonists in reversing acute abstinence complaints.

FIGURE 4.4. Clinical support for dopamine depletion theory.

6. Increased anxiety and suspiciousness
7. Decreased need of sleep
8. Allows postponement of fatigue
9. Increased self-confidence, egocentricity
10. Delusions
11. Physical symptoms of a generalized sympathetic discharge

These effects apply to all methods of cocaine use, but may be more rapid and intense with cocaine smoking or IV use. These acute effects have been linked to cocaine's blockade of the dopamine reuptake transporter (see Figs. 4.5–4.9). The cocaine-induced feeling of increased alertness is reported subjectively and can be confirmed by EEG and ECG (electroencephalogram and electrocardiogram) recordings, which show a general desynchronization of brain waves after cocaine administration. Such desynchronization, which indicates arousal, occurs in the part of the brain that is thought to be involved in the regulation of conscious awareness, attention, and sleep. Despite the feeling of arousal, individuals using cocaine do not gain any particular superior ability or greater knowledge. Their sense of omnipotence is only illusional; they tend to misinterpret their enhanced confidence and lowered inhibitions as signs of enhanced physical or mental acuity.

Cocaine intoxication usually begins shortly after drug self-administration with a "high" feeling. It is characterized as including increased energy, vigor, gregariousness, hyperactivity, restlessness, hypervigilance, talkativeness, anxiety, tension, alertness, grandiosity, stereotyped and repetitive behavior, anger, and impaired judgment. Commonly, tachycardia, pupillary dilation, elevated blood pressure, perspiration or chills, and nausea or vomiting are reported. Occasionally, especially in chronic users, bradycardia and hypotension are reported. The chronic user can demonstrate striking weight loss. Other signs and symptoms are listed below in the *DSM-IV* diagnostic scheme. Problematic chest pain, cardiac arrhythmias, and confusion, seizures, dyskinesias, dystonias, or coma can result in emergency-room visits. Coma, myocardial infarction, cerebrovascular accidents, and epileptic seizures have been reported. Similarly, acute panic, psychosis, and a variety of paranoid states can lead to emergency visits. Cocaine intoxication is associated with the presence of cocaine or its major metabolite in the blood and/or urine (see Fig. 4.10).

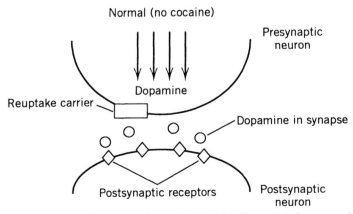

FIGURE 4.5. Effects of cocaine on dopaminergic activity (control study—no cocaine use).

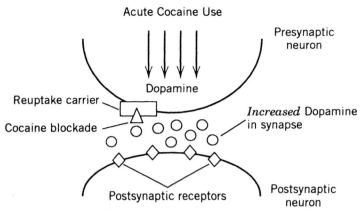

FIGURE 4.6. Effects of cocaine on dopaminergic activity (acute cocaine use).

2. *DSM-IV* **diagnostic criteria for 292.89 cocaine intoxication**

a. Recent use of cocaine.

b. Clinically significant maladaptive behavioral or psychological changes (e.g., euphoria or affective blunting, changes in sociability, hypervigilance, interpersonal sensitivity, anger, stereotyped behaviors, impaired judgment, or impaired social or occupational functioning) that developed during, or shortly after, use of cocaine.

c. Two (or more) of the following, developing during, or shortly after, cocaine use:

   1. Tachycardia

   2. Bradycardia

   3. Pupillary dilation

   4. Elevated or lowered blood pressure

   5. Perspiration or chills

   6. Nausea or vomiting

   7. Evidence of weight loss

   8. Psychomotor agitation or retardation

   9. Muscular weakness, respiratory depression, chest pain, or cardiac arrhythmias

   10. Confusion, seizures, dyskinesias, dystonias, or coma

- Cocaine produces large increases in extracellular dopamine (DA) in the nucleus accumbens.
- Increased extracellular DA is greatest in nucleus accumbens than in other forebrain DA loci.
- Increased extracellular DA is dose-dependent.
- Cocaine levels in extracellular loci are closely related to extracellular DA levels.
- DA increases identically if self-administered or administered by investigator.
- Lower extracellular DA is necessary for reward with chronic cocaine exposure.

FIGURE 4.7. Cocaine and dopaminergic system—1.

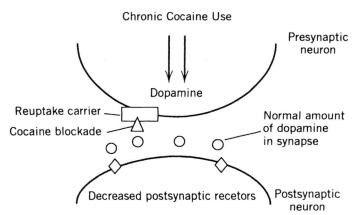

FIGURE 4.8. Effects of cocaine on dopaminergic activity (chronic cocaine use).

    d. The symptoms are not due to a general medical condition and are not better accounted for by another mental disorder.

D. Dependence. Cocaine is the new drug model for all drug dependencies.

    1. Men who abuse cocaine chronically and in high doses may have difficulty maintaining an erection and ejaculating. Many men report experiencing periods of time when they completely lose interest in sex, which is not surprising, perhaps, given the direct effects of cocaine on the primary reward systems of the brain.

E. Withdrawal: Cocaine Abstinence. Until the mid-1980s organized psychiatry discounted the possibility that cocaine use was associated with an abstinence syndrome of any consequence on discontinuation of chronic administration. Observations in humans and more recently, animal studies, support the concept of an important cocaine abstinence state. In humans the acute abstinence state is of variable intensity and symptomatology but includes irritability, anxiety, and depression that can, and often is, self-medicated with cocaine. In animals there are clear behavioral changes after the termination of chronic cocaine use.

    1. *DSM-IV.* Acute withdrawal symptoms (a "crash") are often seen after periods of repetitive high-dose use ("runs" or "binges"). These periods are characterized by intense and unpleasant feelings of marked anergia, dyspho-

---

- DA synthesis rate decreases with chronic cocaine use.
- Cocaine self-administration produces initial burst of DA in nucleus accumbens.
- Nicotine, opiates, Ecstasy and other drugs increase extracellular DA levels in the terminal loci of the mesotelencephalic DA system.
- Drugs that are self-abused by humans are self-administered by animals and produce extracellular DA levels in the terminal projection loci of the mesotelencephalic DA system.
- Naloxone blocks the increased extracellular DA levels produced by opiates and THC.

FIGURE 4.9. Cocaine and dopaminergic system—2.

- Self-administered either intranasally, intravenously, by smoking, or (less commonly) orally. Doses < 10 mg indistinguishable from placebo.
- Intranasal use: Onset of action in 30 s–2 min, slowed by local vasoconstriction. Typical peak levels of ~ 150 ng/mL. Peak blood level, CNS, and CV (cardiovascular) effects occur 15–30 min after use. Drug wears off after 40–60 min, perhaps with postdrug dysphoria. However, detectable blood levels present for 4–6 h after use.
- Intravenous use: Onset of action in 15–30 s; peak effects in 30–50 min; duration of high 15–20 min.
- Smoking (freebase, crack): Onset in 8–10 s; peak effects in 3–5 min; duration of high 15 min.
- Half-life of cocaine is ~ 40–60 min.
- Metabolized largely by plasma cholinesterases to benzoylecgonine, an inactive metabolite typically found in urine for ≤ 48 h after use, maybe longer with sensitive assays.
- Drinking alcohol with cocaine may alter metabolism to form cocaethylene, which appears to be longer-lasting and more cardiotoxic than cocaine itself.
- Cocaine-induced euphoria probably mediated by dopaminergic mechanisms, particularly in circuits originating in ventral tegmentum and innervating frontal lobe, septum, nucleus accumbens, and amygdala.
- Although "kindling" has been reported, acute and chronic tolerance to euphoriant effects are more relevant to abuse. Complete acute tolerance to euphoria, incomplete tolerance to chronotropic effects, kindling for seizures and psychomotor effects in the limbic system.

FIGURE 4.10. Cocaine pharmacology.

ria, irritability, and impulsivity as well as depression, generally requiring several days of rest and recuperation. Depressive symptoms with suicidal ideation or behavior can occur and are generally the most serious problems seen during "crashing" or other forms of cocaine withdrawal. A substantial number of individuals with cocaine dependence have few or no clinically evident withdrawal symptoms on cessation of use with the exception of craving.

a. *DSM-IV* Diagnostic Criteria for 292.0 Cocaine Withdrawl

(1) Cessation of (or reduction in) cocaine use that has been heavy and prolonged.

(2) Dysphoric mood and two (or more) of the following physiological changes, developing within a few hours to several days after criterion 1:
   (a) Fatigue
   (b) Vivid, unpleasant dreams
   (c) Insomnia or hypersomnia
   (d) Increased appetite
   (e) Psychomotor retardation or agitation

(3) The symptoms in criterion 2 cause clinically significant distress or impairment in social, occupational, or other important areas of functioning.

(4) The symptoms are not due to a general medical condition and are not better accounted for by another mental disorder.

The medical consequences of *stimulant withdrawal* appear to the physician as relatively minor and never life-threatening but are perceived by cocaine-dependent persons as the most negative and aversive state.

Behavioral models in animals and the characterization of the cocaine receptor appear to offer promise for understanding the differences between the observed severity of withdrawal and the patient's perception. These models also hold considerable promise in identifying new treatments that might reduce not only cocaine withdrawal distress but also prevent relapse or cocaine euphoria. The fact that not all dopamine uptake inhibitors exert reinforcing properties similar to cocaine suggests that the purified and cloned cocaine recognition site on the neuronal dopamine transporter may lead to new non-addicting treatments for human cocaine addicts.

In summary, even though severe cocaine abuse is characterized by binges alternating with abstinence, the occurrence of a withdrawal dysphoric state with neurovegetative symptoms and anhedonia occurring within hours after discontinuation of cocaine is now accepted by both cocaine users and psychiatrists as the "crash." Use of cocaine to reverse withdrawal is a relief and thereby a positive reinforcer in its own right.

F. Special Populations: Food and Cocaine. According to many users, taking low doses of cocaine is an easy and harmless way to lose weight. Clinicians have found this to be a common claim among women *and* men. Unfortunately for many, cocaine became something far more dangerous than a harmless diet aid. By inactivating the feeding center located in the lateral hypothalamus, cocaine supersedes the primary eating drive, leading to severe loss of appetite and loss of body weight. Many anorexic and bulimic women take amphetamines to suppress appetite. Some of these women progress to using cocaine or methamphetamine. One study of 386 consecutive patients admitted for inpatient substance-abuse treatment revealed that 15% of 143 female patients had a lifetime diagnosis of anorexia or bulima compared to only 1% of males. In this study, women substance abusers with eating disorders were far more likely to abuse stimulants (82%) than opiates (5%). The preference for stimulants in this population suggests (1) a common psychopathology between stimulant abuse and eating disorders, (2) a preference for stimulants among eating-disorder patients as a means of controlling appetite, or (3) a combination of these factors.

VI. AMPHETAMINES

A. Epidemiology. Long-term trends in perceived availability of amphetamines has steadily risen from 57.3% in 1991 to 63% in 1994 in 12th-graders. This coincides with a decreasing perception of harmfulness of daily use. In 1991, 74.1% of 12th-graders considered daily use of amphetamines as harmful, in contrast to 67% in 1994.

B. Intoxication. Amphetamine or cocaine intoxication usually begins with a "high" feeling and includes one or more of the following: euphoria with enhanced vigor, gregariousness, hyperactivity, restlessness, hypervigilance, interpersonal sensitivity, talkativeness, anxiety, tension, alertness, grandiosity, stereotyped and repetitive behavior, anger, and impaired judgment. These behavioral and psychological changes are accompanied by two or more of the following signs and symptoms that develop during or shortly after use noted above for cocaine in the *DSM-IV* scheme. Stimulant effects such as euphoria, increased pulse and blood pressure, and psychomotor activity are most commonly seen. Acute amphetamine intoxication is sometimes associated with confusion, rambling speech, headache, transient ideas of reference, and tinnitus. During intense amphetamine intoxication, paranoid ideation, auditory hallucinations in a clear sensorium, and tactile hallucinations may be experienced. Frequently, the person using the substance recognizes these symptoms as resulting from the stimulants. Extreme anger with threats or acting out of aggressive behavior may occur. Mood changes such as depression with suicidal ideation, irritability, anhedonia, emotional lability, or disturbances in attention and concentration are common, especially during withdrawal.

C. Dependence. See section V. D.

D. Withdrawal. Marked withdrawal symptoms ("crashing") often follow an episode of intense, high-dose use (a "speed run"). These periods are characterized by intense and unpleasant feelings of lassitude and depression, generally requiring several days of rest and recuperation. Weight loss commonly occurs during heavy stimulant use, whereas a marked increase in appetite with rapid weight gain is often observed during withdrawal. Depressive symptoms may last several days and may be accompanied by suicidal ideation.

E. *DSM-IV* Diagnostic Criteria for 292.0 Amphetamine Withdrawal

1. Cessation of (or reduction in) amphetamine (or a related substance) use that has been heavy and prolonged.
2. Dysphoric mood and two (or more) of the following physiological changes, developing within a few hours to several days after criterion 1.
   a. fatigue
   b. vivid, unpleasant dreams
   c. insomnia or hypersomnia
   d. increased appetite
   e. psychomotor retardation or agitation
3. The symptoms in criterion 2 cause clinically significant distress or impairment in social, occupational, or other important areas of functioning.
4. The symptoms are not due to a general medical condition and are not better accounted for by another disorder. Weight loss, anemia, and other signs of malnutrition and impaired personal hygiene are often seen with sustained amphetamine dependence.

SELECTED READINGS

American Psychiatric Association: *Diagnostic and Statistical Manual of Mental Disorders III*, revised, DSM-III-R. Washington, DC: American Psychiatric Press, 1988.

Gawin FH, Kleber HD: Abstinence symptomatology and psychiatric diagnosis in cocaine abusers. *Arch Gen Psychiatry* 43:107–113, 1986.

Gold MS: *Drugs of Abuse: A Comprehensive Series for Clinicians.* Vol III, *Cocaine.* New York: Plenum Medical Book Company, 1993.

Gold MS: *Drugs of Abuse: A Comprehensive Series for Clinicians.* Vol IV, *Tobacco.* New York: Plenum Medical Book Company, 1995.

Gold MS, Vereby K: The psychopharmacology of cocaine. *Psychiatric Ann* 14:714–723, 1984.

Grinspoon L, Bakalar JB: Drug dependence: non-narcotic agents. In HI Kaplan, AM Freedman, BJ Sadock (eds): *Comprehensive Textbook of Psychiatry*, 3rd ed. vol 2. Baltimore: Williams & Wilkins, 1980.

Kokkindis L, McCarater BD: Postcocaine depression and sensitization of brain-stimulation reward: analysis of reinforcement and performance effects. *Pharmacol Biochem Behav* 36:463–471, 1990.

Markou A, Koob GF: Postcocaine anhedonia: an animal model of cocaine withdrawal. *Neuropsychpharmacology* 4:17–26, 1991.

Markou A, Koob GF: Bromocriptine reversees the elevation in intracranial self-stimulation thresholds observed in a rat model of cocaine withdrawal, *Neuropharmacology* 7:213–24, 1992.

Rothman RB: High affinity dopamine reuptake inhibitors as potential cocaine antagonists: a strategy for drug development. *Life Sci* 46:17–21, 1990.

Satel SL, Price LH, Palumbo JM, McDougle CJ, Krystal JH, Gawin F, Charney DS, Heninger GR, Kleber HD: Clinical phenomenology and neurobiology of cocaine abstinence: a prospective inpatient study. *Am J Psychiatry* 148:1712–1716, 1991.

CHAPTER 5

INTOXICATION AND WITHDRAWAL FROM OPIATES AND INHALANTS

Mark S. Gold, M.D.
University of Florida
Brain Institute
Gainesville, Florida

Norman S. Miller, M.D.
University of Illinois at Chicago
Chicago, Illinois

I. OPIATES

A. History. Opiate drugs have been important analgesics and drugs of abuse for centuries. Until very recently, the majority of what we knew about opiates came from historical accounts such as those descriptions of Assyrian "poppy art" dating from 4000 B.C. and from studies of Egyptian, Greek, and Persian cultures. In addition to pain relief, opiates were used for their ability to induce a state of euphoria. In the nineteenth century, millions of Chinese became addicted to opium after smoking, eating, drinking, or sniffing it. In Europe at this time opiates were used as "tonics" usually in pills of two to three grains or dissolved in alcohol and drunk under the name *laudanum*. Notable poets such as Samuel Taylor Coleridge and Elizabeth Barrett Browning, became dependent on opiates. With the availability of parenterally administered opiates and the invention of the hypodermic syringe, opiate addiction and opiate withdrawal distress became major worldwide public health problems. Although the opiate drugs have been around for centuries, heroin, like all drugs of abuse, was at first considered a "new" opiate of great promise. Derived from the poppy plant and first produced in the nineteenth century, its proponents thought it would serve as a cure for morphine and opium addiction. By the twentieth century, opioid addiction was a widespread problem in the United States. In San Francisco, one survey found that by the turn of this century one in every 400 people were abusing opiates.

B. Epidemiology. More recently, the 1991 National Household survey found that 2% of the population had used heroin in their lifetime, and the 1992 National High School Senior survey found a lifetime rate of 1.2%—up from 0.9% in 1991. Opiate emergency-room visits also appear to be increasing. While the prevalence of heroin addiction today in the United States is less than 1%, its impact on the total morbidity and mortality of drugs is significant. Opioids play a disproportionate role in the 6000 deaths attributed to drug

Manual of Therapeutics for Addictions, Edited by Norman S. Miller, Mark S. Gold, and David E. Smith.
ISBN 0471-56176-2 © 1997 John Wiley & Sons, Inc.

abuse. Once heroin addiction develops, the prognosis is often very poor. At least 25% of addicts will die within 10–20 years of active use, usually as a result of suicide, homicide, accidents, and infectious diseases such as tuberculosis, hepatitis, and AIDS. History has taught us that depressants like heroin, the most familiar of the opiate group, often make a "comeback" following a period of extensive stimulant abuse (i.e., cocaine). This resurgence in opiate use appears to be here today. Even though the total number of opiate users in the United States had remained constant for many years, opiate use and addiction remained major public policy and public health problems because of the HIV risk associated with intravenous use, heterosexual transmission to their partners and offspring, and the recent changes in route of administration preference to intranasal. The association between opiate use and HIV infection has been so clearly established with users that use via the intranasal route is now seen as preferable. Sniffing, snorting, or so-called "chasing the dragon" allows users to self-administer opiates by a route that they do not perceive as dangerous.

The most recent heroin outbreaks revealed a new form called "black tar,"or "tootsie roll," that first appeared in the southwestern United States in the mid-1980s and spread through the country. While Mexican or Asian forms of heroin have a purity level of 2–5%, black tar has been reported to be 60–85% pure. Heroin has also been used frequently when injected in combination with cocaine, a technique known as "speed-balling." This dangerous practice was responsible for the death of actor John Belushi, and is increasing in use with the spread of crack.

Although heroin use varies with supply, there are still between 400,000 and 700,000 heroin addicts in the United States. A community survey conducted in the United States in 1991 reported that 6% of the population sampled had used analgesics for nonmedical purposes; 2.5% had used them within the past year; and 0.7% had used them in the past month. The survey also showed that 1.3% had used heroin in their lifetime, and 0.2% had used it in the last year (use in the past month was not reported). Because these statistics only sample people living in fixed residences—not jails or rehabilitation facilities—the statistics reported are probably underestimated. It is not likely that heroin use will diminish because, like other addictive drugs, its sale is also very profitable. Ten kilos (10 kg) costing about $250 can be converted into about $400,000 worth of heroin on the street. One gram (0.3 oz) sells for $50–$400.00. Recent data from the Monitoring for the Future study show that opiate use is quite uncommon among high-school and college students and young adults in the United States. Interestingly, most high-school seniors view the risks of trying heroin once or twice to be slightly less dangerous than using cocaine once or twice (50.9% vs. 57.1%). The most recent data available from the Monitoring for the Future study on heroin use among 8th–12th-graders are shown in Figure 5.1.

A community study conducted in the United States from 1980 to 1985 that used the more narrowly defined *DSM-III* criteria revealed that 0.7% of the adult population had opioid dependence or abuse at some time in their lives. Among those with dependence or abuse, 18% reported use in the last month and 42% reported having had a problem with opioids in the last year. Throughout the twentieth century in the United States, heroin has generally been used by lower socioeconomic groups. But in recent years, the drug has climbed out of the ghetto into the middle class. Some of this is due to the fact that many GIs (general infantrymen) were exposed to the drug in Vietnam. And the drug has accompanied serious polydrug abuse among the middle class, who use it to come off cocaine binges.

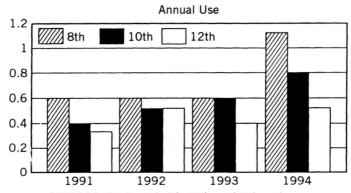

FIGURE 5.1. Heroin use in 8th-, 10th-, and 12th-graders.

C. Opiate Medications. Morphine and heroin have been of considerable scientific interest because of the psychic state they induce; their efficacy as analgesics, antiemetics, and other medicinal agents; and their propensity to produce tolerance and physical dependence (see Table 5.1). The opiates or opioids include morphine, the prototypical μ-opioids, semisynthetics such as heroin and synthetics with morphine-like action (e.g., codeine, hydromorphone, methadone, oxycodone, meperidine, fentanyl). The mixed-agonist/antagonist medications such as pentazocine and buprenorphine, because of their agonist properties, produce similar physiological and behavioral effects. Opioids are among the most commonly prescribed analgesics, anesthetics, antidiarrheal agents, and cough suppressants (see Table 5.2). Heroin is a drug of abuse taken by injection or sniffed or smoked. Fentanyl is also abused primarily by health-care providers and those who are afraid of urine detection. Opioid cough remedies are abused by adolescents.

D. Course. Opioid dependence can begin at any age, but problems associated with opioid use are most commonly first observed in the late teens or early 20s. Factors in opiate drug dependence prominently include pharmacology. First and foremost is the role of opiate drugs as binding with opioid receptors and interacting with the endogenous neuroanatomy of reward. The intense

TABLE 5.1. Opiate Agonists, Antagonists, and Mixed Antagonists

Agonists	Antagonists	Mixed Antagonists
Morphine	Naloxone (Narcan)	Pentazocine (Talwin)
Methadone		
Oxycodone (Percodan)	Naltrexone	Nalbuphine (Nubain)
Meperidine (Demerol)		
Propoxyphene (Darvon)		Buprenorphine (Buprenex)
Heroin		
Hydromorphone (Dilaudid)		Butorphanol (Stadol)
Fentanyl (Sublimaze)		
Codeine		

TABLE 5.2. Comparative Analgesic Potency[a] **of Opioids and Opiates**

Drug	Dosage (mg)	Route
Morphine sulfate	10	IM, SC
	60	Oral
	10	IV
Heroin	3	IV
Hydromorphone (Dilaudid)	1.5	IM, SC
Codeine	120	IM, SC
	180	Oral
Oxycodone (in Percodan)	10–15	IM
	20–30	Oral
Meperidine (Demerol)	75–100	IM, SC
	150–200	Oral
Methadone	10	IM, SC
	10	Oral
Propoxyphene (Darvon)	180–240	Oral
Pentazocine (Talwin)	30–50	IM, SC
Naloxone	0.4	IM, IV
Fentanyl	125 ng	Oral
Diphenoxylate (Lomotil)	40–60	Oral
Paregoric	25 mL	Oral

[a]Tolerance to the analgesic effects of opiates develops rapidly, requiring greater and greater doses that may reach 10 times the initial one.

opiate experience recalled by addicts as "the high" or "the rush" stimulates its own taking in humans just as it does in animals. Even though weeks of opiate administration leave the user with more anxiety, dysphoria, and the emergence of physical abstinence symptoms on discontinuation or preceding self-administration, the lure of opiate euphoria is not easily resisted. The positive effects of the drug experience apparently outweigh the obvious negative effects and numerous risks that the addicts are exposing themselves and of which they are well aware. Addicts generally have concurrent diagnoses, from major depression to alcoholism to antisocial personality disorder. However, these diagnoses do not appear to be the hidden underlying cause of the drug use or addiction. This does not mean that these new and important "other" problems can be ignored. In fact, treatment response rates improve when the depression or major life problems are treated as well.

E. Reinforcement. Endogenous drug reward is great and appears to be the primary factor in sustaining opiate drug use. However, autonomic withdrawal cannot be ignored as contributing to the generalized discomfort reported objectively and subjectively by opiate addicts. The addict's desire to find more opiates to remain "normal," despite numerous health risks, psychiatric, and other problems and other addictions is common. With much of the emphasis on neurobiology, epidemiology, and comorbidity, the overall lack of family support and the level of addiction and other problems in the addict's environment are common.

F. Opioid Systems. Scientists in the early 1970s had preliminary evidence that opiate drugs bind to specific sites in the brain and body that cause the numerous and seemingly diverse effects of opiate drugs. Effects on pupils, diarrhea, cough, mood, pain, respiration, and so on were explained by the opioid receptor theory. This theory correlated the binding of opiates to endogenous opioid receptors in key areas of the brain and body with already recognized functions of these areas (see Table 5.3). While numerous questions remain, such as why every vertebrate and some invertebrates possess opioid receptors, whether endorphins are neurotransmitters or hormones, or why authentic morphine and codeine have been found in the mammalian nervous systems, the identification of these receptors *has* led to the discovery of endorphins, naturally occurring endogenous substances that possess opiate activity. Opioid drugs exert their actions by binding to receptors on cell membranes of neurons and other cells. These opiate receptors are multiple in type and primary functions. They have been divided into mu, kappa, delta, and lambda subtypes. A number of important differences between these subtypes have been identified. Kappa-receptor activation produces analgesia, but unlike mu and delta agonists are not self-administered by laboratory animals. Consistent with this self-administration data, it now appears that the kappa agonists are dysphoric rather than euphoric. Once dependence develops, it is usually continuous over a period of many years, even though brief periods of abstinence are frequent. Relapse following abstinence is common.

G. Diagnostic Criteria for Opioid Intoxication. Intoxication is a common emergency-room, medical emergency. It is accompanied by pupillary constriction and one or more of the following signs: drowsiness (described as being "on the nod") or even coma, slurred speech, and impairment in attention or memory. The classic narcotic overdose, characterized by hypotension, respiratory arrest, and pinpoint pupils is reversed by the opiate antagonist naloxone. Individuals with opioid intoxication may appear comatose or stuperous or

TABLE 5.3. Clinical Effects Induced At Receptor Sites

Mu	Supraspinal analgesia
	Respiratory depression
	Miosis
	Euphoria
Kappa	Spinal analgesia
	Sedation
	Sleep
	Miosis
	Limited respiratory depression
Sigma	Dysphoria
	Delusions
	Hallucinations
	Respiratory stimulation
	Vasomotor stimulation
Delta	Interacts with mu receptor via endogenous opioids and the enkephalins, similar to sigma

simply demonstrate inattention to the environment. Symptoms of untreated opioid intoxication usually last for several hours, a timeframe that is consistent with the half-life of most opioid drugs. Severe intoxication following an opioid overdose can lead to coma, respiratory depression, pupillary dilation, unconsciousness, and death (see Table 5.4). While users are almost obsessed with the pain of withdrawal, death occurs during intoxication and not generally during withdrawal.

1. *DSM-IV* criteria for opioid intoxication

a. Recent use of an opioid.

b. Clinically significant maladaptive behavioral or psychological changes (e.g., initial euphoria followed by apathy, dysphoria, psychomotor agitation or retardation, impaired judgment, or impaired social or occupational functioning) that developed during, or shortly after, opioid use.

c. Pupillary constriction (or pupillary dilation due to anoxia from severe overdose) and one (or more) of the following signs, developing during, or shortly after, opioid use:

(1) Drowsiness or coma

(2) Slurred speech

(3) Impairment in attention or memory

2. User reports. Heroin has another unique property that users call "the rush," describing this initial effect as "better than sexual orgasm." This is followed by the relaxing "nod," which is part of the classic stereotype of the drowsy heroin experience. Once the rush has subsided, and depending on the level of dependence and tolerance, severe withdrawal symptoms can occur. In

TABLE 5.4. Opiates: Agonist/Antagonist Activity

	Agonist	Antagonist	Respiratory Depression Counteracted by Naloxone
Alphaprodine	+		+
Buprenorphine	+	+	Partial
Butorphanol	+	+	+
Codeine	+		+
Fentanyl	+		+
Heroin	+		+
Hydrocodone	+		+
Meperidine	+		+
Methadone	+	+	+
Morphine	+		+
Nalbuphine	+	+	+
Naloxone		+	
Naltrexone		+	
Oxycodone	+	+	+
Paregoric	+	+	+
Pentazocine	+	+	+
Propoxyphene	+	+	+

fact, it is the interplay between the positive reinforcement of heroin's euphoric rush, and the wish to avoid the terrors of opiate withdrawal, that are the real mechanisms of the drug's addicting power. This combination is one of the unique features of heroin addiction. Like other drugs, heroin also fits the addictive model of repeated, compulsive use, preoccupation with the drug, and relapse after treatment. Opiate addicts are also among the most difficult to understand, since the drug is so destructive. Like cocaine, heroin is illicit and mixed or cut with a variety of other chemicals. This is another reason why so many users die suddenly, despite long heroin experience. Heroin induces tolerance quickly, reducing euphoric dose while keeping titral dose constant.

H. Opiate Withdrawal Syndrome. Withdrawal from the classic morphine-like opiate is a syndrome now understood to be the mu-agonist withdrawal syndrome (see Table 5.5). It is quite variable from person to person depending on individual factors as well as the specific opiate used and its dose and duration of self-administration. Naturally, withdrawal intensity will depend on whether the tolerant and dependent person is given an antagonist such as naloxone to provoke withdrawal or whether opiates are slowly discontinued. When antagonists are used to provoke withdrawal, it is somewhat surprising to find significant withdrawal complaints in the user early in the self-administration cycle. Administration of naloxone to animals and addicts has suggested that even single doses of opiates induce some degree of neuroadaptation. As is the case for most drugs of abuse, withdrawal phenomena are easily understood as the opposite of the drug effects. So the mu-agonist's effects of decreased bowel motility are seen in withdrawal as diarrhea, hypotension as hypertension, decreased heart rate and respirations as increases in heart rate and respira-

TABLE 5.5. Classification of Opiates and Opioids

Natural Opium

Opium
    Tincture of Opium
    Paregoric (camphorated opium tincture)
    Morphine
    Codeine

Synthetic Derivatives

Morphine and cogeners	Meperidine and congeners
Morphine	Meperidine, pethidine
Heroin	(Demerol)
Hydromorphone (Dilaudid)	Anileridine (Leritne)
Osymorphone (Numorphan)	Diphenoxylate (lomotil)
Hydrocodone	Fentanyl (Innovar, Sublimaze)
	Loperamide (Imodium)
	Alphaprodine (Nisentil)
Methadone and congeners	Others
Methadone	Pentazocine (Talwin)
L-*a*-Acetylmethadol (LAAM)	Butorphanol (Stadol)
Propoxyphene (Darvon)	Nalbuphine (Nubain)
	Naloxone (Narcan)
	Naltrexone (Trexan)
	Buprenorphine (Buprenex)

TABLE 5.6. Withdrawal Symptoms

	Onset (h)	Peak (h)	End (days)
Morphine	14–20	36–48	5–10
Heroin	8–12	48–72	5–10
Methadone	36–72	72–96	14–21
Codeine	24	—	—
Dilaudid	4–5	—	—
Meperidone	4–6	8–12	4–5

tions, and so forth. Many of the mu-agonist withdrawal syndromes' signs and symptoms appear to be due to a rebound hyperactivity or release from chronic inhibition of the locus coeruleus (LC). Such supersensitivity is reversed by opiates but also by clonidine. The withdrawal syndrome from heroin begins within 12 h of abrupt discontinuation of chronic administration and commonly includes dysphoria, anxiety, yawning, perspiration, lacrimation, rhinorrhea, sleep difficulties, nausea, vomiting, diarrhea, cramps, and fever. In summary, the syndrome looks and feels like "the flu." This acute abstinence syndrome is not life-threatening, although it is sometimes difficult to convince addicts and/or their families that this is a problem that will for the most part pass in less than a week. Clinicians and experienced addicts recognize that the acute withdrawal phase with its dramatic symptoms is generally followed by a longer-lasting protracted syndrome that may last for months and include episodes of sweats, night terrors, dysphoria, drug craving, and malaise. When opioids are rapidly cleared from the mu receptor and become functionally unavailable, as they are by administration of naloxone or naltrexone, neurons in the LC are put into a state of hyperexcitability, also referred to as rebound from chronic inhibition or LC hyperactivity. The resultant noradrenergic hyperactivity and release would be the most critical element in the generation of withdrawal symptoms and signs.

   1. *DSM-IV* **diagnostic criteria for opioid withdrawal.** Acute withdrawal symptoms for a short-acting opioid such as heroin usually peak within 1–3 days and gradually subside over a period of 5–10 days (see Table 5.6). Less acute withdrawal symptoms can last for weeks to months. These more chronic symptoms include anxiety, dysphoria, anhedonia, insomnia, and drug craving. These criteria are necessary for diagnosis:

   a. Either of the following:
      (1) Cessation of (or reduction in) opioid use that has been heavy and prolonged (several weeks or longer)
      (2) Administration of an opioid antagonist after a period of opioid use
   b. Three (or more) of the following, developing within minutes to several days after criterion a:
      (1) Dysphoric mood
      (2) Nausea or vomiting
      (3) Muscle aches
      (4) Lacrimation or rhinorrhea
      (5) Pupillary dilation, piloerection, or sweating
      (6) Diarrhea
      (7) Yawning

(8) Fever

(9) Insomnia

c. The symptoms in criterion b cause clinically significant distress or impairment in social, occupational, or other important areas of functioning.

d. The symptoms are not due to a general medical condition and are not better accounted for by another mental disorder.

(See Table 5.7.)

I. Diagnosis of Opioid Addiction. Typically, the opiate addicted patient is not the most difficult to diagnose. Naloxone (0.4–0.8 mg) can be given to provoke withdrawal and confirm a diagnosis. The diagnosis of opioid addiction is made by using criteria similar to those employed for the diagnosis of other drug addictions. The criteria include a preoccupation with the acquisition of the opioid, compulsive use in spite of adverse consequences, an inability to reduce the amount of use, and a pattern of relapse to opioids after a period of abstinence. The pursuit of opioid drugs is particularly dramatic in the typical addict who first needs to find the money or barter, then who must, with regularity, find and use the drug. Physical examination with special reference to commonly related medical illnesses of the skin and evidence of parenteral use is essential. (see Section I.I, on medical complications of IV drug use, below) In addition, Table 5.3 lists the signs and symptoms of opiate withdrawal.

1. Laboratory confirmation. Classic abstinence symptoms and signs such as nausea, vomiting, and diarrhea; gooseflesh; dilated pupils; perspiration; increased pulse, blood pressure, and respirations; bone and muscle aches; and so forth are present with a strong drive for the drug. Track marks and other physical evidence of parenteral use may be found during the examination of the patient. The patient and loved ones give the story of drug seeking, drug acquisition, and drug taking. Difficulties in sexual functioning are common. Males often experience erectile dysfunction during intoxication or chronic use. Females commonly have disturbances of reproductive function and irregular menses. Laboratory diagnosis is available and reliable when the physician chooses the correct methodology and the correct bodily fluid for the particular opioid being abused. Thin-layer chromatography (TLC) testing, the most inexpensive and most commonly ordered comprehensive testing, will detect high-dose, current use of some opioids. While TLC is usually adequate to detect morphine quinine (a diluent of heroin), methadone, codeine, dextromethorphan, and propoxyphene used within 12 h, another screen, the enzyme-linked immunoassays (EIA), has technical and detection advantages for routine screening. These advantages make EIA comparable in many respects to screening of 25–40 drugs in a single analysis by capillary gas–liquid chromatography/mass spectrometry (GC/MS). EIA screens can detect opiates (morphine, codeine, heroin metabolite, hydrocodone, etc.), methadone, and propoxyphene, even in the microgram- or picogram-per-milliliter (μg/mL or pg/mL) range. EIA tests have gained popularity over the TLC because no extraction or centrifugation is required and the system for comprehensive testing can be automated. Although EIA screening is more costly than TLC, the screens are more sensitive for most drugs and thereby detect lower drug concentrations. For example, TLC sensitivity for opiates is 2000 ng/mL, EIA is 300 ng/mL, and GC/MS is $\leq$ 20 ng/mL. Detectability of opiates such as morphine can be increased to 1–2 days by use of EIA or GC/MS. While GC/MS operates only in the scanning mode, and looking at the full range of

TABLE 5.7. Duration of Action and Abstinence Symptoms of Different Opiates and Opioids

Drug Name	Dose[a] (mg)	Duration[a] (hours)	Addiction Potential	Abstinence Symptoms
Morphine	10	4–5		
Heroin (diacetylmorphine)	3(2–8)	3–4	Like morphine	Like morphine
Hydromorphone (dihydromorphinone, Dilaudid)	1.5	4–5	Like morphine	Like morphine
Oxymorphone (dihydroxymorphinone, Numorphan)	1.0–1.5	4–6	Less than morphine	Less than morphine
Codeine	120 (10–30)	(4–6)	Less than morphine	Less than morphine
Hydrocodone (dihydrocodeine, Hycodan)	(5–10)	(4–8)	Between morphine and codeine	Between morphine and codeine
Dihydrocodeine (Paracodin)	60	4–5	Like morphine	Like morphine
Oxycodone (dihydrohydroxycodeinone, Percodan)	10–15	4–5	Like morphine	Like morphine
Methadone (Dolphine)	7.5–10	3–5	Like morphine	Longer than morphine
Acetylmethadol (LAAM)			Like morphine	Longer than morphine
Propoxyphene (dextropropoxyphere, Darvon)	240	4–5	Less than morphine	Less than morphine
Meperidine (Demerol, Pethidine)	80–100	2–4	Less than morphine	Less than morphine
Levophanol (L-Dromoran)	2–3	4–5	Less than morphine	Less than morphine
Fentanyl (Sublimaze)	0.1	2–6	Like morphine	Like morphine
Pentazocine (Talwin)	3	4–5	Like morphine	Like morphine
Buprenorphine (Buprenex)	0.3	4–6	Less than morphine	Less than morphine

fragmentation is considered absolute identification, the expense of this test makes it suitable only for forensic identification or corroboration of a positive by TLC or EIA. When drug screens are ordered, the physician should be aware that false-negative results occur more frequently than false-positives because of the lack of sensitivity of TLC. A negative test for opiates or drugs by TLC alone is not reliable. Also, a screening test by EIA or radioimmune assay (RIA) may not be totally reliable, if the laboratory set the cutoff for detecting and reporting positives too high or if the sample was taken too late after the drug was used. Finally, some opioids such as fentanyl occur in such small amounts for short periods of time that testing in blood by RIA or GC/MS is necessary.

J.   Opioid Dependence. The classic studies of Bozarth and Wise (1984), which demonstrated the neuroanatomic independence of abstinence symptom generation and drive for the drug, reinforces the clinician's impression that even when abstinence complaints are totally eliminated, the patient can and will likely relapse because of the same sort of craving seen with other drug addictions. Lesion of the locus coeruleus (LC) abstinence areas does not reduce the drive for the drug that is mediated by the mesolimbic DA projections to the nucleus accumbens. Recent studies have reported that the drive for opiates and also the drive for cocaine may both be mediated by the mesolimbic DA projections. Similar work has recently suggested that the opiate model for the dissociation of drug self-administration and abstinence is relevant to all drugs of abuse. Dependence includes signs and symptoms that reflect compulsive, prolonged self-administration of opioid substances that are used for nonlegitimate medical purposes. If a specific medical condition that requires opioid treatment is present, the person with opioid dependence uses the opioid in a pattern and doses that are greatly in excess of the amount needed for pain relief. Persons with opioid dependence tend to develop such regular patterns of compulsive drug use that daily activities are typically planned around obtaining and administering opioids. Opioids are usually purchased on the illegal market, but may also be obtained from physicians by faking or exaggerating general medical problems or by receiving simultaneous prescriptions from several physicians. Maladaptive behavioral or psychological changes (e.g., initial euphoria followed by apathy, dysphoria, psychomotor agitation or retardation, impaired judgment, or impaired social or occupational functioning) may develop during, or shortly after, opioid use.

K.   Medical Complications of IV Drug Use. At the onset of treatment, a full medical evaluation is necessary to identify physical conditions that may affect the outcome of treatment and compromise the health of the addict. Intravenous use is associated with diseases introduced by dirty needles contaminated with the blood of previous users as well as with extra substances in the drug. Less common conditions arising from IV (intravenous) use include cellulitis, cerebritis, wound abscess, sepsis, arterial thrombosis, renal infarction, and thrombophlebitis. The most common, severe complications from IV drug use are bacterial or viral endocarditis, hepatitis, and AIDS. Specifically, the physician should address these issues during medical history and review of systems:

1. Accidents
2. Asthma
3. Breathing problems and sputum
4. Exposure to HIV
5. Head injuries
6. Heart palpitations

7. Hepatitis
8. Memory problems
9. Paresthesia
10. Prior TB, HIV, and hepatitis testing
11. Seizures
12. Sexually transmitted diseases
13. Subacute bacterial endocarditis
14. Tuberculosis
15. Ulcers, abscesses, cellulitis
16. Veins used for IV injection

In addition to the direct effects of opiates, the effects of intravenous self-administration, sharing needles, and the lifestyle of the typical intravenous addict combine to make a variety of major medical illnesses more common among heroin addicts. Naturally, skin abscesses, sclerosed veins ("tracks"), and puncture marks on the lower portions of the upper extremities are common. Veins sometimes become so badly sclerosed that peripheral edema develops and individuals switch to veins in the legs, neck, or groin. When these veins become unusable or otherwise unavailable, individuals often inject directly into their subcutaneous tissue ("skin popping"), resulting in cellulitis, abscesses, and circular-appearing scars from healed skin lesions. Infections may also occur in other organs and include bacterial endocarditis, hepatitis, and human immunodeficiency virus (HIV) infection. Tuberculosis is a particularly serious problem among individuals who use drugs intravenously, especially those dependent on heroin. Infection with the tubercle bacillus is usually asymptomatic and evident only by the presence of a positive tuberculin skin test. However, many cases of active tuberculosis have been found, especially among those who are infected with HIV. The incidence of HIV infection is high among individuals who use intravenous drugs, a large proportion of whom are individuals with opioid dependence. HIV infection rates have been reported to be as high as 60% among persons dependent on heroin in some areas of the United States. Needle sharing among IV users contributes to a higher risk of HIV infection and AIDS in this population and their sexual partners. As of September 1989, there were 21,188 reported cases of HIV infection in intravenous drug users which amounted to 21 percent of all AIDS cases in the United States. Among the 9724 women who had been diagnosed with AIDS, 51% were intravenous drug users and an additional 19% were sexual partners of intravenous drug users. Of the 1859 children diagnosed with AIDS, 58% had mothers who used drugs intravenously or were sexual partners of intravenous drug users.

L. Life Expectancy. In addition to infections such as cellulitis, hepatitis, HIV, tuberculosis, and endocarditis, opioid dependence is associated with a very high death rate—at the level of approximately 10 per 1000 per year among untreated persons. Death most often results from overdose, accidents, injuries, or other general medical complications. Accidents and injuries due to violence that is associated with buying or selling drugs are common. In some areas, violence accounts for more opioid-related deaths than overdose or HIV infection.

M. Clonidine plus Naltrexone. The discovery of clonidine's efficacy in opiate withdrawal not only provided physicians with an effective nonopiate treatment for opiate withdrawal but when linked to naltrexone provides a rapid technique for allowing the patient to go from opiate-dependent to being maintained on naltrexone. Clonidine helped reduce the detoxification process significantly. Clonidine plus naltrexone can reduce the detoxification process from 14 days to 8–24 h. This combination rapidly became new standard treatments that could be added to opiate maintenance, detoxification and abstinence, and drug-free 12-step fellowships and therapeutic communities. Once detoxification on clonidine is accomplished, it is still important that abstinence be maintained. Since relapse is a continuing part of addiction, once detoxified, most addicts still seek drugs. The combination of these two drugs has been shown to be effective in the working and highly motivated opiate addict, especially in conjunction with outpatient therapy and regular attendance at groups such as Narcotics Anonymous.

II. INHALANT-RELATED DISORDERS

A. Epidemiology. Because of their low cost and easy availability, inhalants are often the first drugs of experimentation for young people, and there may be a higher incidence among those living in economically depressed areas. Inhalant use is the most common abuse in a number of geographic areas. Inhalant use may begin by 9 years of age, appears to peak in adolescence, and is less common after age 35 years. Males account for 70–80% of inhalant-related emergency-room visits. Most compounds that are inhaled are a mixture of several substances that can produce psychoactive effects. These volatile substances are available in a wide variety of commercial products and may be used interchangeably, depending on availability and personal preference.

B. Intoxication. Several methods are used to inhale intoxicating vapors. Most commonly, a young person may purchase "whip-its" or simply inhale from a whipped-cream can in the supermarket. Other use forms include using a rag soaked with the substance, and the vapors are inhaled. The substance may also be placed in a paper or plastic bag and the gases in the bag inhaled. The inhalants reach the lungs, bloodstream, and brain target sites very rapidly.

C. *DSM-IV* Inhalant Intoxication. The essential feature of inhalant intoxication is the presence of clinically significant maladaptive behavioral or psychological changes (e.g., belligerence, assaultiveness, apathy, impaired judgment, impaired social or occupational functioning) that develop during, or shortly after, the intentional use of, or short-term, high-dose exposure to, volatile inhalants. The maladaptive changes are accompanied by signs that include dizziness or visual disturbances (blurred vision or diplopia), nystagmus, incoordination, slurred speech, an unsteady gait, tremor, and euphoria. Higher doses of inhalants may lead to the development of lethargy and psychomotor retardation, generalized muscle weakness, depressed reflexes, stupor, or coma.

D. *DSM-IV* Diagnostic Criteria for 292.89 Inhalant Intoxication

1. Recent intentional use or short-term, high-dose exposure to volatile inhalants (excluding anesthetic gases and short-acting vasodilators).
2. Clinically significant maladaptive behavioral or psychological changes (e.g., belligerence, assaultiveness, apathy, impaired judgment, impaired social or occupational functioning) that developed during, or shortly after, use of or exposure to volatile inhalants.
3. Two (or more) of the following signs, developing during, or shortly after, inhalant use or exposure:
    a. Dizziness

      b. Nystagmus

      c. Incoordination

      d. Slurred speech

      e. Unsteady gait

      f. Lethargy

      g. Depressed reflexes

      h. Psychomotor retardation

      i. Tremor

      j. Generalized muscle weakness

      k. Blurred vision or diplopia

      l. Stupor or coma

      m. Euphoria

4. The symptoms are not due to a general medical condition and are not better accounted for by another mental disorder.

Individuals with inhalant intoxication may present with auditory, visual, or tactile hallucinations or other perceptual disturbances (macropsia, micropsia, illusionary misperceptions, alterations in time perception). Delusions (such as believing that one can fly) may develop during periods of inhalant intoxication, especially those characterized by marked confusion; in some cases, these delusions may be acted on with resultant injury. Anxiety may also be present. Repeated but episodic intake of inhalants may first be associated with school problems (e.g., truancy, poor grades, dropping out of school) as well as family conflict.

REFERENCES

Bozarth MA, Wise RA: Anatomically distinct opiate receptor fields mediate reward and physical dependence. *Science* 224:516–517, 1984.

Gold MS: Opiate addiction and the Locus 24. *Psychiatric Clin North Am* 16:61–73, 1993.

Gold MS, Roehrich H: Treatment of opiate withdrawal with clonidine. *Pharmacology* 1741:29–32, 1987.

Gold MS, Miller NS: Seeking drugs/alcohol and avoiding withdrawal: the neuroanatomy of drive states and withdrawal. *Psychiatric Ann* 22:430–435, 1992.

Koob GF, Bloom FE: Cellular and molecular mechanisms of drug dependence. *Science* 242:715–723, 1988.

CHAPTER **6**

DRUG TESTING

Robert L. DuPont, M.D.
President, Institute for Behavior & Health, Inc.
Rockville, Maryland
and
Clinical Professor of Psychiatry
Georgetown University School of Medicine
Washington, DC

I. INTRODUCTION

Drug testing of biological specimens, which objectively identifies specific drug use with varied laboratory procedures, plays a vital role in the prevention and management of addiction to alcohol (ethanol) and other drugs.

II. DRUG TESTING METHODS

Beginning in the 1960s with thin-layer chromatography (TLC) testing in drug-abuse treatment programs, drug testing methods have evolved rapidly into a system based on an initial test, usually an immunoassay, followed when necessary by a confirmation test, usually by gas chromatography / mass spectrometry (GC / MS). Laboratory drug tests that were once done one specimen at a time have now been automated, resulting in falling costs and wider usage.

A. Immunoassays. The standard initial screening test for drugs of abuse is the immunoassay based on the link of a monoclonal antibody to the specific abused-drug molecule. The antibody–antigen linkage is measured using a variety of patented mechanisms, some of which are radioactive isotopes (RIA, ABUSCREEN by Roche Diagnostic Systems), colorimetric changes (EMIT, by Syva) and fluorescence polarization (FPIA, ADx, and TDx by Abbott Diagnostics). Capable laboratories are now high-production centers with sophisticated quality-control procedures. Some immunoassays have been adapted for rapid on-site testing by trained personnel using procedures designed to assure reliability.

 1. Advantages. Easily automated for mass testing but also suitable for on-site small-scale testing. Highly sensitive (e.g., detects drugs at very low concentrations). Low cost (a few dollars per test).

 2. Disadvantages. Cross-reactivity can occur. For example, over-the-counter (OTC) stimulants found in cold medicines cross-react with amphetamine / methamphetamine antibodies.

Manual of Therapeutics for Addictions, Edited by Norman S. Miller, Mark S. Gold, and David E. Smith.
ISBN 0471-56176-2 © 1997 John Wiley & Sons, Inc.

B. GC/MS. This is the highest standard of precise chemical identification in routine practice today. Once reserved for rare forensic tests with slow turnaround times and high costs, modern computers and laboratory technology have brought GC/MS testing into the mainstream of everyday drug testing.

1. Advantages. High sensitivity and high specificity (e.g., detecting drugs at very low concentrations and identifying specific drugs and drug metabolites with no cross-reactivity with other substances).

2. Disadvantages. Must be done at large laboratory (e.g., cannot be used in on-site settings) and relatively expensive (about $30–$75 per test) if confirmation is required. Because GC/MS testing is done at a laboratory that is remote from most specimen collection sites, there is a delay between collection and the result, often 2–3 days or longer.

C. Other Technologies. Thin layer chromatography has been improved since the 1960s, and it offers some advantages, particularly the broad range of substances tested. However, TLC is labor-intensive, is expensive to automate, is not as specific or sensitive as the immunoassays, and does not provide a permanent record of the results for challenged test results (unless a photograph is taken, which is expensive).

III. DRUGS TESTED AND CUTOFF LEVELS

Most drugs of abuse can be identified through drug testing. Although drug abusers could use a virtually limitless variety of chemicals to get high, drug abusers use relatively few substances. Each immunoassay tests for specific drug groups. The number of drugs screened is limited to the immunoassays for the most commonly abused drugs. Standards for workplace testing required by the federal government are limited to five drug classes: marijuana, cocaine, morphine/codeine, amphetamine/methamphetamine, and PCP. In order to limit the interference with legitimate medical practice, routine workplace drug testing does not include barbiturates and benzodiazepines, and it does not identify opiates other than morphine and codeine.

It is important to recognize just how narrow this standard screen is because the abuse of other drugs (including methadone, hydromorphone, oxycodone, LSD, MDMA (Ecstasy), and methylphenidate) is not identified with this screen. Nor does this screen identify the use of medicines that are not controlled substances, (e.g., antidepressants, anticonvulsants, antihypertensives, and birth control medicines).

In settings outside the workplace such as drug treatment, the criminal justice system, and emergency rooms, additional potentially abused drugs may be identified on drug tests. The most common additions to the basic workplace test panel are barbiturates, the benzodiazepines, propoxyphene, and methaqualone. Usually it requires a special order to screen for LSD and MDMA. For most drugs, the parent substance is identified in the test, but for marijuana and cocaine the major metabolites (THC acid and benzoylecgonine, respectively) are identified in urine tests since they are present in higher concentration than the parent compound. In settings where drug tests are often repeated over time and where the consequences of a single positive test are relatively minor, GC/MS confirmation is seldom justified because of its additional costs.

The standard cut-off levels used in urine drug tests reflect a consensus of the scientific community, and are based on manufacturers' specifications so that these products can be used by commercial laboratories. As the technology of immunoassays has increased in sophistication, the number of drugs identified has increased and the limits of detection have decreased. See Table 6.1 for common cutoff levels for workplace urine drug testing. Table 6.2 shows cutoff levels for routine hair and sweat patch tests.

Because marijuana smoke can be an environmental contaminant (e.g., at a rock concert or at a party), concern exists over possible passive exposure producing a positive drug test. The highest concentration recorded in tests that simulate real-life passive exposure is 6 ng/mL (nanograms per milliliter) of urine, well below the lowest commonly used cutoff of 20 ng/mL.

Passive exposure is not a practical issue for other drugs of abuse because, unlike marijuana smoke, they are not environmental contaminants. Crack "smoke" is volatilized particles (not true smoke). Cocaine particles are not spread in the air more than a few feet from the crack pipe.

IV. ALTERNATIVE BIOLOGICAL SPECIMENS

Drugs enter the bodies of drug users by many routes of administration—swallowing, inhaling smoke, snorting into the nose, and injecting into veins or under the skin. The drug user's goal is to get the active drug to the pleasure centers in the brain (ventral tegmental area and nucleus accumbens) where reward takes place primarily through dopamine neurotransmitter systems. Most abused drugs are metabolized in the liver and excreted through the kidneys into the urine. The abused drugs are distributed to every part of the drug user's body, so they can be identified in blood, sweat, and saliva and in such accessible solid tissues as hair and fingernails. At autopsy drug concentrations are also determined for the brain, liver, and other organs. Alcohol is unique among commonly abused drugs because it vaporizes so that it is present in exhaled breath, and not present in hair and fingernails.

A. Urine. Outside forensic tests, urine was the first specimen studied to identify drug use because urine is more easily collected than blood, the drugs and their metabolites are present in relatively high concentrations, and because extracting these substances from blood is more complex and expensive than extraction from urine.

TABLE 6.1. DHHS Cutoff Concentrations for Workplace Urine Tests

	Immunoassay Screen (ng/mL)	GC/MS Confirmation (ng/mL)
Marijuana metabolites	50	15[a]
Cocaine metabolites	150	150[b]
Opiate metabolites	300	300[c]
Phencyclidine	25	25
Amphetamine/methamphetamine	1000	500

[a]In GC/MS Δ-9-tetrahydrocannabinol-9-carboxylic acid
[b]Benzoylecgonine
[c]Morphine/codeine proposed cutoff levels will be 2000 ng/mL for morphine and codeine and 10 ng/mL for 6-MAM.

TABLE 6.2. Cutoff Concentrations for Hair and Patch Tests for Abused Drugs

Hair or Patch	Confirmation Level
Hair	
Opioid metabolites	5 ng/10 mg hair
Amphetamine/methamphetamine	5 ng/10 mg hair
Cocaine metabolites	5 ng/10 mg hair
PCP	3 ng/10 mg hair
Marijuana metabolites	1 pg/10 mg hair
Patch[a]	
Opiate metabolites	10 ng/mL
Cocaine metabolites	10 ng/mL
Amphetamine/methamphetamine	10 ng/mL
PCP	7.5 ng/mL
THC	1 ng/mL

[a]Patch is washed with 2.5 mL of liquid.

Because drug substances leave the blood rapidly, blood is preferable for identifying very recent drug use. However, within a few hours of drug use, the blood concentrations of most abused drugs fall below routine detection levels. In contrast, after the use of psychoactive doses of abused drugs, urine remains positive for 1–3 days. In cases of heavy chronic marijuana use, the urine tests can remain positive for several weeks after the last use of the drug. After a single use of one or two joints of marijuana, all urine samples are negative at 50 ng/mL in about 3 days and at 20 ng/mL in about 5 days. Many subjects have no positive urine samples after even one day has elapsed since the last smoking of one or two marijuana cigarettes.

B. Hair. Hair traps drug chemicals in the protein matrix of the hair as it is formed in the hair follicle, producing a virtual tape recording of the history of drug use. Since it takes about a week for the hair to grow from the base of the follicle to be long enough to clip at the scalp, drug use in the 5–7 days prior to hair sampling is not identified by a hair test. Because scalp hair grows at a rate of about $\frac{1}{2}$ in. per month, a standard $1\frac{1}{2}$-in. hair sample identifies drug use in the prior 90 days.

C. Sweat. Patches applied to the skin capture sweat, which is continuously produced even when a person is not noticeably sweating. Patches can be applied so that they are "tamperproof," meaning that they cannot be removed and replaced without the removal being easily identified. Patches can be applied from a few hours to about 2 or 3 weeks. Sweat patches are becoming available for widespread use. They can identify drug and alcohol use during the period when the patch has been worn.

D. Saliva. Saliva has been used as a tissue for alcohol and other drug testing. Like breath for alcohol testing, saliva is in equilibrium with blood, making it especially useful for identifying very recent use of alcohol and other drugs.

E. Breath. Breath tests are used only for alcohol testing.

F. Other Testing for Abused Drugs. A new technique called IONSCAN, a sort of mechanical sniffer-dog, has been developed for law enforcement and other uses based on an environmental sample (a vacuum or a moist swipe) to test for abused drugs. It is possible to test a person's pocket or hands, or a locker or a car, to identify traces of cocaine, heroin, or other abused drugs. This approach has not been widely used in addiction treatment and other settings where possible drug abusers are being identified, but the technology has promise as a screening device similar to the way metal detectors are used in airports, to screen large numbers of people quickly.

V. CLINICAL APPLICATIONS OF DRUG TESTS

A. What Drug Tests Do and Do Not Do. Drug tests cannot identify either *addiction* or *impairment*. They can reliably detect recent *use* of abused drugs. Because recent nonmedical use is highly correlated with impairment, and other undesirable characteristics such as drug sales, nonmedical drug use is prohibited in many settings including the workplace. Addiction treatment and the criminal justice system also use recent nonmedical drug use as a trigger for sanctions and interventions.

Blood tests reliably determine the concentration of specific drugs present in the blood. Blood concentrations closely correlate to the concentrations of drugs in the brain and other tissues at the time the sample is taken. Concentrations of drugs in other tissues, including urine and hair, do not correlate with brain concentrations of drugs at the time of collection because the samples are based on longer periods of time prior to collection. For urine, this sampling period is measured in hours and for hair it is measured in weeks or months.

Blood tests for abused drugs are especially useful in settings in which acute intoxication and overdose reactions are concerns. Urine tests are most useful when the identification of drug use within the 1–3 days prior to collection is the goal of the test. Hair and sweat patch tests are most useful when longer windows of detection are desired, 90 days for a $1\frac{1}{2}$-in. sample of scalp hair and a few days to 3 weeks when a sweat patch is used.

Breath tests for alcohol use correlate relatively well with current impairment, although impairment because of alcohol or other drug use is a complex function of blood concentration (there is greater impairment at a given blood concentration on the up slope—during absorption—than on the down slope—during elimination—of the blood concentration curve). In addition, tolerance is a major factor in impairment, and impairment varies with the complexity of the behavior being tested (impairment is greatest after drug use for novel and complex activities and least for simple and frequently repeated activities). Blood is most useful in tests for alcohol use and in postaccident testing for drugs of abuse when the critical question is the acute effects of the drug use.

Urine testing is especially useful when an intermediate window of detection is desired, such as with high-risk subjects in the criminal justice system and in addiction treatment settings. Random urine tests seldom identify occasional users but primarily identify frequent users of large doses of illicit drugs because of the short window of detection of urine tests.

Sweat patch testing and hair testing are especially useful in relatively low-risk settings (e.g., when the subject has been abstinent for long periods of time) and when a longer window of detection is desired (e.g., preemployment testing and posttreatment testing). See Table 6.3 for a comparison of blood, urine, hair, and sweat patch testing for drugs of abuse.

VI. LIMITATIONS OF DRUG TESTS

Urine tests are relatively easily cheated by submitting a false sample (freeze-dried urine or urine from someone else who has not used drugs) or by excessive hydration, as well as by using agents that confound the immunoassay screening test since, if the immunoassay screen is negative, no GC/MS test is done. Patch and hair tests are resistant to cheating and are particularly useful in settings in which long-term abstinence is the standard being applied.

Drug tests are valid only for those drugs for which tests are conducted. This means that a person may be intoxicated on alcohol or LSD and still produce a "negative" result following routine urine testing for abused drugs.

There are many clinical settings in which absolute certainty of drug test results is not needed. In these settings, an immunoassay screen is often sufficient without a GC/MS confirmation. Relying on an immunoassay screen alone permits on-site testing and dramatically reduces the cost of testing. Such settings include most drug-abuse treatment and criminal justice testing. Immunoassay screen results for marijuana, cocaine, and PCP are highly likely to be confirmed and are extremely unlikely to be the result of cross-reactivity. Amphetamine/methamphetamine and opiate positives are more difficult to interpret since cross-reactivity with OTC stimulants may trigger an immunoassay positive for amphetamine/methamphetamine. Poppy-seed consumption or the use of codeine or synthetic narcotics such as hydromorphone and oxycodone can trigger a positive test result for opiates on an immunoassay test.

In workplace testing, when termination may be the result of a positive test, or in legal proceedings when a positive test can have serious consequences, it is desirable to have the GC/MS confirmation. The ultimate safety net for a person being drug-tested in critical settings is the retained positive sample that can be subject to retest. To permit retesting in workplace drug-testing programs, the standard practice is to retain positive test samples for one year or longer after collection.

In disputed results, it is possible to retest urine, hair, and patch samples. It is not possible to test a newly collected sample of urine or sweat since a negative test result from the second sample does not invalidate the original test. On the other hand, in cases of disputed results because of the much longer detection window of hair testing, it is possible to take a second hair sample and retest it.

Because poppy seeds contain morphine and codeine, the laboratory test positive result of morphine and/or codeine of a urine test after poppy seed ingestion is not a laboratory error or "false positive" but a true positive. This has been a serious limitation for the usefulness of opiate-positive urine tests. Federal workplace guidelines for drug testing require that all morphine/codeine-positive tests be declared "negative" unless there is independent evidence of heroin use. Sometimes 6 monoacetylmorphine (6-MAM), a unique intermediate metabolite between heroin (diacetylmorphine) and morphine, can be identified in urine. When 6-MAM is found in urine, it is definitive evidence of heroin use, since poppy seeds contain no heroin or 6-MAM. Urine tests of heroin users are often negative for 6-MAM because of its short half-life. In order to reduce the number of laboratory positive test results for opiates as a result of poppy-seed and codeine use, it has been proposed that the opiate cutoff levels be raised to 2000 ng/mL from the current 300 ng/mL and that all workplace urine samples that are positive at this higher level be tested for 6-MAM. Both hair and sweat patches easily identify 6-MAM, so they have the advantage over urine of being able to reliably distinguish heroin use from poppy-seed consumption or codeine use.

TABLE 6.3. Blood, Urine, Hair, and Sweat Patch Testing for Drugs of Abuse

	Blood	Urine	Hair	Sweat Patch
Immunoassay screen	Yes	Yes	Yes	Yes
GC/MS confirmation option	Yes	Yes	Yes	Yes
Chain-of-custody option	Yes	Yes	Yes	Yes
Retained positives for retest option	Yes	Yes	Yes	Yes
MRO option	Yes	Yes	Yes	Yes
Surveillance window	3–12 h	1–3 days	7–90 days	1–21 days
Intrusiveness of collection	Severe	Moderate	None	Slight
Retest of same sample	Yes	Yes	Yes	Yes
Retest of new sample if original test disputed	No	No	Yes	No
Number of drugs screened	Unlimited[a]	Unlimited	5[b]	3[c]
Cost/sample (NIDA-5)	~ $200	~ $15-$30	~ $40-$65	~ $20
Permits distinction between light, moderate, and heavy use	Yes, acutely	No	Yes, chronically	Yes, chronically
Resistance to cheating	High	Low	High	High

	Postaccident and overdose testing for alcohol and other drugs	Reasonable cause and random testing	Preemployment testing	Posttreatment testing
Best applications	Alcohol BAC level	Frequent testing of high-risk groups such as post-treatment follow-up and CJS	Random and periodic testing Testing to determine severity of drug use for referral to treatment Testing subjects suspected of seeking to evade urine-test detection Opiate addicts claiming poppy-seed "false positive"	Maintaining abstinence Opiate addicts claiming poppy-seed "false positive"

[a]Blood testing for alcohol is routine, costing about $25 per sample, but blood testing for drugs is done by only a few laboratories in the country. Blood testing for drugs is relatively expensive, costing about $60 for each drug detected.
[b]Currently hair testing is available only for NIDA-5 (cocaine, opiates, marijuana, amphetamines, and PCP).
[c]Morphine / codeine, cocaine, amphetamine / methamphetamine. Additional sweat patch tests will become available, including marijuana, PCP, and alcohol.

VII. MEDICAL REVIEW OFFICER

When there is a concern that legitimate medical use may have caused a laboratory positive test result, it is desirable to have a *medical review officer* (MRO—a physician trained to interpret drug tests) interview the test subject after the laboratory positive and before reporting to the employer, court, or other requester of the drug test. The MRO decides whether laboratory positives can be explained by legitimate medical use. If so, a "negative" report is made to the employer or other requesting authority. Because the employer sees only the MRO "negative" result, the employee's legitimate medical treatment remains confidential and unknown to the employer as a result of the drug test. MRO review is required of all federally regulated workplace drug tests. If an MRO is not used, great care needs to be exercised in the interpretation of laboratory results of drug tests, especially opiate and amphetamine positives. Workplace drug testing and the role of the MRO are governed by regulations at the state and federal levels.

VIII. SUMMARY

Drug tests using the highest level of modern biotechnology are now routinely carried out in high-volume, sophisticated laboratories. Drug tests offer physicians powerful new tools to detect the use of specific abused drugs. For the full promise of this technology to be realized, it is necessary for physicians to understand how this technology works, what drug test results do and do not mean, and how to use a wide variety of biological specimens to answer important questions about the use of controlled substances.

SELECTED READINGS

DuPont RL: Drugs in the American workplace: conflict and opportunity. Part I: Epidemiology of drugs at work. *Soc Pharmacol* 3:133–146, 1989.

DuPont RL: Drugs in the American workplace: conflict and opportunity. Part II: Controversies in workplace drug use prevention. *Soc Pharmacol* 3:147–164, 1989.

DuPont RL: Laboratory diagnosis. In NS Miller (ed): *Principles of Addiction Medicine*. Chevy Chase, MD: American Society of Addiction Medicine, 1994, section IV, chapter 2, pp 1–8.

DuPont RL, Griffin DW, Siskin BR, Shiraki S, Katze E: Random drug tests at work: the probability of identifying frequent and infrequent users of illicit drugs. *J Addictive Dis* 14:1–17, 1995.

Schwartz RH: Urine testing in the detection of drugs of abuse. *Arch Intern Med* 148:2407–2412, 1988.

US Department of Health and Human Services: Mandatory guidelines for federal workplace drug testing programs. *Fed Reg* April 11, 1988, pp 11979–11989.

US Department of Health and Human Services: *Medical Review Officer Manual—A Guide to Evaluating Urine Drug Analysis*, DHHS Publication (ADM)88–1526. Washington, DC: Superintendent of Documents, US Government Printing Office, 1988.

PART II

PHARMACOLOGIC TREATMENT OF INTOXICATION AND WITHDRAWAL

CHAPTER 7

TREATMENT OF DETOXIFICATION IN ADDICTIVE DISORDERS

Norman S. Miller, M.D.
University of Illinois at Chicago
Chicago, Illinois

Mark S. Gold, M.D.
University of Florida
Brain Institute
Gainesville, Florida

David E. Smith, M.D.
Haight Asbury Free Clinic
San Francisco, California

I. DIAGNOSIS

A. The diagnosis of substance-related disorder (*DSM-IV* definition of addiction) is defined by the behaviors of addiction (preoccupation with acquiring alcohol/drugs, compulsive use, and relapse) and pharmacologic tolerance, and dependence to alcohol/drugs. Alcohol and drug disorders complicate many clinical conditions (e.g., medical, surgical, and psychiatric).

B. Effective treatment for alcohol and drug disorders is available, and evaluation, treatment, and referral by the physician is recommended for patients suspected of having an alcohol and/or drug disorder.

II. ADDICTION

A. Addiction is drug seeking as manifested by a preoccupation with acquiring alcohol and drugs, and by compulsive use (continued use despite adverse consequences and a pattern of relapse or return to alcohol and drug use despite reinstitution of adverse consequences).

B. Addiction is derived from biological drives (hunger, thirst, sex), and reflects an interaction between alcohol and other addicting drugs with neurosubstrates in the brain responsible for reinforced behaviors of the instincts of hunger, thirst, and sex.

Manual of Therapeutics for Addictions, Edited by Norman S. Miller, Mark S. Gold, and David E. Smith.
ISBN 0471-56176-2 © 1997 John Wiley & Sons, Inc.

III. TOLERANCE AND DEPENDENCE

A. Tolerance and dependence to drugs are expected physiologic responses to the pharmacologic effects of drugs, especially if taken chronically. Pharmacologic tolerance to a drug is an adaptive response that is defined as the need to increase the dose to maintain the same effect or the loss of an effect at a particular dose. Pharmacologic dependence is an expected deadaptive response following the cessation of the use of the drugs (withdrawal). The physiologic responses are stereotypic and predictable according to the drug type and pharmacologic properties.

B. Tolerance and dependence are not specific to addiction. Tolerance and dependence often occur in the setting of addictive use but can also occur independently of addictive use, such as regular use of nonaddicting medications.

IV. TREATMENT OF INTOXICATION AND WITHDRAWAL

A. Alcohol

1. Intoxication. Alcohol intoxication is manifested in a broad range of clinical conditions. Commonly, alcohol is used in combination with other drugs. The signs and symptoms of intoxication include clouded sensorium, dysinhibition, impairment in motor and mental functions, poor insight and judgment, lethargy, stupor, and coma.

2. Withdrawal. Typically, the peak period for withdrawal from alcohol is 1–3 days and the duration is 5–7 days. Manifestations of withdrawal are excitatory, and include signs and symptoms of hyperarousal from sympathetic-nervous-system (SNS) stimulation. Signs of alcohol withdrawal are hand and body tremors, diaphoresis, tachycardia and elevated blood pressure, dilated pupils, increase in temperature, seizures, restlessness, behavioral hyperactivity, mental hyperarousal, agitation, ataxia, and clouding of consciousness. Symptoms of alcohol withdrawal are anxiety, panic attacks, paranoid delusions or ideation, illusions, disorientation, visual hallucinations (usually zooscopic), and auditory hallucinations (often derogatory and intimidating).

a. For the majority of alcoholics, the withdrawal from alcohol is mild and requires minimal medical intervention. The single best predictor of future withdrawal from alcohol is the previous history of withdrawal, including the characteristics of past withdrawals, such as presence or absence of seizures or delirium tremens.

3. Treatment. When pharmacologic treatment of alcohol withdrawal is indicated, as in moderate to severe withdrawal, substitution with a pharmacologic agent with cross-tolerance and dependence with alcohol is indicated. Diazepam (Valium) or lorazepam (Ativan) or phenobarbital is usually recommended. The usual initial dosage of diazepam or lorazepam is titrated according to elevations of blood pressure and pulse rate, agitation, and presence of psychosis. In general, diazepam provides a smoother and safer withdrawal because of its longer half-life. Lorazepam is indicated when elimination time for benzodiazepines is prolonged, as in significant liver disease. Suggested parameters and doses are presented in Table 7.1. Thiamine 100 mg

TABLE 7.1. Alcohol Detoxification

	Mild Withdrawal	Moderate Withdrawal	Severe Withdrawal (Delirium Tremens)[a]
Diazepam or lorazepam	(Diazepam) 5–10 mg PO or (lorazepam) 1–2 mg po every 4 to 6 hours PRN for 1 to 3 days	(Diazepam) 15–20 mg PO QID day 1 10–20 mg PO QID day 2 5–15 mg PO QID day 3 10 mg PO QID day 4 5 mg PO QID day 5 or (lorazepam) 2–4 mg PO QID day 1,2 1–2 mg PO QID day 3,4 1 mg PO BID day 5 (may need to adjust based on signs and symptoms of alcohol withdrawal)	(Diazepam) 10–25 mg PO every hour while awake PRN or (lorazepam) 1–2 mg IV every hour while awake PRN for 3–5 days (to sedate)
	Systolic blood pressure > 150	Systolic blood pressure 150–200	Systolic blood pressure > 200
	Diastolic blood pressure > 90	Diastolic blood pressure 100–140	Diastolic blood pressure > 140
	Pulse > 100	Pulse 110–140	Pulse > 140
	Temperature > 100°F	Temperature 100–101°F	Temperature > 101°F
	Tremulousness	Tremulousness	Tremulousness
	Insomnia	Insomnia	Insomnia
	Agitation	Agitation	Agitation

[a]Monitoring in intensive care is recommended for cardiac and respiratory function, fluid and nutrition replacement, vital signs, and mental status. Restraints are indicated in the confused and agitated state to protect the patient from self, and others. (Delirium tremens can be a terrifying and life-threatening state.)

IM or PO QD × 3–7 days, hydration, and magnesium replacement may be indicated according to the severity of the withdrawal state.

B. Tranquilizers, Sedatives, and Hypnotics (e.g., Benzodiazepines, Barbiturates)

1. Intoxication. Tranquilizers (benzodiazepines) and sedatives/hypnotics (barbiturates, ethchlorvynol, glutethimide, and meprobamate) are depressants that suppress brain function. Manifestations of intoxication from sedatives and tranquilizers include sedation, slowed mentation and coordination, confusion, loss of consciousness, and coma. Depressants can cause hypotension, bradycardia, and slowed respiratory rate; as heart conduction slows, cardiac arrhythmias can occur. Prolonged slowing of the respiratory rate can lead to respiratory acidosis, arrest, and death.

2. Withdrawal. Typically, the peak period of withdrawal for short-acting preparations of benzodiazepines (e.g., alprazolam) is 2–4 days, with a duration of withdrawal is 4–7 days; the peak period of withdrawal for long-acting preparations (diazepam) is 4–7 days, with a duration of 7–14 days. Signs of withdrawal are agitation; increased psychomotor activity; muscular weakness; tremulousness, hyperpyrexia; sweating; delirium; convulsions; tachycardia; elevated blood pressure; coarse tremor of tongue, eyelids, and hands; and status epilepticus; symptoms of withdrawal are anxiety, euphoria, depression, incoherent thoughts, hostility, grandiosity, disorientation, euphoria, depression, tactile, auditory and visual hallucinations, and suicidal ideation and thinking (see also Table 7.2).

    a. The signs and symptoms of withdrawal for sedative/hypnotics are similar to those for the benzodiazepines. The treatment of withdrawal is similar for sedative/hypnotics (barbiturates) as for benzodiazepines.

    b. Withdrawal from benzodiazepines is seldom marked by significant elevations in blood pressure and pulse as with alcohol. Supplemental PRN (pro re nata; as-needed) doses are usually not needed for changes in vital signs. The anxiety of withdrawal is usually controlled with a prescribed taper with a long-acting preparation unless objectively it appears that the doses are too low. Caution is urged as drug-seeking behavior must be differentiated from anxiety of withdrawal, and anxiety from other disorders. Only the anxiety of withdrawal or other conditions, when severe, need be treated with increased doses of benzodiazepines. Alternative methods other than use of benzodiazepines for treating the anxiety from another disorder are indicated whenever possible. The prescriber must objectively assess the need for benzodiazepines and be in control of the dispensing of the benzodiazepines or other medications used for withdrawal. The addict by definition is out of control in regard to drug use and cannot reliably negotiate in the schedule for tapering.

3. Treatment. Treatment of withdrawal is aimed at gradually tapering off the depressant drugs or by substituting another depressant drug that shares pharmacologic cross-tolerance and dependence to suppress withdrawal symptoms (see Tables 7.3–7.6).

    a. Benzodiazepines have cross-tolerance and dependence with each other, other sedative/hypnotic drugs, and alcohol. Therefore, benzodiazepines can be substituted for other benzodiazepines and barbiturates and

TABLE 7.2. Signs and Symptoms of Benzodiazepine (Sedative/Hypnotics) Withdrawal

Symptoms of Hyperexcitability	Neuropsychiatric Symptoms		Gastrointestinal Symptoms	Cardiovascular Symptoms	Genitourinary Symptoms
Agitation	Ataxia	Malaise	Abdominal pain	Chest pain	Incontinence
Anxiety	Depersonalization	Myalgia	Constipation	Flushing	Loss of libido
Hyperactivity	Depression	Paranoid delusions	Diarrhea	Palpitations	Urinary urgency, frequency
Insomnia	Fasciculations	Paresthesias	Nausea		
	Formication	Pruritus	Vomiting		
	Headache	Tinnitus tremor			
	Hyperventilation	Visual hallucinations			

TABLE 7.3. Benzodiazepine (Barbiturate) Withdrawal: Benzodiazepine (Barbiturate) Detoxification

Short-acting	7–10-day taper: day 1, diazepam 10–20 mg PO QID with a gradual decremental reduction in dose to 5–10 mg PO QD on last day; avoid PRN; adjustments in dose according to clinical state may be indicated
	or
	7–10-day taper: calculate barbiturate or benzodiazepine equivalence and give 50% of the original dose, and taper (if actual dose is known before detoxification); avoid PRN
Long-acting	10–14-day taper: day 1, diazepam 10–20 mg PO QID with a gradual taper to 5–10 mg PO QD on last day; avoid PRN; adjustments in dose according to clinical state may be indicated
	or
	10–14-day taper: calculate barbiturate or benzodiazepine equivalence and give 50% of the original dose and taper (if actual dose is known before detoxification); avoid PRN

vice versa. The conversion for equivalent doses can be calculated if doses are actually known prior to taper (Table 7.4). A long-acting benzodiazepine is more effective than short-acting preparations in suppressing withdrawal symptoms and in producing a gradual and smooth transition to the abstinent state. In general, greater patient compliance and less morbidity can be expected from the use of the longer-acting benzodiazepines (see Table 7.3).

TABLE 7.4. Phenobarbital Withdrawal Conversion for Benzodiazepines

Benzodiazepine	Dose (mg)	Phenobarbital Withdrawal Conversion (mg)
Alprazolam (Xanax)	0.5–1.0	30
Chlordiazepoxide (Librium)	25	30
Clonazepam (Klonopin)	2	30
Chlorazepate (Tranxene)	15	30
Diazepam (Valium)	10	30
Flurazepam (Dalmane)	30	30
Lorazepam (Ativan)	2	30
Temazepam (Restoril)	15	30
Triazolam (Halcion)	0.25–0.50	30
Quazepam (Doral)	15	30
Estazolam (ProSom)	2	30

TABLE 7.5. Example 1: Phenobarbital Substitution[a]

Day Number	Dose per Day (mg)
1	60 mg TID = 180 mg
2	60 mg TID = 180 mg
3	60 mg TID = 180 mg
4	50 mg TID = 150 mg
5	50 mg TID = 150 mg
6	50 mg TID = 150 mg
7	40 mg TID = 120 mg
8	40 mg TID = 120 mg
9	40 mg TID = 120 mg
10	30 mg TID = 90 mg
11	30 mg TID = 90 mg
12	30 mg TID = 90 mg
13	20 mg TID = 80 mg
14	20 mg TID = 60 mg

[a]*Example*: Patient taking 12 mg of Alprazolam (Xanax) per day = 180 mg Phenobarbital (50% reduction)

TABLE 7.6. Example 2: Benzodiazepine Taper[a]

Day Number	Dose per Day (mg)
1	10 mg QID = 40 mg
2	10 mg QID = 40 mg
3	10 mg QID = 40 mg
4	10 mg QID = 40 mg
5	10 mg TID = 30 mg
6	10 mg TID = 30 mg
7	10 mg TID = 30 mg
8	10 mg TID = 30 mg
9	10 mg BID = 20 mg
10	10 mg BID = 20 mg
11	5 mg BID = 10 mg
12	5 mg BID = 10 mg
13	5 mg QD = 5 mg
14	5 mg QD = 5 mg

[a]*Example*: Patient taking 12 mg of lorazepam (Ativan) per day = 40 mg diazepam (50% reduction).

    b. The duration of the tapering schedule is determined by the half-life of the benzodiazepine or barbiturate that is being withdrawn.

        (1) For short-acting benzodiazepines such as alprazolam, 7–10 days of a gradual taper with a long-acting benzodiazepine or barbiturate is often sufficient: 7 days for low-dose, short-duration use and 10 days for high-dose, long-duration benzodiazepine use. In the case of alprazolam, because of higher rates of withdrawal seizures, the use of phenobarbital substitution is recommended for the taper.

        (2) For the long-acting benzodiazepines, 10–14 days of a gradual taper with a long-acting benzodiazepine or barbiturate is often sufficient; 10 days for low-dose, short-duration use and 14 days for high-dose, long-duration of use. The doses can be given in a QID or TID intervals. The long-acting preparations accumulate during the taper to result in a self-leveling effect of the blood level of the benzodiazepine or barbiturates over time (Table 7.3).

C. Stimulants

1. Intoxication. Common examples of central-nervous-system (CNS) stimulants are cocaine and amphetamines. Their short-term effect is to increase the release of dopamine and other catecholamines to act on postsynaptic receptors, but after prolonged use, they deplete the presynaptic supplies of these neurotransmitters.

Signs and symptoms of cocaine and amphetamine intoxication are sympathomimetic: dilated and reactive pupils, tachycardia, elevated temperature, elevated blood pressure, dry mouth, perspiration or chills, nausea and vomiting, tremulousness, hyperactive reflexes, repetitious compulsive behavior, stereotypic biting or self-mutilation, cardiac arrhythmias, flushed skin, poor self-care, suicidal behaviors, violence and homicide, and seizures. Particularly common and serious psychiatric symptoms during intoxication are depression and suicidal and homocidal ideation.

2. Other drugs and alcohol. Stimulant users frequently use other drugs including alcohol. A careful history, Breathalyzer test, urine toxicology, and continued assessment of clinical state and vital signs are indicated to detect the use of alcohol and other drugs such as opiates, cannabis, and phencyclidine.

3. Withdrawal. Peak period for withdrawal is 1–3 days, and duration is 5–7 days. Signs and symptoms of withdrawal include anhedonia, depression, hyperphagia, hypersomnia, psychomotor retardation, and suicidal thinking and behavior. Ordinarily, these signs and symptoms resolve within days with abstinence. However, at times delusions and/or depression may persist.

Commonly, few withdrawal states from stimulants require pharmacologic intervention. However, severe withdrawal states from stimulants may require consideration of pharmacologic intervention.

Supportive treatments for withdrawal from stimulants are indicated. Observation and monitoring for depression and suicidality are advised.

4. Treatments

    a. Mild to moderate withdrawal. Because of irritability from stimulant withdrawal, diazepam 5–10 mg PO Q4–6h either on a fixed schedule or PRN for 2–3 days is recommended.

    b. Severe withdrawal. For persistent depression, therapy can be initiated with desipramine at a dosage of 50 mg/day and titrated upward every other day in 50-mg increments until a dosage of 150–250 mg/day is attained. The dosage is maintained for 3–6 weeks and discontinued by gradually tapering off the drug over 2 weeks.

5. Treatment of acute toxicity. The treatment of acute overdose due to stimulants is blockage of catecholamine stimulation at the postsynaptic sites of action. Hypertensive episodes and cardiotoxicity are both treated with oral or parenteral doses of a beta blocker such as propranolol (Inderal) as indicated. Psychosis responds to a dopamine blocker, haloperidol, 5–10 mg orally or intramuscularly every 1–6 hours as needed.

D. Opiates

1. Intoxication. During intoxication, centrally, opiate drugs cause a suppression of noradrenergic release. Mood and affect are depressed and inhibited. Important clinically, pupils are constricted and poorly reactive. Peripherally, hypotension and constipation from activation of noradrenergic alpha and beta receptors are common findings. If sufficient amounts of opiates are acutely used, medullary suppression in the brainstem can lead to respiratory suppression and cardiovascular arrest.

  a. During intoxication, opiate suppression can be reversed by naloxone, an opiate antagonist. Naloxone is given intravenously in doses of 0.4–0.8 mg every 20 min as required. The dose is increased as indicated by symptom response until an upper limit of 24 mg is attained over an 8–12-h period.

2. Withdrawal. Peak period of acute withdrawal from opiates is 1–3 days and duration is 5–7 days. Opiate withdrawal, although medically benign and rarely life-threatening, is subjectively distressing and is marked by an intense drive to use more opiates. When opiate receptors are no longer hyperstimulated by opiates (e.g., morphine or heroin), the inhibition of the norepinephrine system through agonist action on α_2 receptors is released. Rebound release of norepinephrine underlies signs and symptoms of withdrawal.

Signs of opiate withdrawal are

  1. Pulse $\geq$ 10 beats per minute (bpm) over baseline or $>$ 90 bpm if there is no history of tachycardia and the baseline is unknown; systolic blood pressure $\geq$ 10 mmHg above baseline or $>$ 160/90 in nonhypertensive patients
  2. Dilated pupils
  3. Gooseflesh, diaphoresis, rhinorrhea, lacrimation, diarrhea
  4. Agitation, insomnia, mood lability
  5. Drug-seeking behavior

Symptoms of opiate withdrawal are intense muscular cramps, anxiety, arthralgia, nausea, malaise, and compelling desire for more opiates.

3. Treatment. Treatment of opiate withdrawal can be accomplished with clonidine or methadone. Those patients for which clonidine is more indicated are intranasal users, outpatients, and those who are motivated for the abstinent drug-free state. Those patients for whom methadone is indicated are intravenous users, inpatients, and those who have medical and psychiatric complications and poor compliance with withdrawal from opiates.

  a. An initial dosage of clonidine 0.4–0.8 mg/day in TID or QID intervals alleviates the withdrawal discomfort and craving from opiates in the first 3–4 days. The dosage is then gradually reduced over 5–7 days.

Hypotension, sedation, and headache are frequent side effects of clonidine (see Table 7.7). If hypotension is significant, the dosage can be reduced until blood pressure stabilizes.

b. Methadone may also be used for detoxification from heroin and methadone itself. Methadone is given in 5–10-mg PO test doses. If pharmacologic tolerance is present (e.g., patient awake, with adequate vital signs), an additional 5–20 mg PO can be given in 24 h. Subsequently, methadone is given 20–30 mg PO QD or BID, and tapered 5–10 mg PO QD (see Table 7.7).

c. Naltrexone may assist the motivated addict to maintain abstinence. Naltrexone is a pure opiate antagonist that blocks the effects of opium-derived compounds. Naltrexone acts competitively as an inhibitor at opiate receptors. The usual dosage is 50 mg orally each morning, prescribed under direct medical supervision. If the patient uses an opiate while taking naltrexone, the effects of the opiate are fully or partially blocked. Thus, the physical reinforcements of continued opiate use can be decreased by naltrexone.

E. Psychedelic Agents

1. Intoxication. Cognitive or memory impairment, disorientation, and confusion often occur in intoxication from psychedelic use. Psychedelic agents also produce EEG changes similar to those seen during REM (rapid-eye-movement) sleep, which may account for the dreamlike quality of the "high" reported by those using this class of drugs.

2. Treatment. The duration of the effects of intoxication following cessation of use can last days to weeks. Supportive care in a quiet environment is often sufficient until the effects of the intoxication subside. Psychedelic agents commonly require combined pharmacologic and psychosocial treatments for the management of intoxication and withdrawal. Lorazepam (Ativan) 1 to 2 mg PO or IV Q1–2h PRN or diazepam (Valium) 5–10 mg PO Q2–4h PRN can be given to calm and sedate.

F. Phencyclidine

1. Intoxication. PCP (phencyclidine) is a dangerous drug. Those under the influence are capable of acts of poor judgment and impulsivity that render themselves and others at significant risk for harm. The most important clinical symptoms of PCP intoxication are hyperactivity, insensitivity to pain, hallucinations, paranoid delusions, and memory loss. Signs include hypertension, tachycardia, eyelid retraction (producing a wide-eyed stare), dry erythematous skin, dilated pupils, nystagmus, and an excitable, angry affect. The duration of the effects of intoxication may last days to weeks following last use. PCP intoxication is a dangerous state to the users and others.

The characteristic superhuman strength of PCP users is related to its actions at opiate receptors and properties of a local anesthetic. Because perception of pain (analgesic and anesthetic action) is reduced, the user is capable of great feats of strength, such as breaking out of restraints and overpowering staff. Insensitivity to pain, disturbed thinking, and increased motor activity make PCP-intoxicated patients threatening to themselves and others.

2. Treatment. Acute symptoms of intoxication and withdrawal are diminished or reversed by haloperidol 5–10 mg intramuscularly or orally every 1–6 h as needed for behavioral control. Lorazepam 1–2 mg IV or diazepam 5–10 mg PO Q1–6 h can be given as needed.

TABLE 7.7. Opiate Detoxification

Heroin/Morphine Withdrawal (Clonidine Substitution)

Standing Dosing
Clonidine: 0.1–0.2 mg PO QID for 3–4 days and taper over 4–7 days

or:

As Needed (PRN) Dosing
Clonidine: 0.1 or 0.2 mg PO every 4–6 h PRN for signs and symptoms of withdrawal for 5–7 days (peak doses are between 1–3 days.)

Check blood pressure before each dose, do not give if hypotensive (for that individual, e.g., 90/60)

Methadone Withdrawal (Clonidine Substitution)

Standing dosing
Clonidine
0.1–0.2 mg PO QID × 14 days
0.1–0.2 mg PO TID × 3 days
0.1–0.2 mg PO BID × 3 days

As needed dosing
Clonidine: 0.1–0.2 mg PO Q 4–6 h PO PRN for signs and symptoms of withdrawal (18–20) days.

Check blood pressure before each dose, do not give if hypotensive (for that individual, e.g., 90/60)

Heroin/Morphine Withdrawal (Methadone Substitution)

Methadone test dose of 10 mg PO in liquid or crushed tablet; additional 10–20 mg doses are given for signs and symptoms of withdrawal every Q 4–6 h after initial dose for 24 h; Range for daily dose is 15–30 mg in 24 h; repeat total first day dose in single or two divided doses (stabilization dose) for 2–3 days, then reduce by 5–10 mg/day until completely withdrawn

Methadone Withdrawal (Methadone Substitution)

Methadone test dose of 10 mg PO in liquid or crushed tablet; Additional 10–20-mg doses are given for signs and symptoms of withdrawal every 4–6 h for 24 h; average dose is 20–30 mg in 24 h; repeat total first-day dose in single or two divided doses QD (stabilization dose), then reduce by 1–5 mg/day until completely withdrawn

G. Nicotine

1. Intoxication. There is a strong association between cigarette and alcohol use. Although the overall prevalence rate of alcoholism is 16% in the general population, 85% of alcoholics smoke cigarettes (inhalation). Moreover, cancer is the third leading cause of death in the general population, with alcohol and cigarettes being associated with several of the major types of cancer (e.g., lung, oropharyngeal, and gastrointestinal).

Nicotine acts on dopamine neurons in the ventral segmentum to produce its addicting effects. Nicotine is the active ingredient that users seek and to which addiction occurs. Inhalation (smoking) is the most common route of administration. Two basic methods of smokeless tobacco use are dipping and chewing. Dipping involves placing moist or drug tobacco between the cheek and gum.

2. Withdrawal. Nicotine dependence is included as a diagnostic category within the "Psychoactive Substance Use Disorders" in *DSM-III-R*. The peak of withdrawal is 1–3 days, and the duration is 1–2 weeks.

3. Treatment of withdrawal

a. Nicotine polacrilex. A nicotine substitute used in the treatment of nicotine withdrawal is nicotine polacrilex or gum. Its alkaline pH permits nicotine absorption across the buccal mucosa. A schedule for tapering gum use is planned after the daily maintenance dose is established. For example, a patient using 15 pieces of 2-mg gum each day during the first week of treatment gradually reduces the number of pieces to 10 per day by the end of the first month and 5 per day by the end of the second month. Patients are typically able to discontinue nicotine gum after 3–6 months of treatment.

Patients who use polacrilex for nicotine replacement and tapering should be counseled regularly about other aspects of nicotine cessation. Unsupervised patients are more likely to use the gum over an extended period of time and nicotine polacriles addiction may result. This is especially common with nicotine addicts who suffer from other drug addictions.

b. Transcutaneous nicotine patches. Nicotine patches are more likely than polacrilex to deliver a steady, predictable, and measurable amount of nicotine. Nicotine patches are manufactured in different diameters according to doses. The transcutaneous method involves applying the large-diameter patch to skin (hairless, dry, clean) for the first week, an intermediate-size patch during the second week, and the smallest patch during the third week. One disadvantage of this method is the development of contact dermatitis (change site each day). Nicotine replacement and fading should be used in conjunction with a recovery program.

c. Clonidine. Clonidine is an antihypertensive medication used to treat nicotine withdrawal. Transcutaneous clonidine is available in 0.1-, 0.2-, and 0.3-mg patches. Clonidine is usually prescribed for a period of 3–4 weeks, with the dose gradually reduced over the detoxification period. As with other forms of treatment for nicotine addiction, clonidine should be used in conjunction with a behavioral recovery program.

4. Treatment of addiction. It must be understood that these pharmacologic agents that treat detoxification of withdrawal do not prevent relapse because of addiction. Behavioral programs are needed to ensure continuous abstinence from nicotine use beyond the withdrawal period.

V. ADDICTION TREATMENT (PREVENTION OF RELAPSE)

1. Treatment of alcohol and drug withdrawal is seldom sufficient to provide sustained abstinence from the use of alcohol and drugs. Further referral to addictions treatment to prevent relapse to alcohol and drugs is indicated concurrently or following treatment of withdrawal.

2. Most treatment programs in the United States consist of variations of the 12-step method of abstinence-based treatment that uses cognitive and behavior techniques to treat the addictions. The 12-step recovery groups such as Alcoholics Anonymous (AA) and Narcotics Anonymous (NA) are used while in treatment and postdischarge during the sustained recovery process.

3. Treatment outcome studies have found that at 1 year postdischarge from abstinence-based treatment programs, 60% of patients have had continuous abstinence from alcohol and drugs. The studies have found that it was important for the patients to attend continuing care in the treatment program and participate in 12-step programs. One-year abstinence rates of 80–90% were achieved when weekly participation in continuing care and / or attendance at AA meetings followed the treatment program postdischarge.

VI. TREATING PSYCHIATRIC COMORBIDITY IN ADDICTION DISORDERS

A. Many patients with addictive disorders will present with psychiatric symptomatology due only to drug or alcohol consumption. However, because psychiatric patients have high rates of addictive alcohol and drug use, further evaluations should be conducted for concomitant addictive disorders among psychiatric disorders.

B. Various models have been proposed and are being implemented to treat addictive comorbidity in psychiatric populations: the serial, parallel, and integrated models.

1. The *serial model* is the traditional practice of treating the psychiatric comorbidity in a psychiatry setting, and then transferring to an addiction setting for the treatment of the addictive disorders. A major disadvantage is that chronically mentally ill patients do not respond well in the confrontative and active group participation used in the addiction treatment settings.

2. The *parallel model* is a newer practice in which the patients reside primarily in a psychiatric setting and are sent to an addiction setting for addiction treatment. In the *serial* and *parallel* models, the staff and sites are separate and the patients must contend with both.

3. The *integrated model* is an attempt to provide addiction and psychiatric treatments in the same milieu by the same staff. The patient receives a core approach to the treatment of both categories of disorders because the staff is trained in psychiatric and addictive treatments. The integrated approach is gaining significant popularity in treating those chronically mentally ill patients with an addictive disorder. In this model, the patient is assigned a case manager who integrates psychiatric and addiction services for their total care. The

patient is closely followed longitudinally for compliance and outcome. Referring physicians need to consider the advantages and disadvantages of the different comorbid treatment settings when making referrals.

SELECTED READINGS

Adams RP, Victor M: *Principles of Neurology,* 3rd edn. New York: McGraw-Hill, 1985.

Clark LT, Friedman HS: Hypertension associated with alcohol withdrawal: assessment of mechanisms and complications of alcoholism. *Clin Exp Res* 9:125–132, 1985.

Cocores JA, Sinaikin P, Gold MS: Scopolamine as treatment for nicotine polacrilex dependence. *Ann Clin Psychiatry* 1:203–204, 1989.

Gold MS, Dackis CA: Role of the laboratory in the evaluation of suspected drug abuse. *J Clin Psychiatry* 47:17–23, 1986.

Henningfield SE: Nicotine medication for smoking cessation. *N Engl J Med* 333(18):1196–1203, 1995.

Jaffe JH: Drug and addiction abuse. In AG Gilman, LS Goodman, TW Rall, F Murad (eds): *The Pharmacological Bases of Therapeutics,* 7th ed. New York: Macmillan, 1985, pp 532–581.

Kannel WB, Sorlie P: Hypertension in Framingham. In O Paul (ed): *Epidemiology and Control of Hypertension.* New York: Station Incontinental Medical Book Corp, 1974.

Klatsky AL, Friedman GD, Siegelaum AB, Gerad MJ: Alcohol consumption and blood pressure. *N Engl J Med* 296:1194–1200, 1977.

Miller NS: *The Pharmacology of Alcohol and Drugs of Abuse and Addiction.* New York: Springer, 1991.

Miller NS: *Principles of Addiction Medicine.* Washington, DC: American Society of Addiction Medicine, 1994.

Miller NS: *Treatment of the Addictions: Applications of Outcome Research for Clinical Management.* New York: Haworth Press, 1995.

Miller NS, Gold MS (eds): *Pharmacological Therapies for Drug and Alcohol Addiction.* New York: Marcel Dekker, 1995.

Parsons OA, Leber WR: The relationship between cognitive dysfunction and brain damage in alcoholics: causal or epiphenomena. *Clin Exp Res* 5:326–343, 1981.

Schuckit MA: Alcoholism and affective disorder: diagnostic confusion. In DW Goodwin, CK Erickson (eds): *Alcoholism and Affective Disorders.* New York: SP Medical and Scientific Books, 1979, pp 9–19.

CHAPTER 8

TREATMENT OF OPIOID DEPENDENCE

Joseph A. Piszczor, M.D.
& William Weddington, M.D.
Westside VAMC
Chicago, Illinois

I. INTRODUCTION

Although the cocaine epidemic may have caused a decrease in illicit opioid use during the 1980s, the number of Americans addicted to opioids is on the rise again. It is estimated that there are currently about 500,000 opioid addicts in the United States (Kreek, 1992). Apart from the problems presented by the addiction proper (e.g., overdose, withdrawal), opioids are responsible for significant morbidity and mortality. Within 10–20 years of initiating use, approximately 25% of all persons addicted to heroin die from suicide, homicide, accidents, or infectious disease such as tuberculosis, hepatitis, and AIDS (Gold, 1995). All clinicians should be knowledgeable of problems associated with opioid addiction as well as current means of addressing them.

II. DEFINITION

Opioids are best defined by their biochemical activity—they are chemicals that act at opioid receptors. This includes the naturally occurring opioids (e.g., morphine, codeine, thebaine), semisynthetic opioids (e.g., oxycodone, fentanyl), and synthetic opioids (e.g., propoxyphene, methadone). There are a number of different opioid receptors; but activity at the mu receptor is responsible for conditions that bring addicts to clinicians. Although the major focus in this chapter is on heroin, a derivative of morphine, clinicians should be aware of health hazards posed by other opioids such as codeine (in preparations such as tylenol No. 3), propoxyphene (Darvon), and methadone.

Opioids may also be classified by their function at the receptor sites. Agonists activate opioid receptors, whereas antagonists displace opioids from receptors and block their activity. Mixed agonists/antagonists produce some effects of opioids at receptors but block others.

III. PHARMACOLOGY

A. Activity. Opioids act principally on the central nervous system and bowel. They relieve pain and anticipatory anxiety, decrease gastrointestinal motility,

Manual of Therapeutics for Addictions, Edited by Norman S. Miller, Mark S. Gold, and David E. Smith.
ISBN 0471-56176-2 © 1997 John Wiley & Sons, Inc.

suppress cough, produce urinary retention, and induce euphoria. Opioids also inhibit the locus coeruleus (LC), a bilateral nucleus in the dorsolateral tegmentum. The LC increases blood pressure and pulse and is activated by pain, blood loss, and cardiovascular collapse. Consisting of only about 18,000 cells, the LC accounts for the origin of almost all noradrenergic afferents in the brain, the most extensive of any network of neural pathways (Gold, 1995). Opioids also activate dopaminergic neurons to the nucleus accumbens, which current research implicates in development of the compulsive nature of addiction.

B. Pharmacokinetics. Activity of opioids depends on their half-lives. Intoxication with short-acting opioids such as heroin (half-life 6–8 h) is generally briefer and more intense, and withdrawal symptoms occur more quickly. Opioids such as methadone (half-life 48–72 h) or LAAM (L-acetyl-α-methadol; half-life 2.6 days), produce effects that are less intense, longer-lasting, and followed by a longer onset of withdrawal symptoms.

Metabolism of opioids is generally by glucuronidation in the liver. In some cases, the metabolites are responsible for activity of the drug. Heroin is rapidly metabolized to morphine. LAAM is metabolized to nor-LAAM and dinor-LAAM, both of which are active at opioid receptors.

C. Routes of Administration. The most common route for heroin users is intravenous injection. However, with advent of the AIDS epidemic, more users snort heroin, which may lead to ulceration of the nasal septum. Heroin may also be smoked in a water pipe. Oral ingestion is the obvious route for addictions to drugs such as codeine (either solid or liquid; cough medicine may be the preferred vehicle or is used if other forms are not available). Often medication containing opioids is readily available from physicians or on the streets. Iatrogenic addiction may be due to prescribing physicians or as a result of a substance user's use of multiple physicians and emergency-room visits.

D. Content of Heroin. Most street heroin is somewhere within 4–20% pure. Clinicians must be aware that heroin is adulterated with quinine, sedating drugs such as diazepam (Valium) and diphenhydramine (Benadryl) to mimic the effects of "nodding out" (the state of lethargy induced by opioids), talcum powder (which may cause microcrystalline inclusions when the insoluble crystals lodge in the capillary bed of the lungs), and human immune deficiency virus (HIV) or hepatitis B virus when users share injection paraphernalia.

IV. CLINICAL STATES

A. Opioid Intoxication. *Diagnostic and Statistical Manual of Mental Disorders*, 4th edition (*DSM-IV*: American Psychiatric Association, 1994) requires the following for opioid intoxication: (1) recent use of an opioid; (2) clinically significant maladaptive behavior or psychological changes during or shortly after opioid use (initial euphoria followed by apathy, dysphoria, psychomotor agitation, or retardation, impaired judgment, or impaired social or occupational functioning); (3) *pupillary constriction* (or pupillary dilation due to anoxia from severe overdose) and one or more of the following signs during or shortly after opioid use—drowsiness, coma, slurred speech, or impairment in attention or memory; and (4) these symptoms are not due to a general medical condition and are not better accounted for by another mental disorder. Although it is not listed in *DSM-IV*, analgesia will also be present.

An opioid-intoxicated patient should be monitored until signs and symptoms of intoxication have resolved. As long as he or she remains alert, no medical intervention is necessary. However, if a patient becomes comatose or if vital signs begin to deteriorate, action must be taken to counteract the overdose (see below). Once patients are no longer intoxicated and require no further monitoring, attempts should be made to engage them regarding the serious consequences of addiction and to persuade them to enter treatment. At a minimum, such patients should be referred to NA (Narcotics Anonymous).

B. Opioid Overdose. Individuals addicted to opioids develop tolerance to many of the effects of opioids, but a lethal dose always exists. Overdose may be accidental due to errors in cutting heroin, a deliberate attempt by someone seeking revenge (e.g., unpaid dealer, retaliation for cooperation with federal narcotics agents), or a suicide attempt by a patient. Opioid overdose is characterized by coma, shock (decreased pulse and blood pressure), decreased respiratory rate (due to decreased sensitivity to CO_2 accumulation), cyanosis, and pinpoint pupils. (*Note:* Dilated pupils in a known opioid overdose are a sign of impending death; dilated pupils are due to severe anoxia.)

C. Acute Opioid Withdrawal. *DSM-IV* requires the following for opioid withdrawal: (1) either cessation or reduction of opioid use that has been heavy and prolonged (several weeks or longer), or administration of an opioid antagonist after a period of opioid use; (2) three or more of the following, developing within minutes to several days after cessation or reduction in opioid usage: dysphoric mood, nausea, vomiting, muscle aches, lacrimation, rhinorrhea, pupillary dilation, piloerection, sweating, diarrhea, yawning, fever, insomnia; (3) these symptoms cause clinically significant distress or impairment in social, occupational, or other important areas of functioning; and (4) these symptoms are not due to a general medical condition and are not better accounted for by another mental disorder. Other symptoms not listed by *DSM-IV* but commonly noted include joint pains (particularly the knees and back), abdominal cramps, hot and cold flashes, anorexia, muscle spasms, kicking movements (particularly bothersome at night), restlessness, anxiety, irritability, depression, hypertension, and tachycardia. Symptomatology varies among patients, but generally one episode of opioid withdrawal for a given patient is similar to other episodes. Resolution of symptoms generally occurs within 5–7 days for short-acting opioids (e.g., heroin, codeine) and within 10–14 days for longer-acting ones (e.g., methadone).

D. Protracted Withdrawal Syndrome from Opioids. Studies (Himmelsbach, 1942; Martin and Jasinski, 1969) indicate that a protracted withdrawal syndrome from opioids occurs in two phases. The first phase lasts 4–10 weeks and is characterized by increases in vital signs (blood pressure, pulse, temperature, respiratory rate) along with pupillary dilation. The second phase follows during weeks 6–9 of abstinence and lasts until weeks 26–30. This phase consists of a decrease in vital signs and miosis. The decrease in respiratory rate is due to decreased responsiveness to CO_2. Other data (Himmelsbach, 1942; Eisenman et al., 1969) indicate that during protracted opioid withdrawal, patients may also be hyperresponsive to stressors and thus more susceptible to return to usage.

E. Opioid Withdrawal in Neonates. Children of opioid-addicted mothers experience a withdrawal syndrome during the first 2 weeks of life. This has not been extensively studied. Questions may be raised regarding specificity of the data because the mothers are typically addicted to or abusing more than one class of drug (e.g., heroin, cocaine, alcohol, nicotine). Symptoms of opioid withdrawal appear within the first 24 h if the mother has been using short-acting opioids. If she has been taking methadone, symptoms generally appear within 3–4 days but may occur up to 3–4 weeks after delivery (Finnegan and Kandall, 1992). An affected infant demonstrates coarse tremors, a high-pitched cry, sleep disturbance, sneezing, increase in muscle tone, sucking of the fist, hyperactive Moro reflex, frequent yawning, and nasal stuffiness (Finnegan and Kandall, 1992). Diarrhea, fever, dehydration, and grand mal seizures have been noted in untreated infants. Fever and dehydration may also lead to infant death if the withdrawal syndrome is not treated.

V. TREATMENT

A. Opioid Intoxication. Opioid intoxication requires close monitoring of mental status and vital signs. When a patient's mental status has cleared sufficiently and vital signs are stable, a clinician should attempt to engage the patient (and his/her support system) in stopping opioid usage and entering treatment. At a minimum, the patient is instructed to attend NA meetings regularly. The patient should also be encouraged to enter a rehabilitation program. Because of the relapsing nature of this illness, neither patients nor clinicians should be discouraged by a history of multiple previous attempts at rehabilitation. Because of denial involved with addictive diseases, success in rehabilitation is not often achieved during the first attempt.

B. Opioid Overdose. The ABC's of cardiopulmonary resuscitation are the first priority. Adequate ventilation must be assured, and stability of the cardiovascular system must be established and maintained. Naloxone hydrochloride (Narcan) is administered intravenously at 0.4 mg every 4 min. A patient usually regains consciousness within seconds and may show some signs or symptoms of opioid withdrawal. Repeated doses of naloxone are given until the patient regains consciousness. A high number of doses of naltrexone may be required if a patient has overdosed on buprenorphine; because of high affinity of buprenorphine for opioid receptor sites, up to 25 doses of naloxone may be required (Jaffe, 1992). Any patient who requires treatment with naloxone should be hospitalized for at least 24 h for further monitoring because of the possibility that that patient has used a long-acting opioid (e.g., methadone, LAAM, propoxyphene). Because naloxone has a half-life of 2–3 h, coma, shock, and respiratory depression may recur if a patient has used a long-acting opioid.

A clinician should be aware that information regarding drug use obtained from a patient may be inaccurate because the patient is either unwilling or unable to estimate quantity and frequency of the substance used. A urine toxicology screen is necessary and provides additional information.

If a patient does not respond to naloxone, possibility of a patient's abuse of other drugs, such as benzodiazepines or barbiturates, should be considered. *Flumazenil* is useful in the event of benzodiazepine overdose; 0.2 mg flumazenil is administered in repeated doses up to a total of 3 mg. Flumazenil is contraindicated if a patient has a seizure disorder, is benzodiazepine-dependent, or has overdosed on tricyclic antidepressants (Becker and Olson, 1995). Ventilatory support must be continued if a patient does not regain consciousness. All patients, whether they regain consciousness with naloxone or not, should be given a full physical examination. Appropriate lab studies, such as serum chemistry including electrolytes, glucose, renal and liver function tests, complete blood count (CBC), arterial blood gas, urinalysis, and urine toxicology screen, should be ordered. CT scanning of the head and/or skull x-rays may also provide important information regarding unresponsive patients.

C. Opioid Detoxification–Short-Term. Short-term opioid detoxification is generally best achieved in an inpatient setting. Unlike social setting detoxification from alcohol (detoxification from alcohol without the use of medication), drug-free detoxification from opioids is unlikely to be successful unless a patient is incarcerated. Patients normally find withdrawal symptoms intolerable and leave to seek relief. Outpatient detoxification may be successful in patients with lesser habits ($20–$30/day) and who are snorting. Patients who use larger amounts of opioids ($40–$100/day) or who administer opioids intravenously are not likely to successfully complete short-term detoxification on an outpatient basis. Again, patients will seek relief if withdrawal symptoms are not being suppressed adequately.

1. Short-term detoxification with oral clonidine. Clonidine is an α_2-adrenergic agonist that suppresses the activity of the locus coeruleus (LC). It thus counteracts hyperactivity of the LC induced by opioid withdrawal. Regimens of clonidine in the literature vary (Kleber, 1994; Jaffe, 1992; Renner, 1994; O'Connor and Kosten, 1994). Between 0.1 and 0.3 mg of clonidine is given to the patient orally every 4–6 h. The initial dose is 0.1 mg Q4–6h, which is increased if withdrawal symptoms are not fully controlled. Recommendations limit the maximum daily amount of oral clonidine to 1.2 mg for outpatients and 2.0 mg for inpatients. Clonidine is tapered by 0.1–0.2 mg/day as withdrawal symptoms subside. Detoxification with clonidine lasts between 5–14 days, depending on type of opioid and daily quantity used.

The two most commonly encountered side effects of clonidine are orthostatic hypotension and sedation. Because of hypotensive effects of clonidine, a patient's blood pressure should be closely monitored. Blood pressure readings should be taken before each dose of oral clonidine. If the systolic BP is < 90 mmHg or if the diastolic is < 60 mmHg, clonidine must be withheld. Because of risk of patient falls, it is preferable that usage of clonidine be monitored on an inpatient basis. Sedation is the other major side effect of clonidine. Unfortunately, this has little effect on sleep disturbances, which patients often report during withdrawal.

Any patient who is being treated for opioid withdrawal with clonidine as an outpatient [*Note*: We do not recommend this, but the procedure has been studied (Kleber et al., 1985).] should be warned of potential risks involved while operating heavy machinery or driving a car. It is preferable that detoxification with clonidine be done in a day-hospital setting rather than during outpatient visits, with at least daily checking of a patient's blood pressure.

Clonidine does not treat all symptoms of opioid withdrawal; ancillary medication is usually required. The following medications may be used to treat symptoms as indicated: ibuprofen 600 mg Q6h or 800 mg Q8h as needed for muscle aches and joint pains; cyclopropomide (Bentyl) 20 mg Q6–8h for stomach cramps; quinine (Quinamm) 260 mg QHS for muscle spasms (particularly "jumpy legs" during the nighttime); a benzodiazepine (e.g., lorazepam 2 mg) Q4h PRN anxiety; a sleeping pill (e.g., triazolam 0.25 mg, diphenhydramine 50 mg) QHS PRN sleep [*Note*: Tricyclics negate the action of clonidine (Jaffe and Kleber, 1989), so sedating tricyclics such as amitriptyline cannot be used concurrently with clonidine.]; loperamide (Imodium) 2 mg or attapulgite (Kaopectate) 30 mL PRN after each loose bowel movement PRN diarrhea; and propoxyphene (65 or 100 mg) as a replacement opioid to relieve the intensity of the withdrawal symptoms.

2. Short-term detoxification with clonidine transdermal patch. Clonidine transdermal patches may be preferable to oral clonidine because they provide consistent availability of the medication as opposed to the peaks and troughs with oral medication (Burant, 1990; Ling and Wesson, 1990; Spencer and Gregory, 1989). Two clonidine transdermal patches No. 2 (three may be necessary if the patient weighs > 150 lb) are applied on the first day of treatment. Because it takes 24–48 h for clonidine patches to become effective, one may supplement with oral clonidine (0.1–0.2 mg Q6–8h as tolerated for the first day or two only), while closely monitoring blood pressure. Alternately, only two patches are used. One clonidine transdermal patch No. 2 is applied the first day of treatment, and a second clonidine patch No. 2 is applied the following day (Piszczor J, Kuhs L, and Showalter C: unpublished data). A patient may also require ancillary medications listed under the section on short-term treatment of withdrawal with oral clonidine. If opioid withdrawal is prolonged over one week, one should change each patch on the seventh day of use. (*Note*: Clonidine patches have two components—a small square patch, which contains the active medication, and a larger, round, flesh-colored patch, which acts as a covering. If a patient experiences no relief with clonidine, one should check to see that both parts of the patch have been applied. Occasionally, only the outer patch, which contains no medication, has been applied.) Blood pressure must be checked regularly every 6–8 h. Occasionally, patients will complain of itching or skin irritation at the patch site. This side effect is usually controlled with *diphenhydramine (Benadryl)* 25–50 mg Q4–6h.

Use of oral clonidine or the transdermal patches is not approved by the Food and Drug Administration (FDA) for use in detoxification from opioids. However, there is extensive research supporting its effectiveness and safety (Gold, 1995). Research studies have generally employed oral clonidine, but there is information in the medical literature on use of clonidine transdermal patches (Spencer and Gregory, 1989; Burant, 1990; Ling and Wesson, 1990).

As noted above with oral clonidine, clonidine transdermal patches are ineffective if a patient has recently been taking a tricyclic antidepressant (TCA).

3. Short-term detoxification with methadone. Methadone maintenance for opioid addiction is strictly regulated by the FDA and the Drug Enforcement Agency (DEA). Methadone may be dispensed only in hospitals and outpatient clinics licensed by the FDA and the DEA. Short-term detoxification with methadone is limited to 30 days. Detoxification may be performed on an inpatient drug unit or in an outpatient methadone clinic.

There are several regimens for short-term detoxification in the literature (Kleber, 1994; Jaffe, 1992; Lowinson et al., 1992; O'Connor and Kosten, 1994; Schuckit, 1989). During the first 2–3 days of detoxification, the patient is stabilized on a given dose of methadone. On the first day, a patient receives an initial dose of 15–20 mg. If this does not suppress symptoms, another 5–10 mg of methadone may be given an hour later. Alternately, the methadone dose may be repeated 12 h later. Most patients will not require more than 40 mg on the first day. On the second day, the same methadone dose is given unless the patient has experienced significant withdrawal symptoms or is oversedated. Once a patient is stabilized on a given dose, methadone is decreased by 10–20% per day. Alternately, methadone may be decreased by 5–10 mg per day. Detoxification is halted or slowed if the patient experiences significant opioid withdrawal symptoms.

Methadone may not be used on an inpatient medical or psychiatric unit for opioid withdrawal unless the patient has been admitted for another primary diagnosis (hepatitis, trauma, etc.). If a patient is unable to remain hospitalized in order to complete the detoxification (e.g., unavailability of a formal detoxification unit; limits on length of stay), arrangements should be made before the patient is discharged to complete the detoxification as an outpatient or to enter methadone maintenance in a licensed methadone clinic.

4. Long-term detoxification with methadone. Federal regulations allow a 180-day detoxification from opioids with methadone even if a patient does not otherwise qualify for methadone maintenance (see below). After a patient is stabilized on a dose of methadone, the dose is gradually decreased over 6 months. According to federal regulations, the dose on the first day of treatment cannot exceed a total of 40 mg—an initial dose of 30 mg, supplemented by 10 mg more if symptoms are not suppressed. After the first day of treatment, the dose of methadone can be increased by 10 mg every 3 days if necessary. Once a stabilizing dose has been achieved, a variety of regimens are recommended for detoxification (Kleber, 1994; Senay, 1994). In general, dose of methadone is decreased by 5–10 mg/wk. Once methadone dose has been lowered to 20–25 mg/day, decrease in dosage should be no more than 5 mg/wk.

D. Long-Term Treatment of Opioid Dependence (Drug-Free). A patient who has been detoxified from opioids should become involved in a life-long program of recovery. Without such involvement, relapse is a strong probability.

Early recovery takes place in either an inpatient or an outpatient rehabilitation program. Both inpatient and outpatient programs consist of educational seminars, group therapy, one-to-one counseling, medication management by physicians when necessary, family therapy, peer support, and attendance at 12-step meetings (NA).

After completion of a rehabilitation program, patients are encouraged to maintain contact with the treating facility through group therapy, between once a week to once a month, depending on how well they are progressing in recovery. Continued urine toxicology screening is also valuable to focus a patient on the goal of abstinence.

Attendance at 12-step meetings (NA) and having a sponsor, a mentor who is also in the program, are crucial to any recovery program. Patients who do not follow through with these resources consistently report relapse.

Some patients may also benefit from taking *naltrexone* (*ReVia*—formerly known as Trexan), an opioid antagonist. Naltrexone blocks opioid receptors and prevents a patient from experiencing euphoria with opioid use. However, naltrexone also blocks the analgesic effects of opioids. Because naltrexone will precipitate withdrawal if given too soon after the start of detoxification, naltrexone is administered after a patient has been opioid-free for at least 7 days for short-acting opioids and at least 10–14 days for longer-acting opioids such as methadone. A dose of naltrexone 150 mg every third day will provide adequate opioid receptor blockade; however, for ease of patient compliance, 50 mg/day is preferable. Before starting naltrexone, a patient may be administered a naloxone challenge, in which a single dose of *naloxone* (0.4–0.8 mg) is injected intramuscularly and the patient is monitored for any sign of opioid withdrawal (Greenstein et al., 1992). Alternately, a starting dose of naltrexone 25 mg is given. If there are no signs of opioid withdrawal, naltrexone 50 mg is administered daily. Further increases in dosage are not required. With this dose, a patient's opioid receptors are blocked for 3 days, during which time he/she cannot experience euphoria with opioids. Naltrexone therapy usually requires a highly motivated patient. Many patients will reject naltrexone therapy. Also, many patients will note that the medication cost ($3–$4 per pill) is prohibitive. In either case, issues of a patient's denial and resistance should be addressed.

Because of a 19% incidence of hepatotoxicity in patients treated with naltrexone doses 6 times the daily recommended dose of 50 mg, clinicians should monitor liver function tests prior to starting naltrexone and every 6 months thereafter. Generally, patients note no side effects with methadone. The most frequent complaints with naltrexone therapy are symptoms of opioid withdrawal. Such symptoms indicate that treatment with naltrexone was probably initiated before opioid detoxification was complete.

E. The Pregnant Patient. Because detoxification of a pregnant patient is more likely to result in fetal loss than withdrawal experienced by a newborn infant in the first few weeks of life, it is recommended that pregnant opioid addicts be placed on methadone for the duration of their pregnancy. If detoxification becomes necessary or if a mother insists, it should be done between weeks 16 and 32 of gestation. Methadone dosage should be decreased by no more than 5 mg every 2 weeks (Finnegan and Kandall, 1992). Medical care for the mother, intensive prenatal care, and psychosocial support are also necessary treatment for the opioid-dependent mother. Since methadone crosses the placental barrier, an infant will be born physically dependent on opioids. Such infants should be monitored and treated for any signs or symptoms of neonatal opioid withdrawal.

F. Treatment of Neonatal Abstinence Syndrome Due to Opioids. The following is a summary of the recommendations by Finnegan and Kandall (1992), who have comprehensively reviewed this phenomenon.

Because not all infants develop neonatal abstinence syndrome following intrauterine exposure to opioids, treatment is not initiated until signs of opioid withdrawal develop. The neonate should be monitored in a hospital for at least 4 days and up to 7–10 days if there is indication that the home situation will not be conducive to appropriate care of the child by the mother (e.g., unstable social situation at home or polydrug abuse). Before the neonate is discharged from the hospital, the mother should be instructed regarding signs of opioid abstinence syndrome and advised to bring the child to the hospital should signs of withdrawal develop. A return-to-clinic visit should be scheduled a few days following discharge.

Any neonate who develops an opioid abstinence syndrome should be admitted to the hospital. There may be stepwise progression of the syndrome. Because an infant may suffer fever, diarrhea, vomiting, and subsequent dehydration, careful monitoring of fluid and electrolyte balance as well as caloric intake is essential.

Paregoric is preferred to phenobarbital if the abstinence syndrome is due exclusively to opioid withdrawal because paregoric is more effective in controlling seizures in this patient population. *Paregoric* 0.2 mL Q3h is given as a starting dose. Dose of paregoric is increased by 0.05 mL to a maximum of 0.35 mL Q3h. A patient's progress is monitored by recording opioid abstinence scores. Once a stabilizing dose of paregoric has been achieved, it is continued for another 5 days. After that, the dose of paregoric is decreased by 0.05 mL every other day. During the decrease, paregoric is still administered every 3 h.

If there is polydrug abuse, phenobarbital is the preferred drug to treat the withdrawal syndrome. Schuckit (1989) recommends 8 mg/kg in divided doses 3 or 4 times a day. Treatment is continued for 10–20 days, with gradual reduction in dose of phenobarbital toward the end of the period.

G. Long-Term Treatment of Opioid Dependence with Long-Acting Opioids

1. Methadone maintenance. Although methadone maintenance still remains controversial to some because patients are actively administered an opioid, the HIV epidemic has resulted in a resurgence of interest in methadone. Only 10% of intravenous drug users (IVDUs) in continuous treatment with methadone prior to 1978 are HIV-positive, whereas 47% of those not in methadone treatment are HIV-positive (Gordis, 1988). Moreover, patients successfully maintained on methadone have decreased arrests, increased employment, and increased stability in their relationships.

Methadone maintenance is strictly regulated by the FDA and the DEA, which specifically license clinics offering treatment with methadone. Patients must have at least one year of continual opioid usage and must show at least two signs of physical opioid withdrawal to qualify for methadone maintenance. Initial medical screening for entrance into a program must include a history and physical examination and lab work [complete blood count, serum chemistry including electrolytes, BUN (blood urea nitrogen), creatinine, and liver function tests, serologic test for syphilis (RPR, VDRL), urinalysis, chest x-ray, and electrocardiogram where appropriate, as well as PPD screening for tuberculosis (or chest x-ray with a history of previous positive PPD). HIV testing is also strongly encouraged but not required. Initial dose of methadone on the first day of treatment may be as high as 30 mg and may be supplemented with another dose of 10 mg if the 30-mg dose of methadone does not adequately suppress symptoms. Methadone dose can go no higher than 40 mg on the first day. Generally the daily methadone dose is increased on subsequent days until adequate suppression of opioid abstinence symptoms results. Studies indicate that blood levels of 150–600 ng/mL of methadone result in significant decrease in use of other opioids (Dole, 1988). Reaching this blood level usually requires a dose of 60–100 mg/day (Weddington, 1995). At these blood levels, euphoria from heroin use is blocked. However, regulations and policies vary from state to state and may not take into account these research findings.

Methadone is not hepatotoxic. Side effects include excess sweating, decreased libido and sexual performance, chronic constipation, sleep abnormalities, and drowsiness. The latter may be dose-related and are treated by lowering the dose of methadone gradually, provided urine toxicology remains negative. Side effects of methadone generally disappear within the first 6 months of treatment.

In a patient population at high risk for tuberculosis, clinicians should be aware that isoniazid and rifampin increase metabolism of methadone and usually necessitate an increase in methadone dosage to maintain an effective blood level.

2. LAAM maintenance. LAAM (L-α-acetyl methadol) has recently been approved for long-term opioid maintenance. LAAM maintenance is similar to methadone maintenance. However, because of its longer half-life, LAAM is not dispensed more frequently than once every other day. A patient is thus required to attend a treatment clinic only 3 times a week—for example, Monday, Wednesday, and Friday, with the Friday dose increased by 20–40%. LAAM maintenance is particularly useful for patients who are working or who have other difficulties with daily attendance (e.g., the chronically ill or disabled). No take-home doses of LAAM are allowed, which addresses the problem of diversion with methadone when patients have take-home privileges. The main disadvantage of LAAM is that, because of its long half-life (2–

3 days), it takes 1–2 weeks for a patient to experience the full effect of the drug. Any patient who is unable to tolerate this and supplements LAAM with heroin or with another CNS depressant (e.g., benzodiazepines or alcohol) may suffer a fatal overdose. Thus, it may be preferable to stabilize a patient on methadone initially. Following stabilization, a patient is then placed on LAAM maintenance at 1.2–1.3 times the dose of methadone.

VI. MEDICAL COMPLICATIONS

Major and minor medical problems are consequent to opioid usage, apart from the clinical states discussed above. Although opioids themselves are nontoxic to tissue, injected pathogens and adulterants create multiple medical problems. Infectious complications of opioid usage include HIV infection, subsequent AIDS, hepatitis B infection, cellulitis, endocarditis, osteomyelitis, infection of the fascia of the hands, pyomyositis, tetanus, upper respiratory infections secondary to decreased cough reflex, skin abscesses, meningitis, brain abscesses, septicemia, pyelonephritis, cerebritis, and tuberculosis. Other complications include sclerosed veins, contractures of the hands, thrombophlebitis, microcrystalline inclusions in the lungs from talcum powder and starch used as diluents, edema of the extremities, false-positive test for syphilis, nephrotic syndrome, renal infarction, and accidents. These complications often cause a patient to present for medical treatment. Although some patients are beyond engaging in treatment at the time, a clinician should not be discouraged by this but should continue to encourage the patient to stop drug use and to enter treatment.

VII. MEDICAL USE OF OPIOIDS

Clinicians should not be reluctant to prescribe opioids in appropriate doses when required by a patient's condition. The general population does not become addicted to opioids when they are used for severe pain (e.g., dental procedures, severe trauma, cancer). However, care must be used when prescribing these medications to persons with a history of addictive disorders. If a patient with a known addiction to substances—whether alcohol, prescription drugs, or street drugs—requires narcotic medication for the control of pain, it should be for a period of time consistent with the patient's medical condition. However, a patient currently dependent on opioids will require higher doses of opioids for pain because of acquired tolerance.

If a patient on methadone or LAAM maintenance is hospitalized, his/her current dose of methadone or LAAM should be verified by the treating methadone clinic. Dose of LAAM can be converted to a daily dose of methadone and should be administered on the second day following the last dose of LAAM and every day thereafter. The patient should be maintained on that dosage of methadone throughout the hospital stay, unless medically contraindicated. The dose of methadone should not be increased to treat pain during the time a patient is hospitalized. Nonnarcotic analgesics or other opioids can be used instead. Detoxification from methadone should occur only at a patient's insistence and after consultation with staff in the patient's methadone clinic.

REFERENCES

Becker CE, Olson KR: Management of the poisoned patient. In BG Katzung (ed): *Basic and Clinical Pharmacology,* 6th ed. Norwalk, CT: Appleton & Lange, 1995, pp 899–911.

Burant D: Management of withdrawal. In BB Wilford (ed): *Syllabus for the Review Course in Addiction Medicine.* Washington, DC: American Society of Addiction Medicine, 1990, pp 173–194.

Department of Health and Human Services Food and Drug Administration: Methadone: rules, proposed rules, and notice. *Fed Reg* 54:8953–8979, 1989.

Dole VP: Implications of methadone maintenance for theories of narcotic addiction. *JAMA* 260(20): 3025–3029, 1988.

Eisenman AJ, Sloan JW, Martin WR, Jasinski DR, Brooks JW: Catecholamine and 17-hydroxycorticosteroid excretion during a cycle of morphine dependence in man. *J Psychiatric Res* 7:19–28, 1969.

Finnegan LP, Kandall SR: Maternal and neonatal effects of alcohol and drugs. In JH Lowinson, P Ruiz, RB Millman, JG Langrod (eds): *Substance Abuse: A Comprehensive Textbook,* 2nd ed. Baltimore: Williams & Wilkins, 1992, pp 628–656.

First MB (ed): *Diagnostic and Statistical Manual of Mental Disorders,* 4th ed. Washington, DC: American Psychiatric Association, 1994, pp 247–255.

Gold MS: Pharmacological therapies of opiate addiction. In NS Miller, MS Gold (eds): *Pharmacological Therapies for Drug and Alcohol Addictions.* New York: Marcel Dekker, 1995, pp 159–174.

Gordis E: A commentary by NIAAA director Enoch Gordis, M.D. *Alcohol Alert* 1:2–4, 1988.

Greenstein RA, Fudala PJ, O'Brien CP: Alternative pharmacotherapies for opiate addiction. In JH Lowinson, P Ruiz, RB Millman, and JG Langrod (eds): *Substance Abuse: A Comprehensive Textbook,* 2nd ed. Baltimore: Williams & Wilkins, 1992, pp 562–573.

Himmelsbach CK: Clinical studies of drug addiction: physical dependence, withdrawal, and recovery. *Arch of Intern Med* 69:766–772, 1942.

Hutchings DE: Opiates during pregnancy; neurobehavioral effects in the offspring. In GG Nahas, C Latour, N Hardy, P Dingeon (eds): *Physiopathology of Illicit Drugs: Cannabis, Cocaine, Opiates.* Oxford: Pergamon Press, 1991, pp 285–294.

Jaffe JH: Drug addiction and drug abuse. In AG Gilman, LS Goodman, TW Rall, F Marad (eds): *The Pharmacological Basis of Therapeutics,* 8th ed. New York: Pergamon Press, 1990, pp 522–573.

Jaffe JH: Opiates: clinical aspects. In JH Lowinson, P Ruiz, RB Millman, JG Langrod (eds): *Substance Abuse: A Comprehensive Textbook,* 2nd ed. Baltimore: Williams & Wilkins, 1992, pp 186–194.

Jaffe JH, Kleber HD: Opioids: general issues and detoxification. In American Psychatric Association: *Treatments of Psychiatric Disorders: A Task Force Report of the American Psychiatric Association.* Washington, DC: American Psychiatric Association, 1989, pp 1309–1331.

Kleber HD: Opioids: detoxification. In M Galanter, HD Kleber (eds): *The American Psychiatric Press Textbook of Substance Abuse Treatment.* Washington, DC: American Psychiatric Press, 1994, pp 191–208.

Kleber HD, Riordan CE, Rounsaville B, Kosten T, Charney D, Gaspara J, Hogan I, O'Connor C: Clonidine in outpatient detoxification from methadone maintenance. *Arch Gen Psychiatry* 42:391–394, 1985.

Kreek MJ: Pharmacological treatment of opioid dependency. In G Buhringer, JJ Platt (eds): *Drug Addiction Treatment Research.* Malabar, FL: Krieger Publishing, 1992, pp 389–406.

Ling W, Wesson DR: Drugs of abuse—opiates. *West J Med* 152:565–572, 1990.

Lowinson JH, Marion IJ, Herman J, Dole VP: Methadone maintenance. In JH Lowinson, P Ruiz, RB Millman, JG Langrod (eds): *Substance Abuse: A Comprehensive Textbook,* 2nd ed. Baltimore: Williams & Wilkins, 1992, pp 550–561.

Martin WR, Jasinski DR: Physiological parameters of morphine dependence in man: tolerance, early abstinence, and protracted abstinence. *J Psychiatric Res* 7:9–16, 1969.

O'Connor PG, Kosten TR: Management of opioid intoxication and withdrawal. In NS Miller, MC Doot (eds): *ASAM: Principles of Addiction Medicine.* Chevy Chase, MD: American Society of Addiction Medicine, 1994, section 11, chapter 5, pp 1–6.

Renner JA: Pharmacotherapy of alcoholism and substance abuse. In *Syllabus for Psychopharmacology.* Boston: Harvard Medical School, Department of Continuing Medical Education, 1994, pp 526–539.

Schuckit MA: *Opiates and Other Analgesics, Drugs and Alcohol Abuse,* 3rd ed. New York: Plenum Publishing, 1989, pp 118–142.

Senay EC: Opioids: methadone maintenance. In M Galanter, HD Kleber (eds): *The American Psychiatric Press Textbook of Substance Abuse Treatment.* Washington, DC: American Psychiatric Press, 1994, pp 209–221.

Spencer L, Gregory M: Clonidine transdermal patches for use in outpatient opiate withdrawal. *J Substance Abuse Treatment* 6:113–117, 1989.

Weddington W: Methadone maintenance. In NS Miller, MS Gold (eds): *Pharmacological Therapies for Drug and Alcohol Addictions.* New York: Marcel Dekker, 1995, pp 411–417.

CHAPTER 9

TREATMENT OF ADDICTIVE DISORDERS

Robert M. Swift, M.D., Ph.D.
Brown University
Providence, Rhode Island

I. INTRODUCTION

The task of the patient in recovery is to develop skills to avoid psychoactive substances, to develop better methods of coping with stress and distress, and to improve self-esteem and self-efficacy. Pharmacologic treatment can be used to assist recovery as a component of a comprehensive treatment program that includes psychosocial therapies, such as counseling and self-help groups. Pharmacotherapies may reduce drug craving, decrease protracted withdrawal symptoms, and decrease the "high" of illicit drugs. They have been demonstrated to reduce relapse and improve long-term abstinence. Pharmacotherapies can also treat comorbid psychiatric disorders that provide part of the impetus for drinking. Types of pharmacologic therapies used in long-term treatment and rehabilitation are depicted in Table 9-1.

II. ALCOHOL DEPENDENCE

A. General Considerations. Pharmacologic agents are important adjuncts in the treatment of alcohol withdrawal, reducing withdrawal signs and symptoms and medical morbidity. Several pharmacologic agents have shown efficacy as adjuncts in the treatment of alcohol dependence, decreasing drinking and reducing relapse in patients in rehabilitation treatment. Pharmacologic agents should always be used as adjuncts in treatment, as part of a comprehensive treatment program that addresses the psychological, social and spiritual needs of the patient.

B. Maintenance Therapy with Benzodiazepines. While benzodiazepines (chlordiazepoxide, diazepam, etc.) have been shown to be efficacious in the treatment of alcohol withdrawal, the use of maintenance benzodiazepines to reduce drinking and to prevent relapse remains controversial. In the past, some alcoholics were maintained on daily doses of benzodiazepines, barbiturates, or other sedatives in a poorly monitored and uncontrolled fashion. This uncontrolled use sometimes led to the development of benzodiazepine dependence or combined alcohol and benzodiazepine dependence. At the present time, the use of benzodiazepines or other sedatives for maintenance treatment is strongly discouraged by most addiction professionals.

Manual of Therapeutics for Addictions, Edited by Norman S. Miller, Mark S. Gold, and David E. Smith.
ISBN 0471-56176-2 © 1997 John Wiley & Sons, Inc.

TABLE 9.1. Pharmacotherapies Used for Prophylaxis

Maintenance treatment with a cross-tolerant agent (e.g., methadone maintenance treatment for opioid dependence, nicotine gum for nicotine dependence

Administration of an agent to block the drug "high" (e.g., naltrexone for opioid dependence and alcohol dependence)

Aversive therapy (e.g., disulfiram treatment in alcoholism)

Administration of an agent to suppress craving (e.g., naltrexone in alcohol dependence)

Pharmacotherapy of comorbid psychiatric disorders (e.g., antidepressants in comorbid depression and alcoholism

C. Aversive Therapy: Disulfiram. Disulfiram (Antabuse) is an irreversible inhibitor of the enzyme acetaldehyde dehydrogenase, and is used as an adjunctive treatment in selected alcoholics.

1. Disulfiram–alcohol reaction. If alcohol is consumed in the presence of disulfiram, the toxic metabolite acetaldehyde accumulates in the body, producing tachycardia, skin flushing, diaphoresis, dyspnea, and nausea and vomiting. Hypotension and death may occur if large amounts of alcohol are consumed. This unpleasant reaction provides a strong deterrent to the consumption of alcohol. The medication is most effective for those who believe in its efficacy and who are compliant with treatment.

2. Use of disulfiram. The typical dose of disulfiram is 250 mg once daily. Daily doses of 125–500 mg are sometimes used, depending on side effects and patient response. The optimal duration of treatment is unknown—most patients use the medication for brief periods of high risk of relapse; however, some patients use the medication continuously for years. Some clinicians administer a small dose of alcohol to patients receiving disulfiram in order to experience a disulfiram–alcohol reaction. This is thought to provide a stronger deterrent to future alcohol drinking.

3. Precautions. Alcohol present in foods, shaving lotion, mouthwashes, or OTC medications may produce a disulfiram reaction. Thus, patients started on disulfiram must be advised to avoid all forms of alcohol. Disulfiram may have interactions with other medications, notably anticoagulants and phenytoin. It is contraindicated in patients with liver disease. A complete blood count and liver function tests should be monitored prior to starting disulfiram therapy and periodically during treatment.

D. Naltrexone to Reduce Alcohol Craving

1. General considerations. The opioid neurotransmitter system has been strongly implicated in mediating alcohol consumption. In clinical trials with recently abstinent human alcoholics, naltrexone-treated subjects had lower rates of relapse to heavy drinking, consumed fewer drinks per drinking day, and had lower dropout than did the placebo group. Subjects receiving naltrexone also report decreased "craving" and decreased "high" from alcohol.

2. Use of naltrexone in alcohol dependence. The usual dose of naltrexone is 50 mg/day, with a range of 25–150 mg/day. The most common side effects include anxiety, sedation, and nausea in approximately 10% of patients. There also exists a potential issue of hepatic toxicity with the drug. Although high doses of naltrexone (300 mg/day) have been associated with hepatotoxicity, few deleterious hepatic effects have been observed with a 50-mg daily dose of naltrexone. However, naltrexone should probably be avoided in patients with hepatitis or severe liver disease. It is recommended that liver functions be monitored prior to naltrexone treatment, at 1 month and periodically thereafter. Naltrexone should only be used in the context of a comprehensive alcoholism treatment program, which includes counseling and other psychosocial therapies.

3. Serotonergic medications. Manipulations that increase central serotonergic function appear to reduce ethanol consumption in animals and humans.

a. Buspirone (Buspar) is a nonbenzodiazepine anxiolytic medication that has partial agonist activity at the 5HT-1a receptor and 5HT-2 receptor, as well as having dopamine receptor antagonist activity. Buspirone reduces alcohol consumption in some alcoholic patients, particularly those with anxiety disorders. Alcoholic subjects receiving buspirone reduced their drinking, experienced less craving, and improved their social and psychological status. The effective doses for alcoholism is 10–20 mg TID.

b. Selective serotonin reuptake inhibitors (SSRIs). Examples are fluoxetine (Prozac), sertraline (Zoloft), and fluvoxamine which augment serotonergic function, and also appear to modestly reduce alcohol consumption. Several human studies on heavy drinkers found SSRIs to reduce overall alcohol consumption by approximately 15–20%. The effective daily doses are somewhat higher than those used typically in depression (e.g., 60 mg fluoxetine, 200 mg sertraline).

4. Acamprosate (calcium acetylhomotaurine). This is a structural analog of γ-aminobutyric acid (GABA), and has agonist effects at GABA receptors and inhibitory effects at N-methyl-D-aspartate (NMDA) receptors. In clinical trials with alcoholics, acamprosate reduced relapse drinking and craving for alcohol and had minimal side effects. The medication has been approved in several European countries for the prevention of alcoholic relapse, and is currently under clinical testing in the United States.

III. OPIOIDS

A. General Considerations. The most widely used pharmacologic treatments for opioid-dependent individuals include pharmacologic maintenance treatments with the opiate agonists methadone and l-α-acetylmethodol (LAAM), maintenance with the partial opiate agonist buprenorphine, and opiate antagonist therapy with naltrexone. All of these medications are best used in the setting of a structured, maintenance treatment program, which includes monitored medication administration, periodic, random urine toxicologic screening to assess compliance, and intensive psychological, medical, and vocational services.

B. Agonist Substitution Treatments. These maintain opioid dependence in a safe and controlled manner. Substitution treatments reduce use of illicit opiates by increasing drug tolerance, thereby decreasing the subjective effects of illicitly administered opiates, and by stabilizing mood, thereby decreasing self-medication. Substitution treatments also provide an incentive for treatment so that patients may be exposed to other therapies.

1. Methadone maintenance. Methadone is a synthetic opiate, which is orally active, possesses a long duration of action, produces minimal sedation or "high," and has few side effects at therapeutic doses.

a. Efficacy. Many studies have shown the efficacy of methadone maintenance in the treatment of addicts who are dependent on heroin and other opiates. Methadone treated patients show increased retention in treatment, improved physical health, decreased criminal activity, and increased employment. Methadone is most effective in the context of a program that provides intensive psychosocial and medical services, and flexibility in methadone dosing. The use of methadone for maintenance is highly regulated by government agencies.

b. Dosing. Methadone is dissolved in a flavored liquid, and is administered to patients daily, under observation. Long-standing program participants are allowed "take-home" doses of methadone, which they may self-administer. Doses of methadone usually range from 20 mg/day to over 100 mg/day. Higher doses are shown to be generally associated with better retention in treatment. Urine toxicologic screening is performed randomly and periodically to assess compliance with treatment. Counseling and other rehabilitative services are provided on a regular basis.

2. ʟ-α-acetylmethadol acetate (LAAM). This is a long-acting, orally active opiate with pharmacologic properties that are similar to methadone. Studies on LAAM have shown it to be equal or superior to methadone maintenance in reducing IV drug use, when used in the context of a structured maintenance treatment program. The advantages of LAAM include a slower onset of effects and a longer duration of action than methadone. This allows LAAM to be administered only 3 times per week, and potentially reduces the use of take-home medications that may be diverted to illegal uses. Patients treated with LAAM should be started on 20 mg administered 3 times weekly, with the dose increased weekly in 10-mg increments as necessary. Doses of ≤ 80 mg 3 times weekly are safe and effective.

3. Buprenorphine. This is a partial agonist opiate medication (mixed agonist–antagonist), originally used medically as an analgesic. The drug has both agonist and antagonist properties; agonist properties predominate at lower doses, and antagonist properties predominate at higher doses.

a. Efficacy. In the setting of a structured treatment program, daily dosing of buprenorphine is effective in the maintenance treatment of narcotics addicts. Buprenorphine may also reduce cocaine use (see below).

b. Dosing. Medication doses usually range from 4 mg/day to ≤ 16 mg/day, administered sublingually, since the medication is not effective orally. Advantages of buprenorphine include a milder withdrawal syndrome on discontinuation and less potential for abuse, as agonist effects diminish at higher doses. Opioid dependent patients may be started on 2–4 mg buprenorphine immediately after opiates are discontinued, and the dose of buprenorphine titrated to 8–16 mg over several days.

C. Antagonist Therapy. Antagonist therapy reduces the use of illicit drugs by blocking the effect of the drugs at neurotransmitter receptors, leading to decreased use. There is some evidence that opiate antagonists may block craving for drugs other than opiates, as well.

1. Naltrexone. This is an orally active opioid antagonist, approved for the treatment of opiate dependence and narcotic addiction. Naltrexone blocks the intoxicating effects of opioids and has few effects in individuals not dependent on opioids. The usual dose of naltrexone is 50 mg/day, administered orally, although 3 times weekly dosing with 100, 100, and 150 mg has also been shown to be effective. High doses of naltrexone have been associated with hepatotoxicity; however, few deleterious hepatic effects are observed using a 50-mg/day dose of naltrexone. Other possible side effects include anxiety, sedation, and nausea in some patients. Naltrexone therapy has been shown to be most effective in highly motivated individuals with good social supports.

2. Naloxone challenge. Patients receiving naltrexone must be opiate-free for a period of approximately 2 weeks, or may experience severe opiate withdrawal symptoms. Opiate abstinence can be assessed with urine toxicology screens and by naloxone (Narcan) challenge test. Naloxone 0.2 mg is injected subcutaneously, and the patient is observed for 20 minutes. If no withdrawal is observed, 0.6 mg is injected. If no withdrawal is observed, the patient is suitable for naltrexone.

IV. COCAINE DEPENDENCE

A. General Considerations. Several pharmacologic agents have been tested as adjuncts in the treatment of cocaine dependence, with the goal of reducing craving and relapse. While some agents—including the antidepressant desipramine, the dopamine agonist bromocriptine, the stimulant methylphenidate, and the partial opioid antagonist buprenorphine—have shown initial promise, follow-up studies with these agents have not demonstrated widespread success.

1. Desipramine. This has been shown to be efficacious for some cocaine users, in reducing craving and helping them to remain abstinent, even when depression is not present. The doses used have been similar to those used in the treatment of depression (50–150 mg/day, usually at night). The major side effects include sedation and dry mouth.

2. Bromocriptine. This is a dopamine agonist used in the treatment of Parkinson's disease and prolactin-secreting pituitary tumors. Low doses of bromocriptine (0.125 mg Q6h) have been reported to be helpful in reducing craving and discomfort in the early stages of cocaine abstinence, but not all studies have shown effectiveness. Amantadine, mazindol, and other dopamine agonists have not been found to be particularly effective.

3. Methylphenidate. This is a psychomotor stimulant with noradrenergic and dopaminergic effects. Some researchers have reported that methylphenidate may reduce cocaine relapse, particularly in those who also have attention deficit hyperactivity disorder. The doses used are 5–20 mg administered TID. Since methyphenidate is a controlled substance, careful selection of patients is necessary.

4. Buprenorphine. This is a partial opiate agonist that has been used for analgesia and maintenance treatment in opiate addicts (see above). Patients with combined opiate and cocaine dependence, receiving buprenorphine maintenance treatment, show significant reductions in their use of cocaine, compared to patients receiving methadone maintenance.

V. NICOTINE DEPENDENCE

A. General Considerations. Tobacco dependence is a major public health problem because of its association with cancers and cardiovascular disease. Patients who are unable to quit smoking on their own and to remain abstinent may be helped by pharmacotherapies including nicotine replacement therapy and antidepressants.

B. Nicotine Replacement. The principle of nicotine replacement therapy is to provide the nicotine-dependent patient with nicotine in a form not associated with the carcinogenic and irritant elements in tobacco products. Two methods of nicotine administration have been approved: nicotine gum and the transdermal nicotine patch. A third method, intranasal nicotine, is under consideration by government agencies. While nicotine replacement has been used primarily for detoxification and relief of withdrawal symptoms during smoking cessation, some patients use nicotine replacement in a maintenance fashion.

1. Nicotine Gum. Nicotine gum consists of 2 mg nicotine complexed to a polacrilex resin matrix, also containing sweeteners and flavors. The gum is placed in the mouth and chewed *slowly* to release the nicotine from the matrix. When tingling of the mouth or tongue is perceived, chewing should cease for a short period of time, while still holding the gum in the mouth. Too rapid chewing releases excess nicotine and may cause nausea and other side effects. The gum is chewed for 20–30 minutes and then may be discarded. This method produces nicotine blood levels that rise and fall, partially mimicking smoking. The gum is available by prescription in units of 96 pieces.

2. Nicotine transdermal patches. The nicotine patch consists of various doses of nicotine (7, 14, and 21 mg) impregnated into an adhesive patch for transdermal administration. This method produces nicotine blood levels that are relatively constant throughout the period of application. One patch is applied to uncovered skin each 24-h period, and the previous patch is discarded. Some individuals wear the patches during the daytime only, and remove them while asleep. Side effects include irritation from the patch and nicotine effects (nausea, cardiac effects, etc.). It is important that patients not use tobacco products while using the patch, as toxic nicotine blood levels may occur. The patches are available by prescription.

3. Antidepressants. Several clinical studies have shown a high incidence of major depression occurring within days to weeks following smoking cessation and nicotine withdrawal. Patients with a personal or family history of affective illness appear to be at most risk for depression. Antidepressants have been shown to reduce the prevalence of depression and to improve the chances of remaining abstinent from nicotine. Antidepressants reported as effective include desipramine, doxepin, and buproprion (Wellbutrin). The dose of antidepressant is similar to that used for depression.

VI. PHARMACOLOGIC TREATMENT OF COMORBID PSYCHIATRIC DISORDERS

A. General Considerations. Affective disorders, anxiety disorders, and psychotic disorders are frequently observed in patients with addictive disorders. The treatment of the patient with comorbid psychiatric and substance-abuse diagnoses (dual diagnosis) presents a particular challenge to the clinician. The presence of a comorbid psychiatric disorder may result in resistance to addiction treatment because of the need to use drugs and alcohol for self-medication. Appropriate pharmacologic treatment of the psychiatric disorder reduces the need for self-medication and improves the ability to respond to psychosocial treatment. Detailed treatment recommendations are presented in Chapter 13.

SELECTED READINGS

Brewer C: Recent developments in disulfiram treatment. *Alcohol Alcohol* 28(4):383–395, 1993.

Bruno F: Buspirone in the treatment of alcoholic patients. *Psychopatholoy* 22(suppl 1):49–59, 1989.

Fuller RK, Branchley L, Brightwell DR, Derman RM, Emrick CD, Iber FL, James KE, et al: Disulfiram treatment of alcoholism. A Veterans Administration cooperative study. *JAMA* 256(11): 1449–1455, 1986.

Gawin FH, Ellinwod EH Jr: Cocaine and other stimulants. Actions, abuse and treatment. *N Engl J Med* 318(18):1173–1182, 1988.

Gorelick DA: Serotonin uptake blockers and the treatment of alcoholism. *Recent Devel Alcohol* 6:267–279, 1989.

Kleber HD, Morgan C: Treatment of cocaine abuse with buprenorphine. *Biol Psychiatry* 26:637–639, 1989.

Ladewig D, Knecht T, Leher P, Fendl A: Acomprosate—a stabilizing factor in long-term withdrawal of alcoholic patients. *Ther Umsch* 50(3):182–188, 1993.

Liskow BL, Goodwin DW: Pharmacological treatment of alcohol intoxication, withdrawal and dependence: a critical review. *J Stud Alcohol* 48:356–370, 1987.

Litten RZ, Allen JP: Pharmacotherapies for alcoholism: praising agents and clinical issues. *Alcohol Clin Exp Research* 15(4):620–633, 1991.

O'Malley SS, Jaffee AJ, Chang G, Schottenfeld RS, Meyer RE, Raunsaville B: Naltrexone and coping skills therapy for alcohol dependence. *Arch Gen Psychiatry* 49:881–887, 1992.

Resnick RB, Schuyten-Resnick E, Washton AM: Assessment of narcotic antagonists in the treatment of opioid dependence. *Annu Rev Pharmacol Toxicol* 20:463–474, 1980.

Senay EC: Methadone maintenance treatment. *Internatl J Addictions* 20:803–821, 1985.

Volpicelli JR, Alterman Al, Hayashida M, O'Brien CP: Naltrexone in the treatment of alcohol dependence. *Arch Gen Psychiatry* 49:876–880, 1992.

PART

TREATMENT IN SPECIFIC POPULATIONS

CHAPTER 10

TREATMENT OF ACUTE EMERGENCIES

Sajiv John, M.D.
University of Chicago
Chicago, Illinois

The psychiatrist is frequently called to the emergency room to evaluate a patient who has developed complications of drug or alcohol use, especially intoxication or withdrawal states. Medical complications, accidents, injuries, suicidal behaviors, and violence often accompany these states. Drugs of addiction may worsen preexisting medical conditions or interact adversely with prescribed medication. Drug addiction can present in a variety of ways and affect cognition, mood, perception, or behavior. It is therefore incumbent on the psychiatrist, internist, family practitioner, or other physician to be aware of the signs and symptoms of common withdrawal or overdose emergencies and their management. This chapter deals with the presentation and management of emergencies related to drug and alcohol use, some of the complications of abuse, and harmful interactions between drugs of addiction and medication.

I. GENERAL PRINCIPLES

A. Drug toxic patients seldom can organize their thinking clearly, and rarely can give a clear history. Therefore obtain as many details as possible from friends, paramedics, or the police.

(1) The initial history in every case of an alcohol or drug emergency must include the following:

(a) The pattern of use: whether continuous or intermittent.

(b) Symptoms of withdrawal such as delirium tremens (DTs) and seizures both currently and in the past.

(c) Psychosocial issues that may have contributed to or resulted from use, such as family and job problems, driving under the influence, and arrests.

(d) Significant medical illness arising as a consequence of or independent of use.

(e) Concurrent psychiatric illness, especially depression and anxiety disorders.

(2) A thorough physical examination should follow in every case. The examination should also look for frequent complications such as injuries, pneumonia, or liver failure in the alcoholic; nystagmus and

Manual of Therapeutics for Addictions, Edited by Norman S. Miller, Mark S. Gold, and David E. Smith.
ISBN 0471-56176-2 © 1997 John Wiley & Sons, Inc.

hypertension in the PCP user; and ataxia, nystagmus, and ophthalmoplegia in Wernicke's encephalopathy.

(3) Laboratory tests should include a CBC, serum chemistry, blood alcohol level, and a urine toxicology screen in every case. Other tests including prothrombin time, chest x-rays, and CT scans, may follow depending on the clinical picture.

B. Attention to the ABC's is crucial. Maintenance of an intact airway is first priority. Alert and awake patients usually are able to maintain their airway; while drowsy, comatose, or actively-seizing patients may need the chin-lift/jaw-thrust maneuver, oral or nasopharyngeal airways, or endotracheal intubation.

C. Assessment of breathing using clinical features, pulse oximetry, or arterial blood gas estimation should follow. This may lead to continued observation, administration of nasal oxygen, manual bag–valve–mask ventilation, or endotracheal intubation depending on the clinical picture.

D. Circulatory failure necessitates intravenous access, fluid administration, and vasopressors if needed.

E. Removal of the drug from the gut may be attempted using activated charcoal, ipecac, lavage, or whole-bowel irrigation. The exact method

TABLE 10.1. Common Drugs of Addiction

Drug	Other Names	Duration of Action (h)
Opiates		
Morphine	MS Contin, Roxanol	3–6
Heroin	Diacetylmorphine, horse, smack	3–6
Meperidine	Demerol, mepergan Pethidine	3–6
Methadone	Dolophine, Methadose	12–24
Stimulants		
Cocaine	Coke, crack, snow	1–2
Amphetamine	Speed, dexedrine	2–4
Methylphenidate	Ritalin	2–4
Sedative Hypnotics		
Barbiturates	Phenobarbital, amytal, seconal	1–16
Benzodiazepines	Diazepam, Ativan, Halcion	4–8
Chloral hydrate	Noctec	5–8
Methaqualone	Quaalude	4–8
Glutethimide	Doriden	4–8
Hallucinogens		
LSD	Acid, microdot	8–12
Phencyclidine	PCP, angel dust, hog	Days
Cannabis		
Marijuana	Pot, grass, Acapulco gold	2–4
Hashish	Hash	2

varies depending on the clinical condition and preference. Generally, in symptomatic patients where ingestion has occurred within 2 h of presentation, lavage or ipecac should be used followed by charcoal. If asymptomatic, or if ingestion has occurred more than 2 h from presentation, charcoal alone may be used. If an agent known to slow GI motility has been ingested, lavage or ipecac may be tried even 2 h after ingestion. Both lavage and ipecac should be used with caution in the drowsy or agitated patient because of the risk of aspiration.

F. Restraint, both physical and chemical, may need to be used in the agitated patient who is a danger to self or others. Two commonly used drugs are lorazepam (Ativan) 1–2 mg IM/IV and haloperidol 2–10 mg IM/IV; both can be repeated every 15–30 min until adequate control is obtained. Lorazepam is commonly the first drug used as it acts quickly, is not metabolized in the liver, does not significantly affect respiration, and has antiseizure action. It is preferable to give drugs vigorously until the desired effect appears and then to titrate the dose based on the clinical picture. This is better than an agitated, inadequately treated patient out of control in the emergency room (ER).

G. Always try to build a relationship with the patient, however difficult that may be; orient the patient; introduce familiarity in the form of a family member or friend; and assess the potential for suicide and violence. Every effort must be made to work with the patient and family. However, patients can be held against their wishes if there is clear evidence that judgment is impaired or that a potentially life-threatening illness or injury is present. Careful documentation of the risk involved and test results that contributed to the decision is crucial.

H. Finally, many patients have been using multiple drugs when they present to the emergency room. The clinical picture may be modified as a result. Table 10.1 lists common drugs of abuse, including their other names and duration of action.

II. ALCOHOL

A. Clinical Features

1. Intoxication. The degree of intoxication typically varies according to the blood level of alcohol and the patient's previous experience with it. Some important blood levels include: (1) 100 mg/dL—the legal limit for intoxication in most states, (2) 300–400 mg/dL—usually stuporous, (3) 400–500 mg/dL—usually unconscious, and (4) $\geq$ 500 mg/dL—associated with death.

2. Withdrawal. This may range from mild symptoms with craving, sleep disturbance, and signs of autonomic arousal that settle in a few days to a full-blown delirium tremens with a fluctuating level of consciousness, marked autonomic signs, several metabolic abnormalities, auditory and visual hallucinations, and a mortality rate of $\leq$ 10% in spite of treatment. Seizures that may be solitary (33%) or a flurry (65%) usually occur in the first 24–48 h and are grand mal in type.

B. Complications. Injuries include head, spine, bone, or soft-tissue injuries that occur during fights while intoxicated, and accidents, which typically are motor-vehicle crashes and falls. Subdural hematomas and the Wernicke–Korsakoff syndrome must always be looked for. Respiratory compromise following aspiration of secretions or vomitus is well known, as are pneumonia, hypoglycemia, hypoxia, hypothermia, and hypomagnesemia. Hepatic dysfunction, including encephalopathy, can occur. Gastrointestinal complications include GI bleeds, ulcers, diarrhea, pancreatitis, cirrhosis, and portal hypertension with esophageal varices.

C. Interactions. See Table 10.2.

D. Management. Outpatient treatment is appropriate for patients with mild withdrawal symptoms, who demonstrate good judgment, have some family support, are not suicidal, and do not have a serious medical complication. These patients are typically treated with a parenteral dose of thiamine 100 mg, a multivitamin, folic acid 1 mg, and a benzodiazepine—usually chlordiazepoxide (librium) or diazepam, generally not more than 5–20 mg/day in divided doses. After a period of observation they are discharged from the ER with at least a few days' supply of medicines, instructed to return if symptoms worsen, and scheduled for a follow-up appointment. The mild to moderately intoxicated patient is essentially managed similarly and allowed to become sober before being discharged. It is safer to wait for the blood alcohol level to fall below 100 mg/dL and for the patient to be able to answer questions and walk without assistance before being discharged. Generally nonalcoholics eliminate alcohol at the rate of approximately 15 mg/dL/h, while alcoholics do so at a rate of 30–50 mg/dL/h.

Inpatient treatment is indicated for more seriously ill patients and includes the following:

1. Vitamins—thiamine 100 mg is given parenterally in the ER and repeated for the next 4–5 days.

2. Benzodiazepines are now agents of choice for sedation. Chlordiazepoxide 10–20 mg, diazepam 5–20 mg, or oxazepam 20–30 mg are given every 2–4 h until withdrawal symptoms are controlled. Usually not more than 100 mg a day is required. Doses of drugs are best titrated depending on the picture rather than a set dose being given. Lorazepam 1–2 mg, which can also be given IM, and oxazepam are used if significant hepatic dysfunction exists. Vital signs and level of consciousness must be monitored frequently.

3. Fluid and electrolyte abnormalities must be corrected.

4. *Withdrawal seizures* are treated with diazepam 5–10 mg IV or lorazepam 1–2 mg IV. Phenytoin in a dose of 15 mg/kg IV has also been used. Prophylactic use of an anticonvulsant is not indicated for alcohol-withdrawal seizures. About 2% of patients develop status epilepticus, needing more aggressive therapy. These typically are epileptic patients who have discontinued their medication.

5. *Delirium tremens* usually occurs within 24–72 h of abstinence and includes sympathetic overactivity, fever, a fluctuating level of consciousness, hallucinations, and agitation. Treatment of DTs is best done in a medical setting and includes parenteral sedation with benzodiazepines, vitamins, fluid replacement, aggressive treatment of hyperthermia, close monitoring for seizures, and antibiotics for infections. Restraint is often needed. Despite treatment, DTs still have a mortality rate of 5–10%.

6. The *Wernicke–Korsakoff syndrome* occurs most often in the nutritionally compromised alcoholic and is due to thiamine deficiency. The acute stage, or Wernicke's encephalopathy, consists of ocular manifestations, including horizontal or vertical nystag-

TABLE 10.2. Interactions Between Alcohol and Other Agents

Agent	Effect
Other CNS depressants (benzodiazepines, barbiturates, tricyclic antidepressants, anti-psychotics, opiates)	Drowsiness, stupor, coma
The Disulfiram (antabuse) reaction	Occurs shortly after alcohol ingestion; includes flushing, headache, nausea, vomiting, sweating, and chest pain, which may progress to breathing difficulty, confusion, arrhythmias, shock and death; disulfiram-like reactions may occur with *metronidazole, griseofulvin,* and *oral antidiabetics*
Induction of hepatic enzymes	Decreased effectiveness of phenytoin, anticoagulants, tricyclic antidepressants
Oral antidiabetics and insulin	Can potentiate effect

mus and weakness or paralysis of extraocular muscles, ataxia, and confusion with a good prognosis if treated early. Korsakoff's psychosis features predominantly anterograde with some degree of retrograde amnesia and confabulation with a poor prognosis. Treatment consists of supplemental thiamine, 100 mg IV in the acute situation. Giving glucose before thiamine could worsen the picture.

7. The *antabuse reaction* is treated symptomatically with careful monitoring for and treatment of hypotension, respiratory compromise, and arrhythmias. Benadryl 50 mg parenterally may be useful.

8. *Alcoholic ketoacidosis* is a metabolic acidosis with an elevated anion gap without significant hyperglycemia and no evidence for other etiologies such as salicylate toxicity, ethylene glycol ingestion, uremia, and lactic acidosis. This condition is typically seen in chronic nutritionally compromised alcoholics, and pancreatitis may occur as a complication. It is treated with vitamins and glucose along with correction of dehydration and electrolyte abnormalities.

III. OPIATES

A. Clinical Features

1. **Intoxication.** The patient who has overdosed on opiates typically presents with stupor and miosis (abnormal pupillary contraction). Other features

include respiratory depression, pulmonary edema, orthostatic hypotension, urinary retention, and decreased peristalsis. This typical picture is seen with morphine, heroin, and methadone. The predominant symptom can vary depending on the specific opiate used. Further, many opiates are mixed with other drugs leading to presentations that are colored by the other drug used. Pulmonary edema, which may rapidly lead to respiratory arrest and death, is seen in propoxyphene overdose. Myoclonic jerks leading on to generalized seizures can occur with meperidine overdose. Codeine is rarely lethal if used alone; however, it is often mixed with aspirin, glutethimide, caffeine, or phenacetin, all of which can color the picture. Fentanyl usually presents with drowsiness and responds to naloxone; however, it is not picked up with standard toxicology screens because of its chemical structure. Pentazocine, which causes sclerosis of veins and local infections if injected, is a mixed agonist–antagonist; the initial high can therefore be followed by dysphoria, anxiety, hallucinations, and seizures.

2. Withdrawal. This can begin by 6 h and is usually complete in 7–10 days. Early symptoms include anxiety, sleep disturbance, yawning, sweating, nasal discharge, and lacrimation. This is usually followed by gooseflesh, abdominal cramping, fluctuating autonomic signs, and diarrhea. Symptoms peak in 2–3 days and can include leukocytosis, ketosis, and electrolyte imbalance. Opiate withdrawal is usually more uncomfortable than dangerous.

B. Interactions. See Table 10.3.

C. Management

1. Intoxication. Supportive care is crucial. Monitoring respiratory function is the first priority as death is usually due to respiratory failure. Endotracheal intubation and ventilatory support is required for falling oxygen saturation. Pulmonary edema, if present, is believed to be due to hypoxic damage causing increased capillary permeability and responds to positive end expiratory pressure. If hypotension does not respond to ventilatory support, then fluids and pressor agents need to be used.

Definitive treatment involves the administration of naloxone, a true antagonist devoid of partial agonist activity. Naloxone can be administered subcutaneously, IM/IV, and via the endotracheal tube. It is usually given in a dose of 0.4 mg IV push and reverses opiate effects for up to 45 min. If no response occurs a second dose of 2 mg IV should be given and can be repeated every 2–3 min until a response occurs or a total dose of 10 mg over 15–20 min is given. The maximum dose recommended is 10 mg; lack of response to this dose should lead one to look for another cause of coma. If response does occur, naloxone will need to be repeated in doses of 0.4–2 mg as the half-life of most opiates is longer than that of naloxone. Continuous infusion using rates of 0.2–0.8 mg/h can be used for long-acting opiates to prevent a relapse of symptoms as the effect of naloxone wears off. If naloxone is given to a regular user, an acute withdrawal syndrome may be precipitated. While this should not discourage the physician from using the drug in an acute overdose situation involving a regular user, smaller doses (0.1 mg) can titrate reversal better.

2. Withdrawal. This is commonly accomplished using methadone or clonidine.

a. Methadone. Methadone should be administered when a withdrawing addict manifests at least two of the following symptoms: tachycardia, fluctuating blood pressure, dilated pupils, sweating, gooseflesh, rhinorrhea, or lacrimation. The usual initial dose is 10 mg; it can be repeated every 4 h, and only

TABLE 10.3. Interactions Between Opiates and Other Agents

Agent	Effect
Monoamine oxidase (MAO) inhibitors	Severe, immediate reactions can occur with hypertension, muscle rigidity, excitation, and sweating when *meperidine* is administered to patients taking MAO inhibitors; the mechanism is unclear, it has not been reported with other narcotic analgesics, morphine is the narcotic analgesic of choice in patients receiving MAO inhibitors; concurrent administration of MAO inhibitors and any *opiate* may result in hypotension, and exaggeration of CNS and respiratory depressant effects
Other CNS depressants (benzodiazepines, barbiturates, tricyclics, antipsychotics, tetrahydrocannibinols and alcohol)	Drowsiness, stupor, or coma
H2 receptor antagonists	
Cimetidine and ranitidine	Increased sedation and respiratory depression (decreased hepatic clearance)
Ranitidine	Confusion, disorientation, and agitation with high-dose morphine
Stimulants	
Dextroamphetamine	Increased euphoriant effects, variable effects on respiration
Methylphenidate	Increased analgesia and decreased sedation

rarely is a dose of > 40 mg per 24 h needed. Patients maintained on > 40 mg of methadone prior to detoxification may need higher doses. The total dose given over the first 24 h is administered the next day in two divided doses and then tapered by 5 mg/day beginning with the morning dose until completely withdrawn. It is always given in liquid or crushed form under supervision. If the patient is dependent on methadone and CNS depressants, the methadone is maintained and the depressant withdrawn first.

   b. Clonidine. An α_2-adrenergic agonist that suppresses many of the withdrawal symptoms of opiates is usually given in a dose of 10–20 μg/kg/day in three divided doses, adjusted to prevent symptoms of withdrawal and hypotension. After stabilization for 4–14 days depending on the half-life of the opiate, it is tapered over 4–5 days and stopped. Sedation and hypotension are potential problems; further, it does not help craving and insomnia.

IV. STIMULANTS

A. Clinical Features. The two commonly used stimulants are cocaine and amphetamine.

1. Intoxication. This usually begins with feelings of euphoria and self-confidence accompanied by increased heart rate and blood pressure, elevated temperature, and dilated pupils. Higher doses may lead to stereotyped movements, formication (the sensation of bugs under the skin), irritability, restlessness, and lability. A paranoid psychosis with persecutory delusions; auditory, visual, and tactile hallucinations; and potential violence can develop. Acute intoxication may produce hyperthermia and seizures.

2. Withdrawal. Classic withdrawal symptoms do not occur, although regular users may experience a significant dysphoria also called the "crash," which is usually short-lived, although it may occasionally last several weeks.

B. Complications

1. CNS. The most common neurologic complication is seizures. These are typically grand mal in type, of short duration, are temporally related to cocaine use, and can occur in both first-time and chronic users. Status epilepticus may occur. Seizures generally are benign and without residual deficits. Syncopal episodes and headaches may occur. Catastrophic events such as intracranial hemorrhage or infarction may also occur.

2. Cardiovascular. Myocardial ischemia and infarcts are well recognized. This complication is not dose-related, may occur during withdrawal as well as during use, and may occur minutes to days after use of cocaine. Myocardial infarcts rarely follow amphetamine use. Cocaine has type 1 antiarrhythmic properties, can cause QRS and QT prolongation on the EKG, and may lead to both atrial and ventricular arrhythmias. Aortic dissection and rupture have been described.

C. Interactions. See Table 10.4.

D. Management

1. Intoxication

a. General measures. These include removal from the nares if insufflated and gastric lavage followed by charcoal if recently ingested. If renal and hepatic function are normal, forced acid diuresis using ammonium chloride 500 mg Q4h can speed up excretion. There is a risk of myoglobinuric renal failure secondary to rhabdomyolysis if this method is used, and some authors would not recommend it.

b. Treatment of stimulator effects. Treat central stimulatory effects as they will often decrease the peripheral manifestations such as hypertension and tachycardia. High fever should be treated vigorously with ice baths or cooling blankets. Patients should be sedated using benzodiazepines. Seizures are treated with diazepam 5–10 mg IV slowly, repeated every 5 min up to a total

**TABLE 10.4. Interactions Between Stimulants
and Other Agents**

Agent	Effect
Alcohol and marijuana	Blood pressure elevation, increased potential for cardiovascular toxicity; ethanol may potentiate cocaine hepatotoxicity
Cardiovascular agents	
Guanethidine, methyldopa	Antagonism of antihypertensive effect
Quinidine	Higher chance of an arrhythmia
Beta blockers	Increased vascular resistance, decreased coronary flow, and increased incidence of angina
Psychotropics	
Tricyclics	Enhanced effects
MAO inhibitors	Severe hypertension and hyperpyrexia
Antipsychotics	Decreased effectiveness

of 30 mg. Phenobarbital and phenytoin can be used for status epilepticus. Persistent seizures with hyperthermia are an indication for neuromuscular paralysis as acidosis and later rhabdomyolysis can result. Antipsychotics may worsen hyperthermia and lower seizure threshold and are best used only for psychotic symptoms. Haloperidol is the agent most favored.

    c. Cardiac complications

        1. Hypertensive crisis is typically treated with beta blockers such as propranolol 1 mg IV over 1 min repeated every 1–5 min up to 6 mg. If blood pressure does not respond to beta or mixed alpha/beta blockade, it can be effectively controlled with sodium nitroprusside 0.5–3 μg/kg/min titrated to response.

        2. Both atrial and ventricular cardiac dysrhythmias can occur. Atrial tachycardias can be treated with propranolol or verapamil. Ventricular dysrhythmias respond to lidocaine, although caution must be shown as lidocaine can lower seizure threshold and may exacerbate the cardiac depressant effect of cocaine. Ventricular ectopy responds to propranolol. Acidosis, if present, should always be corrected.

        3. Myocardial ischemia—patients with chest pain following cocaine use should always be treated like patients with chest pain who have not used the drug.

    2. Withdrawal. As mentioned earlier, the crash features dysphoria and craving and is time-limited. If, however, it lasts more than a few weeks, the possibility of an underlying affective illness must be considered, and antidepressant treatment may be indicated.

V. SEDATIVE/HYPNOTICS

These commonly refer to the benzodiazepines and the barbiturates, although there are several other agents that cannot be classified as either. All these drugs have sedative and anxiolytic properties, can be abused, and can cause psychological and physical dependence.

A. Clinical Features

1. Intoxication. *Benzodiazepine overdose* presents typically with mild to moderate CNS depression. Tachycardia, hyper- or hypotension, hyperreflexia, nystagmus, hallucinations, and seizures have also been described, as have extrapyramidal effects and dystonic reactions. *Barbiturate overdose* can present with progressive CNS depression and cardiorespiratory failure, the intensity of which depends on the amount ingested. Pupils are usually reactive and in midposition. Hypotension, pulmonary edema, hypothermia, and gastric paralysis are well described. Skin blisters are seen in 6% of barbiturate intoxications and in 50% of patients dying from overdose. *Chloral hydrate* toxicity also features gastritis because of its corrosive effect on the GI tract, and hypotension with arrhythmias from its negative inotropic effect. *Glutethimide* (*Doriden*) has intrinsic anticholinergic activity. *Meprobamate* can produce severe hypotension and gastrointestinal bezoars that require endoscopic removal in large doses. *Ethchlorvynol* (*Placidyl*) can cause severe respiratory depression. *Methaqualone* (*Quaalude*) overdose is different as patients are hyperreflexic and hypertonic and can have seizures and rhabdomyolysis. Cardiac and respiratory depression is less intense.

2. Withdrawal. The onset of withdrawal from sedative/hypnotic drugs will depend on the duration of action of the drug used. Withdrawal may begin as early as 12 h after the last dose in the case of short-acting barbiturates while

TABLE 10.5. Interactions Between Sedative Hypnotics and Other Agents

Agent	Effect
Other CNS depressants (alcohol, tricyclic antidepressants, antipsychotics)	Increased drowsiness
Induction of enzymes (Cytochrome P450 in the liver)	Lower levels of oral anticoagulants—tricyclics, antipsychotics, corticosteroids, disopyramide, estrogens, metronidazole, cyclosporine, antibiotics—chloramphenicol and tetracycline; antitumor agents—cyclophosphamide and lomustine; anticonvulsants—carbamazepine, lamotrigine, and vigabatrin; many beta blockers, verapamil, and theophylline

they may appear as late as 7–10 days after the last dose of diazepam. Early symptoms include restlessness, anxiety, nausea and abdominal cramps that can progress to tachycardia, postural hypotension, hyperreflexia, tremor, insomnia, and nightmares. Seizures and delirium may also occur.

B. Interactions. See Table 10.5.

C. Management

1. Intoxication

(a) General supportive management is crucial in the overdose situation. Aggressive airway management and control of hypotension with fluids and pressor agents, if needed, is life-saving. Gastric lavage and repeated administration of charcoal may be of benefit if performed early.

(b) *Flumazenil* is a pure benzodiazepine antagonist with a half-life of 1 h necessitating frequent dosing. It is usually given as 0.2 mg IV over 30 s followed in 30 s by 0.3 mg over a further 30 s. If the patient is still drowsy, further 0.5-mg doses are given at 1-min intervals to a total dose of 5 mg. Resedation after an initial response can be treated with 1-mg boluses to 3 mg/h. Continuous infusion of 0.5 mg/h has been tried with success. Seizures and cardiac arrhythmias are potential side effects; both appear related to the sudden withdrawal of benzodiazepines and are more likely to occur in mixed overdose states, especially with tricyclic antidepressants. Flumazenil is best avoided if there are serious signs of overdose with tricyclic antidepressants, in cases where a known hypersensitivity to benzodiazepines or flumazenil exists, and in cases where benzodiazepines were given to control a life-threatening situation.

(c) The rate of elimination of barbiturates can be increased by forced alkaline diuresis, hemodialysis, and hemoperfusion. Alkaline diuresis, which is useful in increasing the excretion of long-acting drugs, is performed by administering sodium bicarbonate 50 mequiv (milliequivalents) IV push followed by 150 mequiv in 1 L D5W infused to maintain a pH of > 7.5 and urine output of 3–4 ml/kg/h. Cardiac and renal function must be normal. Hemodialysis may be useful in cases of long-acting drugs, while hemoperfusion may help intermediate- and short-acting agents. Forced diuresis is best avoided in ethchlorvynol poisoning due to the possibility of pulmonary edema developing.

(d) In hypotension from chloral hydrate toxicity pressors such as dopamine, dobutamine, epinephrine, norepinephrine, and isoproterenol should be avoided as their beta agonist activity can potentiate arrhythmias. Phenylephrine (a pure alpha agonist) can be used. Lidocaine, phenytoin, beta blockers, and overdrive pacing can be used for arrhythmias.

(e) Hypertonicity and seizures in methaqualone toxicity respond to benzodiazepines, phenytoin, and paralytics.

2. Withdrawal. General supportive measures and management of seizures and delirium are similar to that described in alcohol withdrawal.

A longer-acting drug such as phenobarbital for barbiturates and diazepam or clonazepam for benzodiazepines is usually substituted. This drug is then slowly withdrawn.

VI. PHENCYCLIDINE

A. Clinical Features

1. Intoxication. Patients who have used low-dose PCP (< 5 mg) usually present with incoordination, blurred vision, and horizontal nystagmus. With increasing doses, additional symptoms include slurred speech, increased muscle tone, hyperreflexia, and catalepsy. Overdose with > 20 mg can lead to seizures, hypertension, respiratory depression, coma, and death. Other symptoms include auditory and visual hallucinations, depersonalization, euphoria, anxiety, depression, and agitation. Increased bronchial and salivary secretions are seen. The effects usually settle in 4–8 h.

2. PCP-induced psychosis. This can occur in both the naive and the regular user and may last several days, very rarely months. Patients often present with paranoid delusions, are hyperactive and can be unpredictably assaultive. Over the next 5–15 days symptoms gradually settle and gain control over their behavior.

3. Withdrawal. Phencyclidine use can result in dependence, abuse, and intoxication, but no withdrawal syndrome.

B. Management

1. General measures

(a) Begin with assessment of the ABCs. One possible complication here is laryngospasm and prolonged paralysis from succinylcholine due to PCP's ability to inhibit pseudocholinesterase.

(b) Restraint, both physical and chemical, is frequently needed. PCP is a dissociative drug, and patients seldom respond to attempts to talk them down. Benzodiazepines are most often used for sedation; their antiseizure activity is also helpful. As antipsychotics such as haloperidol can lower seizure threshold and worsen anticholinergic toxicity, they are best avoided.

(c) Gastrointestinal decontamination is recommended. Nasogastric suction and charcoal will remove PCP if used recently even if smoked or insufflated as it is trapped in acid stomach secretions. The possibility of further agitation must be kept in mind.

(d) Urine acidification is often needed. PCP is trapped in an acid urine at pH < 5. This is accomplished using ammonium chloride 2.75 mequiv/kg in 60 mL of saline every 6 h through the nasogastric tube along with ascorbic acid 2 gm in 500 mL of IV fluid every 6 h. This method has recently fallen into disfavor as agitation, seizures, and hyperthermia can all produce acidosis and rhabdomyolysis. Acidification of urine may worsen acidosis and exacerbate myoglobin precipitation in the kidney.

2. Specific treatment

(a) Seizures are treated with benzodiazepines such as diazepam (Valium) or lorazepam (Ativan).

(b) Hypertension most often responds to control of agitation or seizures. Sodium nitroprusside can be used if rapid control is needed.

(c) PCP-induced psychosis is managed using the same general measures mentioned above. Haloperidol is the neuroleptic of choice in doses of ≤ 5 mg/h, taking care to avoid high doses for reasons mentioned earlier. Low-potency drugs such as chlorpromazine (thorazine) and thioridazine (mellaril) are best avoided.

VII. MARIJUANA

A. Clinical Features

1. Intoxication. Initial features include relaxation, friendliness, and alteration in time perception. Common physical findings include tachycardia and conjunctival injection. Adverse reactions include

    (a) Acute episodes of panic typically seen in the inexperienced user

    (b) Delirium usually seen after oral ingestion of large doses

    (c) Flashbacks that may last several months

2. Withdrawal. Like PCP, cannabis can produce dependence, abuse, and intoxication but no significant withdrawal, though mild symptoms including irritability, insomnia, nausea, vomiting, and diaphoresis have been described in chronic high-dose users who stop the drug.

B. Management. Management essentially includes reassuring patients that they are not mentally ill and that symptoms will settle in a few hours, and to prevent harm to the patients or others. Use of psychotropic medication is usually unnecessary.

VIII. HALLUCINOGENS

Hallucinogens are classified into two groups of drugs: the *psychedelics*, which are agents that alter mood and perception without affecting reality testing and include lysergic acid diethylamide (LSD), mescaline, psilocybin, and cannabis; and the *dissociative anesthetics*, such as PCP, which produce true hallucinations that cannot be differentiated from reality.

A. Clinical Features

1. Intoxication. Symptoms begin 30–45 min after ingestion of LSD and last up to 12 h. Altered mood states and sensory perceptions including synesthesias, which is the mixing of sensations, are common, as are sympathomimetic effects such as mydriasis, tachycardia, hypertension, and hyperthermia. Anxiety, panic attacks, and an acute toxic psychosis can occur. Respiratory failure, coma, and a transient coagulopathy have been described in patients who have insufflated large (milligram-range) quantities. Seizures and death have not been reported, and all patients made a full recovery.

Psychoactive substances found in mushrooms include psilocybin found in the genus *Psilocybe* and ibotenic acid and muscimol found in *Amanita muscaria*. Toxic symptoms are essentially that produced by LSD, except that psilocybin can also produce seizures, while amanita poisoning can produce an anticholinergic syndrome. Mescaline is found in the peyote cactus, and doses of 20 mg/kg can produce vasodilation, bradycardia, and respiratory depression, all of which are believed to be related to histamine release.

2. Withdrawal. Hallucinogens do not produce a withdrawal syndrome.

B. Management. Hallucinogen toxicity is managed conservatively. Benzodiazepines are preferred for sedation, and antipsychotics are best avoided due to their anticholinergic effects. Hypotension from mescaline toxicity is treated with fluids; bradycardia, with atropine or isoproterenol.

IX. SUICIDE

Many studies have confirmed that alcohol and drug addiction is a major risk factor for suicide, as both cause and precipitant. Suicidal ideation may be influenced in at least three ways: (1) alcohol and drugs may pharmacologically impair judgment and cognition and depress mood, (2) multiple crises and disrupted interpersonal relationships predispose to suicidal thinking, and (3) finally, the alcoholic and drug addict often has comorbid psychiatric disorders that have suicide as a significant risk factor. Over 50% of suicidal patients found in a general survey of hospital admissions were associated with drug and alcohol addiction. The lifetime prevalence of alcohol and drug addiction in the general population is 18%; this figure may be several times higher in adolescent suicides. Several studies have suggested that suicidal patients generally receive less aggressive care than do nonsuicidal patients. These figures make it imperative that the risk of suicide be assessed in every patient who presents to the emergency room.

A. Risk Factors. The presence of one or more of the following risk factors increases the chance of suicide occurring.

(1) The young (in their 20s) of both sexes and the older male are especially prone to commit suicide.

(2) White males are most likely to commit suicide, although the rate for black males is increasing.

(3) Being separated, divorced or widowed.

(4) Lack of social support and presence of a suicide note. Up to 15% leave a suicide note.

(5) Being unemployed or retired.

(6) Being in poor physical health with an acute or chronic illness increases relative risk.

(7) Suicide risk is highly correlated with multiple drug and alcohol addiction; the drugs most commonly used are alcohol, opiates, sedatives, amphetamines, cocaine, and marijuana. Phencyclidine and hallucinogens are used only rarely.

(8) Presence of comorbid psychiatric disorders is associated with a greater prevalence of suicide. The common psychiatric disorders include depression, borderline personality disorder, mania, and schizophrenia.

(9) A prior history of suicidal behavior and recent loss or separation is also a significant predictor.

(10) Methods used include hanging, drowning, jumping, and use of firearms in the high-risk category, while cutting or piercing gas and poison indicate less risk. Easy access to lethal methods significantly increases risk.

B. Treatment. Patients at high risk need to be admitted for treatment. Intensive outpatient intervention is effective for patients at lower risk. In most cases depression, hopelessness, anxiety, and paranoia will diminish over time with abstinence. Psychotropic medication is not indicated in the majority of cases.

However, antidepressants should be instituted in situations where dangerous levels of depression and suicidal thinking persist.

X. VIOLENCE

Violence is becoming frequent in our society today, and mental health professionals are being asked to predict and treat violence in their patients. In spite of clear limitations in our ability to predict violence, psychiatrists can be held legally liable for unfortunate outcomes. It is therefore crucial to assess the potential for violence in patients, especially in an emergency-room setting.

A. Risk Factors. The following factors have been shown to be especially associated with the risk of violence:

(1) A history of past violent behavior has repeatedly been shown to be the best predictor of violence and should be asked for in every case.

(2) One's "gut reaction" must never be ignored. This can be cultivated through experience.

(3) In the emergency situation contextual cues are important. A patient who is agitated, threatening, intoxicated, loud, and brought in by the police is more likely to be violent than one who is relaxed, cooperative, sober, speaks normally, and comes in voluntarily.

(4) The intoxicated or delirious patient has clearly been shown to be potentially violent.

(5) Seriously mentally ill patients who are noncompliant with medication.

(6) In general, men are more likely to be violent than are women. However, some studies have shown that staff on inpatient and emergency services underrespond to threats and escalating behavior by female patients. Up to 30% of male psychiatric patients with a history of violence become violent within one year of discharge. Females with major mental illness are over 25 times more likely than are females in the general population to be convicted of violent crimes.

(7) Close to 50% of murdered women and 12% of murdered men are killed by sexual partners in domestic-violence incidents. Of female psychiatric patients seen in the emergency room, 25% are battered by a male partner, while only 8% of domestic-violence cases are correctly diagnosed by physicians. This makes assessment of domestic violence imperative in every case.

B. Management. The single most important intervention is to be aware of and assess the potential for violence in every case. Other important interventions include

(1) Medical evaluation, including vital signs, a good physical examination, and basic lab work such as blood count and chemistry is vital in ruling out organic factors. Toxicology screens, especially in younger and more aggressive patients, helps detect drugs of abuse. PCP, cocaine, and amphetamines can be associated with violence.

(2) An escalating patient can be offered empathy, verbal limits, and medication in sequence. A lack of response will necessitate seclusion followed by restraint and finally involuntary medication. One usually starts with the least restrictive alternative but may have to be more restrictive initially if violence is imminent.

(3) Presence of adequate security personnel in the examining room or nearby is an excellent deterrent.

(4) Treatment of cofactors that predict violence is crucial.

    (a) The pychotic patient needs a neuroleptic without further delay. Haloperidol 5–10 mg PO or IM is a good choice if the patient is not already on a neuroleptic. In that case the dose can be increased.

    (b) Low-dose (1–2 mg) haloperidol is useful in the agitated delirious patient.

    (c) Agitation, intoxication, and withdrawal can be safely managed with a benzodiazepine such as lorazepam 1–2 mg PO or IM.

(5) Dispositions include

    (a) Protective custody, which can be set up in conjunction with the local police and is ideal for patients who are primarily antisocial and violent as they seldom benefit from admission.

    (b) Hospitalization for patients who are violent and have a psychiatric illness.

    (c) Finally, the patient may be discharged home if found safe enough to leave. Family or caregivers should be contacted and management options discussed in detail.

(6) If it is determined that a patient is violent or potentially violent, the psychiatrist has a duty to protect the potential victim. This responsibility can be discharged through admission to a psychiatric facility; the responsibility then falls on the admitting hospital or by notifying the local law-enforcement agency and warning the potential victim.

(7) Documentation must be detailed in every case and must include the assessment made, conclusions drawn, and treatment administered. If the patient is released, details of contact made with local police and potential victims must also be recorded.

SUGGESTED READINGS

Hales RE, Yudofsky SC, Talbott JA (eds): Alcohol and other psychoactive substance use disorders. In *Textbook of Psychiatry*, 2nd ed. Washington, DC: American Psychiatric Press, 1994.

Hyman SE, Tesar GE (eds): *Manual of Psychiatric Emergencies*, 3rd ed. Boston: Little, Brown and Company, 1993.

Miller NS: The pharmacological treatment of the acute intoxication and detoxification of alcohol and drugs of abuse and addition. In *The Pharmacology of Alcohol and Drugs of Abuse and Addiction*. New York: Springer-Verlag, 1991.

Miller NS: *Principles of Addiction Medicine*. Washington, DC: American Society of Addiction Medicine, 1994.

Miller NS, Owley T, Erickson A: Working with drug/alcohol-addicted patients in crises. *Psychiatric Ann* 24(11):592–597, 1994.

Shader RD (ed): *Manual of Psychiatric Therapeutics*, 2nd ed. Boston: Little, Brown and Company, 1994.

Slaby AE, Martin SD: Drug and alcohol emergencies. In NS Miller (ed): *Comprehensive Handbook of Drug and Alcohol Addictions*. New York: Marcel Dekker, 1991.

CHAPTER 11

TREATMENT OF COMORBID MEDICAL COMPLICATIONS

Jonathan M. Rubin, M.D.
Assistant Professor
Department of Emergency Medicine
Medical College of Wisconsin
Milwaukee, Wisconsin

David G. Benzer, D.O.
Associate Clinical Professor
Departments of Psychiatry and Pharmacology
Medical College of Wisconsin
Milwaukee, Wisconsin

I. ALCOHOL

A. General Considerations

Awareness of the complications of alcohol abuse is important not only to aid in the diagnosis and treatment of the complications themselves but also to draw awareness to an underlying alcohol problem. Although factors other than alcohol can cause many of the disorders listed, it is important to consider alcoholism in patients who present with any of these disorders.

B. Chronic Conditions

1. Gastrointestinal

a. Reflux esophagitis. Alcohol significantly relaxes the tone of the lower esophageal sphincter and also decreases peristalsis of the distal esophagus, resulting in contact of gastric contents with the lower esophagus.

b. Esophageal bleeding. Bleeding is frequently noted in alcoholics. The two main causes are reflux esophagitis and esophageal varices. Varices result from portal hypertension, which causes the veins of the distal esophagus to dilate. In addition, Mallory–Weiss tears of the esophagus following protracted vomiting can occur.

c. Gastritis. Alcohol disrupts the barrier function of the gastric mucosa, resulting in inflammation of the stomach lining. Gastritis is a frequent cause of GI bleeding in alcoholics.

d. Intestinal malabsorption. Alcohol impairs the absorption by the small intestine of numerous substances, including thiamine, folic acid, vitamin B_{12}, and some fats. The resulting increased osmotic load, as well as alcohol's ability

Manual of Therapeutics for Addictions, Edited by Norman S. Miller, Mark S. Gold, and David E. Smith.
ISBN 0471-56176-2 © 1997 John Wiley & Sons, Inc.

to stimulate jejunal propulsion, results in diarrhea. The diarrhea usually resolves within 1 week of cessation of alcohol consumption.

e. Pancreatitis. It is estimated that alcohol is responsible for 30–60% of all cases of pancreatitis. The pathogenesis of alcoholic pancreatitis is not well defined, but may include the toxic effect of alcohol on pancreatic acinar cells, precipitation of proteinaceous material in the pancreatic ducts, or the reflux of digestive enzymes into pancreatic ducts. Acute pancreatitis presents with abdominal pain, nausea, and vomiting in conjunction with alcohol abuse. Chronic alcoholic pancreatitis is often associated with the late sequelae of the disease, including pancreatic calcification, diabetes mellitus, and manifestations of exocrine function abnormalities.

f. Hepatitis. Inflammation of the liver is caused by the toxic effects of alcohol and acetaldehyde, its primary metabolite. Patients most commonly present with right-upper-quadrant pain, fever, jaundice, leukocytosis, and abnormal liver function tests.

g. Cirrhosis. Cirrhosis represents the formation of fibrous tissue within the liver parenchyma as a result of prior tissue damage. This liver scarring causes an increased resistance to hepatic venous blood flow, giving rise to portal hypertension, the major consequence of cirrhosis. The manifestations of portal hypertension include esophageal varices, splenomegaly, ascites, dilation of superficial abdominal wall veins (caput medusae), peripheral edema, and internal hemorrhoids. Liver disease is the leading cause of death among alcoholics.

h. Hepatorenal syndrome. Hepatorenal syndrome is characterized by oliguria with increased serum creatinine in a patient with alcoholic liver disease. The prognosis is poor for patients with this syndrome.

2. Cardiovascular

a. Hypertension. Alcohol is a major risk factor for the development of hypertension. The degree of both systolic and diastolic hypertension is directly related to the amount of alcohol consumed. The mechanism is unclear, but may involve alcohol's effect as a pressor or its ability to evoke a withdrawal syndrome as blood levels fall. In alcoholics, when alcohol consumption stops, blood pressure falls; if drinking resumes, blood pressure rises again.

b. Cardiomyopathy. Degenerative change of cardiac muscle leads to the gradual development of cardiomegaly, ultimately progressing to symptomatic left ventricular failure. The etiology is unclear and may be due to alcohol alone or to other coexisting factors.

3. Pulmonary

a. General considerations. Alcohol interferes with normal pulmonary physiology in three major ways. First, alcohol impairs mechanical respiratory defenses (tracheal mucociliary action, glottic closure, and cough reflex). Next, alcohol reduces pulmonary bacterial clearance by decreasing surfactant production and depressing ciliary movement. Finally, alcohol impairs cellular immunologic defenses.

b. Bacterial pneumonia. Alcoholics are prone to bacterial pneumonia due to alcohol's interference with normal respiratory defense mechanisms. Malnutrition, poor dental hygiene, and tobacco use also play a role. The bacteria most commonly seen are *Streptococcus pneumoniae, Haemophilus influenzae, Klebsiella pneumoniae,* and gram-negative organisms.

c. Aspiration pneumonitis. Pneumonitis, lung abscess, and empyema can all follow aspiration of oropharyngeal secretions and / or gastric contents. Poor glottic closure together with alterations in the level of consciousness place the alcoholic at risk for aspiration. The pathogens most commonly seen in aspiration are *Peptostreptococcus, Fusobacterium,* and *Bacteroides* species.

d. Tuberculosis. Pulmonary tuberculosis (TB) has been occurring with greater frequency in patients who are dependent on alcohol, as well as other drugs.

4. Hematologic

a. General considerations. Ethanol leads to direct toxic changes in the hematopoietic system, including vacuolization of marrow precursor cells, decreased marrow cellularity, and erythrocyte megaloblastic changes.

b. Macrocytosis. Elevation of the mean corpuscular volume (MCV) to the range of 100–110 μm^3 is often the earliest laboratory indicator of alcoholism and usually is present without anemia. This toxic macrocytosis is characterized by the presence of round macrocytes as opposed to the macroovalocytes seen in folate deficiency. Alcoholic macrocytosis resolves slowly within 2–3 months of cessation of alcohol consumption.

c. Folate deficiency. Alcoholism is the most common cause of folate deficiency in the United States. Megaloblastic anemia from folate deficiency can be diagnosed by the presence of macroovalocytes and hypersegmented neutrophils on the peripheral smear with decreased serum and erythrocyte folate levels. Treatment consists of folate replacement and abstinence from alcohol use.

d. Iron-deficiency anemia. In alcoholics, iron-deficiency anemia most commonly results from gastrointestinal bleeding. The MCV, however, may be only slightly decreased or normal, due to the concurrent macrocytosis. The serum ferritin level is the test of choice to diagnose iron deficiency.

e. Leukocytes. Alcohol has numerous direct toxic effects on white blood cells, including inhibition of neutrophil production, impairment of chemotaxis, and reduction of both the number of circulating T lymphocytes and their ability to respond to antigenic stimulation. The defects in cell-mediated immunity are further exacerbated by malnutrition and liver disease.

f. Platelets. Alcohol exerts a toxic effect on platelet production by the bone marrow. With abstinence from alcohol, rebound thrombocytosis and increased platelet aggregation occur.

5. Endocrine

a. Pseudo–Cushing's syndrome. Alcohol-induced elevation of plasma cortisol levels results in signs and symptoms of corticosteroid excess, including edema, hypertension, truncal obesity, hirsutism, weakness, fatigue, bruising, and muscle wasting. Unlike true Cushing's syndrome, the findings resolve within several weeks of stopping alcohol consumption.

b. Gonadal disturbances. Female alcoholics experience irregular menstrual cycles and early menopause. Alcohol-induced testicular atrophy contributes to sexual dysfunction in males.

6. Neurologic

a. Dementia. Alcoholic dementia is characterized by cognitive impairment persisting at least 3 weeks after the cessation of alcohol intake. Deficits must be present in cognitive functions other than memory alone, such as visuospatial, abstracting, and learning. Cortical atrophy is often associated.

b. Wernicke–Korsakoff syndrome. The syndrome is caused by thiamine deficiency and is not exclusive to alcoholism. Wernicke's encephalopathy presents with the triad of oculomotor dysfunction (bilateral abducens nerve palsy), ataxia, and confusion. Treatment consists of parenteral thiamine (initial dose 100 mg), with up to 1 g given over the first 12 h. Glucose administration can precipitate Wernicke's encephalopathy in the presence of thiamine deficiency. Untreated, the encephalopathy often evolves into a chronic phase: Korsakoff's psychosis. The psychosis, also known as *alcohol amnestic disorder*, is characterized by both retrograde and anterograde amnesia with sparing of intellectual function. Confabulation is a key feature of the psychosis. Up to 50% of patients with Korsakoff's psychosis do not improve significantly.

c. Seizures. Seizures in alcoholics may be directly related to either alcohol withdrawal or to alcohol addiction in the absence of acute intoxication or withdrawal and without other organic causes of epilepsy. In addition, alcohol may lower the seizure threshold in patients with a preexisting seizure disorder. The pathogenesis of "alcoholic epilepsy" is poorly understood, but may include hypomagnesemia, cerebral atrophy, or abnormal cerebral microcirculation. Treatment of alcohol-induced seizures is controversial, but treatment mainstays consist of phenytoin and/or benzodiazepines.

d. Stroke. Alcohol significantly increases the risk of hemorrhagic stroke. The risk may be related to alcoholic liver disease and coagulopathy.

e. Polyneuropathy. Alcoholic polyneuropathy results from nutritional deficiencies and is seen in late-stage alcoholics. Presenting symptoms are usually lower-extremity pain, paresthesias, and weakness. As the disease progresses, motor deficits and muscle atrophy occur. Treatment consists of abstinence from alcohol, vitamin B–complex supplementation, and adequate nutrition.

f. Hepatic encephalopathy. Impaired hepatocellular function can cause a toxic brain syndrome due to the accumulation of unmetabolized nitrogenous waste products. The disorder is characterized by alterations in consciousness and behavior along with fluctuating neurologic signs, including asterixis, a characteristic flapping tremor. Elevation of the serum ammonia level is also noted. Treatment is aimed at eliminating or correcting precipitating factors (such as gastrointestinal hemorrhage, electrolyte abnormalities, or benzodiazepine use) and decreasing serum ammonia levels by decreasing the absorption of protein and nitrogen products from the intestine. Lactulose (30–50 mL hourly until diarrhea occurs, then 15–30 mL TID) decreases ammonia absorption from the gut, while neomycin (0.5–1 g Q6h) decreases endogenous ammonia production by gut bacteria.

g. Cerebellar degeneration. Manifested by truncal ataxia and wide-based gait, cerebellar degeneration is found at autopsy in almost one-third of chronic alcoholics. Etiology may be a combination of nutritional deficiency and direct toxic effect of alcohol. Treatment consists of adequate nutrition and abstinence from alcohol.

h. Marchiafava–Bignami disease. Demyelination of the corpus callosum results in a wide range of neuropsychiatric symptoms, including impairment in language, gait, and motor skills. The disease is thought to be due to nutritional deficiencies from late-stage alcoholism. Diagnosis is based on clinical presentation, but may be confirmed with MRI.

7. Nutritional/Metabolic

a. General considerations. Alcoholics represent the single largest group of patients with nutritional deficiencies in the United States. Alcohol not only takes the place of more nutritional substances but it also causes the malabsorption of nutrients such as D-xylose, thiamine, folic acid, and vitamins A, D, B_6, and B_{12}.

b. Alcoholic hypoglycemia. Hepatic glycogen reserves are eventually depleted by the consumption of inadequate quantities of carbohydrates. In addition, alcohol acutely impairs gluconeogenesis. The result is alcoholic hypoglycemia, an infrequent but serious complication of alcoholism. Clinically the patient presents with tachycardia, diaphoresis, tremulousness, and agitation. The syndrome is usually seen within 12 h of alcohol consumption. Treatment consists of glucose replacement, both orally and intravenously (25 g of 50% dextrose solution). Glucagon is ineffective due to the lack of glycogen stores.

c. Alcoholic ketoacidosis. The syndrome is most commonly seen in the alcoholic who has been binge drinking. The patient usually presents with abdominal pain but may also complain of nausea, vomiting, and anorexia. Physical findings include tachypnea, diaphoresis, and orthostatic hypotension. Mental status may range from normal to comatose. Laboratory testing reveals an elevated anion-gap metabolic acidosis. The condition is caused by alcohol's ability to impair ketogenesis, with a resultant rise in serum fatty-acids in a starved patient. When alcohol use ceases, ketogenesis is unblocked and the free fatty-acid metabolism produces an excess of ketone bodies. Treatment consists of intravenous hydration with glucose-containing solutions.

d. Hypophosphatemia. Alcoholism is one of the most common causes of hypophosphatemia. Etiologic factors include poor nutritional intake, diarrhea, and phosphorus wasting secondary to hypomagnesemia. Symptoms range from none to rhabdomyolysis, red cell dysfunction, cardiac failure, and CNS dysfunction. Treatment consists of phosphorus replacement.

e. Hypomagnesemia. Hypomagnesemia in alcoholism is caused by inadequate nutritional intake, malabsorption, and renal wasting of magnesium. Magnesium depletion presents with muscle cramping, tremulousness, and seizures. Mild depletion responds to adequate nutrition, while severe depletion requires parenteral replacement.

8. Miscellaneous

a. Alcohol withdrawal. Physical addiction is characterized by a withdrawal syndrome that occurs as the blood alcohol concentration declines. The main features of the syndrome are tremulousness, diaphoresis, agitation, tachycardia, and hypertension. Some patients may progress to a more severe form of withdrawal with toxic psychosis, disorientation, hallucinations, and seizure; this latter syndrome is known as *delirium tremens* (DTs). The mainstays of treatment are the benzodiazepines (most commonly diazepam 5–10 mg IV); for patients with refractory symptoms, phenobarbital is the second-line drug.

b. Carcinoma. While alcohol's exact role in the pathogenesis of cancer has not been determined, increased risk of cancer of the liver, esophagus, nasopharynx, and larynx is associated with chronic heavy alcohol consumption.

c. Myopathy. Acute alcoholic myopathy most often occurs in binging alcoholics and is probably caused by the direct toxic effect of alcohol on muscle tissue. The disorder is characterized by a spectrum of severity, ranging from an asymptomatic course with transient elevation of serum creatine kinase levels, to a severe form with muscular pain and swelling, myoglobinuria, and muscle necrosis. The disease is usually self-limited and resolves over 1–2 weeks. Chronic alcoholic myopathy is a progressive syndrome associated with late-stage alcoholism. The usual presentation is muscle atrophy and weakness, especially of the hips and shoulders. Treatment of these myopathies consists of correction of nutritional and fluid and electrolyte imbalances as well as stopping alcohol use.

C. Interactions

1. Tobacco. Alcoholics with nutritional deficits who use tobacco may experience tobacco–alcohol amblyopia, an ophthalmologic syndrome consisting of decreased visual acuity, including scotomas and difficulty distinguishing colors. These defects usually respond to vitamin therapy.

2. Anticoagulants. Significant interactions between alcohol and anticoagulant medications have not been observed. Chronic alcohol use may decrease serum warfarin levels due to enzyme induction. Alternatively, the long-term hematologic and hepatic effects of alcohol use enhance the effect of anticoagulants.

3. Anticonvulsants. Valproic acid poses a hypothetical risk of additive liver toxicity with alcohol; clinically this has not been observed.

4. Nonsteroidal antiinflammatory drugs (NSAIDs). NSAIDs worsen the gastric irritation produced by alcohol. Acetaminophen toxicity is enhanced by alcohol-induced liver changes.

5. Antidepressants. Tricyclic-induced psychomotor impairment is enhanced by alcohol. Chronic alcohol use increases the elimination of tricyclics.

6. Sedative/hypnotics. Additive or synergistic depression of the level of consciousness is the most important interaction between the two drugs. Pharmacokinetic interactions are variable but are probably not clinically significant.

7. Histamine (H_2) antagonists. The bioavailability of alcohol is increased by cimetidine and ranitidine through impairment of the activity of gastric antidiuretic hormone.

8. Antipsychotics. Alcohol acutely raises serum levels of chlorpromazine by decreasing its elimination.

II. TOBACCO

A. Chronic Conditions

1. Cardiac disease. Premature atherosclerotic coronary artery disease is the most important consequence of smoking. A dose–response relationship exists between coronary artery disease risk and cigarette smoking; the overall mortality rate in 2-pack/day smokers is increased twofold compared to nonsmokers. Sudden cardiac death is 2–3 times more likely to occur in 35–54-year-old male cigarette smokers than in nonsmokers.

2. Chronic obstructive pulmonary disease (COPD). Chronic bronchitis and emphysema are felt to be due to the effect of tobacco smoke on pulmonary immune function, proteolytic enzymes, and ciliary function. Treatment consists of oxygen supplementation (usually 1–12 L/min via nasal cannula) and nebulized bronchodilators (albuterol, metaproterenol, and ipratropium metered-dose inhalers). For acute exacerbations of lung disease, short-course steroids (prednisone 40–60 mg daily) and antibiotics are frequently added to the regimen.

3. Gastrointestinal disorders. Gastric and duodenal ulcer disease is more prevalent in male than female cigarette smokers and causes more deaths in male smokers than nonsmokers. Smoking impairs peptic ulcer healing and decreases the tone of the lower esophageal and pyloric sphincters.

4. Carcinoma. Many cancers are linked to smoking, including lung, larynx, oral cavity, esophagus, stomach, bladder, pancreas, and uterine cervix. The cancer risk is most likely related to the tar component of cigarette smoke rather than to nicotine or carbon monoxide. Cigarette smoking is the single most important cause of cancer mortality in the United States.

B. Interactions. The components of tobacco smoke induce hepatic microsomal enzyme systems that play an important role in the metabolism of many diverse drugs. For example, cigarette smoking increases the metabolism of propranolol, propoxyphene, and theophylline. Insulin absorption may also be decreased in smokers.

III. SEDATIVE/HYPNOTICS

A. Chronic Conditions

1. Withdrawal reaction. Between 40–50% of patients who use benzodiazepines chronically develop minor withdrawal symptoms with drug cessation. Symptoms may appear within 12–16 h of the last dose of a short-acting barbiturate or as late as 7–10 days after a drug such as diazepam with a long half-life. Symptoms include myalgias, agitation, restlessness, insomnia, and generalized anxiety. Insomnia and nightmares have been noted. More severe withdrawal reactions can occur, and may cause seizures, delirium, and death. Treatment consists of administration of the drug to which the patient is tolerant.

B. Interactions. The barbiturates cause induction of hepatic microsomal enzymes and affect the metabolism of a wide array of medications, including warfarin, digitalis, oral contraceptives, beta blockers, quinidine, phenytoin, and tricyclic antidepressants. Unlike the barbiturates, the benzodiazepines do not affect hepatic metabolism.

IV. DRUGS OF ADDICTION

A. General Considerations. Frequently the complications of drug use are directly related to the route of administration. Parenteral use introduces bacteria (from the skin, drug, and/or needles) and is associated with endocarditis, skin and soft-tissue infections, and osteomyelitis. Parenteral drug abuse is the second leading cause of AIDS in the United States. Vascular lesions such as aneurysms and thrombophlebitis can also be seen. Drug adulterants can damage heart valves and cause renal failure and granuloma formation. Intranasal drug use is associated with rhinorrhea and sinusitis, as well as damage to the nasal mucosa, with mucosal atrophy and septal necrosis resulting. Inhalation can cause pulmonary inflammatory changes and barotrauma (pneumothorax, pneumomediastinum, and pneumopericardium.)

B. Cocaine

1. Chronic conditions

a. General considerations. Most of the significant medical complications resulting from cocaine use (i.e., cardiac and neurologic) are related to the drug's acute effects. However, several complications resulting from chronic abuse have been recognized.

b. Nasal septal perforation. Seen primarily with insufflation of cocaine, perforation of the nasal septum probably results from a combination of the sharp edges of the cocaine crystal, repeated episodes of mucosal vasoconstriction and tissue hypoxia, and mucosal anesthesia and trauma. Symptoms include epistaxis, nasal crusting, pain, and eventually whistling on inspiration.

c. Alterations in pulmonary function. Use of freebase cocaine has been found to result in impaired carbon monoxide diffusing capacity.

d. Chronic heart failure. Several cases of dilated cardiomyopathy in chronic users of cocaine have been described. While cocaine's role in this disorder is not well established, patients with pheochromocytoma experience similar cardiac effects.

e. Hepatic effects. Animal studies have demonstrated periportal inflammation and necrosis related to chronic cocaine use, but only isolated reports have described similar injury patterns in humans.

f. Endocrine effects. In men who are chronic cocaine users, impotence and gynecomastia have been noted. Females may experience amenorrhea, infertility, and galactorrhea. Lactation may be a sign of cocaine dependence, since chronic cocaine use depletes dopamine (which inhibits prolactin secretion), resulting in rebound elevation of prolactin levels.

g. Headache. Headache is frequently seen in patients with cocaine dependence. While many cocaine-related headaches are signals of serious intracranial pathology (especially hemorrhage), there is evidence that cocaine induces a withdrawal headache through its effect on serotonin levels in the central nervous system.

h. Psychiatric. With chronic cocaine use, a syndrome consisting of visual and auditory hallucinations together with paranoid ideation may develop.

2. Interactions

a. Alcohol. The acute effects of cocaine intoxication are enhanced by alcohol through the formation of cocaethylene, a psychoactive metabolite of cocaine. Alcohol and cocaine have a synergistic effect on the degree of tachycardia produced. Alcohol may also increase cocaine's toxic hepatic effects.

C. Marijuana

1. Chronic conditions

a. Pulmonary effects. As compared to tobacco smoke, marijuana smoke contains higher levels of carbon monoxide and tar, and results in greater amounts of tar retained in the respiratory tree. Both acute and chronic bronchitis can be seen with regular marijuana use.

b. Genitourinary. Reports indicate that in males, marijuana use may cause decreased testosterone levels, as well as decreased sperm counts and motility, but these effects have not been confirmed.

c. Psychiatric. Although not specific to marijuana, an amotivational syndrome has been described, consisting of apathy, loss of ambition, inattention, impaired memory, and deterioration of school and work performance.

d. Withdrawal reaction. Mild withdrawal states have been reported in chronic marijuana users, with treatment seldom required. Signs and symptoms include tremor, sweating, nausea, vomiting, diarrhea, irritability, anorexia, and sleep disturbances.

2. Interactions

a. Tobacco. Impairment of single-breath carbon monoxide diffusion capacity is greater in patients who smoke both marijuana and tobacco than in those who smoke tobacco alone.

D. Opiates

1. Chronic conditions

a. Narcotic bowel syndrome. Opioid compounds reduce bowel motility and frequently cause constipation with chronic use. The presenting complaint in narcotic bowel syndrome is often an acute exacerbation of chronic abdominal pain. The pain is usually generalized and cramping in nature. Vomiting may be present. Plain x-rays demonstrate ileus and may suggest mechanical small-bowel obstruction. The pathophysiology of the disorder is thought to involve not only the pharmacologic effects of the opiate but also the gastrointestinal effects of withdrawal. Clonidine has been successfully used to treat the syndrome; its beneficial effect is probably due to its ability to relax intestinal smooth muscle and to diminish opiate withdrawal.

b. Withdrawal reaction. A withdrawal syndrome is well described in patients with physical addiction to opiates. Symptoms include nausea, diarrhea, coughing, lacrimation, rhinorrhea, diaphoresis, muscle twitching, and piloerection. Diffuse body pain, insomnia, and yawning also occur. Mild elevations in temperature, heart rate, respiratory rate, and blood pressure are also seen. Symptoms usually occur within 8–16 h of the last dose, with peak effects seen within 36–72 h. Treatment consists of rest, adequate nutrition, and administration of opiate medication (methadone 10 mg by mouth) to decrease symptoms. Another approach is to administer clonidine (usual oral dose 0.3 mg 2–4 times a day), which is effective at decreasing autonomic nervous system dysfunction.

2. Interactions. Interactions with other substances are most important in acute intoxication states, but have little significant effect on the complications of opiate use.

E. Inhalants

1. Chronic conditions

a. Dilated cardiomyopathy. Trichloroethylene (found in shoe-cleaning fluid and some correction fluid) has been associated with dilated cardiomyopathy, which results in congestive heart failure.

b. Hepatic necrosis and/or failure. Liver disease is associated with the chronic use of benzene and carbon tetrachloride.

c. Renal failure. Chloroform, carbon tetrachloride, and toluene are associated with renal dysfunction and renal failure.

d. Bone-marrow suppression. Benzene toxicity suppresses bone-marrow production of hematologic precursor cells.

2. Interactions. Significant interactions between inhalants and other medications have not been reported.

F. Hallucinogens

1. Chronic conditions

a. Psychiatric. Chronic users of lysergic acid diethylamide (LSD) are at risk for development of schizophreniform psychosis and derangements in memory function, problem solving, and abstract thinking.

2. Interactions. Significant interactions between the hallucinogens and other medications have not been reported.

SELECTED READINGS

Benzer DG: Medical consequences of alcohol addiction. In NS Miller (ed): *Comprehensive Handbook of Drug and Alcohol Addiction*. New York, Marcel Dekker, 1991.

Engel CJ, Benzer DG: Medical complications of drug addiction. In NS Miller (ed): *Comprehensive Handbook of Drug and Alcohol Addiction*. New York: Marcel Dekker, 1991.

Wartenberg AA: Medical disorders associated with certain drugs. In NS Miller (ed): *Principles of Addiction Medicine*. Chevy Chase, MD: American Society of Addiction Medicine, 1994.

CHAPTER 12

TREATMENT OF COMORBID SURGICAL DISORDERS

Robert A. Littrell, M.D.
& Gordon L. Hyde, M.D.
University of Kentucky
Louisville, Kentucky

I. INTRODUCTION

A. Role of the Surgeon. Although surgeons are rarely responsible for long-term treatment of addictive disease, they are routinely called on to provide treatment for patients with such disease, either diagnosed or undiagnosed. Sensitivity to issues unique to addiction, knowledge of surgical and medical complications characteristic of addicted patients, and knowledge of special treatment considerations is necessary for the appropriate management of such patients. Without such knowledge, surgeons may fail to identify an addictive illness, fail to prevent life-threatening episodes of drug withdrawal, fail to plan appropriately for common medical and surgical complications, or otherwise unknowingly perpetuate or worsen an addiction.

B. Prevalence of Addictive Disease in Surgical Patients. As many as 20–30% of patients admitted for inpatient surgery are either abusing alcohol or are alcohol-dependent. Among trauma patients who have changes in mental status on admission, as many as 84% may have positive drug screens. Although drug screens are not pathognomonic for addiction, positive screens may raise the suspicion that an addictive disease is present. Only about 50% of patients identified by the surgeon to have a significant problem with alcohol are referred to long-term treatment. However, long-term patient survival may depend more on proper management of the addictive disorder than on the surgical procedures.

II. DIAGNOSIS IN ADDICTIVE DISORDERS

A. General Pharmacologic Considerations in Surgical Management of Addicted Patients. The physiologic elimination of many drugs routinely used by surgeons is affected by alcohol, nicotine, and other drugs of abuse. Alcohol, the most commonly abused drug associated with significant impairment in physical and social function, has significant effects on the pharmacokinetics of many drugs. Acute drug–alcohol interactions are listed in Table 12.1 and chronic interactions are listed in Table 12.2.

Manual of Therapeutics for Addictions, Edited by Norman S. Miller, Mark S. Gold, and David E. Smith.
ISBN 0471-56176-2 © 1997 John Wiley & Sons, Inc.

TABLE 12.1. Acute Alcohol-Drug Interactions

Drug	Effect	Mechanism
H₂ Antagonists[a]	← Peripheral ethanol concentration	Inhibition of gastric alcohol dehydrogenase
Cytochrome 450–eliminated drugs[b]	← Peripheral drug concentration, ← therapeutic or toxic effects	Competitive inhibition of hepatic Cytochrome P450
Acetaminophen	→ Hepatotoxicity	Inhibition of hepatic breakdown of APAP to toxic metabolites
Acetaldehyde dehydrogenase inhibitors[c]	Disulfuram reaction (nausea, headache, vomiting, etc.)	Inhibition of acetaldehyde dehydrogenase ← acetaldehyde concentration
Monoamine oxidase inhibitors	Hypertensive crisis	Release of norepinephrine caused by high tyramine concentration in some beers and wines
CNS depressants	Potentiated effects	Additive CNS depression
Nonsteroidal anti-inflammatory drugs	Potentiated GI toxicity	Additive GI toxicity
Antidiabetics	Poor diabetic control	Ethanol produces fluctuations in blood glucose
Vasodilators	Potentiated effects can lead to vascular collapse	Additive hypotensive effects

[a]Except famotidine
[b]Barbiturates, benzodiazepines, tricyclic antidepressants, opiates, warfarin, phenytoin.
[c]Chloramphenicol, cephalosporins, metronidazole, griseofluvin, quinacrine, disulfuram, sulfonylurea, hypoglycemic agent

TABLE 12.2. Chronic Alcohol-Drug Interactions

Drug	Effect	Mechanism
Highly plasma-protein-bound drugs[a]	← Free concentration, ← therapeutic or toxic effects	→ Plasma proteins secondary to alcoholic liver disease
Cytochrome P450–eliminated drugs[b]	→ Therapeutic effect	← Clearance secondary to enzyme induction
Acetaminophen	← Hepatotoxicity	Enzyme induction ← formation of toxic metabolites

[a]quinidine, lorazepam
[b]barbiturates—benzodiazepine, propranolol, tolbutamide, warfarin, phenytoin, isoniazid.

B. Preoperative Evaluation. Despite common misperceptions, addicts are found in all socioeconomic, age, racial, and occupational groups. Thoughtful preoperative evaluation for drug dependencies in all patients can prevent life-threatening and costly treatment complications. Such an evaluation begins with screening all patients for drug addictions. The following items should be included in a comprehensive preoperative evaluation.

1. Complete history

   a. Social. Specific attention should be given to alcohol or other drug dependencies in the patient's family. Patients should be asked about frequency of substance use, past withdrawal episodes, and whether they are currently in recovery. The preoperative period is the most appropriate period to administer the SMAST (Table 12.3), CAGE (Table 12.4), or Ethanol Trauma Scale (Table 12.5) questionnaires.

   b. Medical. Patients with drug addictions have a higher rate of coexisting medical conditions. Conditions such as cirrhosis, ascites, gastric ulcers, and hypertension are very common among alcoholics. Chronic back pain, headaches, or other chronic pain syndromes are also associated with drug dependencies. Drug addicts neglect nutrition and may be at high risk for both common and chronic infections such as hepatitis and HIV.

   c. Surgical. If the patient or the patient's family has a history of gastrointestinal surgical procedures, especially those involving the liver and esophagus, the surgeon should look for addictive illness. Surgical procedures related to trauma may also indicate addiction.

TABLE 12.3. The SMAST Questionnaire[a]

1. Do you feel you are a normal ethanol user?
2. Do friends or relatives think you are a normal ethanol user?
3. Have you ever attended a meeting of Alcoholics Anonymous?
4. Have you ever lost friends or boyfriends/girlfriends because of ethanol use?
5. Have you ever gotten into trouble at work because of ethanol use?
6. Have you ever neglected your obligations, family, or work for 2 or more days in a row because of ethanol use?
7. Have you ever had delirium tremens (DTs), had severe shaking, heard voices, or seen things that weren't there after heavy ethanol use?
8. Have you ever gone to anyone for help about your ethanol use?
9. Have you ever been hospitalized because of ethanol use?
10. Have you ever been arrested for drunk driving or driving when using ethanol?

[a]A score of six positive answers justifies a diagnosis of probable alcohol dependency.
Source: Adapted from Pokorny AD, Miller BA, Kaplan HB: The brief MAST: a shortened version of the Michigan Alcoholism Screening Test. *Am J Psychiatry* 129:344, 1972.

TABLE 12.4. The CAGE Questionnaire*a*

1. Have you felt the need to C*ut* down on your drinking?
2. Have you been A*nnoyed* by criticism of your drinking?
3. Have you felt G*uilty* about your drinking?
4. Have you ever had a morning E*ye*-opener after a night of drinking?

*a*The CAGE questionnaire yields a relatively high number of false-negative results. However, two or more positive responses justify a diagnosis of alcohol dependency and the accuracy rate increases to 90% when three or four answers are affirmative.

Source: Adapted from Mayfield D, McLeod G, Hall P: The CAGE questionnaire: validation of a new alcoholism screening instrument. *Am J Psychiatry* 131:1121, 1974.

d. Psychiatric. Psychiatric disorders are present in a significantly higher number of patients with alcoholism and other drug dependencies. Identification of psychiatric disorders in a patient or a patient's family can be an indication of high risk for addictive illness.

2. Complete physical examination. A thorough physical examination is essential in the evaluation of the surgical patient with alcoholism or drug addiction. The surgeon should look for signs of withdrawal and hyperadrenergia (tension tremors, hypertension, tachycardia, PACs, diaphoresis, and fever). Among younger patients these signs may be minimal, but as addicted persons age, all the physical signs become more apparent. The patient should also be examined for signs of traumatic injuries (bruises, ecchymosis), chronic liver disease (jaundice, hepatomegaly, spider angiomata, testicular atrophy, gynecomastia, asterixis), and neurologic disease (nystagmus, ataxia, ophthalmoplegia, and asterixis, as well as confusion).

TABLE 12.5. The Ethanol Trauma Scale*a*

1. Have you had any fractures or dislocations of your bones or joints?
2. Have you been injured in a traffic accident?
3. Have you injured your head?
4. Have you been injured in an assault or fight (excluding sports injuries)?
5. Have you been injured while using ethanol?
6. Is anyone in your family ethanol-dependent?
7. Are you dependent on tobacco?
8. Did you start using ethanol or tobacco before age 18?

*a*The probability is more than 70% that patients with an elevated MCV who respond affirmatively to more than one of these questions are alcohol- or ethanol-dependent.

Source: Adapted from Skinner HA, Holt S, Schuller R, et al: Identification of alcohol abuse using laboratory tests and a history of trauma. *Ann Intern Medicine* 101:847, 1984.

3. Laboratory evaluations

a. Drug screens. Routine urine or blood drug screens can identify drug ingestion in the hours preceding the test and, in some cases (e.g., marijuana), drug use in the recent past. Although a positive drug screen does not indicate addiction, the presence of large quantities of a single drug or of multiple drugs of abuse is a good indicator of potential problems. Blood alcohol levels of $>$ 200 mg/100 mL in a conscious patient indicate tolerance and strongly suggest the diagnosis of alcoholism. Levels of $>$ 300 mg/100 mL in a conscious patient are virtually diagnostic of alcoholism. The results of drug screens must be considered in the context of other significant findings.

b. Electrolytes. Alterations in electrolytes can indicate secondary problems such as malnutrition, dehydration, and trauma.

c. Liver function tests (LFTs). Malnutrition and hepatitis secondary to drug addiction can produce elevated LFTs. Both alcohol and narcotic abuse are also associated with elevated liver enzymes.

d. Electrocardiogram. Abuse of sympathomimetics such as amphetamines and cocaine can produce tachycardia following acute drug or alcohol ingestion as well as in alcoholic withdrawal syndromes. Alcohol and other drugs of abuse may produce characteristic arrhythmias. It is not uncommon to find evidence of previously undetected myocardial infarctions among cocaine addicts who otherwise seem to be low-risk patients.

III. INTERACTION WITH SURGICAL DISORDERS

A. Intraoperative Management

1. Anesthetic technique. The primary factor in selection of an anesthetic agent is the magnitude of end-organ dysfunction related to drug use. Pharmacokinetic and pharmacodynamic alterations in drug response caused by organ dysfunction should be considered when selecting general anesthetics. Opioids and benzodiazepines are not necessarily contraindicated for patients with addictive disease. Tolerance may necessitate the use of higher doses of these drugs to achieve a suitable effect. Regional anesthetic administration may be preferable to general anesthesia because drug-induced alterations in pharmacokinetics and pharmacodynamics are less important. Regional anesthesia may also be used in conjunction with general anesthesia to reduce the amount of general anesthetic needed.

B. Acute Postoperative Management

1. Analgesia. Addictive disease is not an appropriate rationale for withholding potentially addictive postoperative analgesics. The addicted patient may have increased analgesic requirements due to the development of tolerance and cross-tolerance. Furthermore, provision of adequate pain relief in the acute postoperative period is central to good postoperative recovery for all patients but may be especially important for addicted patients who may also be experiencing symptoms of withdrawal. Withdrawal symptoms such as hyperadrenergia mimic the body's physiologic response to pain and may compromise postoperative recovery.

Recovering addicts are often concerned about the postoperative use of potentially addictive analgesics. Sound preoperative education is necessary to assure that the patient understands the importance of postoperative pain control and to allay unfounded fears of relapse.

TABLE 12.6. Guidelines for the Treatment of Addicted Patients with Chronic Pain

Written treatment plan for managing pain and related symptoms

Periodic reassessment of treatment plan with modifications as needed

Outline of treatment course in medical chart

Use of outside professional consultation (addiction specialists, psychologists, psychiatrists, pain management specialists, neurologists, neurosurgeons, etc.)

Ongoing relationship with patient's pharmacist

Continuous assessment for the presence of addictive behaviors

Use of nonpharmacologic treatments (e.g. physical therapy)

---

2. **Monitor for withdrawal syndrome.** Withdrawal can be a formidable problem in postoperative patient care. Surgeons must be keenly aware of the signs and symptoms of withdrawal in order to detect it early and to provide appropriate intervention immediately. Chapter 3 contains detailed descriptions of substance-specific withdrawal syndromes as well as treatment guidelines for such syndromes. The most effective treatment for withdrawal syndromes is prevention. Detection of addictive disorders in the preoperative period can, therefore, be vital to preventing postoperative complications.

C. **Chronic Postoperative Management.** Although administration of potentially addictive agents in the immediate postoperative period offers little risk for relapse or development of chronic dependence, chronic use of such agents may be problematic even in the absence of preexisting addictive illness. Preexisting addictive illness is generally a contraindication for the use of potentially addictive pain control drugs. When pain persists beyond the immediate postoperative period, pharmacologic treatment should focus on nonaddictive agents such as nonsteroidal antiinflammatory drugs (NSAIDs), salicylates, acetaminophen, and antidepressants. Opioids and sedative/hypnotics should be avoided not only because of the likelihood of addiction but also because their use might trigger a relapse to their drug of choice (such as alcohol). If these agents are absolutely necessary, they should be prescribed for well-defined periods with fixed doses and fixed, scheduled administration times. To closely monitor patients with addictive disorders for relapse and other patients for the development of addiction, the surgeon should follow the guidelines outlined in Table 12.6.

IV. COMBINED TREATMENT OF ADDICTIVE AND SURGICAL DISORDERS

A. **Bleeding Varices.** Endoscopic evaluation and sclerotherapy are indicated for bleeding varices. Pitressen (0.4 unit per minute intravenously) or a balloon tamponade may be useful. Shunts like the new TIPs procedure should be considered for patients with recurrent bleeding. Transplantation may have a role in very rare instances of acute bleeding.

B. **Liver Failure.** Diuretic therapy and peritoneal venous shunting are useful procedures for ascites. Transplantation is currently being offered earlier for patients with jaundice who qualify (Table 12.7). Transplantation should be

TABLE 12.7. Guidelines for Liver Transplantation in Alcoholic Patients

1. Candidates must have a life expectancy of <12 months without transplantation
2. Candidates must have enough social support to assure assistance in alcohol rehabilitation and in immunosuppressive treatment after the operation
3. Candidates must have achieved a minimum period of abstinence to be established by individual hospitals and their transplantation teams
4. Candidates must not currently be using alcohol or drugs
5. Candidates must not have symptoms of behavioral problems or psychiatric illnesses that could interfere with adherence to a postoperative medical regimen

Source: Criteria for Medicare coverage of adult liver transplantation—HCFA. Final notice. *Fed Reg* 56(71):15006–15008, 1991.

considered when death is imminent, when reversible damage to the central nervous system is inevitable, and when the quality of life has deteriorated to an unacceptable level. Studies indicate that the 3-year survival rate for liver transplantation is approaching 70% and should be considered for patients who are abstinent and seem likely to remain so.

C. Pancreatitis. Occasionally alcoholic patients who are in severe pain from chronic relapsing pancreatitis and have quit drinking are candidates for pancreatectomy and operative intervention may be helpful in some circumstances.

SELECTED READINGS

American Psychiatric Association: *Diagnostic and Statistical Manual of Mental Disorders. DSM-IV,* 4th ed. Washington, DC: American Psychiatric Association, 1994.

Beattie C, Mark L, Umbricht-Schneiter A: Anaesthesia and analgesia. In *Principles of Addiction Medicine.* Chevy Chase, MD: American Society of Addiction Medicine, 1994.

Clark HW: Policy and medical-legal issues in the prescribing of controlled substances. *J Psychoactive Drugs* 23:321, 1991.

Lieber CS: Interaction of ethanol with drugs, hepatotoxic agents, carcinogens and vitamins. *Alcohol Alcohol* 25:157, 1990.

Mattila MJ: Alcohol and drug interactions. *Ann Med* 22:363, 1990.

Maull KI, Kinning LS, Hickman JK: Culpability and accountability of hospitalized injured alcohol-impaired drivers. A prospective study. *JAMA* 252:1880, 1984.

Mayfield D, McLeod G, Hall P: The CAGE questionnaire: validation of a new alcoholism screening instrument. *Am J Psychiatry* 131:1121, 1974.

Moore RD, Bone LR, Geller G, et al: Prevalence, detection, and treatment of alcoholism in hospitalized patients. *JAMA* 261:403, 1989.

Rall TW: Hypnotics and sedatives: ethanol. In AG Gilman, TW Rall, AS Nies,

P Taylor (eds): *Goodman and Gilman's Pharmacological Basis of Therapeutics,* 8th ed. New York: Pergamon Press, 1990.

Silverman JJ, Peed SF, Goldberg S, et al: Surgical staff recognition of psychopathology in trauma patients. *J Trauma* 15:544, 1985.

Skinner HA, Holt S, Schuller R, et al: Identification of alcohol abuse using laboratory tests and a history of trauma. *Ann Intern Med* 101:847, 1984.

CHAPTER 13

TREATMENT OF COMORBID PSYCHIATRIC DISORDERS

Norman S. Miller, M.D.
& Philip G. Janicak, M.D.
University of Illinois at Chicago
Chicago, Illinois

I. INTRODUCTION

Although there are relative contraindications for the use of pharmacologic agents in addictive disorders alone, these agents can be used as indicated for comorbid psychiatric disorders in patients addicted to drugs and alcohol. The use of pharmacologic and nonpharmacologic treatments for addictive disorders and attendant psychiatric comorbidity requires an independent status for each disorder. (See *DSM-IV*.)

II. PSYCHOTROPICS FOR ADDICTIVE DISORDERS

A. Antidepressants

1. Only limited studies are available investigating the use of antidepressants in the treatment of addictive disorders or for the psychiatric complications of alcoholism and drug addiction. In general, antidepressants do not appear to alter the course of alcoholism or the symptoms of depression from the alcoholism.

2. Results from controlled studies have not confirmed a role for antidepressants in cocaine addiction.

B. Lithium

1. Lithium has been used in both uncontrolled and controlled trials for depressed and nondepressed alcoholics. While early open-label and uncontrolled studies suggested improved abstinence in alcoholics, especially those with a history of affective disorder, the criteria for alcoholism and depression differed widely, methods for measuring treatment response varied, and dropout rates were 30–59%.

2. In a multisite, double-blind, placebo-controlled study, the effect of lithium versus placebo in 200 randomly assigned alcoholics with no other psychiatric illness was compared to 200 alcoholics with a diagnosis of major depressive disorder or dysthymic dis-

Manual of Therapeutics for Addictions, Edited by Norman S. Miller, Mark S. Gold, and David E. Smith.
ISBN 0471-56176-2 © 1997 John Wiley & Sons, Inc.

order. Although no significant differences were found among the four groups (i.e., depressed alcoholics on lithium or placebo and nondepressed alcoholics on lithium or placebo), the depressed alcoholics on lithium tended to show the poorest abstinence rate.

C. Antipsychotics

1. Antipsychotics have not been investigated extensively in the treatment of addictive disorders. Theoretical consideration suggests that dopamine (DA) blockade should intensify the drive to drink or to use other drugs by reducing the stimulation of DA to postsynaptic neurons in the reinforcement area. The putative "addiction substrate" is specifically the mesolimbic pathway that contains DA neurons extending from the ventral tegmentum to the nucleus accumbens. Clinically, there is no indication that neuroleptics alter the course of alcoholism or drug addiction alone without a psychiatric comorbidity.

D. Benzodiazepines. Benzodiazepines and their agonists have not been extensively studied as a substitute for alcohol, ostensibly because of the clinical and research experience showing that alcoholics tend to relapse to alcohol while on benzodiazepines. Further, benzodiazepines as a class are addicting and produce significant pharmacologic tolerance and dependence. Recent controlled studies found that symptoms of anxiety, depression, and insomnia worsened despite continued use of benzodiazepines. Thus, these findings do not support the value of long-term benzodiazepine therapy.

III. TREATMENT FOR THE COMORBID DISORDERS

A. Need to Treat Multiple Disorders

1. It is widely acknowledged that the treatment of addictive disorders can be difficult without adequate treatment of the psychiatric disorder. For instance, a schizophrenic patient who is hallucinating and delusional, but who also uses alcohol or drugs, cannot participate in treatment for the addiction without adequate control over the psychosis. Likewise, a manic patient who is euphoric and delusional, an anergic depressive patient, or an agoraphobic patient addicted to alcohol and/or other drugs will have difficulty cooperating with addiction treatment.

2. Nonpharmacologic treatment of a comorbid addictive disorder is necessary for a schizophrenic, manic, depressive, or phobic patient to enhance compliance with psychiatric treatments. It is known that poor control of the addictive disorder can lead to an unfavorable prognosis for the concurrent psychiatric disorder. The prognosis of combined psychiatric and addictive disorders follows more closely that of the addictive disorders. Thus, treatment of the addictive disorder seems necessary to improve the course of either disorder.

B. Limitations of Pharmacologic Agents in Addicted Populations

1. Pharmacologic agents have limitations in the addicted population. Medications may impair cognition and blunt feelings, sometimes subtly. Clinicians treating addictive disorders advo-

cate that the alcoholic or addict needs a clear sensorium and access to emotions to make fundamental changes in them. The recovering alcoholic or drug addict must take an active part in changing attitudes and in abandoning the long-held belief that alcohol and / or drugs can "treat" life problems and uncomfortable psychological states.

2. Symptoms such as anxiety and depression in recovering addicts might be vital to recovery, and pharmacotherapy to treat such symptoms must be considered carefully in this context. Clinically, anxiety and depression can provide the motivation to change when the sufferer otherwise has little awareness of the need to alter behavior. A commonly used expression to explain this practice among recovering individuals is "no pain, no gain."

B. Standard of Care

1. After detoxification and stabilization with pharmacologic agents, the current treatment of choice for addictive disorders is nonpharmacologic. Further, several studies have shown that treating addictive disorders with abstinence alone results in improvement of the psychiatric syndromes associated with the alcohol and / or drug use or addiction. Severe syndromes induced by alcohol that may meet criteria for major depressive and anxiety disorders in *DSM-IV* resolve within days to weeks with abstinence. Likewise, manic syndromes induced by cocaine resolve within hours to days, and schizophrenia-like syndromes (e.g., hallucinations and delusions) induced by cocaine and PCP often resolve within days to weeks with abstinence.

2. Further studies are needed to confirm the clinical experience that psychiatric symptoms (including anxiety, depression, and personality disorders) respond to specific treatment of the addiction. For example, cognitive behavioral techniques employed in the 12-step treatment approach have been effective in the management of anxiety and depression associated with addiction.

IV. PSYCHOTROPICS FOR COMORBID PSYCHIATRIC DISORDERS

A. General Aspects

1. Because alcohol and drugs can induce almost any psychiatric symptom or sign or mimic any psychiatric disorder, their effects must always be considered before a comorbid or dual diagnosis is established or treated.

2. With an understanding of the interactions between psychiatric syndromes and alcoholism or drug addiction, a rational approach can be applied to the use of pharmacologic therapies in comorbid disorders. The use of medications for psychiatric symptoms should begin only after the knowledge of the natural history of the addictive disorder and other psychiatric disorders is clarified. Further, skill must be developed to identify the respective roles of addictive and other psychiatric disorders in the generation of psychiatric symptoms.

3. Generally, psychiatric symptoms induced by alcohol or drugs resolve within days to weeks. Moreover, studies show that non-

anxious and nondepressed alcoholics continue to drink despite alcohol-induced anxiety and depression and not because of these symptoms. Alcohol use was negatively correlated with depressive episodes in nonalcoholics with bipolar or unipolar disorders. While alcohol consumption was elevated in the manic phase, so were other hyperactive behaviors. In many studies, the prevalence rates for anxiety and affective disorders in alcoholics were not greater than that for nonalcoholics.

4. A retrospective history of psychiatric symptoms can often lead to an inflated diagnosis of these disorders because of rationalizations and minimizations regarding drinking and drug use by the individual. Typically, psychiatric symptoms are emphasized by both the patient and the psychiatric examiner.

5. Longitudinal observation frequently clarifies the role of alcohol and drugs in the production of anxiety, affective, psychotic, or personality symptoms, particularly if objective criteria are relied on in addition to the addict's subjective report. Also, specific treatment of addictive disorders can result in improvement of mood, psychotic behavior, and personality disturbances if related to the alcohol or drug use. Mood lability and personality states can be a manifestation of addictive disorders, and treatment of the addictive disorder can lead to stabilization of these psychiatric symptoms.

B. Anxiety Disorders

1. General approach

a. Prevalence rates for the comorbidity of anxiety and addiction disorders range from 5–20% in epidemiologic and clinical studies.

b. These antianxiety agents can also oversedate and dull the individual's reaction to internal and external influences. Because anxiety in recovery can be critically important for emotional growth, the individual must feel a certain amount of anxiety to motivate change in behavior, attitudes, and emotions. The expression "emotional growth" is related to the anxiety or discomfort a recovering individual feels while undergoing the process of change to reach a more mature state.

c. Depressants (e.g., alcohol) can produce anxiety during withdrawal, and stimulants (e.g., cocaine) can produce anxiety during intoxication. Because alcoholics and drug addicts are in a relatively constant state of withdrawal (it is impossible to maintain a constant blood level), they regularly experience anxiety from pharmacologic withdrawal (dependence). As the alcohol and drug use become more chronic, the anxiety from pharmacologic dependence can become increasingly severe. Relapse and/or periods of abstinence (sometimes prolonged—weeks or months) must be considered (confirmation of abstinence with laboratory drug testing, if necessary) before the effects of depressant or stimulant drugs in inducing anxiety can be ruled out. It can take weeks or months for these effects to subside completely, although a period of only a few days to weeks is often sufficient in clinical practice.

d. Treatment is indicated when the anxiety persists after adequate effort in a recovery program for addiction. A thorough evaluation to assess whether the individual is abstinent, using continuing treatment and/or attending self-help meetings, and using other forms of addiction therapy is usually necessary before a diagnosis of psychiatric comorbidity can be definitively established. After such an evaluation, treatment of the anxiety disorder can proceed separately from similar symptoms arising from the addictive disorder.

2. Pharmacologic therapies

a. The ideal medication works against abnormal anxiety but not against the "normal" anxiety needed for recovery. Some of the physical symptoms of anxiety include sweating, tremors, palpitations, muscle tension, and increased urination. Psychological symptoms include nervousness, feelings of dread or impending doom (apprehension), unpleasant tenseness, and many more.

b. The most common agents used in anxiety disorders are benzodiazepines and antidepressants. The benzodiazepines most frequently used are alprazolam and lorazepam. Diazepam and clonazepam are used less often. Because the benzodiazepines can cause significant problems in addicted and nonaddicted patients, they are not generally recommended for alcoholics and drug addicts or for long-term treatment of anxiety or depressive disorders.

c. Antidepressants such as imipramine and nortriptyline and SSRIs such as fluoxetine have a low addiction potential and can be used with relative safety in either the addicted or the nonaddicted patient. They differ in their tendency to produce sedation and anxiety and have a withdrawal syndrome of their own. Because of its anticholinergic properties, imipramine is more sedating, but nortriptyline and the SSRIs can produce anxiousness in some individuals and sedation in others. Not all individuals react the same way to these medications.

d. When medications are used, a specific target symptom should be the focus. Also, medications should be tried in time-limited intervals, such as weeks to months. A drug holiday should then be attempted to see if the medication is still necessary.

e. The patient should be instructed that the medications will not "cure" the addiction, that treatment of anxiety will not control the addiction, and that treatment of the addiction will not necessarily ameliorate the anxiety disorder. In essence, the addiction must be treated independently of the anxiety disorder and vice versa.

C. Depressive Disorders

1. General approach

a. Prevalence rates for the comorbidity of depressive and addictive disorders range from 5–25% in epidemiologic and clinical studies.

b. Depressive disorders include major depressive and dysthymic disorders, which can occur independently with addictive disorders, or similar depressive symptoms can be induced by alcohol and drug disorders. Depression can be viewed as protective and associated with "healing" in many conditions involving emotions. For example, a grief reaction is an expected experience after a loss, with depression an essential emotion in this process. Recovery from an addictive disorder has been compared to a grief reaction because of losses suffered by the addict (e.g., alcohol, drugs, relationships). Likewise, and analogous to the role of anxiety, depression is also a part of the healing process the addict experiences during recovery from addictive disorders.

c. Depressant drugs (e.g., alcohol) can produce depression during intoxication, and stimulant drugs (e.g., cocaine) can produce depression during withdrawal. These effects may be prolonged with certain drugs that linger in the body (i.e., stored in fat), such as cannabis and benzodiazepines. These drugs can produce depression or anxiety that is indistinguishable from other psychiatric causes of depression. Therefore, they must be considered causative whenever depression is present, and the possibility of addiction must be assessed when these drugs are identified. While depression may persist for weeks or months, it often resolves within days with abstinence from these drugs. Major depressive disorder is more common in older individuals and in females and can be difficult to distinguish from the depression induced by alcohol or drugs.

2. Pharmacologic therapies

a. The use of medication is recommended if the depression persists beyond a few weeks of drug withdrawal or arises during confirmed abstinence (laboratory drug testing may be necessary to confirm abstinence). The risk of suppressing normal depressive processes during recovery versus the benefit from suppressing depression that is interfering with function must be weighed, as is the case with anxiety disorders.

b. Antidepressants are the mainstay of treatment for depression. The target symptoms are a sad mood, tearfulness, appetite and sleep disturbances, and other neurovegetative symptoms. Depression can be found in many conditions, including a variety of psychiatric and medical disorders.

c. Depressive disorders are thought to have a significant biological component, including deficiencies in such CNS neurotransmitters as serotonin, norepinephrine, and dopamine. Interestingly, these neurotransmitters are also affected by alcohol and other drugs of addiction. These agents are thought to act by enhancing the activity of these neurotransmitters, ultimately alleviating depression and stabilizing mood. Examples of several different antidepressants distinguished by their actions on neurotransmitters are given in Table 13.1.

D. Bipolar Disorders

1. General approach

a. Prevalence rates for the comorbidity of bipolar and addictive disorders range from 30–60% in epidemiologic and clinical studies.

b. Mania is a condition associated with elevated mood, grandiosity, hyperactive behavior, poor judgment, and lack of insight. The manic patient

TABLE 13.1. Biochemical Activity[a] **of Commonly Used Antidepressant Drugs**

	Norepinephrine	Serotonin	α-Adrenergic
Amitriptyline	1	2	3
Doxepin	2	1	2
Desipramine	3	0	1
Nortriptyline	2	<1	1
Fluoxetine	0	3	2
Trazodone	0	1	2

[a]<0, no effect; 1, mild, moderate; 3, major.

will show excesses such as spending sprees, sexual promiscuity, intrusiveness, and abnormal alcohol and drug use. A manic episode can follow, precede, or alternate with depressive episodes.

c. The manic state can be produced by stimulants (e.g., cocaine) during intoxication, and during withdrawal from depressants (e.g., alcohol). A period of confirmed abstinence is usually necessary before mood-stabilizing drugs are started. Generally, a period of a week or two may be required for the role of drugs in inducing manic symptoms to be properly assessed.

2. Pharmacologic therapies

a. Mood stabilizers control bipolar disorder in patients with or without comorbid addictive disorder. These medications can control either the manic or depressed phase, or both.

b. Manic episodes can occur cyclically, alternatively, and concurrently with depressed episodes. One theory of the pathogenesis of bipolar disorder is thought to involve the neurotransmitter norepinephrine (i.e., excessive in mania and deficient in depression).

c. Lithium is a natural salt, available in the carbonate form and slow-release preparations. Its exact mechanism of action is unknown, but it can be effective in reducing or preventing the recurrence of manic and depressive episodes. Lithium carbonate must be taken daily in doses of 600–2400 mg to achieve plasma levels in the 0.5–1.5-m equiv/L range.

d. Anticonvulsant mood stabilizers include divalproex sodium and carbamazepine. They can be effective in controlling mania and, some evidence suggests, in comorbid addictive disorders as well. One theoretical explanation for their mechanism of action for carbamazepine involves suppression of mood centers in the limbic system that act like seizure foci. In this context, a "kindling" model has been proposed for both mood and addictive disorders.

E. Psychotic Disorders

1. General approach

a. Prevalence rates for comorbidity of schizophrenic and addictive disorders range from 40–80% in epidemiologic and clinical studies.

b. Schizophrenia is a chronic illness characterized by bizarre thinking and behavior. Hallucinations and delusions are "positive" symptoms of the psychotic process, while symptoms such as social withdrawal and poverty of emotions are "negative" symptoms (or deficit syndrome). Conventional neuroleptics are more effective for positive symptoms, whereas behavioral, group, and individual psychotherapy are more effective for the negative symptoms. Newer agents such as clozapine and risperidone may be more effective in treating both the positive and negative symptoms.

c. Psychosis can be caused by stimulant drug use during intoxication and depressant drug/alcohol use during withdrawal. A period of weeks or months may be necessary to assess the effects of drugs of addiction, but as with anxiety, depression, or mania, medications can be started at almost any time if the psychosis is persistent and waiting is not possible. Moreover, the greater the number of psychiatric admissions, the greater the probability of a chronic mental disorder associated with the comorbid addictive disorder.

TABLE 13.2A. Potencies and Side-Effect Profiles of Various Psychotropic Drugs

Antipsychotic	Sedative Effect	Anticholinergic Effect	Hypotensive Effect	Extrapyramidal Effects	Addiction Potential
Chlorpromazine	High	Medium	High	Medium	Medium
Thioridazine	High	High	High	Low	Medium
Fluphenazine	Medium	Low	Low	High	Low
Perphenazine	Low	Low	Low	High	Low
Trifluoperazine	Medium	Low	Low	High	Low
Thiothixene	Low	Low	Low	High	Low
Loxapine	Medium	Medium	Medium	High	Low
Droperidol	Low	Low	Low	High	Low
Haloperidol	Low	Low	Low	High	Low
Molindone	Medium	Medium	Low	High	Low
Risperidone	Low	Low	Medium	Low	Low
Clozapine	Low	Low	Medium	Low	Low

TABLE 13.2B. Potencies and Side Effects of Various Psychotropic Drugs

Antidepressant	Sedative effect	Anticholinergic effect	Hypotensive effect	Extrapyramidal effects	Addiction potential
Amitriptyline	High	High	High	Low	Medium
Amoxapine	Low	Low	High	Low	Low
Desipramine	Low	Low	Medium	Low	Medium
Doxepin	High	Medium	Medium	Low	Medium
Imipramine	Medium	Medium	High	Low	Medium
Nortriptyline	Low	Low	Medium	Low	Low
Bupropion	Low	Low	Low	Low	Low
Trazodone	Low	Low	Low	Low	Low
Fluoxetine	Low	Low	Low	Low	Low
Venlafaxine	Low	Low	Low	Low	Low
Sertraline	Low	Low	Low	Low	Low
Paroxetine	Low	Low	Low	Low	Low
Nefazodone	Low	Low	Low	Low	Low

TABLE 13.2C. Potencies and Side-Effect Profiles of Various Psychotropic Drugs

Antianxiety agent	Sedative effect	Anticholinergic effect	Hypotensive effect	Extrapyramidal effects	Addiction potential
Alprazolam	High	Low	Low	Low	High
Buspirone	Low	Low	Low	Low	High
Lorazepam	High	Low	Low	Low	High
Clonazepam	High	Low	Low	Low	High
Diazepam	High	Low	Low	Low	High

2. Pharmacologic agents. High- or moderate-potency neuroleptics are generally the agents of choice in the treatment of schizophrenia (e.g., haloperidol or thiothixene). The potency is determined by the drug's ability to block the action of the neurotransmitter dopamine at postsynaptic DA_2 receptor sites (see Tables 13.2A–C).

V. ADVERSE EFFECTS

A. Antianxiety Agents. While benzodiazepines are useful in the short term, their efficacy wanes with long- term use, probably because of the development of pharmacologic tolerance and dependence. Importantly, benzodiazepines can be addicting, particularly in those already addicted to other substances.

B. Antipsychotic Agents. Antipsychotics can produce sedation and hypotension (at times causing lightheadedness and syncope in some individuals), particularly with postural changes. Conventional neuroleptics produce acute extrapyramidal reactions, which include pseudoparkinsonism, dystonia, and akathisia. Dystonia usually responds to treatment with anticholinergic drugs such as benztropine or diphenhydramine. Akathisia is the subjective feeling of anxiety and tension causing the patient to feel compelled to move about restlessly. This symptom usually requires a beta blocker as a decrease in the antipsychotic dose does not work. Alternatively, switching to risperidone may accomplish the intended effect while avoiding intolerable neurologic syndromes.

C. Antidepressants

1. Antidepressants, particularly the tricyclics, can produce sedation, hypotension, syncope, and other anticholinergic effects. The SSRIs can produce anxiousness, sedation, insomnia, and gastrointestinal upset. A withdrawal syndrome has also been reported with most antidepressant medications.
2. The SSRIs are preferred in patients with comorbid addiction because of their lack of addiction potential, anticholinergic effects on the sensorium, and risk of lethal effects from overdose.

D. Cognitive State in Recovery

1. The recovering alcoholic or addict must have a clear mind and a stable mood. Medications have a tendency, sometimes subtly and other times obviously, to dull the sensorium and thinking and / or blunt or disrupt the emotional state. Addicts must eventually change and control feelings to remain sober and also to comply with psychiatric management. The addict's ability to use the 12 steps of Alcoholics Anonymous (AA) and accept psychiatric advice will depend on clear thinking and emotional balance, which is stressed as central to the recovery process in AA.
2. Accordingly, the use of medications should be conservative, taking into consideration the pros and cons of their expected positive and negative effects. Unfortunately, few psychiatric medications are totally free of mood-altering properties.

E. Dosing. Because of the inherent susceptibility to drug effects by alcoholics and drug addicts, it is important to use the lowest effective doses as possible. Also, the intervals for administration should be selected to reduce effects on cognition and feelings.

SELECTED READINGS

Alterman AI, Erdlen FR, Murphy E: Alcohol abuse in the psychiatric hospital population. *Addict Behav* 6:69–73, 1981.

American Psychiatric Association. *Diagnostic and Statistical Manual, 4th ed.* Washington, DC: American Psychiatric Association, 1994.

Bernadt MW, Murray RM: Psychiatric disorder, drinking and alcoholism: what are the link? *Br J Psychiatry* 148:393–400, 1986.

Blankfield A: Psychiatric symptoms in alcohol dependence: diagnostic and treatment implications. *J Substance Abuse Treatment* 3:275–278, 1986.

Brown SA, Schuckit MA: Changes in depression among abstinent alcoholics. *J Stud Alcohol* 49:412–417, 1988.

Ciraulo DA, Alderson LM, Chapron DJ, Jaffe JH, Subbarao B, Kramer PA: Imipramine disposition in alcoholics. *J Clin Psychopharmacol* 2:2–7, 1982.

Ciraulo DA, Jaffe JH: Tricyclic antidepressants in the treatment of depression associated with alcoholism. *J Clin Psychopharmacol* 1:146–150, 1981.

Dorus W, Ostrow DG, Anton R, et al: Lithium treatment of depressed and nondepressed alcoholics. *JAMA* 262:1646–1652, 1989.

Drake RE, Osher FC, Wallach MA: Alcohol use and abuse in schizophrenia: a prospective community study. *J Nerv Ment Dis* 177:408–414, 1989.

Fawcett J, Clark DC, Gibbons RD, et al: Evaluation of lithium therapy for alcoholism. *J Clin Psychiatry* 45:494–499, 1984.

Fine J, Miller NS: Methodological approach to psychiatric and addictive disorders in drug and alcohol dependence. In NS Miller (ed): *Comorbidity of Addictive and Psychiatric Disorders.* New York: Haworth Press, 1993.

Hoffmann NG, Miller NS: Treatment outcome for abstinence-based programs. *Psychiatric Ann* 22:402–407, 1992.

Janicak PG, Davis JM, Preskorn SH, and Ayd F Jr: *Principles and Practice of Psychopharmacotherapy.* Baltimore, MD: Williams & Wilkins, 1993.

Keso L, Salaspuro M: Inpatient treatment of employed alcoholics: a randomized clinical trial on Hazelden-type and traditional treatment. *Alcohol Clin Exp Res* 14:584–589, 1990.

Kline NS, Wren JC, Cooper TB, Varga E, Canal O: Evaluation of lithium therapy in chronic and periodic alcoholism. *Am J Med Sci* 268:15–22, 1974.

Kofoed L, Kanie J, Walsh T: Outpatient treatment of patients with substance abuse and coexisting psychiatric disorders. *Am J Psychiatry* 143:867–872, 1986.

Liskow BI, Goodwin DW: Pharmacologic treatment of alcohol intoxication, withdrawal and dependence: a critical review. *J Stud Alcohol* 8:356–370, 1987.

Merry J, Reynolds CM, Bailey J, Coppen A: Prophylactic treatment of alcoholism by lithium carbonate. *Lancet* 2:481–482, 1976.

Miller NS: The psychiatric consequences of alcohol and drugs of abuse and addiction. In NS Miller (ed): *The Pharmacology of Alcohol, Drugs of Abuse and Addiction.* New York: Springer-Verlag, 1991, pp 77–88.

Miller NS: Comorbidity of psychiatric and alcohol/drug disorders: critical overview and future directions for "dual diagnosis." *J Addict Dis* 12:5–16, 1993.

Miller NS, Gold MS: Abuse, addiction, tolerance and dependence to benzodiazepines: in medical and nonmedical populations. *Am J Alcohol Drug Abuse* 17:27–39, 1991.

Miller NS, Gold MS: The psychiatrist's role in integrating pharmacologic and nonpharmacologic treatments for addictive disorders. *Psychiatric Ann* 22:436–440, 1992.

Miller NS, Mahler JC, Belkin BM, Gold MS: Psychiatric diagnosis in alcohol and drug dependence. *Ann Clin Psychiatry* 3:79–89, 1991.

Miller SI, Frances RJ, Holmes DJ: Psychotic medications. In WR Miller (ed): *Alcoholism Treatment Approaches.* Elmsford, NY: Pergamon Press, 1990, pp 231–241.

Penick EC, Powell BJ, Nickel EJ, et al: Comorbidity of lifetime of psychiatric disorder among male alcoholics. *Alcohol Clin Exp Res* 18:1289–1293, 1994.

Rickels K, Schweizer E, Case G, Greenblatt DJ: Long-term therapeutic use of benzodiazepines, I: effects of abrupt discontinuation. *Arch Gen Psychiatry* 47:899–907, 1990.

Schuckit MA: Alcoholism and other psychiatric disorders. *Hosp Commun Psychiatry* 43:53–57, 1982.

Schuckit MA: *Dual Diagnosis: Psychiatric Picture Among Substance Abusers. Principles of Addiction Medicine.* Washington, DC: American Society of Addiction Medicine, 1994.

Schuckit MA, Montero MG: Alcoholism, anxiety, depression. *Br J Addiction* 83:1373–1380, 1988.

Schweizer E, Rickels K, Case G, Greenblatt DJ: Long-term therapeutic use of benzodiazepines, II: effects of gradual taper. *Arch Gen Psychiatry* 47:908–915, 1990.

Schweizer E, Rickels K, Weiss S, Zavodnick S: Maintenance drug treatment for panic disorder, I: results of a prospective, placebo-controlled comparison of alprazolam and imipramine. *Arch Gen Psychiatry* 50:51–60, 1993.

Tamerin JS, Mendelson JH: The psychodynamics of chronic inebriation: observations of alcoholics during the process of drinking in an experimental group setting. *Am J Psychiatry* 125:886–899, 1969.

Walsh EC, Hingson RW, Merrigan DM, et al: A randomized trial of treatment options for alcohol abusing workers. *N Engl J Med* 325:775–782, 1991.

Young LD, Patel M, Keller MH: The effect of lithium carbonate on alcoholism in 20 male patients with concurrent major affective disorder. *Currents Alcohol* 8:175–181, 1981.

CHAPTER 14

TREATMENT OF ADDICTIVE DISORDERS IN WOMEN

Laura J. Miller, M.D.
Assistant Professor
Department of Psychiatry
University of Illinois at Chicago
Chicago, Illinois

For many years, most studies of addiction were done exclusively with male subjects. It was assumed that the findings in men would apply to women. More recently, studies comparing women to men have found significant gender differences in the epidemiology, clinical presentation, pharmacology, and sociocultural aspects of addiction. These gender differences have important implications for identifying and treating women with addictive disorders.

I. GENDER DIFFERENCES IN THE EPIDEMIOLOGY OF ADDICTIVE DISORDERS

A. As a group, women drink alcohol less and use illegal drugs less than men.

B. As a group, women overuse prescribed addictive drugs more than men.

C. Women's use of addictive substances has increased over the last few decades, especially among young women of childbearing age. This trend is exemplified by data on nicotine addiction; the prevalence of smoking in men has continued to fall since the mid-1960s, while the prevalence in women has remained the same. By 1986, lung cancer had surpassed breast cancer as the leading cause of cancer death in women.

D. As compared with alcoholic men, alcoholic women have a more rapid deterioration; they begin drinking at a later age, but appear for treatment at about the same age and with the same severity of illness.

II. GENDER DIFFERENCES IN THE CLINICAL PRESENTATION OF ADDICTION

A. In women, medical complications of alcoholism appear sooner in the course of the disease than they do in men. These include liver disease,

---

Manual of Therapeutics for Addictions, Edited by Norman S. Miller, Mark S. Gold, and David E. Smith.
ISBN 0471-56176-2 © 1997 John Wiley & Sons, Inc.

hypertension, anemia, malnutrition, and gastrointestinal disease. In addition, there is some evidence for a dose–response relationship between alcohol intake and the likelihood of developing breast cancer.

B. Women are more likely than men to be addicted to multiple substances. This gender difference is especially pronounced in the concomitant use of alcohol with benzodiazepines or other prescription drugs.

C. Addicted women are more likely than addicted men to have a concomitant psychiatric disorder. The most common associated disorder for women is major depression. Suicide attempts are about 4 times more frequent in alcoholic women than in nonalcoholic women. Bulimia and drug addiction also commonly occur together.

D. Women with alcoholism have significantly lower self-esteem than men with alcoholism.

E. Women with addictive disorders have significantly higher incidences of past sexual abuse, rape, and being the victim of violence than do nonaddicted women.

F. Women with addictive disorders exhibit significantly fewer antisocial behaviors than do men with addictive disorders.

G. Women alcoholics are more likely than men to do their drinking in private.

H. Women smokers are more likely than men to seek help to quit.

I. For women, fear of weight gain is a major factor in initiating smoking, and in failure to quit smoking.

III. GENDER DIFFERENCES IN THE PHARMACOKINETICS OF ADDICTIVE SUBSTANCES

A. A given dose of ethanol produces a higher blood alcohol concentration in women, on average, than in men. Factors that contribute to this include:

1. In women, total body water is a lower percentage of total body weight.

2. Women have lower levels of gastric alcohol dehydrogenase, which means that less ethanol is metabolized in the stomach, and more is absorbed into the bloodstream.

B. In men, blood alcohol concentrations after a given dose of ethanol tend to be the same day to day. In women, there is more variability. Some of the variability may be linked to the menstrual cycle.

C. The clinical implications of these differences are that most women react more intensely to a given amount of alcohol than do most men, and that women can less reliably predict the effect a drink will have on them.

IV. SOCIOCULTURAL INFLUENCES ON WOMEN WITH ADDICTIVE DISORDERS

A. There is, in many cultural contexts, a greater social stigma attached to women using addictive substances as compared to men. This seems particularly true for alcohol. This is partly protective, as there is less social pressure for women to drink. However, the stigma poses a formidable barrier to seeking treatment.

B. For women, social-role deprivation (i.e., women who are unmarried, unemployed, and have no children to care for, or women who have lost previously important family roles) is associated with a higher incidence of problem drinking.

C. For certain subcultures of women, addictive substances become associated with female camaraderie and the passage from girlhood into womanhood. For example, immigrant women from India, New Guinea, and Southeast Asia commonly chew betel-nut quid, a highly addictive mixture with significant health hazards. This practice is almost entirely confined to women, and typically begins when a woman first gives birth to a child.

D. Women are more likely than men to relate the onset of their addiction to a stressful event in their lives.

E. Despite the recent increase in prevalence of addictive disorders in women, the ratio of men to women in addiction treatment programs has remained constant. This seems strongly influenced by social factors that disproportionately affect women, such as financial barriers, lack of childcare, and fear of child-custody loss.

F. For women, there is a strong correlation between the use of addictive substances and the addictions of significant people in their lives, more so than for men. Notable examples are women's drinking patterns being tied to those of their spouses, and daughters' smoking habits being significantly linked to their mothers' smoking status.

V. EFFECTS OF ADDICTION ON FEMALE SEXUAL AND REPRODUCTIVE FUNCTION

The effects of addiction on sexuality are complex. They include physiologic effects of addictive substances on sexual functioning, cultural beliefs about the effects of these substances on sexual functioning, the effects of addiction in sexual partners, and the use of sexuality to obtain drugs.

A. A long-standing cultural myth attributes aphrodisiac and sexually disinhibiting qualities to addictive substances such as cocaine, alcohol, marijuana, heroin, and LSD. Studies have demonstrated that a number of addictive drugs physiologically depress sexual functioning.

B. Nevertheless, many women, especially alcoholic women, report subjectively experiencing greater sexual arousal, desire, and enjoyment while drinking.

C. At the same time, alcoholic women *and* spouses of alcoholic men report significantly more overall sexual dissatisfaction than do other women.

D. A related cultural belief is that intoxicated or addicted women are promiscuous. There is some empirical support for this belief with respect to alcoholic women, many of whom report that drinking renders them more likely to have sex with partners they would otherwise avoid. However, few lighter drinkers report these behavioral changes with drinking.

E. Addiction is closely linked with sexual victimization, including unwanted sexual advances by others who are intoxicated, and supporting illicit-drug habits by prostitution.

F. Chronic alcohol, cocaine, or heroin use may inhibit ovulation and cause irregular menstrual cycles. This intermittent impairment of fertility, combined with poor judgment and planning related to addiction, may contribute to a lack of family planning and unwanted pregnancies. The offspring of such pregnancies are at high risk of adverse effects of the addiction (see Chapter 15).

G. Women with premenstrual dysphoria tend to increase their use of addictive substances before their menstrual periods. Further, drug addiction is correlated with a higher incidence of menstruation-related symptoms.

VI. IDENTIFICATION OF ADDICTIVE DISORDERS IN WOMEN

A. There are several factors that make it more difficult to identify addiction in women as compared with men. They include the following:

1. Because of the greater cultural stigma against women drinking, women tend to drink more while alone.

2. Alcoholic women, as a group, drink less than alcoholic men. A woman may report drinking what sounds (to a clinician accustomed to standards developed in studies of men) like a relatively small amount, and may have more severe consequences than expected. This is due in part to gender differences in pharmacokinetics (see Section III) and in part to combined alcohol/benzodiazepine addiction in many women.

3. Women are less likely to get into public fights while intoxicated, and are less likely to be arrested while intoxicated. As a group, they are less likely to be employed than addicted men, and therefore are less likely to go through employee assistance programs. For men, these are common routes of entry into addiction treatment.

4. Healthcare providers may be subject to cultural gender biases, and as a result are less likely to suspect drug addiction in women than in men.

5. Women may fear, often correctly, that custody of their children will be in jeopardy if they reveal addiction in order to enter treatment.

B. The following measures can facilitate identification of addiction in women:

1. Since women have a higher incidence of comorbid medical and psychiatric problems, screening among hospital and clinic patients is a productive means of identification.

2. Another helpful means of identifying addicted women is to routinely assess the spouses or partners of men in addiction treatment programs.

3. Public policy that emphasizes treatment access rather than punitive measures is likely to facilitate identification of addicted women.

VII. TREATMENT CONSIDERATIONS FOR WOMEN WITH ADDICTIVE DISORDERS

Women are underrepresented in addiction treatment programs. This may be due, in part, to the design of traditional treatment delivery systems. Factors to consider in developing programs responsive to women's needs include the following:

A. *Providing childcare.*

B. *Identifying and treating comorbid disorders.* One tradition in addiction treatment holds that it is problematic to focus on other problems until the addiction is controlled. However, for women with significant comorbid conditions, such as eating disorder, sexual abuse, major depression, or domestic violence, it is essential to simultaneously address those conditions. Unless these comorbid disorders are treated, their presence renders addiction treatment less effective, and the woman is more vulnerable to relapse. Treatments for addiction and comorbid conditions must be integrated with one another, rather than compartmentalized.

C. *Identifying addiction to prescription drugs,* and communicating with prescribing physicians.

D. *Decreasing financial and emotional dependence on addicted partners,* and attempting to bring addicted partners into treatment.

E. *Addressing adverse effects of addiction on the woman's children and family life.* Interventions can include
   1. Psychoeducation about effects of addictive drugs on fetuses, children, and family structure.
   2. Parenting skills training.
   3. Intensive in-home family rehabilitation. This involves a counselor spending 20–30 h per week in the patient's home for 4–6 weeks, assisting the family with communication and household management, and helping the family connect with community resources.

F. *Providing education on the effects of addiction on reproduction, sexuality, and risk of sexually transmitted diseases.* Integrated family planning services are extremely useful.

G. *Self-esteem and assertiveness training.*

H. *Women role models and sponsors.*

Although all this can be provided in mixed-gender programs, women-only programs are a viable alternative. Programs particularly geared to lesbian women are also helpful for this high-risk population.

SELECTED READINGS

Beckman LJ: Self-esteem of women alcoholics. *J Stud Alcohol* 39:491, 1978.

Blume S: Women, alcohol, and drugs. In NS Miller (ed): *Comprehensive Handbook of Drug and Alcohol Addiction.* New York: Marcel Dekker, 1991.

Klassen AD, Wilsnack SC: Sexual experience and drinking among women in a U.S. national survey. *Arch Sexual Behav* 15:363, 1986.

Schmidt C, Klee L, Ames G: Review and analysis of literature on indicators of women's drinking problems. *Br J Addiction* 85:179, 1990.

Van Thiel DH, Gavaler JS: The adverse effects of ethanol upon hypothalamic-pituitary-gonadal function in males and females compared and contrasted. *Alcoholism: Clin Exp Res* 6:179, 1982.

Weisner C, Schmidt L: Gender disparities in treatment for alcohol problems. *JAMA* 268:1872, 1992.

Wilsnack RW, Cheloha RL: Women's roles and problem drinking across the lifespan. *Soc Problems* 34:231, 1987.

Winick C: Substances of use and abuse and sexual behavior. In JH Lowinson, P Ruiz, RB Millman (eds): *Substance Abuse: A Comprehensive Textbook,* 2nd ed. Baltimore: Williams & Wilkins, 1992.

CHAPTER 15

TREATMENT OF ADDICTIVE DISORDERS DURING PREGNANCY

Laura J. Miller, M.D.
Assistant Professor
Department of Psychiatry
University of Illinois
Chicago, Illinois

Rubeena Mian, M.D.
Department of Psychiatry
Chicago, Illinois

I. ADDICTION DURING PREGNANCY: GENERAL CONSIDERATIONS

A. Background Information

1. A high prevalence for use of addictive drugs during pregnancy is found in all socioeconomic classes. In the United States, about 20% of pregnant women smoke cigarettes, 19% drink alcohol, and 5% use illicit drugs. A much higher prevalence is found in pregnant adolescents, and among mentally ill pregnant women.

2. Since about 50% of pregnancies in the general United States population are unplanned, and since drug addiction often causes irregular menstrual periods, many women in the critical early stages of pregnancy (and their clinicians) may be unaware that they are actually pregnant.

3. Psychoactive substances, including addictive drugs, freely cross the placenta as a result of the same properties that allow them to cross the blood–brain barrier. Further, most drugs have a longer half-life in the fetus than in the mother, since fetal metabolic pathways have not fully matured. Addictive drugs also pass into breast milk, and into breast-feeding babies in variable amounts.

4. Use of addictive drugs during pregnancy contributes to many other risk factors that adversely affect pregnancy outcome. These include insufficient prenatal care, inadequate nutrition, increased likelihood of infection, increased risk of violence, diminished financial resources, and diminished social support.

B. Evaluation of Drug Addiction during Pregnancy.
A thorough history of drug use should be obtained for all pregnant or potentially pregnant women. In addition

1. A high index of suspicion for addiction during pregnancy, warranting urine testing, should be maintained in cases where

Manual of Therapeutics for Addictions, Edited by Norman S. Miller, Mark S. Gold, and David E. Smith.
ISBN 0471-56176-2 © 1997 John Wiley & Sons, Inc.

a. A woman has not sought prenatal care until late in the pregnancy, or not at all until labor.

b. A woman is failing to gain expected weight, and/or her uterine size (or fetal image on ultrasound) is smaller than expected for gestational age.

c. A woman is demonstrating marked mood lability and/or irritability (this may be erroneously attributed to the pregnancy itself).

d. A woman's obstetric history includes prior unexplained pregnancy complications, or babies born with problems common in drug-exposed neonates.

e. A woman's financial difficulties are worse than expected given her income, even taking into account the increased financial demands of pregnancy.

f. A woman is not planning ahead for her baby.

g. A woman's spouse or partner is addicted, or the woman is otherwise in close contact with others who are addicted to drugs.

h. A woman has lost custody of prior children related to sequelae of drug addiction.

2. Evaluation should include assessment of comorbid problems commonly seen in pregnant women with addiction. These include

a. Psychiatric disorders, such as mood disorders, eating disorders, anxiety disorders, posttraumatic stress disorders, and psychotic disorders.

b. Use of other addictive substances, including prescription drugs and nicotine.

c. Sequelae of sexual and physical abuse, including current domestic violence.

d. Medical complications of drug addiction.

e. Sexually transmitted diseases, including HIV infection.

f. Sexual dysfunction.

3. In addition to a thorough history and physical examination, the following laboratory studies are useful during pregnancy besides those normally checked in patients with addictive disorders:

a. Blood type and antibody screen (to test for maternal/fetal blood type incompatibility).

b. Rubella titer, hepatitis B surface antigen, HIV test, and syphilis serology. These are all infections that, if present during pregnancy, can affect the fetus or neonate.

c. One-hour glucose screen. Fasting blood glucose is measured and compared with blood glucose drawn 1 h after the patient drinks a 50-g glucose solution. This screens for gestational diabetes mellitus.

d. Pelvic/abdominal ultrasound. For accurate dating of pregnancy, since many addictive substances cause irregular menses. Ultrasound examinations can also detect some fetal abnormalities associated with addiction.

C. Treatment of Drug Addiction during Pregnancy

1. A cornerstone of addiction treatment during pregnancy is adopting a nonpunitive attitude. Approaches that invoke legal sanctions, threats of child-custody loss, and guilt induction tend to drive women away

from care, including prenatal care. A nonjudgmental, factual explanation of the impact of drug addiction on pregnancy and parenting is essential.

2. A top priority, even in women who deny the problematic aspects of their addiction and do not otherwise seem ready for treatment, is the institution of good prenatal care. Prenatal obstetric care improves maternal and neonatal outcome, even in the presence of ongoing drug use. In addition to standard prenatal care, more frequent ultrasounds are warranted to assess for accurate gestational age and intrauterine growth retardation. Nonstress tests (NSTs) to assess fetal well-being may be needed weekly during the month before the due date. Delivery should occur in a facility with a neonatal intensive-care unit, to handle potential neonatal complications of intrauterine drug exposure.

3. Another intervention that can dramatically improve outcome, even with ongoing drug use, is teaching about safe sex and, for IV drug users, access to sterile needles. These measures can decrease the likelihood of HIV infection in both mother and fetus.

4. There is growing evidence that inadequate nutrition can potentiate the teratogenicity of addictive substances. Nutritional counseling and monitoring can greatly improve pregnancy outcome. An especially important nutrient during pregnancy is folate. Folate deficiency, common with alcoholism, increases the risk of neural tube defects in offspring. Folate is present in standard prenatal vitamins, and is in ample supply in a healthy, balanced diet. Checking weight weekly can help monitor overall nutritional adequacy. Although normal weight gain is variable during pregnancy, most well-nourished women gain about a pound a week after the first trimester, for a total weight gain of approximately 25 pounds.

5. For women who are receiving obstetric care, use of a peer leadership team is a useful way to help pregnant women enter addiction treatment. Such a team might include a recovering addict and an addiction counselor, supervised by a social worker, who visit patients in the obstetric clinic or ward and invite them to participate in addiction treatment.

6. Standard therapeutic approaches to addiction, such as AA and NA, may need to be supplemented by specific psychotherapeutic attention to issues raised by the pregnancy. These often include
   a. Grieving past custody loss: A "vicious cycle" can develop in which custody loss triggers additional drug use, which, in turn, renders future custody loss more likely.
   b. Newly emergent reactions to past sexual abuse.
   c. Unresolved interpersonal conflicts that influence the patient's reactions to the baby. These include difficulties in the relationship with the father of the baby, and / or financial dependence on an addicted partner.

7. Since planning and judgment can be adversely affected by addiction, specific attention to planning for the baby's needs, and planning to prevent unwanted future pregnancies, is important. This may include
   a. Building a support network.
   b. Finding a pediatrician.
   c. Arranging services, such as WIC (Women, Infant, and Children's Program, which provides nutritional support), childbirth, and par-

enting classes. The latter are especially important, because babies affected by in utero drug exposure may have physical and behavioral abnormalities that make their care more difficult.

d. Helping the woman plan child care arrangements to enable her to continue her treatment postpartum.

e. Family planning and birth control.

f. Education about potential effects of active drug use on the woman and her fetus.

8. Pharmacologic agents are often used to treat certain sequelae of addiction (see Chapters 7–13). During pregnancy, the risks of those agents for both the patient and her fetus must be weighed against the risks of not using pharmacotherapy. Risks of specific pharmacologic agents during pregnancy are outlined in the relevant sections below.

9. Alternative nonpharmacologic therapies, most notably acupuncture, are beginning to be used for pregnant women with addictive disorders. Further study is needed in order to assess efficacy.

10. Pain during labor can be managed just as it would be for women without addictive disorders. Administering potentially addictive substances, such as benzodiazepines and opiates, on a temporary basis for pain is unlikely to contribute to addiction.

D. Drug Addiction and Parenting

1. Active drug addiction may impair parenting capabilities in many ways, including

   a. Impairing judgment.

   b. Draining financial resources.

   c. Creating a chaotic and unpredictable environment for children.

   d. Producing direct physical hazards for the child (e.g., ingestible drugs or needles within reach of toddlers, passive intoxication via smoke inhalation)

   e. Promoting abuse and neglect.

2. It is essential to realize that the effects of drug addiction on parenting are highly variable. Drug addiction per se does not constitute a sufficient reason to remove a child from the custody of the addicted parent(s). Parenting capability must be assessed in each individual case.

3. Addiction treatment programs designed with children in mind are ideal for women addicted during pregnancy. Pregnancy and postpartum addiction units, where women can receive treatment throughout pregnancy and then live with their newborns, have been very effective. Access to treatment is greatly enhanced by "one-stop shopping" models of healthcare delivery, where addiction treatment, medical care, gynecologic care, psychiatric care, pediatrics, family planning, and nutritional and financial support services are all coordinated and in one place. Mothers with infants and young children, especially if impoverished, have great difficulty keeping and coordinating multiple separate appointments for healthcare.

4. Assessment of mother–infant interaction in the newborn period can identify early maladaptive patterns and prevent them from becoming chronic. This is particularly important for those addicted mothers who have unrealistic ideas about babies' capabilities, who are depressed and unresponsive to babies' cues, and who have babies with physical and / or neurobehavioral abnormalities.

5. Ongoing communication between a pediatrician and those treating the mother's addiction promotes the well-being of both mother and baby. This communication should ideally be established during the pregnancy.

6. High rates of depression are found in pregnant, drug-addicted women, particularly older women. Depression and child-custody loss are highly correlated with one another in addicted women. Causality seems to go in both directions; depression impairs parenting capability, and custody loss triggers depression.

II. ALCOHOL DURING PREGNANCY

Drinking alcohol during pregnancy risks permanent harm to offspring. The U.S. Surgeon General recommends that women who are pregnant or considering pregnancy abstain from using any alcoholic beverages. Yet, alcohol use among women has increased during the last half century, especially among young women of childbearing age. Although the overall consumption of alcohol during pregnancy in the United States is declining, it is declining less among pregnant women who are smokers, unmarried, less educated, or younger and are already at high risk of poor pregnancy outcome.

A. Adverse Effects of Alcohol during Pregnancy

1. **Fetal alcohol syndrome.** This is a specific recognizable pattern of malformation seen in 2–10% of offspring exposed to alcohol in utero, or about 1 in 300 live births in the United States. It is diagnosed when the following abnormalities are present:
   a. Growth retardation (weight, length, and/or head circumference below the 10th percentile).
   b. Characteristic facial anomalies, with at least two of the following signs:
      i. Microophthalmia and/or short palpebral fissures.
      ii. Indistinct or absent philtrum, thin upper lip, or flattened maxillary area.
      iii. Microcephaly.
   c. CNS dysfunction (neurologic abnormality, intellectual impairment, and/or developmental delay).
   d. There is also an increased likelihood of nonspecific congenital anomalies, infections, and neoplasms.

2. **Fetal alcohol effects.** These are partial expressions of fetal alcohol syndrome associated with lower levels of alcohol intake. They are seen in 30–40% of offspring exposed to alcohol in utero, or about 1 in 100 babies born in the United States. They are about 3 times more likely to occur when pregnant women continue drinking than when they stop drinking during the course of the pregnancy. They include
   a. Spontaneous abortion
   b. Premature birth
   c. Stillbirth
   d. Long-term behavioral and developmental effects

B. Assessment of Alcohol Addiction during Pregnancy. Many women will spontaneously reduce or discontinue alcohol consumption during pregnancy, as a result of adverse physiological effects or out of concern for the fetus. However, there is a subset who have great difficulty in doing so. Further, due to the tremendous social stigma attached to drinking during pregnancy, much alcohol use during pregnancy remains undisclosed. Physicians who miss the diagnosis of alcoholism during pregnancy may treat its physical and emotional manifestations symptomatically with prescription sedatives and tranquilizers, creating additional drug dependence and teratogenic risk. Straightforward, nonjudgmental, thorough history-taking is essential.

1. **History.** Assess alcohol use in women who are pregnant or potentially pregnant, and those considering pregnancy. In addition to standard history-taking, the following are relevant for this population:

   a. The T-ACE (see Table 15.1) is a brief set of screening questions designed for use in prenatal populations. Its questions can reliably identify pregnant women whose level of alcohol intake is sufficient to seriously damage the embryo or fetus.

   b. Obtain a history of past alcohol use during pregnancies, and sequelae in offspring.

   c. While obtaining a family history of alcohol addiction, also assess the effects of the patient's drinking on her family members and her parenting capabilities, and assess her partner's drinking habits.

   d. Assess for common comorbid conditions (see Section I.B, list item 2).

2. **Physical examination**

   a. Physical complications of alcohol need to be evaluated, as women develop late stages of physical damage more rapidly than males, and these physical problems may adversely affect pregnancy outcome.

   b. Symptoms and physical signs of alcohol withdrawal can sometimes be confused with concomitants of pregnancy (see Table 15.2).

   c. Physical signs of alcohol-related liver disease (e.g., palmar erythema) can sometimes be confused with concomitants of pregnancy.

TABLE 15.1. The T-ACE Screening Instrument for Detection of Prenatal Risk Drinking

T	How many drinks does it take to make you feel high (TOLERANCE)? (2 points if >2 drinks)
A	Have people *Annoyed* you by criticizing your drinking? (1 point if "yes")
C	Have you felt you ought to *Cut down* on your drinking? (1 point if "yes.)
E	Have you ever had a drink first thing in the morning to steady your nerves or get rid of a hangover (*Eye-opener*)? (1 point if "yes")

*a*These four questions detect "risk drinking." that is, alcohol intake potentially sufficient to damage the fetus (≥1 oz of absolute alcohol per day). A total score of ≥2 is considered "high risk."

TABLE 15.2. **Signs and Symptoms of Pregnancy versus Alcohol Withdrawal**

Symptoms and Signs Common to Both Pregnancy and Alcohol Withdrawal	Symptoms and Signs of Alcohol Withdrawal Not Commonly Associated with Pregnancy
Hypertension (preeclampsia or eclampsia)	Agitation
	Distractibility
Nausea and vomiting	Fever
Restlessness	Hallucinosis
Seizures (in eclampsia)	Impaired memory
Sleep disturbance	Marked diaphoresis
Tachycardia	Tremor
Tachypnea and respiratory alkalosis	

3. Laboratory tests

    a. Urine pregnancy tests are highly accurate ($> 99\%$) and can detect pregnancy as soon as a menstrual period has been missed.

    b. Mean corpuscular volume (MCV) can help distinguish alcohol-related anemia (typically, low hemoglobin and hematocrit with high MCV) from pregnancy-related anemia (low hemoglobin and hematocrit with normal or low MCV).

C. Treatment of Alcohol Addiction during Pregnancy. Psychosocial interventions are as described in Section I.C. When such measures are insufficient to contain withdrawal symptoms or maintain abstinence, pharmacologic intervention is an important adjunct. The following are guidelines for the use of pharmacologic agents in pregnant women with alcoholism:

1. Alcohol withdrawal. Severe withdrawal agitation, hypertension, tachycardia, and / or seizures pose risks to the woman and her fetus and may require pharmacologic treatment when supportive measures are insufficient. Commonly used medications for treating symptoms of alcohol withdrawal include the following.

    a. Benzodiazepines. Benzodiazepines are used to decrease agitation and treat withdrawal seizures. They are also commonly used during labor to decrease the need for analgesia. Diazepam, chlordiazepoxide, and lorazepam are the most extensively studied during pregnancy. Their use during pregnancy poses the following risks:

        i. High doses (≥ 30 mg of diazepam or the equivalent) administered during labor are likely to cause transient neonatal toxicity. This manifests itself as "floppy-baby syndrome," consisting of hypotension, hyporeflexia, lethargy, difficulty sucking, poor respiratory effort, and difficulty maintaining body temperature. These symptoms usually remit spontaneously, with no lasting sequelae if managed supportively. If symptoms are severe, they can be reversed with the benzodiazepine inhibitor flumazenil. Since flumazenil has a short half-life, close observation for at least 24 h is warranted to determine whether repeat doses are needed.

ii. IV administration of benzodiazepines, indicated for intractable seizures, can contribute to kernicterus, because as the solution in which IV benzodiazepines are stored is a sodium benzoate/benzoic acid buffer that displaces bilirubin from albumin. Oral preparations are preferred whenever feasible.

iii. If benzodiazepine use has been prolonged, neonatal withdrawal can result in transient hypertonia, hyperreflexia, and tremor (see Section VI).

iv. In sum, the risks of untreated withdrawal seizures and severe agitation far outweigh the risks of benzodiazepines during pregnancy.

b. Carbamazepine. Sometimes used as an alternative to benzodiazepines to treat withdrawal symptoms, especially when concomitant epilepsy or bipolar mood disorder warrant its use. Considerations for its use during pregnancy include the following:

i. There is a slightly increased risk of spina bifida and minor congenital anomalies with first trimester exposure. For this reason, it should be avoided during the first trimester of pregnancy if there is a nonteratogenic alternative. If carbamazepine is needed, daily folate administration may decrease the risk of neural tube defects. α-Fetoprotein serum levels, a screening test for neural tube defects, should be done if there has been first trimester exposure.

ii. There is an increased risk of neonatal cerebral hemorrhage, due to lowering of vitamin K–dependent clotting factors. This can be prevented by administration of 20 mg vitamin K PO to the mother in the last 1–2 months of pregnancy and 1 mg vitamin K IM to the baby at birth.

iii. Clinical serum levels of *carbamazepine* may be misleading because protein binding is decreased. Either clinical condition or levels of free carbamazepine should guide dosing.

c. β-adrenergic blocking agents. These are used to control withdrawal hypertension and tachycardia. Considerations for their use during pregnancy include the following:

i. *Propranolol* and *atenolol* have been widely used to treat hypertension during pregnancy; they decrease the chances of poor fetal outcome from hypertension regardless of whether it is caused by alcohol withdrawal. Beta blockers are not teratogenic, and pose less risk to both mother and fetus than does untreated hypertension.

ii. Atenolol is sometimes preferred, as it is a selective beta-blocking agent and therefore does not block β_2 receptors in the uterine wall. Although propranolol does block β_2 receptors, it does not contribute to premature labor.

d. Antipsychotic agents. These are used for severe alcohol hallucinosis and among pregnant women with psychotic disorders with concomitant alcoholism. Considerations for their use during pregnancy include the following:

i. High-potency agents are preferred, especially haloperidol and trifluoperazine, which have been relatively well studied during pregnancy, have fewer anticholinergic side effects for both mother and fetus, and have not been associated with teratogenicity. Pregnant alcoholic women are especially vulnerable to the side effects of lower-potency phenothiazines such as chlorpromazine, which include hypotension and liver damage. Further, phenothiazines may increase the risk of nonspecific congenital anomalies with first-trimester exposure, especially in conjunction with nicotine. Newer antipsychotic agents have not yet been systematically investigated for teratogenicity.

ii. In rare instances, neonatal withdrawal syndrome can occur after prolonged use of neuroleptics during pregnancy. Symptoms include hypertonia, tremor, poor motor maturity, irritability, hyperreflexia, irregular respiration, a shrill cry, abnormal posturing, and tongue thrusting. These symptoms resolve over several months, and can be alleviated by diphenhydramine elixir.

iii. Women who have low calcium levels due to increased fetal demand, and poor nutrition due to alcoholism, may have increased risk of extrapyramidal symptoms (EPSs). Since agents used to treat EPSs increase the risk of side effects and teratogenicity, maintaining adequate calcium intake is essential for pregnant alcoholic women taking antipsychotic medication.

e. Other agents. Chloral hydrate and barbiturates are sometimes used to treat withdrawal agitation. During pregnancy, these agents have no demonstrable advantage over benzodiazepines and are no safer for the fetus.

2. Prophylactic treatment for alcohol addiction. Prophylactic agents sometimes used in nonpregnant women include disulfiram and lithium. These are not recommended for this use during pregnancy, since in most cases the risks outweigh potential benefits.

a. Risks of disulfiram use during pregnancy

i. When combined with even small amounts of alcohol, disulfiram may increase the risk of congenital anomalies.

ii. If alcohol is consumed with disulfiram, acetaldehyde accumulates. This causes hypotension, which may lead to maternal shock, decreased placental perfusion, and potentially fetal demise.

iii. Lead poisoning—a metabolite of disulfiram, diethyldithiocarbamate, is a chelating agent that binds lead to form a lipophilic complex that can cross the blood–brain barrier. If a pregnant woman on disulfiram is exposed to lead (e.g., from lead-based paint chips, homemade alcoholic beverages, occupational sources, or soldering), there is an increased risk of intellectual impairment and/or behavior changes in the offspring.

b. Risks of lithium use during pregnancy

i. In the absence of alcohol, lithium is at most a weak cardiac teratogen. However, its teratogenicity in some animal species increases dramatically in the presence of alcohol; it is not known whether this is the case in humans.

ii. Rarely, fetal diabetes insipidus can result in polyhydramnios.

iii. There are rare instances of neonatal thyroid dysfunction, which is transient and reversible.

iv. The risk of prematurity is increased with lithium use.

    v. The risk of neonatal macrosomia may be increased by lithium use.

    vi. Neonatal lithium toxicity is rare, but can occur even when the mother is at therapeutic levels. Signs include poor suck and Moro reflexes, abnormal respiratory pattern, cyanosis, hypotonia, cardiac arrhythmias, hypoglycemia, and poor myocardial contractility.

c. Guidelines for administration of lithium during pregnancy. Given the potential risks, and uncertain efficacy, lithium is not recommended in pregnancy solely for alcohol prophylaxis. However, it may be necessary in a woman with concomitant lithium-responsive bipolar mood disorder. The combination of untreated mania and alcoholism presents greater risk to the pregnancy and the fetus than does lithium alone. When prescribing lithium during pregnancy, the following guidelines will minimize risks:

    i. If possible, avoid lithium during days 20–45 after conception, which will minimize the risk of cardiac malformations. ECT is an alternative during this period. If lithium must be given or was already given, then obtain an ultrasound at 16 weeks' gestation to assess cardiac formation.

    ii. Monitor lithium levels frequently. Keep doses as low as possible. However, as pregnancy progresses, fluid volume increases, and higher doses of lithium may be required.

    iii. Towards the end of pregnancy, lithium should be given in small and divided doses to avoid toxic peaks in the neonate.

    iv. At the expected date of confinement, or at the onset of labor, the lithium dose should be cut in half. This decreases the risk of maternal lithium toxicity secondary to the sudden decrease in fluid volume. Serum lithium level can be rechecked 2 weeks after delivery, and the dose adjusted accordingly.

III. COCAINE DURING PREGNANCY

Survey data suggest that cocaine use has increased among women of childbearing age in the United States. Prevalence estimates of cocaine use during pregnancy vary widely, ranging from 3 to 50%, depending on the population studied. About 60% of pregnant women who use cocaine do not receive prenatal care.

Cocaine readily crosses the placenta. When a pregnant woman uses cocaine a day or two before delivery, the newborn excretes cocaine for 12–24 h and excretes the metabolite benzoylecgonine of cocaine for up to a week.

A. Adverse Effects of Cocaine during Pregnancy

1. Adverse effects on the pregnant woman

    a. Cocaine increases sympathetic-nervous-system (SNS) activation, causing increased heart rate, blood pressure, and myocardial O_2 demand. During pregnancy, heart rate and O_2 demand are already elevated; in some pregnant women, blood pressure is elevated as well. Further, cocaine levels at a given dose are more unpredictable during pregnancy due to altered pharmacokinetics. Of note, levels of cholinesterases, the enzymes that metabolize cocaine, are decreased during pregnancy. The additive effects of cocaine and pregnancy may increase the risk of myocardial infarction, cardiac arrhythmias, or cerebral hemorrhage in the pregnant woman.

b. If a woman is intoxicated with cocaine during labor, the pain of labor may be intensified, and analgesics may be less effective.

2. Adverse effects on the fetus and neonate. Many abnormalities have been reported in offspring exposed to cocaine in utero. For most of these abnormalities, it is not yet known whether cocaine itself caused the problem. Most cocaine-exposed fetuses have also been exposed to other addictive substances, had poor prenatal care, inadequate nutrition, and increased exposure to infection, so poor outcomes may be multifactorial. Further, patterns of cocaine use during pregnancy are widely variable. However, existing data suggest the following as likely specific effects of cocaine:

a. Cocaine constricts uterine blood vessels, resulting in decreased placental perfusion and ultimately in fetal hypoxemia.

b. Fetal hypertension and tachycardia can occur through direct action of cocaine or as a response to cocaine-induced fetal hypoxemia.

c. Labor is more likely to be premature and/or precipitous with cocaine use. There is also a high incidence of placental abruption. These complications may be due to cocaine inhibiting catecholamine uptake by the pregnant uterus, thus increasing uterine contractility. Fetal distress during labor, as evidenced by tachycardia, bradycardia, and/or meconium staining, may be more common with cocaine exposure, but this is less clear.

d. Intrauterine growth retardation, including reductions in birth weight, length, and head circumference, is more likely with cocaine use than without. Head circumference may be reduced proportionally more than weight and length, resulting in microcephaly. Growth retardation correlates more with the duration of cocaine use than with the dose or frequency of use.

e. Neonates who were exposed to cocaine in utero may exhibit transient symptoms and signs, including cardiac tachyarrhythmias, EEG evidence of cerebral irritation, tremor, increased muscle tone, hyperactive deep tendon reflexes, irritability, and impaired homeostasis. These abnormalities are most apparent on the second day of life, are rarely severe, and occur in a minority of cocaine-exposed infants.

f. Although there are case reports of physical congenital anomalies after in utero cocaine exposure, there are no systematic studies identifying cocaine as a human teratogen. There is some evidence linking in utero cocaine exposure with destructive cerebral lesions, presumably due to cocaine's vascular effects causing infarctions and hemorrhages. Animal studies demonstrate that in utero cocaine exposure can cause abnormal neuronal migration and differentiation; it is unknown whether this is the case in humans.

g. It is not clear whether cocaine use increases the risk of spontaneous abortion stillbirth and sudden infant death syndrome (SIDS).

3. Adverse long-term behavioral effects of in utero cocaine exposure. Anecdotal reports describe a variety of difficulties in learning, social interaction, and behavior among children who were exposed to cocaine *in utero*. There are insufficient data to conclude whether this is a direct effect of cocaine. However, it is clear that the offspring of women addicted to cocaine are at high risk of psychological morbidity regardless of whether it is a direct physiologic effect of cocaine.

B. Treatment of Cocaine Addiction during Pregnancy. Treatment considerations include those outlined in Section I.C. In addition, there are several pharmacologic agents specifically used for treatment of cocaine intoxication or craving. Considerations for their use during pregnancy include the following:

1. Desipramine. Desipramine has shown some effectiveness as an anticraving agent for cocaine addiction (see Chapter 19). It is also highly effective for patients with concomitant major depression. It is among the antidepressant agents most widely studied during pregnancy.

>   a. Studies to date have revealed no increased risk of congenital anomalies after in utero exposure to desipramine.
>   b. Some of the common side effects of desipramine enhance the normal physiologic changes of pregnancy, making them more difficult to tolerate. These include constipation, tachycardia, orthostatic hypotension, and sedation. If orthostatic hypotension is significant, placental perfusion can be compromised.
>   c. Some newborns exhibit withdrawal symptoms after prolonged in utero exposure to desipramine. These may include irritability, tachypnea, tachycardia, tremor, and clonus. When these occur, they are generally mild, transient, and self-limited. In very rare instances, seizures can result. When withdrawal symptoms are clinically significant, they can be eliminated by giving the newborn small doses of desipramine and gradually tapering the dose.
>   d. Some common side effects of desipramine can also affect the fetus or newborn. These include difficulty with urination, constipation, sedation, and tachycardia. It is very rare for these to be severe, but occasionally there has been urinary retention, functional intestinal obstruction, or tachyarrhythmias.
>   e. As pregnancy progresses, usually a given dose of desipramine results in a lower serum concentration of desipramine. This is primarily because the volume of distribution increases as total body water content increases. Monitoring serum levels, and adjusting the dose accordingly, can prevent relapse due to subtherapeutic levels.
>   f. There are no studies to date assessing whether in utero desipramine exposure causes enduring behavior changes.

2. Amantadine. Amantadine is sometimes used to reduce cocaine craving (see Chapter 19). There are few data available about its use during pregnancy. A survey of pregnant women with Parkinson's disease found that each of the women using amantadine had pregnancy complications. Because of the paucity of data, amantadine is not currently recommended as an anticraving agent during pregnancy.

3. Bromocriptine. Bromocriptine, also used to reduce cocaine craving, has been studied extensively during very early pregnancy, but not late pregnancy. This is because it is commonly used as a fertility drug, and is discontinued as soon as pregnancy is diagnosed.

a. Existing studies demonstrate no adverse effects on offspring exposed in the first trimester to bromocriptine.

b. If given during the first few weeks postpartum to women with a diathesis for psychotic or mood disorders, bromocriptine may trigger postpartum psychosis.

c. Because of a relative paucity of data about prolonged use during pregnancy, and its propensity to trigger psychosis in a vulnerable population, it is usually best to find alternative treatments for cocaine addiction during pregnancy.

4. Other agents. Benzodiazepines, carbamazepine, and antipsychotic agents are sometimes used as part of the pharmacologic treatment of cocaine intoxication or relapse prevention (see Chapter 19). The use of these agents during pregnancy is discussed in Section II.

IV. NICOTINE DURING PREGNANCY

It has been estimated that 20–25% of pregnant women in the United States continue to smoke during pregnancy. Heavy smokers (> 1 pack/day) are more likely to continue smoking throughout pregnancy. Nevertheless, pregnancy can serve as a strong motivator to quit smoking for many women.

A. Effects of Cigarette Smoking on the Fetus. Cigarettes expose smokers to many potential toxins, including nicotine and carbon monoxide. These are suspected to contribute to reproductive disturbances due to vasoconstriction and reduced oxygen availability. Risks that increase significantly as a result of smoking include

1. Spontaneous abortion (rate doubles for smokers).
2. Prematurity.
3. Low birth weight. Smoking accounts for 25% of low birth weights. This is dose-related; the greater the number of cigarettes smoked, the greater the decrease in birth weight.
4. Perinatal mortality, including deaths related to abruptio placentae, placenta previa, premature rupture of the membranes, and intrauterine growth retardation.
5. Sudden infant death syndrome (SIDS).
6. Low Apgar scores (> 2 packs/day).
7. CNS excitability (increased startle reflex, tremor, and increased tone) in the first month of life.
8. Intellectual deficits, hyperactivity, and impaired attention in older offspring.

B. Treatment of Nicotine Addiction during Pregnancy. Treatment considerations include those outlined in Section I.C. Pregnancy is often a time of high motivation to quit smoking. Multicomponent programs combining cessation techniques with counseling, skills training, and emotional support can be highly effective. It is important to counsel women about the effects of smoking not only during pregnancy but also on offspring after birth. When supportive and behavioral methods of smoking cessation are insufficient, one must assess whether nicotine replacement systems will improve maternal and fetal outcome. Considerations for the use of nicotine replacement systems during pregnancy include

1. Nicotine replacement systems pose less risk to the fetus than cigarette smoking. Smoking delivers not only nicotine, but also carbon monoxide and thousands of other substances, to both the woman and her fetus. Nicotine replacement systems deliver nicotine alone. It is not known whether nicotine itself has any direct teratogenic effects in humans.

2. Nicotine polacrilex gum provides smaller daily doses, and greater individual dose titration, than does the transdermal nicotine patch. For these reasons, it is preferred during pregnancy for women who can use it properly.

3. For pregnant women who do use transdermal systems, patches that can be removed at bedtime are recommended to decrease the total nicotine dose.

4. Clonidine is sometimes used to promote smoking cessation in nonpregnant patients. It is not recommended for this use during pregnancy, because of unclear efficacy in conjunction with increased risks to the fetus. These include behavioral teratogenicity and increased risk of preterm labor.

V. OPIATES DURING PREGNANCY

Approximately 2–3% of babies born in the United States are exposed to opiates in utero. Addiction to "street heroin" is commonly accompanied by multiple other problems posing risks to the pregnant woman and her baby: poverty, poor nutrition, lack of prenatal care, use of other addictive substances, exposure to HIV and other serious medical conditions, psychiatric disorders, homelessness, and involvement in abusive relationships. Further, "street heroin" use is typically characterized by repeated cycles of intoxication and withdrawal, which are also experienced by the fetus. For these reasons, the effects of "street heroin" use on a fetus are dramatically different from the effects of methadone maintenance.

A. Adverse Effects of "Street Heroin" Use during Pregnancy. The following risks are increased in "street heroin" addicts:

1. Spontaneous abortion (miscarriage).
2. Intrauterine growth retardation.
3. Premature labor, with resultant complications.
4. Stillbirth.
5. Fetal hypoxia, especially during opiate withdrawal.
6. HIV and other infections transmitted to the fetus.

B. Assessment of Opiate Addiction during Pregnancy

1. Recognizing withdrawal. Some of the symptoms of withdrawal overlap with normal concomitants of pregnancy. These include insomnia, anxiety, sweating, cramps, nausea, vomiting, and malaise. A careful history of drug use, along with a physical examination looking for signs of heroin addiction, and laboratory screening, are essential to avoid missing the diagnosis.

2. Use of opiate antagonists. In the nonpregnant state, opiate antagonists are sometimes used to assess whether opiate intoxication is present. Sudden opiate withdrawal poses risks of fetal distress and/or demise, so is contraindicated during pregnancy. During pregnancy, narcotic antagonists should be used only to treat life-threatening narcotic overdoses.

C. Treatment of Opiate Addiction during Pregnancy. Treatment considerations include those outlined in Section I.C. In conjunction with supportive treatment, methadone significantly reduces the risks of opiate addiction during pregnancy. Treatment options include methadone maintenance, or methadone detoxification.

1. Methadone maintenance. This is the preferred treatment for most women during pregnancy. It decreases the risk of resuming street heroin use, and eliminates the peaks and troughs of maternal drug levels.

a. Benefits of methadone maintenance compared to street heroin

These include

    i. Improved nutrition.

    ii. Improved prenatal care.

    iii. Fewer obstetrical complications.

    iv. Greater likelihood of the opiate-dependent woman leaving a drug-seeking environment.

    v. Less use of other addictive substances.

    vi. Less illegal behavior, such as prostitution and theft.

    vii. Less risk of HIV infection for both mother and infant.

    viii. Increased birth weight.

    ix. Improved ability to plan for, and care for, baby.

b. Withdrawal. Methadone's long elimination half-life results in a more prolonged, severe, and often delayed onset of neonatal abstinence syndrome. However, these are transient symptoms posing far less long-term risk than the sequelae of street heroin exposure.

c. Techniques of methadone maintenance during pregnancy

    i. Methadone taper—ideally this should be begun on an inpatient or a specialized unit and continued in an intensive program providing psychosocial support.

    ii. Dosing—most clinicians recommend using enough methadone to eliminate withdrawal signs. As pregnancy progresses, total body water content increases, methadone's half-life decreases, and dosage requirements may increase. Using more than 20 mg of methadone per day increases the risk of neonatal abstinence syndrome, so some clinicians advocate using low dose methadone maintenance (a maximum of 20 mg/day) during pregnancy. However, if the woman is symptomatic at too low a dose, it increases the risk of fetal distress from withdrawal, and the risk that the woman will use additional opiates and/or other drugs.

    iii. When nonstress tests (NSTs) are needed, they should be scheduled before methadone doses. Nonstress tests are used to identify potential fetal distress by recording a tracing of fetal heart rate changes in accordance with fetal movements. Methadone may suppress measures of fetal reactivity and give a false impression of fetal distress on the nonstress test.

2. Methadone detoxification

a. Contraindications to methadone detoxification during pregnancy. This is not the treatment of choice for the great majority of pregnant addicts, because of the high risk of resuming street heroin use, and because of potential risks of withdrawal for the fetus. However, it is a useful treatment option for women who

    i. Are highly motivated. Pregnancy can be a time of increased motivation, although even the risk of custody loss is not a sufficient motivator for many women.

    ii. Cannot get into a treatment facility unless detoxified. This is an admission prerequisite in some facilities.

    iii. Live in an area where a methadone maintenance program is unavailable.

    iv. Have failed methadone maintenance, or have had other babies with severe withdrawal after methadone maintenance.

b. Techniques of methadone detoxification during pregnancy

    i. The second trimester may be the optimal time to initiate detoxification. In the first trimester, withdrawal may increase the risk of miscarriage. After the 32nd week of pregnancy, withdrawal may increase fetal activity and decrease fetal oxygenation, which can cause fetal hypoxia, resulting in increased fetal distress or demise.

    ii. Ideally done on an inpatient unit where addiction services are closely coordinated with obstetric services.

    iii. Coordinate with the supplying pharmacy in order to ensure timely preparations of methadone dosages.

    iv. Estimate the equivalent dose of methadone from the amount of prior heroin use. Administer this dose for 3–4 days, observing for symptoms and signs of withdrawal, and adjust the dose accordingly. Because of the risks of withdrawal for the fetus, during pregnancy it is recommended to err on the side of administering more methadone rather than to allow symptomatic withdrawal.

    v. Taper methadone slowly, at a rate of about 0.2–1.0 mg every other day (alternate days). Depending on the starting dose, detoxification may take 8 weeks or more. The more rapid end of this range should be instituted only if there are no withdrawal signs or symptoms present, and if the fetus is showing no signs of distress.

    vi. Perform frequent fetal monitoring; this can include maternal vital signs and fetal heart tones twice a day (or continuous fetal monitoring if available), and obstetric examinations with nonstress tests once a week. If it is too early in the pregnancy for fetal heart tones to be detectable, then pay close attention to subjective symptoms of withdrawal and monitor the fetus with ultrasound as indicated.

    vii. If there are any signs of fetal distress, maintain the methadone dose rather than continuing detoxification.

    viii. Discuss and implement long-term treatment plans. If available, specialized residential programs for pregnant addicted women are optimal.

3. Management of labor and delivery

    a. Withdrawal during labor. This increases the risk of fetal distress and demise. During labor, women addicted to opiates should be given a dose of

TABLE 15.3. Withdrawal Manifestations in Opiate-Addicted Newborns

General	CNS	Respiratory	Gastrointestinal
Irritability	Seizures	Rhinorrhea, sneezing	Salivation, hiccups
Poor sleep, yawning	Tremors, twitching	Respiratory distress	Vomiting, diarrhea
Fever, dia- phoresis	Increased tone, reflexes	Respiratory alkalosis	Weight loss
Skin mottling	Hyperactivity		Failure to gain weight
Hypothermia	High-pitched cry		
Increased sucking			

methadone that eliminates withdrawal symptoms, regardless of whether they were previously on methadone maintenance.

b. Anesthesia and analgesia. Management of the pain of labor is the same as for a woman who is not addicted to opiates.

D. Neonatal Abstinence Syndrome

1. Clinical manifestations. Opiate withdrawal in the neonate (see Table 15.3) is often referred to as the neonatal narcotic abstinence syndrome. Its prominent signs and symptoms reflect CNS hyperirritability. Initially, the infant appears restless, then develops tremors when disturbed. Over time, tremors occur spontaneously. The infant may develop a high-pitched cry, increased muscle tone, and hyperreflexia. Feeding may be difficult because of an ineffectual sucking reflex. Along with vomiting and diarrhea, this may lead to weight loss or failure to gain weight. The neonate is also prone to dehydration, electrolyte imbalance, respiratory distress, tachypnea, and respiratory alkalosis. Abnormal sleep patterns, yawning, sneezing, mottling, and fever all may be present.

2. Onset. Time of onset varies from minutes after birth to 2 weeks after birth. Influential factors include the amount of opioid used, plasma level of the drug, whether multiple drugs were used, timing of use before delivery, labor, anesthesia, analgesia, maturity of the fetus, nutritional status, and intrinsic disease in the infant. In the majority of cases, symptoms appear within 48–72 h after birth. Usually neonatal narcotic abstinence syndrome is not seen when the mother has been drug-free for a week or more prior to delivery. Methadone withdrawal may be delayed as compared with heroin because of methadone's longer elimination half-life.

3. Duration. Withdrawal symptoms can last 2–3 weeks after birth and in subacute form for 4–6 months.

4. Severity. Withdrawal symptoms may be mild and transient, gradually increasing in severity, or biphasic with a course of withdrawal, improvement, and then an exacerbation.

5. Frequency. The frequency of neonatal narcotic abstinence syndrome is 55–94% for babies of opiate-dependent mothers, and higher for methadone than for heroin.

6. Differential diagnosis. Neonatal withdrawal signs may overlap with other medical conditions, including

    a. Infection

    b. Hypoglycemia

    c. Hypomagnesemia

    d. CNS hemorrhage

    e. Anoxia

    f. Pregnancy (see Table 15.4).

7. Treatment. With adequate treatment, the severity of withdrawal does not relate to developmental outcome. Pharmacologic agents used to treat neonatal withdrawal do not adversely affect outcome.

    a. Recommended supportive treatment is as follows. For mild symptoms, observe in a hospital setting for 3–4 days. Polydrug abuse or methadone use may warrant longer observation. Maintain a calm, quiet, warm environment. Gentle handling, swaddling, and frequent small feedings are helpful. A pacifier can relieve irritability and help with the increased sucking urge experienced by these babies. Maintain fluid and electrolyte balance.

    b. Pharmacotherapy is indicated when any of the following are present:

       i. Seizures.

      ii. Weight loss and dehydration from diarrhea and/or vomiting.

     iii. Fever unrelated to an infection.

     iv. Poor feeding, with failure to gain weight.

      v. Severe hyperactivity, irritability, or inability to sleep.

     vi. A score of ≥ 8 on the 21-symptom Neonatal Abstinence Scoring System for three consecutive scorings, or if an average of any 3 is greater than 8 (see Table 15.5).

    c. Pharmacotherapy for neonatal abstinence syndrome should be administered and monitored by an experienced pediatrician. Typically, phenobarbital is recommended for poly-drug-dependent neonates and paregoric, for opiate-addicted neonates.

8. Prognosis. The prognosis for recovery from the acute phase of abstinence is good. No long-term sequelae have been identified.

TABLE 15.4. Neonatal Abstinence Syndrome Overlapping with Pregnancy

Signs and Symptoms Common to Pregnancy and Opiate Withdrawal	Signs and Symptoms Seen in Opiate Withdrawal That Are Not Concomitants with Normal Pregnancy
Anxiety	Dilated pupils
Insomnia	Gooseflesh
Sweating	Tremor
Cramps	Diarrhea
Nausea and vomiting	
Malaise	

VI. SEDATIVE/HYPNOTICS DURING PREGNANCY

It is estimated that 22–28% of pregnant women in the United States take sedative drugs during pregnancy. The most commonly used agents are benzodiazepines and barbiturates.

A. Adverse Effects of Benzodiazepine Use during Pregnancy

1. Morphologic teratogenicity. There is no consensus about whether the use of benzodiazepines during pregnancy increases the risk of congenital anomalies in offspring. In some studies, but not others, diazepam has been associated with increased likelihood of oral clefts. No other benzodiazepine has been implicated as a teratogen. A dramatic increase in the use of benzodiazepines among women of reproductive age in the past few decades has not produced a corresponding increase in oral clefts. In conclusion, diazepam is at most weakly associated with increased risk of oral clefts. However, its uncontrolled use in addicted patients with other risk factors may be more hazardous than its prescribed use.

2. Behavioral teratogenicity. One group of researchers has found delays in mental and motor development in toddlers prenatally exposed to benzodiazepines. However, these studies had significant methodologic flaws. Other studies have found no effect of benzodiazepines on IQ, even in high-risk populations.

3. Toxicity. Newborns exposed to high-dose benzodiazepines in late pregnancy (the equivalent of ≥ 30 mg of diazepam) often exhibit "floppy-baby syndrome" at birth. Signs include lethargy, poor suck and respiratory efforts, hypotonia, hyporeflexia, and difficulty maintaining body temperature. Benzodiazepine toxicity can be diagnosed in utero; fetal monitoring shows decreased beat-to-beat cardiac variability and absence of normal accelerations.

4. Withdrawal. Hypertonia, hyperreflexia, and tremor, which are seldom apparent immediately at birth but appear within several hours, can be manifestations of benzodiazepine withdrawal after prolonged intrauterine exposure.

B. Adverse Effects of Barbiturates during Pregnancy

1. Teratogenicity. Barbiturates are weak human teratogens. They may slightly increase the risk of major congenital anomalies, but the only clear association is with minor craniofacial anomalies that usually disappear by age 4.

2. Malpresentation. Barbiturates can decrease fetal movement, thus increasing the risk of breech or other abnormal presentations during labor.

3. Toxicity. This resembles benzodiazepine intoxication (see above).

4. Withdrawal. Sudden, unsupervised barbiturate withdrawal during pregnancy, or at birth for the neonate, can result in severe symptoms, including status epilepticus and fetal or neonatal respiratory distress. Untreated severe withdrawal can result in death for either the woman, the fetus, or both.

C. Treatment of Sedative/Hypnotic Addiction during Pregnancy

1. Ideally, treatment should be initiated in an inpatient setting where addiction services can work in close collaboration with obstetric services.
2. In most cases, the standard approach of substituting a long-acting agent, then initiating slow, controlled withdrawal, is opti-

TABLE 15.5. Neonatal Abstinence Scoring System

System	Signs and Symptoms	Score	A.M.	P.M.	Comments
CNS disturbance	Excessive high-pitched (or other) cry	2			Daily weight:
	Continuous high-pitched (or other) cry	3			
	Sleeps <1 h after feeding	3			
	Sleeps <2 h after feeding	2			
	Sleeps <3 h after feeding	1			
	Hyperactive Moro reflex	2			
	Markedly hyperactive Moro reflex	3			
	Mild tremors disturbed	1			
	Moderate–severe tremors disturbed	2			
	Mild tremors undisturbed	3			
	Moderate–severe tremors undisturbed	4			
	Increased muscle tone	2			
	Excoriation (specific area)	1			
	Myoclonic jerks	3			
	Generalized convulsions	5			

Metabolic vasomotor respiratory disturbances	Sweating	1											
	Fever <101° (99-100.8°F or 37.2-38.2°C)	1											
	Fever >101° (≥38.4°C)	2											
	Frequent yawning (>3–4 times / interval)	1											
	Mottling	1											
	Nasal stuffiness	1											
	Sneezing (>3–4 times / interval)	1											
	Nasal flaring	2											
	Respiratory rate >60 / min	1											
	Respiratory rate >60 / min with retractions	2											
Gastrointestinal disturbances	Excessive sucking	1											
	Poor feeding	2											
	Regurgitation	2											
	Projectile vomiting	3											
	Loose stools	2											
	Watery stools	3											
	Total score												
	Initials of scorer												

Source: Finnegan LP: Neonatal abstinence syndrome: assessment and pharmacotherapy. In FF Rubalteli, B Granati (eds): Neonatal therapy: an update. Amsterdam: Excepta Medica, 1986.

mal. The initial dose can be reduced by 5–10% per day, or slower if signs of withdrawal develop. However, in the first trimester, it may be preferable to avoid diazepam because of its possible association with oral clefts. Lorazepam has a theoretical advantage over other benzodiazepines during pregnancy, because of its lack of accumulation in the fetus, although this has not been shown to produce better outcomes. Clonazepam, another long-acting agent, has been relatively well studied during pregnancy and has no known teratogenic effects.

3. Maternal, fetal, or neonatal benzodiazepine toxicity can be treated with the benzodiazepine inhibitor flumazenil. Flumazenil has a short half-life, so close observation should be maintained for at least 24 h after the first dose to see whether repeat doses are needed.

SELECTED READINGS

Benowitz NL: Nicotine replacement therapy during pregnancy. *JAMA* 266:3174, 1991.

Chasnoff IJ: Drug and alcohol effects on pregnancy and the newborn. In NS Miller (ed): *Comprehensive Handbook of Drug and Alcohol Addiction.* New York: Marcel Dekker, 1991.

Finnegan LP, Kandall SR: Maternal and neonatal effects of alcohol and pregnancy. In JH Lowinson, P Ruiz, RB Millman (eds): *Substance Abuse: A Comprehensive Textbook*, 2nd ed. Baltimore: Williams & Wilkins, 1992.

James ME, Coles CD: Cocaine abuse during pregnancy: psychiatric considerations. *Gen Hosp Psychiatry* 13:399, 1991.

Levy M, Spino M: Neonatal withdrawal syndrome: associated drugs and pharmacologic management. *Pharmacotherapy* 13:202, 1993.

Miller LJ: Detoxification of the addicted woman in pregnancy. In NS Miller (ed): *Principles of Addiction Medicine.* Chevy Chase, MD: American Society of Addiction Medicine, 1994.

Miller LJ, Raskin VD: Pharmacological therapies in pregnant women with drug and alcohol addictions. In NS Miller, MS Gold (eds): *Pharmacological Therapies for Drug and Alcohol Addictions.* New York: Marcel Dekker, 1995.

Serdula M, Williamson DF, Kendrick JS, Anda RF, Byers T: Trends in alcohol consumption by pregnant women, 1985 through 1988. *JAMA* 265:876, 1991.

Sokol RJ, Martier SS, Ager JW: The T-ACE questions: practical prenatal detection of risk- drinking. *Am J Obstet Gynecol* 160:863, 1989.

CHAPTER 16

TREATMENT OF ADDICTIVE DISORDERS IN PEDIATRIC AND ADOLESCENT POPULATIONS

Peter D. Rogers, M.D., M.P.H., F.A.A.P.; Susan Speraw, Ph.D., R.N.;
Dennis Westmeier, B.A., C.C.D.C., I.C.R.C.; and Joseph Jolly, M.D.
Division of Adolescent/Young Adult Medicine
T. C. Thompson Children's Hospital
Chattanooga, Tennessee

In the war on drugs, the most vulnerable of all the casualties has been the young. Most children and adolescent substance abusers have had a core of emotional pain that predated their drug use. Young people in emotional pain with no coping skills often make poor choices. These children and adolescents often find that their pain is anesthetized when they use drugs and alcohol.

The use of certain drugs is once again on the rise, although alcohol abuse is still the major public health problem among adolescents.

It is clear that in the past, many of the adolescents who have been treated for substance abuse relapsed because they were not properly assessed, diagnosed, and placed in the appropriate level of care.

The treatment of substance-abusing adolescents must not only focus on their use of drugs and alcohol but also on identifying and treating the emotional pain that is often the precipitating cause of their drug or alcohol dependence. Also, the drug-using teenager must learn what recovery is and how to attain it.

I. EPIDEMIOLOGY

The epidemiologic data presented are based on the findings of the National High School Survey on Drugs Use (NHSSDU), published January 31, 1994. This survey is a summary of drug and alcohol use among 50,000 high-school students in 400 schools. The survey has been done annually on high-school seniors since 1975, and has included data collected from 8th- and 10th-graders since 1991. The NHSSDU does not include those teenagers who have dropped out of school.

The results of this survey show a sharp rise in marijuana use at all three grade levels throughout the country, as well as increased usage of stimulants, LSD, and inhalants.

There has also been an increase in cigarette smoking in all three grade levels. More importantly, there has been a softening of the attitudes and beliefs

Manual of Therapeutics for Addictions, Edited by Norman S. Miller, Mark S. Gold, and David E. Smith.
ISBN 0471-56176-2 © 1997 John Wiley & Sons, Inc.

regarding the dangers associated with, as well as personal disapproval of, drug use.

From 1979 to 1991 there had been a steady decline in illicit-drug use. However, since 1991, the use of illicit drugs has been *increasing*.

A. Marijuana. In 1993, the proportion of 8th-graders who used marijuana had increased by 50% over the prior 2 years. The proportion of 10th-graders who used marijuana increased by 25%, and the proportion of high-school seniors who used marijuana increased by 20%.

In the same year, 2.5% of high-school seniors reported smoking marijuana daily. This is in comparison to 2% in 1991 and 10% in 1979. In 1993, 16% of high-school seniors smoked marijuana at least one time per month, as compared to 11% of 10th-graders and 5% of 8th-graders.

B. LSD. Use of LSD has been increasing gradually at all three grade levels. In 1981, the peak year for LSD use, 2.5% of high-school seniors used LSD at least one time. In 1984, 1.5% of high-school seniors used LSD at least one time per month. In 1993, 2.4% of high-school seniors used LSD at least one time per month. If this trend continues, use of LSD will be at an all-time high within 2 years. Because of the uniquely high tolerance associated with LSD use, the drug is rarely used more than 2–3 times per week. Use of LSD is now more common in high-school students than is cocaine.

C. Inhalants. Use of inhalants, including gasoline, aerosols, and glue, has also increased at all three grade levels over the past 2 years. Inhalants are remarkable in that they are most likely to be used in the earlier grade levels. In 1987, the peak year for inhalants use, 2.8% of high-school seniors used inhalants in the previous month. In 1993, 2.5% of high-school seniors used inhalants in the previous month, compared to 3.3% of 10th-graders and 5.7% of 8th-graders.

D. Stimulants. Stimulant (amphetamine) use began to fall after 1981. However, over the past 2 years stimulant use has risen at all three grade levels.

E. Cocaine. Cocaine use reached a peak among high-school seniors in 1985, with 6.7% using cocaine in the previous month. In 1987, 3.4% of high-school seniors had used cocaine in the previous month, and in 1993 1.3% of high-school seniors had used cocaine in the previous month. Lifetime and annual use seem to have reached a plateau since 1991.

F. Alcohol and Cigarettes. The so-called legal drugs remain the most widely used at all grade levels. Two-thirds of 8th-graders and almost nine-tenths of high-school seniors have tried alcohol. Episodes of heavy drinking (>5 drinks on one occasion) also remain common. In 1993, 2.5% of high-school seniors drank daily, compared to 7% of seniors in 1979. However, in 1993, 28% of seniors had greater than 5 drinks on one occasion during the prior 2 weeks. This number was 14% for 8th-graders and 23% for 10th-graders. Statistics for drinking have changed little since 1991, but seniors have had a longer-term decline in episodes of heavy drinking.

Cigarette use has been steady for high-school seniors over the past decade, but is now on the increase. The rate of daily smoking has risen in all three grade levels in 1993, from 7 to 8% among 8th-graders, 12 to 14% among 10th-graders, and from 17 to 19% among high-school seniors.

G. Over-the-Counter Drugs. There are no epidemiologic data available on the use of OTC such as caffeine pills, ephedrine ("white crosses"), phenylephrine and other "diet" pills, and medications with a high alcohol content such as

Nyquil. Over-the-counter drugs are substances commonly abused by adolescents.

H. Racial and Ethnic Differences. Black students report the lowest rate of use for virtually all drugs. In long-term trends, blacks have shown a continuing decline in smoking as well as the slowest rate of increase in inhalant use. In addition, blacks have not shown the increase in LSD use seen among whites and Hispanics.

I. Demographic Comparisons. The trends of increased use of marijuana, LSD, stimulants, and inhalants has occurred across most sectors of society, without concentrations in large cities or particular regions.

J. Conclusions. Over the past 2 years drugs use among American high-school students has increased, with a sharp rise in the use of marijuana, LSD, inhalants, and amphetamines. Alcohol remains the most widely used drug in all age groups and is responsible for more morbidity and mortality than all other drugs combined.

II. ASSESSMENT OF CHILDREN OR ADOLESCENTS AND THEIR FAMILIES

A. Planning the Interview. Establishing "ground rules" for the interview is an essential prerequisite to completing an interview of children or adolescents and their families. Very often all family members have fears and misgivings about the intentions of the interviewer. They may fear that they are being "set up" for reporting to the authorities, severe disciplinary action, personal embarrassment, or ridicule. The purposes of the interview, the expectations of all participating parties, and basic ground rules related to confidentiality and legal reporting mandates must be addressed in order to create an atmosphere or environment conducive to self-disclosure and complete honesty.

1. **Basic ground rules**
    a. Information gathered during the interview will become part of the permanent record and will be shared with the medical evaluation team, including physicians, nurses, social workers, and counselors.
    b. Since secrecy and "secrets" are common among substance-abusing children and adolescents, it is important for the health provider to avoid the reality or appearance of collusion with the patient. While confidentiality will be protected, there will be no "secrets" regarding substance abuse between the health provider and the patient.
    c. Both the child or adolescent and their parents have the right to refuse to answer any question, although openness and honesty are strongly encouraged in the interest of providing the most accurate assessment and the development of the most effective treatment plan.

2. **Confidentiality limits.** There are limits to confidentiality which the provider is mandated by law to observe.
    a. A parent, guardian, and at times the legal authorities such as police or child-protective agencies, must be informed (1) if the child is engaged in behavior that is injurious or life-threatening (such as substance abuse), or if there is suicidal intent on the part of the patient; (2) if the patient is homicidal; and (3) if disclosure

of physical, sexual, or emotional abuse is made to the healthcare provider, or if there is strong suspicion of abuse.

b. Limits to confidentiality are in force in every state of the Union, and are applied to members of *all* health professions. To fail to report suspected abuse, or to inform responsible parties in the event of danger to self or others, is to jeopardize one's professional license. Reporting these things is not optional; it is not at the discretion of the provider, and these limits to confidentiality are not negotiable under circumstance.

c. Parents are accorded the same right to confidentiality with regard to their personal lives, and with regard to the details of their interpersonal relationships, but the same limits of confidentiality are applied to them.

3. **General guidelines for the interview**

a. The patient and parents should be interviewed both individually and as a family unit. There are times when persons are willing to say things privately that they will not say in a group. Yet at other times the comments of one group member stimulate further discussion. Therefore, both approaches to the interview are essential components of assessment.

b. During the course of these interviews questions may be repeated several times. Avoid the temptation to omit repetitious questions. Such questions reworded or repeated over time frequently elicit different responses and often serve to expand the database with critical information or important details about how different family members view the same problem.

c. As rapport and trust are developed, the patient and family will be more self-disclosing, and give added detail or depth to their responses.

d. At times children and adolescents may present as either completely innocent ("I don't know what they are talking about; I never used drugs in my life.") or very angry and defensive ("I don't want to be here, and you can't make me talk to you."). Both approaches to the interviewer are intended to protect themselves and their family from disclosure and additional pain by keeping the health provider at a safe distance.

4. **Qualities in the interview that will increase effectiveness in interviewing**

a. Unconditional positive regard for the patient and family means that the healthcare provider conveys unqualified respect for the inherent worth and dignity of the patient and family as persons, and a willingness to help them with their problems.

b. Acceptance is an attitude which is nonjudgmental. Although substance abuse is not endorsed by the provider, neither is negative, degrading judgment or guilt inflicted on the patient. The healthcare provider accepts the patient's description of activities with professional detachment.

c. Genuineness is a general feeling of interest in the patient, conveyed with personal warmth and openness, within the context of a professional attitude and presentation. Genuineness also includes using language that is easily understandable to the patient (particularly important when dealing with children and adolescents). It is of little merit to use medical jargon or complex terminology to "impress" patients. The genuine healthcare provider will speak the "language" of the client.

d. Empathy differs from sympathy. Empathy means that the health provider attempts to understand the experience of the patient as the patient views it. Empathy is seeing life from the perspective of the other person, while sympathy means feeling sorry for someone else. What the patient and family need from a health provider is empathy, an attempt to understand the patients' life experiences as they themselves see it.

e. Concerning competence and professionalism, patients and families will answer many questions and provide much information if the interviewer appears self-confident and assured. Therefore, the interviewer must be willing to accept calmly whatever information the patient presents. If the patient or family detects that the health provider is reluctant or uncomfortable discussing certain issues, they will avoid total disclosure, and will tell the interviewer what they think the interviewer wants to hear.

f. Self-awareness is critical to an effective interview. Healthcare providers who are speaking with the children or their families must be aware of their own personal response to the situation. Being aware of our own personal issues and "sensitive" areas helps to separate our own anguish from the patient's distress. It is also important to note that what is of critical importance is the patient's history and life experience.

B. Interview of the Child or Adolescent. Children and adolescents who abuse substances usually do so in order to cope with very real emotional pain. This emotional pain often relates to long-standing family problems, which may include substance abuse in one or both parents. In order to survive in such problem families, children unconsciously adopt ways of relating to other family members which are intended to relieve stress in the family. A key purpose of the interview is to identify the roles children play in their families, how they feel about themselves, and, in a broader scope, the quality of their relationships with peers, God, or a higher power.

1. **Key interview questions about parent–child relationships**

   a. "If your father were in the room with us, and I asked him to describe you, what would he say?" After the answer is given, repeat the question using "mother." This question will elicit information about the way the adolescent views his/her relationship with the parents.

   b. "To what extent do you think your parents care or are concerned about you?"

   c. "Do they spend as much time with you as you would like them to?" "What do you do when you are together?"

   d. "Do you think that they care about your future?"

2. **Friendships and relationships with peers**

   a. "If you like someone of the same age and sex, and would like to have this person as a friend, why would he/she want to be your friend?"

   b. "If you like someone about your age of the opposite sex, and would like to date this person, why would this person want to go out with you?"

c. "If you were to spend time with a friend or out on a date, what kind of activities would you most likely do?

3. A "spiritual assessment" to identify what spiritual benefits or resources are sustaining or supportive in a child's life

a. "Do you go to church?" is often a nonthreatening way to approach this subject.

b. "If you go to church, how meaningful is it for you?"

c. "When you think of God, how do you imagine God to be?"

d. "How do you think God feels about you and your family?"

e. "Do you pray?" "If you pray, what do you pray for?"

f. "Sometimes people get frustrated or angry with God about things that happen in their life. Has this ever happened to you?" If so, "Tell me about it."

g. "How have your thoughts or feelings about God and God's relationship to you changed as you have gotten older?"

4. Questions concerning belief in Satan, or involvement in satanic rituals or worship. Young people involved in satanic worship often are experiencing a pathologic alienation from "prosocial" values and may need special, long-term treatment.

a. "Have you ever heard of satanic worship, or devil worship?" If so, "Tell me what you know about it."

b. "To what extent have you or your friends or family ever been involved with it?"

5. Questions regarding possible physical or sexual abuse

a. "Has anyone ever touched you or done anything to you that you think is wrong or made you uncomfortable?" is a question to be asked of teenagers of both sexes.

b. Even a vague denial of this question must be pursued. Children and adolescents may be shameful or fearful of revealing abuse, and reluctant to identify a perpetrator who may be known and loved by them (it is not uncommon for abuse to be perpetrated by a family member, and for a child to have ambivalent feelings about the abuse and the abuser).

c. A positive response must be followed with questions to determine (1) when the abuse took place, (2) who perpetrated the abuse, (3) what exactly happened during the abuse, and (4) whether the person is continuing to be involved with children or have access to children in any way.

d. If an abuse history is identified, it must be reported to the authorities if the child is a minor, or if the perpetrator continues to have access to children in any way (a parent, grandparent, a baby-sitter, a teacher, a minister).

6. A history of suicidality or homicidality

a. "Have you ever tried to kill or hurt yourself?"

b. If "yes," identify details such as when the attempt(s) took place, method used, and outcome (hospitalization, nothing happened).

c. "Have you ever thought about suicide?" If so, "Did you plan how you would do it?"

d. "Are you suicidal now? Do you wish you were dead?" If the response is "yes," must ask for degree of intent, the presence of a plan and the means to carry out the plan, the presence of a suicide note.

e. "Have you ever thought about harming anybody else?" If so, explore as above.

f. In the event of active suicidal or homicidal intent there is a mandated duty to warn the family, the police, and/or the intended victim.

7. The presence of "family secrets": or "personal secrets"

a. Secrets are things that a young person will not readily discuss because of feelings of shame or guilt.

b. Exploration for "secrets" is critical because these secrets may be the source of the pain the child or adolescent is seeking to escape through drug use.

c. Some common "personal" secrets include being sexually active; having had an abortion, rape, homosexual affair, or experimentation; smoking; or having done things under the influence of alcohol or drugs that the child or adolescent would not normally have done.

d. Common "family secrets" include such things as one or both parents engaging in extramarital affairs, substance abuse in one or both parents, domestic violence, divorce, adoption, gay or lesbian members of the family, or such things as cheating on one's income taxes.

e. Secrets need to be flushed out during treatment so that the teenager is allowed to express the feelings associated with these secrets, however painful, and to eventually learn nonchemical coping skills to deal with the pain of their secrets.

f. To give the adolescent the opportunity to speak about secrets will not "put ideas in their head." Rather, it affords the opportunity to talk about their concerns, gives them permission to do so, and acknowledges that they may have worries that are difficult and awkward to discuss.

g. Initial inquiry regarding "secrets" may not evoke an honest response, or may elicit only partial disclosure. With the development of rapport, disclosure may increase.

8. Explore for the use of drugs or alcohol in the parent(s)

a. "Does anyone in your family drink or use drugs?"

b. "How do you feel when you know your parent has been drinking?"

c. "Has anyone in the family ever told them they drink or use drugs too much?"

d. "Have they ever tried to quit or cut back on drug or alcohol use?"

e. "Has anyone in the family ever gone to a support group or organization such as Alcoholics Anonymous?"

f. "Has anyone in the family ever been in drug or alcohol treatment, sometimes called "detox" or "rehab"?

9. Questions regarding other risk-taking behaviors

a. A child or adolescent who has been identified as exhibiting one risk-taking behavior, such as substance abuse is commonly involved in other risk-taking behaviors, such as having multiple sex partners.

b. Direct questioning often works best, and also "gives permission" for more complete honesty rather than protective or defensive denial.

c. "How many different sex partners have you had in the past year?"

d. "Have you ever prostituted for money or for drugs?"

e. "Have you ever had sex for drugs?" "Have you had sex with your dealer?"

f. "Have you ever had sex with someone you didn't know?"

g. "Have you had sex with someone who might be using, or who you think has used, IV drugs?"

h. "When you had sex, did you use any form of protection for disease (such as a condom) or birth control?" "How often did you use protection?"

i. "Have you ever had blood testing for HIV infection?" "When was the most recent test?"

Depending on the answers to these questions, HIV testing may need to be considered. If the patient has self-injected drugs, HIV testing should be done.

10. Four common "family roles" typically assumed by the child in a substance-abusing family system

a. Lost child. This is the child who is often the isolated, withdrawn, quiet "loner." The child seeks to remain essentially invisible to escape the wrath of the parents and to avoid causing trouble.

b. Hero. This is the child who does everything well, who feels "driven" to achieve. The child usually earns good grades, participates in many activities, and in general, makes the family look good. The child's job is to "save" the family.

c. Mascot. The "family clown" keeps the atmosphere in the home cheerful. If an argument erupts, the mascot moves into action, making everyone laugh and forget their troubles.

d. Scapegoat. This is the child who is identified as the problem, who takes on himself/herself all the troubles of the family. The attention of the parents is focused on the "bad" child, so they avoid examination and confrontation of their own interpersonal problems.

e. Questions to ask about family roles

(1) In most families people take on certain roles or "jobs" that they perform for the family. These are ways that they help keep the family moving. Some of these roles are . . . (explain the above). "who has these roles in your family?"

(2) "Who makes most of the really big decisions in your family?"

(3) "What happens if other people disagree with the decision?"

(4) "Who do you go to for help and advice if you have a really serious problem?"

(5) "Who takes care of someone who is sick?" "Who decides when it is time to go to the doctor?" "Who takes a sick child to the doctor?"

(6) "Who do you tell information if you want the 'news' to get out and be spread to everybody?"

(7) "Who do you go to with a really big secret that you don't want anybody to know?"

(8) "Who decides how money is spent?"

C. Interviewing the Family. Knowledge of family history and the family context in which the adolescent has been raised and lives will provide important clues to the origins of the substance-abusing behavior, and can direct future treatment planning.

1. General guidelines specific to the family interview

a. Include siblings as part of the interview process if they are available. Often siblings are more knowledgeable about what is happening in the identified patient's life than are the parents.

b. Defer to the natural authority of the parents by asking for their input first. However, if one person (such as one of the parents) is particularly resistant to the idea of intervention or family involvement, it may be useful to begin by eliciting the opinions or feelings of that person. Such a strategy may serve to "hook" them into the process, demonstrate that you view their contribution as valuable, and acknowledge their importance to the process.

c. Allow every person to have an opportunity to express their perspective on the situation, even the youngest of siblings, grandparents who live at home with the family, or live-in baby-sitters. Each has a unique view of family dynamics that must be shared.

d. Every person's opinion or viewpoint on what is happening in the family is equally valuable.

2. Key questions to include in the family interview

a. Questions about family history

(1) How long have the parents been together? How did they meet and decide to be together as a couple?

(2) What are the parents' occupations, ages, and levels of education?

(3) When were children born? What are the current ages, whereabouts, and activities of all children and stepchildren?

(4) Information about each parent's family of origin: age and health status of the child's grandparents, aunts, uncles, and cousins.

(5) History of substance use (drugs, alcohol, including prescription drugs) among any relatives, or of illness related to chronic substance use (such as cirrhosis).

(6) Does anyone in the family use substances "more than they would like?" Has anyone ever suggested attending a support group such as AA or Al Anon?

(7) History of significant changes in the family (relocation or migration, births, deaths (including the death of pets, friends, relatives), divorce, or remarriage.

(8) How did family members adjust to these changes?

b. Questions about the substance-abusing child

(1) When did the family members first notice a problem or change in behavior to suggest substance abuse?

(2) Has the school reported any behavior problems at school?

(3) What has been the pattern in the child's grades?

(4) Has the child been truant? Engaged in behaviors such as running away, stealing, or lying?

(5) What is the nature of the child's relationships with peers? Can they make and keep friends? What do other family members think about the child's friends?

(6) What do the parents know about the child's friends?

(7) Have there been any noted changes in personality (such as more belligerent, "high-strung," nervous, disinterested in life, depressed)?

(8) Does the child smoke cigarettes? Marijuana?

(9) Do any of the friends of their child use drugs or alcohol?

c. Questions about the parents

(1) What is the quality of the parents' relationship? Is there tension in the home? (This question should be asked both in the family group as well as privately of the parents.)

(2) What is the incidence and nature of family violence?

(3) In cases where there are stepparents, does the child visit with the biological parent? What is the nature of the child's relationship with that parent? What is the nature of the child's visitation with the parent; what do they do when they are together?

(4) Does either of the parents now drink too much or use drugs (including prescription medications)? Have they done so in the past? Has either parent ever belonged to a self-help group such as Alcoholics Anonymous or Narcotics Anonymous? Have they ever tried to cut down on the amount of drugs or liquor that they consume? (This should also be asked both in the family group and of the parents meeting privately.)

(5) What is the family's involvement within the greater community (church and civic groups, Little League, Girl Scouts, etc.)?

(6) How often do they attend church or other religious service? How satisfying do they find their religious affiliation experience?

3. Family interaction patterns that contribute to substance abuse. The interviewer should keep in mind that the following factors may be present in the family or impact in a negative way on the substance-abusing child as a member of the family.

a. Inadequate self-differentiation of family members

(1) Persons who are poorly differentiated have their actions guided by emotions and the reactions of others rather than by their own rational thoughts, personal values, or decisions. Individuals who are poorly differentiated may use substances to dull emotional pain that comes from the perceived disapproval of others.

(2) Children and adolescents, by virtue of their age and developmental level, are often poorly differentiated from their parents.

(3) In substance-abusing families, adults in the system are also often poorly differentiated from their own families of origin and each other.

    b. Presence of triangles

        (1) Under stress, a two-person emotional system (such as a husband and wife) will draw into the system a third person (such as an adolescent who is accustomed to playing the role of the "scapegoat") to lower the intensity of stress and anxiety and gain greater stability.

        (2) When a child is drawn into the system to form the stable triangle, one of two things may happen. Either one or both of the parents may direct their emotion to the "scapegoat" child (becoming critical or angry with the child), rather than directing this legitimate emotion toward their spouse. In another common variant of the triangle, the child has learned from experience that by engaging in a particular behavior (such as overt substance abuse) the parents will stop their attacks on each other as their attention is diverted to focus on the "problem" of the child.

        (3) If the presence of triangles is not identified by the interviewer, the danger is that the problems of the parents and family can be overlooked, and the child will be identified as "the problem."

    c. Presence of the multigenerational transmission process

        (1) In the natural history of the family unit, it is thought that an individual will marry another person who approximates their own emotional development. Thus, individuals who are poorly differentiated and highly governed by their emotions are likely to marry others who have similar difficulties.

        (2) Troubled parents then serve as role models of maladaptive coping for their children.

        (3) The use of substances as a means of coping with stress may be repeated in subsequent generations.

    4. Involvement of the family. Families serve as the context in which substance-addicting behavior exists, and it is within the family context that treatment must also occur. Because children are dependent on their families for physical care and support, they cannot be treated in isolation. The family must be part of the entire process.

III. DIAGNOSIS OF ADOLESCENT CHEMICAL DEPENDENCE

The hallmark of adolescent substance dependence is continued use of the substance(s) despite harmful consequences experienced as a result of the substance(s) abused. For example, continued use of drugs and/or alcohol by an adolescent despite academic, family, legal, or emotional problems experienced as a result of the substance abuse is essential to making the diagnosis of adolescent chemical dependence.

    The *DSM-IV* lists seven criteria for making the diagnosis of substance dependence. Three of the criteria must be met in order to make the diagnosis. These criteria are clearly not adolescent-specific. These criteria are listed below with comments added to make them more age-specific for those between the ages of 12 and 18 years.

A. Criteria for Substance Dependence (*DSM-IV*). A maladaptive pattern of substance use, leading to clinically significant impairment or distress, as manifested by three (or more) of the following, occurring at any time in the same 12-month period:

1. *Tolerance,** as defined by either of the following:

   a. A need for markedly increased amounts of the substance to achieve intoxication or desired effect.

   b. Markedly diminished effect with continued use of the same amount of substance.

   (*Author's note: Tolerance* as defined above is appropriate for adults and adolescents abusing cannabis, alcohol, narcotics, benzodiazepines, sleeping pills, and stimulants. However, with teenagers tolerance is not quite so dramatic with abuse of inhalants and LSD. The frequency of use of inhalants and psychedelic drugs is important.)

2. Withdrawal, as manifested by either of the following:

   a. The characteristic withdrawal syndrome for the substance.

   b. The same (or a closely related) substance is taken to relieve or avoid withdrawal symptoms.

   (*Author's note:* For teenagers, because they do not characteristically abuse drugs or alcohol as long as their adult counterparts, withdrawal is less physiological distress but more emotional lability.)

3. The substance is often taken in larger amounts or over a longer period than intended.

   (*Author's note:* Although this phenomenon is seen with adolescent substance abusers, we consider it one of the less important criteria in making the diagnosis of adolescent chemical dependence.)

4. There is a persistent desire or unsuccessful effort to cut down on control substance use.

   (*Author's note:* Many adolescent substance abusers believe that they can quit anytime they want to and have often never attempted to quit or cut down on use.)

5. A great deal of time is spent in *activities* necessary to obtain the substance, use the substance or recover from its effects.

   (*Author's note:* Adolescent "hangovers" are mercifully brief, and therefore they spend less time than adults recovering from their use of drugs or alcohol.)

6. Important social, occupational, or recreational activities are given up or reduced because of substance use.

   (*Author's note:* In adolescents, academic performance, and family relationships are the most dramatic areas of the child's life that are affected adversely.)

7. The substance use is continued despite knowledge of having a persistent or recurrent physical or psychological problem that is likely to have been caused or exacerbated by the substance.

   (*Author's note:* Of all the criteria, this one is probably the least useful when attempting to document adolescent chemical dependence in terms of physical problems. Adolescents do have psychological problems that are exacerbated by substance abuse.)

As stated, the criteria for making the diagnosis of chemical dependence in the *DSM-IV* has little utility for those of us working with chemically dependent adolescents. A separate set of criteria needs to be devised that would be unique to adolescents, stressing the importance of continued use of substances despite harmful consequences in the areas of family life, school performance, legal problems, depression, and psychosocial functioning.

IV. CHOOSING THE LEVEL OF TREATMENT

Once an adolescent is diagnosed or suspected of being chemically dependent, a further assessment of this young person must be done in order to choose the appropriate level of care to which the child should be admitted if treatment is indicated.

The assessment should include the following areas, although there is considerable overlap in all the areas.

1. *Emotional Stabilization.* Most adolescents do not need a medical detoxification, but will need a period of time to be stabilized emotionally before effective treatment is begun. During the assessment, it must be determined if this initial stabilization should be done in an inpatient or outpatient setting.

2. *Biomedical Conditions and Complications.* Adolescents who are heavily abusing drugs or alcohol must be considered at high risk for such medical problems as hepatitis, bronchitis, HIV infection, sexually transmitted diseases (STDs), and medical or dental problems associated with poor nutrition. Ideally, a thorough history and physical examination by a physician should be part of the assessment.

3. *Emotional/Behavioral Condition or Complications.* A mental status exam must be performed during the assessment in order to choose the appropriate level of care. It must be determined whether the adolescent has any disturbance of mood or conduct, or, possibly, a thought disorder. The mental status may dictate that the adolescent be admitted to a treatment program that has a major psychiatric component. It must be determined during the assessment if the adolescent can cooperate with peer interaction, maintain behavioral stability, and avoid uncontrollable behavior that endangers self or others.

4. *Treatment Acceptance or Resistance.* It must be determined whether the adolescent admits to having a substance abuse problem and is genuinely willing to cooperate with a treatment program. If the teenager does not express a genuine commitment to recovery and will require monitoring and motivating strategies, an inpatient treatment program may be the initial recommendation.

5. *Recovery Environment.* Before choosing an appropriate level of treatment, it must be determined whether the family is emotionally capable of supporting this child during early treatment. A chaotic family sabotages the patient's efforts to change. If there is a substance-abusing family member, this is an indication that the adolescent receive inpatient treatment. Also, if there is no peer support for recovery, the adolescent should be treated, at least initially, in an inpatient setting.

V. ADOLESCENT TREATMENT AND RECOVERY

The treatment of the substance-abusing adolescent must be multidimensional. Because of life stressors plus the substance abuse, young people entering chemical-dependence treatment have been negatively affected in every sphere of their lives: emotional and behavioral, psychosocial, spiritual, and physical.

Adolescents entering treatment for substance abuse are profoundly unhappy and lack a positive self-image.

Chemical-dependence treatment for adolescents requires assessing the adolescent in his/her total environment and evaluating how the adolescent and his/her environment interact with and impact each other. Adolescents, although resilient, have neither broad-based coping mechanisms nor the independence to effectively change their environment. They are truly dependent in a wider sense on their environment and on those who dwell there. Consequently, adolescent treatment must, of necessity, involve treatment strategies designed to address the adolescent in a holistic manner. Of paramount importance in the group and individual therapy sessions, is to allow the adolescent to explore his/her feelings and to practice expressing them assertively and appropriately in a secure setting.

Beside the level of care provided for the adolescent, two additional components are vitally important: the family involvement in the treatment process and continuing care. Family involvement increases the likelihood of family reintegration and provides the family an opportunity to involve themselves in their own recovery process, thereby being of support to the adolescent in his/her recovery. Experience demonstrates that adolescents who remain in continuing care for 1–2 years have a greater recovery rate than do those who terminate treatment on discharge from inpatient, day, and/or outpatient treatment.

The continuing-care program gives the adolescent the opportunity to share personal difficulties in the recovery process with other adolescents who may have varying lengths of time in recovery. A continuing-care program allows adolescents to continue therapy for problems initially addressed as a more restrictive level of care. The long-range benefit of the continuing-care process for adolescents clearly warrants a major emphasis. It may well be the most significant therapeutic modality to prevent relapse or to minimize the intensity and severity of relapse should such occur.

Adolescent treatment is most effective when treatment services are available on an integrated and coordinated continuum-of-care basis to include

1. *Inpatient treatment*—patient requires medical management and supervision.
2. *Day treatment*—patient needs medical monitoring only and has a sufficiently stable environment to be allowed to live at home.
3. *Outpatient*—has no need for routine medical intervention and whose level of resistance and/or lack of awareness is not so high as to preclude treatment benefit.
4. *Continuing care*—patient completed a formal treatment program and is able to maintain abstinence and behavioral responses to participate in a minimum of once-weekly groups, focusing on issues to continue progress toward lifestyle changes.

The level of care (levels 1–3) initially accessed is dependent on the intensity and severity of one's chemical use, and the presence of emotional or behavioral disturbances contributed to by one's chemical use, and/or the presence of other acute emotional disturbances. Adolescents can be transitioned between or among the levels above depending on their needs and/or progress in responding to the goals and objectives of the plan of treatment.

A. Objective per Level

1. Inpatient treatment

a. Provide a safe, secure, and structured environment in which the adolescent can be detoxified.
b. Provide individualized treatment and therapy to meet the medi-

cal, emotional, behavioral, and addiction needs of the adolescent.

c. Provide the therapeutic intervention designed to enhance the adolescent's ability to assume responsibility for his/her addiction and concomitant problems.

d. Provide educational services that permit the adolescent to maintain his/her standing in school, to address deficiencies that have caused him/her to fall behind as a result of addictive and emotional behavioral problems, and to provide opportunities to the adolescent to prepare for alternatives to a high-school diploma.

e. Provide family therapy designed to educate family or significant others about addiction and relapse to provide support to family members in supporting adolescents in recovery, and to involve them in the treatment and continuing care of the adolescent.

2. **Day treatment (8 h/day in structured treatment setting; remaining time in family setting)**

   a. Provide individualized treatment and therapy to meet the emotional, behavioral, and addiction needs of the adolescent.

   b. Provide therapeutic interventions designed to enhance the adolescent's ability to assume responsibility for his/her addiction and concomitant problems.

   c. Provide educational services that permit the adolescent to maintain his/her standing in school, to address deficiencies that have caused him/her to fall behind as a result of addictive and emotional behavioral problems, and to provide opportunities to the adolescent to prepare for alternatives to a high-school diploma.

   d. Provide family therapy designed to educate family or significant others about addiction and relapse to provide support to family members in supporting adolescent in recovery, and to involve them in the treatment and continuing care of the adolescent.

   e. Provide secure, structured environment for adolescent to evaluate emotional and behavioral changes while interacting with family and social network.

   f. Develop strategies to enable the adolescent to cope with his/her responses to the actions or reactions of others in the family or social environment.

   g. Provide adolescent with relapse prevention techniques—identifying triggers, recognizing them as they are experienced, and developing strategies for overcoming them as they are encountered.

   h. Prepare the adolescent emotionally and behaviorally to benefit from treatment at a less intense level of care.

   i. Provide family therapy designed to educate family or significant others about addiction and relapse to provide support to family members in supporting the adolescent to recovery, and to involve in their treatment and continuing care of the adolescent.

3. **Outpatient treatment (1½ h 2–3 times per week)**

   a. Develop individualized treatment strategies designed to encourage changes in

      I. Lifestyle

      II. Attitudes

      III. Behavior

      b. Provide treatment strategies designed to teach adolescents about the disease of addiction and its negative impact on major age-related developmental experiences and its exacerbation of problems, which may have existed prior to the use of mood-altering substances.

      c. Provide adolescent with relapse prevention techniques—identifying triggers, recognizing them as they are experienced, and developing strategies for overcoming them as they are encountered.

4. Continuing care (≥1½ h 1 time per week)

      a. Continue treatment strategies not completed during the treatment modalities outlined above.

      b. Provide a setting in which adolescents can share difficulties regarding maintaining appropriate attitudes and behaviors.

      c. Monitor the adolescent involvement in 12-step and other support-group involvement as outlined in the continuing-care plan.

      d. Maintain contact with family regarding progress and directly involve them when intervention seems appropriate.

B. Ultimate Objective of Recovery. The adolescent should never think that there is an endpoint to recovery. The worst thing about being chemically dependent is the relationships that are prevented or destroyed by dependence on drugs or alcohol. These relationships are with self, others, and God.

What recovery is, then, is not using drugs and alcohol, and working on these relationships so that these young people will become responsible, confident human beings.

SELECTED READINGS

ASAM (American Society of Addiction Medicine): *Patient Placement Criteria for the Treatment of Psychoactive Substance Dependence.* Washington, DC, 1991.

Diagnostic and Statistical Manual of Mental Disorders, 4th ed. Washington, DC: American Psychiatric Association, 1994.

Miller NS (ed): *Principles of Addiction Medicine.* Chevy Chase, MD: American Society of Addiction Medicine, 1994.

Rogers, PD, Werner M (eds): Adolescent substance abuse. *Pediatric Clin North Am* W. B. Saunders. April 1995.

Schydlowner M, Rogers PD: Adolescent substance abuse and addictions. *Adolescent Medicine State of the Art Reviews* Hanley and Belfus, June 1993.

CHAPTER 17

TREATMENT OF GAMBLING, EATING, AND SEX ADDICTIONS

Jennifer P. Schneider, M.D., Ph.D.
El Dorado Medical Associates
Tucson, Arizona

Richard Irons, M.D.
Menninger Clinic
Topeka, Kansas

I. INTRODUCTION

Advances in research on the neurobiochemistry of addiction have shown a number of stimulatory and inhibitory pathways to be operative within and on a pleasure/satiety center, currently thought to be innervated by the medial forebrain bundle and located in the nucleus accumbens. Sexual disorders are often obsessive and compulsive in nature, with fantasy, euphoric recall, magical thinking, and ritualized behavior presenting as significant contributing factors. Mood-altering behavior may be seen in the substance addict who experiences an anticipatory "high" or feeling of well-being after obtaining a supply of the preferred drug (such as cocaine or heroin), even before the agent is administered. Fantasy, urge, and behavior-induced mood alterations are well documented and closely associated with compulsive gambling, sexual and/or romantic relationships, and binge eating; these are referred to as the *process addictions*. Urges or behaviors in these areas may be combined or alternated with substance abuse or addiction. Many will refer to this as dual addiction or cross-addiction. In other patients, the behavioral addiction remains a circumscribed personal expression of powerlessness and unmanageability devoid of association with substance use, abuse, or dependence.

A. A Family Disease. These are primary disorders that tend to run in families; the evolution of compulsive and maladaptive behaviors is often learned in the family system. Most patients suffering from one of these addictive disorders come from families where chemical addiction or alcoholism is found. Many sex addicts and gamblers will be found to have substance abuse or dependency themselves. Profound shame, unconscious denial, unspoken secrets, and rationalization abound within the family. Family members find behaviors that help them escape from the obvious problems at home. For example, in one family, the father's alcoholism may have led the mother to try to bolster self-esteem through excessive involvement in work or children's activities or through episodes of compulsive shopping.

One child may have become the family hero and eventually a compulsive

Manual of Therapeutics for Addictions, Edited by Norman S. Miller, Mark S. Gold, and David E. Smith.
ISBN 0471-56176-2 © 1997 John Wiley & Sons, Inc.

worker who speculates on commodities and periodically flies off to Las Vegas—with disastrous financial consequences, evolving into a pathologic gambler. Another child may have developed an eating disorder, while a third may have indulged in a series of devastating sexual affairs. Of course, all the children vowed that "I will never become an alcoholic," and family shame and consternation are reinforced when yet another family member succumbs to addictive disease.

Some individuals from an addiction-based family system may have a propensity for behavior that provides a sense of excitement, such as gambling, using stimulants, or participating in high-risk stunts. Others may prefer sedation through self-medication with alcohol or satiation through sexually exploitative relationships or compulsive overeating. Still others escape via fantasy, use of psychedelic drugs, preoccupation with work, or compulsive religious practice pursued to excess. When kept in balance, these activities may provide comfort and status, assuaging the sense of unworthiness. But when carried to extremes, they often represent a personal variation on the theme of addiction. Flawed self-perceptions may result in self-destructive or self-defeating actions or judgments that harm self or others.

II. ADDICTIVE SEXUAL DISORDERS

A. Presentation. Patients who have an addictive sexual disorder will commonly present to the clinician in one or more of the following ways:

1. Signs and symptoms of a substance-related disorder. In the course of evaluation or treatment of chemical dependence or alcoholism, the patient reveals a sexual history consistent with an additional diagnosis of an addictive sexual disorder.

2. A pattern of multiple substance addiction relapses. In the process of intensive review, addictive sexual behavior is found to be a significant factor associated with or preceding substance relapse.

3. Acute relationship crisis precipitated by disclosure or discovery of secret sexual behavior outside the relationship, particularly when this is a recurring theme.

4. Unexpected diagnosis of an STD in the patient or sexual partner.

5. Legal consequences resulting from impropriety in personal life (e.g., arrest for solicitation, public indecency, sexual assault, or domestic violence associated with "marital rape").

6. Professional or work-related consequences (e.g., a sexual harassment complaint; professional sexual misconduct; loss of position, status, or employment associated with physical absences; or lost productivity related to sexual activity or desire).

7. Financial crisis associated with diversion of resources for telephone sex lines, pornography, prostitution, "keeping" or "entertaining" sexual partners, or payments made (bribery or extortion) to keep sexual indiscretions from becoming known.

B. Diagnostic Criteria for Addictive Sexual Disorder. Each of the following should be present:

1. *DSM-IV* criteria met for one of the following: paraphilia, sexual disorder not otherwise specified (NOS), or impulse-control-disorder NOS.

2. Addictive features present as indicated by (a) loss of control over a sexual behavior, (b) continued sexual behavior despite significant adverse consequences, *and* (c) obsession or preoccupation with the fantasies, urges, or behavior.

3. Has reached the establishment phase of addictive behavior for a period of at least six months (see Section II.G., below, on natural history).

4. The focus of attachment is usually on relationships wherein the partners are viewed as narcissistic projection—objects to be used for self-aggrandizement and self-gratification and then discarded when they are no longer needed. The goal of entering a relationship is to have sex or romance, rather than sex or romance being part of a relationship. The patient may identify with the term "love" or "relationship" addict. Types of nonparaphilic compulsive sexual behavior include compulsive cruising and multiple partners, compulsive fixation on an unattainable person, compulsive masturbation, compulsive multiple love relationships, and compulsive sexuality within a relationship.

C. Physical Manifestations. Sexual addicts may present with a variety of complications to their physical health such as genital injury as a direct result of sexual activity; STDs, including hepatitis, HIV infection, herpes simplex, gonorrhea, syphilis, and chlamydia; physical injuries associated with engagement in high-risk sexual behaviors or sadomasochistic activity; unnecessary surgeries (such as breast implants, hair transplants, plastic surgery, liposuction) used to enhance sexual appeal; binge–purge cycles in an attempt to regulate weight; abuse of agents reputed to be sexual performance enhancers (amyl nitrite, other inhalants, yohimbine, papaverine); and unwanted pregnancies or the complications of abortions.

D. Comorbid Mental Disorders

1. Commonly associated *DSM-IV* Axis I comorbid mental disorders include mood disorders, posttraumatic stress disorder, dissociative disorders, and adjustment disorders.

2. Self-destructive and self-defeating behavior is not unusual, including suicidal ideation or suicide attempts, substance abuse, or progression to dependence, attempts at "geographic cures" (believing that a change in environment will solve the problem), and engagement in other high-risk behaviors.

3. Addictive sexual disorders are frequently associated with significant maladaptive personality traits or meet the criteria for an Axis II personality disorder. "Defects in character" discovered in the 12-step approach to treatment commonly include narcissistic, hysterical, borderline, dependent, or antisocial features. Many cases involving sexual impropriety are associated with and at least partially attributable to characterologic pathology, particularly when exploitation, assault, or sexual offense is involved. It is sometimes appropriate to diagnose a personality disorder during assessment or treatment. This can be the primary diagnosis, or the patient can be viewed as having comorbid conditions involving an Axis I diagnosis and an Axis II diagnosis of characterologic pathology. Defects of character and other types of self-destructive or self-defeating behaviors are often seen as part of addictive disease. If a patient is capable of honesty and at least

partial insight, able to identify characterologic defects, and work with them in steps 4–9 of a 12-step program, such defects are treatable utilizing addiction model treatment and therapy. Dramatic characterologic change is not infrequently seen as part of personal transformation achieved through dedicated participation in 12-step programs, insight-oriented or analytic therapy, and other avenues that promote spiritual awakening.

E. Comorbidity with Substance-Related Disorders. Many patients who satisfy these criteria are found to have active substance addiction and require treatment for both addictions in order to prevent relapse to either. The use of alcohol and other drugs in conjunction with sexual activity is associated with an increased risk of HIV infection, even when drugs are not injected. Common associations between substance abuse and addictive sexual disorders can be seen in Table 17.1.

F. Cultural and Gender Differences. Because certain sexual behaviors (e.g., multiple extramarital affairs or use of prostitutes) may be normative in some cultures but less acceptable in others, diagnosis of an addictive sexual disorder must take into consideration the cultural milieu. Gender and sexual orientation differences in the definition of normative behaviors are also relevant. For example, dressing in clothing of the opposite gender, and emphasizing one's sexual body parts by wearing revealing clothing are behaviors much more acceptable in women than in men. Addictive sexual disorders are found in both sexes, although men seeking treatment outnumber women 3 : 1. Men and women differ somewhat in the addictive sexual patterns they display: Using Carnes' (1991a, pp. 42–43) categories of behavior patterns, sexually addicted men are more likely than women to have anonymous sex, pay for sex, participate in voyeurism, have paraphilias, or engage in sexual exploita-

TABLE 17.1. Cross-Addiction

Drugs are used ritualistically as part of addictive disease to
  Reenact sexual scenarios from movies, books, fantasy, or past experience
  Create mood and enhance sexual pleasure
  Decrease inhibitions and fears
  Treat sexual dysfunction or performance anxiety
  Permit, excuse, or rationalize expression of sexual aggression
  Provide an excuse for shameful or objectionable behavior

Drugs are given to potential sexual partners to
  Re-enact sexual scenarios from movies, books, fantasy, or past experience
  Increase vulnerability or decrease inhibitions
  Overcome resistance or objections
  Manipulate and control events
  Promote emotional numbness
  Distort reality and memory
  Provide compensation for services

tion. Women are more likely than men to engage in fantasy sex, seductive role sex, trading sex, and pain exchange. Women are more likely than men to refer to themselves as "relationship" or "love" addicts and may identify as "women who love too much," a term popularized by Norwood (1985). With regard to characterologic pathology, sexually addicted women are markedly less likely than men to have antisocial personality disorder, but have a higher incidence of dependent, borderline, and hysterical personality features (Carnes, 1991a).

G. Natural History of Untreated Addiction. Carnes (1989, p. 77) described the progression of untreated sexual addiction. The initiation phase is characterized by an exceptionally intense impact of observed or experienced sexual activities during development as an adolescent and young adult. At some point, sex becomes the "drug of choice," used to escape or cope. Catalytic environments and catalytic experiences lead to the establishment phase, in which there is repetition of an addictive cycle of preoccupation, ritualization, and sexual acting out, then despair, shame, and guilt, which are alleviated by renewed preoccupation. With time, the addiction may escalate, with greater intensity, more frequency, more risk, and greater loss of control. Intermittently the behavior may deescalate, at times through the means of substituting another addictive behavior (such as a period of heavy drug use), or it may progress to the acute phase where the individual becomes alienated from significant others and is constantly preoccupied with the addiction cycle. In some, the addiction becomes immutable and behavior is limited only by opportunity, physical consequences, or incarceration.

H. Assessment. A diagnostic workup includes the following elements:

1. The basic database needed for evaluation includes a medical history and physical examination; biopsychosocial history; relationship history and marital status, family, growth, and development history; and a comprehensive sexual history. The Sexual Addiction Screening Test [SAST (Carnes, 1989)] is helpful as a self-evaluation tool. The more comprehensive Sexual Behavior Inventory is particularly useful and may be obtained from Patrick Carnes, c/o Del Amo Hospital, Torrance, CA. In addition, the clinician should administer a substance use screening self-evaluation such as the MAST (Michigan Alcohol Screening Test) supplemented by a clinical interview and corroborating information from collateral sources.

2. Psychological testing is particularly contributory with patients presenting with strong defenses or denial. The MMPI-2 and/or MCMI-II or III, and a cognitive screening test, such as the Shipley, have been commonly employed. The MMPI (Minnesota Multiphasic Personality Inventory) will commonly indicate elevations on scale 4 (PD), which should initially be considered manifestations of the sexual behavior. Some clinicians have found that other minor subscales such as the McAndrews are helpful.

3. Advanced assessment approaching forensic standards is required when legal problems or professional sexual misconduct are involved. Additional psychologic testing should include projectives such as the Rorschach (comprehensive system), TAT (Thematic Apperception Test), Sentence Completion, and the DeRogatis or Abel Screen. Multidisciplinary assessment is strongly encouraged in these situations.

4. Optional tests that are of value in selected cases include penile plethysmography, Abel Card Sort, Myers-Briggs Type Indicator (for relationship dysfunction), and advanced neuropsychological testing.

I. Differential Diagnosis. A variety of other mental disorders are associated with excessive sexual behavior. Frequent and infrequent *DSM-IV* Axis I diagnoses associated with sexual excesses are presented in Table 17.2. It is helpful to complete the differential diagnosis on Axis I before considering Axes II and III. Sexual disorders, impulse control disorders, and paraphilias, when identified, should be described as precisely as possible. If the NOS category is utilized, it is important to use appropriate descriptors that define the features seen. In our experience the most frequent features noted in addition to specific paraphilic behaviors are those of addiction, exploitation, predation, romantic attachment, coercion, professional misconduct, sexual offense, and sexual assault. The severity of the disorder, duration, current level of activity, and amenability to treatment should also be presented. In the differential diagnosis of sexual improprieties and excesses, Axis II characterologic disorders and traits are often contributory, or may be considered the primary etiology especially of paraphilic sexual behavior.

J. Treatment. Because a large percentage of persons with addictive sexual disorders are also chemically dependent, the initial decision often facing the treatment professional is which addiction to treat first. By the time many sex addicts seek help for this disorder, they are already in recovery from their substance dependence. If not, then regardless of which addiction is primary, the substance dependence must be treated first and intensively, or else sex addiction treatment is unlikely to be successful.

    1. Initial treatment. Decisions about inpatient versus outpatient primary care for addictive sexual disorders can be based on criteria analogous to the American Society of Addiction Medicine's Patient Placement Criteria for the Treatment of Psychoactive Substance Use Disorders. Inpatient admission is appropriate for those who are unlikely to be able to engage in treatment as

TABLE 17.2. Differential Diagnosis of Excessive Sexual Behaviors

Common
> Paraphilias
> Sexual disorder NOS
> Impulse control disorder NOS
> Bipolar affective disorder (type I or II)
> Cyclothymic disorder
> Post-traumatic stress disorder
> Adjustment disorder (disturbance of conduct)

Infrequent
> Substance-induced anxiety disorder (obsessive-compulsive symptoms)
> Substance-induced mood disorder (manic features)
> Delusional disorder (erotomania)
> Obsessive–compulsive disorder
> Gender identity disorder
> Delirium, dementia, or other cognitive disorder

outpatients, are a danger to themselves or others, or have significant concurrent medical or psychiatric conditions requiring closer observation and intensive treatment. Early treatment, both inpatient and outpatient, is similar to that of chemical dependence, comprising education about addiction in general and about sex addiction in particular, a combination of group and individual therapy, introduction to 12-step programs and to mutual-help meetings, and, if possible, involvement of family members in a family program of education and confrontation. Shame, a major issue for sex addicts, is best addressed in a group, where other recovering persons can provide support, confrontation, and shame reduction. Early in the treatment it is suggested that patients refrain from all sexual activities, including masturbation, for 30–90 days. This enables them to learn that they can indeed survive without sex, and allows them to get in touch with feelings that have been avoided and covered up with sexual activity. When they stop all sexual activity, some addicts report psychological withdrawal symptoms.

2. Psychotherapy. This is often of significant value following primary treatment, especially ongoing therapy for shame, childhood trauma, false beliefs, and the consequences of past actions; all can facilitate recovery. In the early recovery period, sex addicts and their partners frequently have sexual and interpersonal difficulties, often to a greater degree than they had during the active addiction phase. Therapists can provide support and reassurance during this phase. If the compulsive sexual behavior was same-sex, as is quite common even among men who identify themselves as heterosexual, therapists can help patients work through conflicts regarding sexual orientation.

Sex therapy is generally most effective at a later stage of treatment, in the second year and beyond. When treating patients with addictive sexual disorders, sex therapists may need to set aside some of their beliefs (views on masturbation, for example) and countertransference. It is important to carefully define and rigorously monitor the recovery boundaries of clients and of the professional–client relationship.

By the time sex addicts seek help, their marriage or relationship is often in great turmoil. Communication is lacking, and distrust, anger, and resentment are pervasive. Couples counseling by a therapist supportive of the sex-addiction treatment model can facilitate forgiveness and rebuilding of trust. Such counseling is unlikely to be effective, however, as long as the significant other persists in viewing himself/herself solely as the victim. The significant other should be encouraged to obtain individual therapy to deal with their own dependence issues, fear of abandonment, external locus of control, and low self-esteem, as revealed through therapy and supplemented by participation in their own mutual help recovery program.

3. Pharmacotherapy. Pharmacotherapy has a definite place in the treatment of addictive sexual disorders. Some addicts report that the selective serotonin reuptake inhibitors (SSRIs) such as fluoxetine, sertraline, paroxetine, and fluvoxamine modulate the intensity of their sexual preoccupation and suppress compulsive fantasies, and allow them to fully participate in treatment and self-help groups. For others, the tendency of the SSRIs to inhibit orgasm is a benefit. SSRIs are also useful in treating concurrent primary clinical depression. Some clinicians have found that other classes of antidepressants, including MAO (monoamine oxidase) inhibitors and bupropion have been helpful when other agents have been ineffective. Valproic acid, carbamazepine, and lithium hydrochloride are useful especially when cyclothymic or bipolar affective disorders are present. Progestational agents are occasionally used in the treatment of sex offenders.

4. Recovery. Recovery from sexual addiction is sometimes viewed as more analogous to recovery from eating disorders than to recovery from chemical dependence. Unlike the goal in treatment of chemical dependence, which is abstinence from use of all psychoactive substances, the therapeutic goal in addictive sexual disorders is abstinence only from compulsive self-destructive, and self-defeating, sexual behavior. Development of healthy sexuality is a primary goal that is usually achieved only through commitment to a program of continued recovery and therapy.

K. Continuing Recovery

1. Course of recovery over time. Compared with recovery from drug dependence, there is generally a greater period of time before improvement in the quality of life in recovery is experienced. The first year is often characterized by great turmoil (Carnes, 1991). Most relapses, if they occur, take place in the second 6 months. Health, legal, occupational, and relationship consequences of the addiction take their greatest toll during the first year. Because sex addicts were often sexually abused as children and because they have distorted ideas about sex, they generally lack experience that facilitates development of healthy sexuality. In the second and third years of recovery, significant growth can be seen. There is improvement in career status, finances, friendships, and self-esteem. It is possible to define and work for healthy sexuality and intimacy in relationships. In the fourth and fifth years, relationships with the significant other, with parents, and with children mature.

Partners of sex addicts follow a similar path, except that they experience their worst health problems and relapses to other addictions during the first 6 months of their partner's treatment. By the second 6 months partners begin experiencing improvement in self-image, career status, and communication with the partner. This means that for a couple working for recovery in the first year, each may be at a different phase, contributing to relationship stress. Couples need to be counseled to avoid making relationship decisions during this period; the couple relationship typically finds significant improvement only after this time.

2. Contingency contracting. In the process of defining and appreciating ritualized behaviors and awareness of powerlessness over compulsive sexual thoughts and actions, patients become ready and able to define certain sexual behaviors they are willing to avoid as part of a continuing care contract. Engagement in one of these behaviors is considered either a "slip" or a relapse, depending on the behavior involved and the circumstances. The use of behavior modification, such as the use of "the three-second [3-s] rule" to limit the length of time one focuses on an object or thought associated with sexual desire, and the use of arousal reconditioning, are also useful for some recovering addicts. Delineating healthy and necessary boundaries in a written contract is usually therapeutic.

Some subgroups of sexually exploitative professionals have a better prognosis than others for return to professional practice. In contrast to professionals who have exhibited exploitative behavior primarily as an expression of Axis II characterologic disorder, sexually addicted professionals who have successfully completed comprehensive assessment and primary treatment can often return to work without compromising public health and safety.

Irons (1991) published a set of proposed contractual provisions for reentry. Such a contract can be part of a binding legal stipulation between the professional and a state professional licensing board or other regulatory agency, and can define a standard of care for potentially impaired healthcare professionals.

3. Mutual support groups. Like other addicts, sex addicts need ongoing support for establishing and maintaining a healthy lifestyle and avoiding relapse. Regular attendance at 12-step meetings (see below) significantly reduces the risk of return to addictive sexual behavior. The 12 steps of Alcoholics Anonymous have been adapted for use in programs for sexual disorders. Programs modeled after Al-Anon, the mutual-help program for families and friends of alcoholics, are also available in many cities. Group support can be a powerful tool for overcoming the shame that most sex addicts and their family members feel. As with other relatively new 12-step programs, caution is in order because some meetings are less healthy than others. Table 17.3 provides the addresses of the national offices of the 12-step programs. Because recovery from addictive sexual disorders includes abstinence only from the addictive behaviors, the definition of "sexual sobriety" has room for interpretation. The various 12-step programs listed differ primarily in their definition of sexual sobriety. For Sexaholics Anonymous (SA), it is limited to sex within marriage. In the other programs, members define their own recovery plans and determine which behaviors to avoid. The members of Sexual Compulsives Anonymous (SCA) are primarily gay men and lesbian women. The two recovery programs for family members, S-Anon and COSA, have no significant differences. Recovering Couples Anonymous (RCA) is a program for couples recovering from all addictions; approximately 50% of the members are recovering from addictive sexual disorders. Attendance at 12-step programs for partners of sex addicts can facilitate recovery.

4. Relapse management and prevention. Lapses and relapses in the addictive sexual disorders often have more severe consequences than in substance dependence; for instance, a single recurrence of exhibitionism may lead to arrest or imprisonment, or another sexual encounter may precipitate the end of a marriage. Accordingly, relapse prevention is a key component of treatment of sex addiction. The value of contingency contracting is often discov-

TABLE 17.3. 12-Step Programs for Sexual Addiction

For addicts

Sexaholics Anonymous, P.O. Box 11910, Nashville, TN 37222-1910, (615) 331-16901

Sex Addicts Anonymous, P.O. Box 70909, Houston, TX 77270, (713) 869-4902

Sex & Love Addicts Anonymous, P.O. Box 119, New Town Branch, Boston, MA 02258, (617) 332-1845

Sexual Compulsives Anonymous, Old Chelsea Station, P.O. Box 1585, New York, NY 10013-0935, (800) 977-HEAL

For family members

S-Anon, P.O. Box 11242, Nashville, TN 37222-1242, (615) 833-3152

COSA, P.O. Box 14537, Minneapolis, MN 55414, (612) 537-6904

Co-SLAA, P.O. Box 1449, Brookline, MA 02146

For couples

Recovering Couples Anonymous, P.O. Box 11872, St. Louis, MO 63105, (314) 830–2600

ered through confrontation of violations of the agreement prior to major relapse. "Tightening" and revision of contracts are important aspects of relapse management.

5. Other Resources. Professionals seeking additional information on addictive sexual disorders can contact the National Council on Sexual Addiction and Compulsivity, located at P.O. Box 161064, Atlanta, GA 30321-19998. Their help-line telephone number is (770) 968-5002. Patients seeking information for themselves and family members can be referred to the books for laypersons by Carnes (1989), Earle and Crow (1989), Kasl (1989), Schneider (1988), and Schneider and Schneider (1991).

III. COMPULSIVE GAMBLING

A. Presentation. While pathologic gambling does not involve the use of a substance, research completed by numerous investigators has noted its addictive features. Pathologic gamblers will customarily indicate that what they seek is "action." The term refers to an aroused, euphoric state comparable to the euphoria or "high" obtained from the use of cocaine or other drugs. They also describe a "rush" commonly associated with adrenergic symptoms and tachycardia, often experienced during a period of anticipation of a winning result or in preparation for gambling. Elevated levels of norepinephrine have been found in compulsive gamblers, consistent with an aroused, hyperadrenergic state of sure betting. Recovering gamblers have described their disorder as being "hooked on their own adrenaline." Patients who have a gambling disorder will commonly present to the clinician with problems in one or more of the following areas:

1. Signs and symptoms of a substance-related disorder. A history of high-risk behavior in the course of evaluation and treatment of chemical dependence or alcoholism reveals the presence of compulsive gambling. In a patient presenting a history of multiple relapses into substance use, compulsive gambling, secrecy, and social isolation are found to be significant contributory factors.

2. A pattern of multiple financial crises and unexplained disappearance of significant sums of money or valuable possessions. The individual may also engage in "bailout" behavior, turning to family or others for help with a desperate financial situation that was caused by gambling.

3. Acute relationship crisis precipitated by disclosure of secret squandering of family assets, or resources squandered while engaging in "bailout" or "chasing losses." Sexual infidelities are not uncommon. Patients often present themselves after most, if not all, significant family and personal relationships have been alienated or destroyed through financial and emotional exploitation.

4. Legal consequences resulting from inability to meet demands for payments on debts or other financial obligations. At this juncture, the patient has usually exhausted credit resources and the patience of creditors. Ready means to raise cash through manipulation and exploitation of friends and relatives as well as pawn shops and credit cards have been maximized. In desperation, the patient may resort to antisocial behavior such as forgery, fraud, theft, or embezzlement, to obtain money. Arrest and/or incarceration may bring about reflection on the true cause of affliction and an earnest desire to find sobriety.

5. Professional or work-related consequences. The individual may have

recently jeopardized or lost a significant relationship, job, or educational or career opportunity because of gambling. Speculation in stocks, commodities, or other high-risk financial ventures is not unusual. This may cause patients to recall past losses and unexplored grief, bringing them to the experience of powerlessness, and a desire for assistance.

6. Health crisis associated with the pain and suffering associated with the consequences and repercussions from gambling behavior. Mood disorders, anxiety disorders, and other manifestations of impulse control may become acute and require immediate care. Stress-related medical disorders may become symptomatic or poorly controlled despite medical management. During evaluation, the presence of pathologic gambling as a primary contributing factor may be discovered.

B. Diagnostic Criteria for Addictive Gambling Disorder

1. *DSM-IV* criteria met for "pathologic gambling" require the presence of 5 of 10 identified types of behavior, and the absence of mania or hypomania. The essential feature of pathologic gambling is persistent and recurrent maladaptive gambling behavior that disrupts personal, family, or vocational pursuits.

2. *Addictive features:* Each of the diagnostic criteria for pathologic gambling from the *DSM-IV* reflects one of the following features commonly seen in substance dependence:
   a. Progression and preoccupation
   b. An indication of tolerance
   c. Withdrawal
   d. Use as an escape
   e. Chasing losses analogous to gulping drinks
   f. Lies and deception
   g. Illegal acts
   h. Family and/or job disruption
   i. Desire for rescue
   j. Loss of control

   Identification of multiple addictive features associated with powerlessness and unmanageability meets these criteria.

3. The individual must have reached the *losing or desperation phase* of addictive behavior for a period of at least 6 months (see Section III.G., on natural history)

C. Physical Manifestations.
Compulsive gamblers may present with a variety of physical complaints or signs associated with stress-related disorders (such as hypertension or ulcer disease), substance-related disorders, or the result of physical trauma sustained as a consequence of failure to make payments to creditors.

D. Comorbid Mental Disorders

1. Commonly associated *DSM-IV* Axis I mental disorders include depressive disorders, posttraumatic stress, dissociative disorders, adjustment disorders, and anxiety disorders. Individuals with pathologic gambling tendencies will often be found to have a variety of significant symptoms that may require treatment. In two studies of male inpatients (one outpatient treatment study, and the other a Gamblers Anonymous survey), 50–76% of the respondents were found to meet the diagnostic criteria for major depression or a bipolar affective disorder. There is a higher than expected rate of anxiety and panic disorders.

2. Self-destructive and self-defeating behavior is not unusual, including suicidal plans, substance abuse or progression to dependence, attempts at geographic cures, and engagement in other high-risk behaviors. Studies have identified suicide attempt prevalence rates as high as 15–24%.

3. Addictive gambling disorders are often associated with sufficient significant maladaptive personality traits or meet the criteria for an Axis II personality disorder. "Defects in character" discovered in the 12-step approach to treatment are commonly found to include narcissistic, hysterical, borderline, dependent, or antisocial features.

E. Comorbidity with Substance-Related Disorders. Many patients who satisfy these criteria are found to have active substance addiction and require treatment for both addictions in order to prevent relapse to either. Published studies on pathologic gamblers have revealed prevalence rates of alcohol and other substance-related disorders ranging from 47 to 52%. The use of alcohol and other drugs in conjunction with gambling distorts reality, decreases inhibitions, helps rationalize or justifies losses, and is used to celebrate wins. Survey investigations of patients in chemical-dependence treatment have found that 9–14% could be diagnosed as pathologic gamblers, and an equivalent percentage as problem gamblers.

F. Gender Differences. According to Dr. Sheila Blume, men tend to gamble for the action and women are more likely to gamble for escape or to cope with depression. Women also feel more stigmatized and are even more reluctant to seek help than are male gamblers.Women are underrepresented in treatment programs and constitute only 2–4% of the membership of Gamblers Anonymous.

G. Natural History of Untreated Addiction. The individual may be preoccupied with gambling, often through recalling past gambling experiences, planning the next gambling venture, or thinking of ways to get money with which to gamble. Most pathologic gamblers say that they are seeking "action" even more than money. Increasingly larger bets, or greater risks, may be needed to continue to produce the desired level of excitement. Pathologic gamblers often continue to gamble despite repeated efforts to control, cut back, or stop the behavior. There may be restlessness or irritability when attempting to cut down or stop gambling. The individual may gamble as a way of escaping from problems or to relieve feelings of helplessness, guilt, anxiety, or depression. A pattern of "chasing" one's losses may develop, with an urgent need to keep gambling, often with larger bets or the taking of greater risks, to undo a loss or series of losses. The individual may abandon his/her gambling strategy and try to win back losses all at once. Although all gamblers may chase for short periods, it is the long-term chase that is more characteristic of pathologic gamblers. As the disorder progresses, the individual may lie to family members, therapists, or others to conceal the extent of involvement with gambling. Dr. Robert Custer described three classic phases in compulsive gambling: the winning phase, the losing phase, and the desperation phase. These phases are not uniform or sequential in all cases. Stock market and commodity speculators represent over 20% of the gamblers he has diagnosed. So many compulsive gamblers are employed within the brokerage field that it should be considered an occupational hazard. What often pushes gamblers over the edge into desperation is an illogical loss. Bettors lose by what they consider a fluke, or suffer large losses when they abandon their usual strategies or self-imposed rules for engagement. Over time, compulsive gamblers develop highly ritualized behaviors. These personal rituals take on increasing importance with daily life becoming increasingly focused around their maintenance.

H. Assessment. A diagnostic workup includes the following elements.

1. Basic database. This includes medical history and physical examination; biopsychosocial history; relationship history; family, growth, and developmental history; employment history; and a comprehensive history of gambling and other high-risk behavior. Factual data, including credit reports, commodity and stock trading records, as well as checking account and credit card records, is often of great benefit in confronting denial and resistance. Without sufficient information from collateral sources, it is often difficult, if not impossible, to define the nature and extent of pathologic gambling, nor the severity of the disorder. Self-evaluation tests, such as the South Oaks Gambling Screen or the 20 questions offered in the "Combo" book of Gamblers Anonymous, are very useful.

2. Differential diagnosis. This includes attention-deficit/hyperactivity disorder, the manic phase of bipolar affective disorder, and engagement in professional gambling wherein the risks are limited and discipline regarding the behavior is maintained.

I. Treatment. Most compulsive gamblers cannot acknowledge the need for help until their addictive behavior has made their lives intolerable. This may include any number of consequences such as the loss or threatened loss of family, job, or possessions. Loss of freedom, fear of prosecution, overwhelming debts, bankruptcy, or IRS (Internal Revenue Service) consequences may result in hitting bottom. Some come to a total loss of self-respect, or attempt to drown their self-pity in alcohol or other drug use and find themselves in chemical-dependence treatment or detoxification centers, afraid to return to old patterns. Others suffer stress-related medical or psychological illnesses that can no longer be ignored and know that unless they stop their gambling compulsion, nothing will change. Reaching a crisis point is usually the event that leads to an acceptance of powerlessness over gambling and the willingness to accept help. Pathologic gambling is a treatable illness.

1. Initial treatment. The best-known treatment center in the country is at South Oaks Hospital in Amityville, New York. Sheila Blume, M.D., the Clinical Director at South Oaks, can be reached at (516) 264-4000. U.S. military veterans can often get inpatient services through the VA (Veterans Administration) system. One such facility offering treatment is in Miami, Florida. Most insurance carriers will not pay for treatment. In Gamblers Anonymous, completion of a fearless and searching financial inventory is as important as the customary 12-step moral inventory. These inventories identify areas important to the newcomers. Defects can be recognized, and growth can be measured. Because money is an integral part of pathologic gambling, the compulsive gambler must use the financial inventory, together with the moral inventory to begin and continue true characterologic change and promote spiritual awakening. The initial financial inventory and participation in GA usually sets the stage for a "pressure group" meeting, wherein new members can receive experience, strength, and hope from the group in preparation for putting their lives in order. Without complete honesty and accuracy, such meetings and other types of interventions are generally useless, and omissions of crucial data often become an excuse to return to gambling or for geographic escape. Compulsive gamblers are at least initially fiscally irresponsible, and until they have time in recovery and learn how to handle money responsibly, they should be relieved of as many financial duties and credit privileges as possible.

2. Psychotherapy. Individuals seeking counseling are encouraged to seek a therapist who has been trained and certified in the treatment of pathologic gambling.

3. Pharmacotherapy. The use of selective serotonin reuptake inhibitors (SSRIs) in this disorder has met with variable success. Antianxiety agents, particularly benzodiazepines, should be used with caution and in limited quantities because of the propensity for medicating feelings associated with consequences, and the risk of iatrogenic addiction.

J. Continuing Recovery

1. Contingency Contracting. Contingency contracting as described in the section on addictive sexual disorders is often crucial and often of significant benefit in the treatment of pathologic gambling. The contract should be geared to foster and promote establishment of responsibility and honesty in the gambler, with positive reenforcement for constructive progress. It should be made clear that the contract does not constitute a bailout. Concrete provisions regarding supervision of financial affairs and possession of money or negotiable financial instruments such as credit cards are crucial, as well as those regarding the payment of debts and family expenses, and addressing actual or potential legal problems.

2. Monitoring. The behavioral parameters to be monitored must be outlined with precision, and the individuals assigned to the monitoring role must be prepared to invoke the defined consequences for noncompliance. Most compulsive gamblers will at some point test the contract and the conviction of those in control or authority to enforce the terms.

3. Mutual support groups. Available resources, including regional counseling and treatment options, may be obtained by calling the Florida Council on Compulsive Gambling at (800) 426-7711, or the National Council on Compulsive Gambling national hotline at (800) GAMBLER. They can provide information on local meetings of Gamblers Anonymous and Gam-Anon, the organization that offers help and support for spouses, families, or close friends of compulsive gamblers.

4. Relapse management. Compulsive gambling is viewed as a chronic relapsing disease. Relapse is not uncommon, and often has severe consequences. The patient may relapse through a switching of addictions to a different type of high-risk behavior or may resort to the use of mood-altering substances. The desire to use geographic, occupational, or relationship changes to "cure" current distress is extremely common. As in other addictive disorders, relapse can be a source of education and growth in recovery if properly appreciated by the patient, managed by the clinician, and disclosed to the patient's sponsor and GA homegroup.

IV. EATING DISORDERS

The *DSM-IV* describes only two specific eating disorders—*anorexia nervosa* and *bulimia nervosa*—and in addition, describes a proposed new diagnosis, *binge-eating disorder*. However, eating disorders can also be considered within an addiction model framework, within which eating disorders occur on a continuum, from rigid control over intake at one end, to loss of control on the other. In all cases there is marked preoccupation with food and weight, and continuation of the behavior despite significant adverse consequences. Like alcohol and substance abuse, eating disorders have very high rates of chronicity, relapse, recurrence, and psychosocial morbidity. For obesity, as for alcoholism, a genetic component is clear; several studies of twins and adoptees show that obesity is significantly influenced by genetics (Bouchard et al., 1990; Stunkard et al., 1986, 1990).

Patients who experience loss of control over their eating or starvation continue abnormal eating behaviors despite adverse consequences; are obsessed with food, cooking, and eating rituals; demonstrate the essential features of addiction; and may be usefully treated for their eating disorder within the addiction model. This is particularly true for those patients who have other comorbid addictions. Some studies have shown high levels of endogenous opiates in the CSF (cerebrospinal fluid) of anorectics and a weight gain when opiate effect is inhibited by naltrexone administration, suggesting that anorexia is, in effect, an addiction to fasting. Like alcoholics and other addicts, anorectic patients often deny the illness, making it difficult to prevent relapse even after treatment.

A. Presentation. Eating disorders that alter body morphology are immediately apparent, although patients with anorexia tend to conceal their emaciation by dressing in multilayered clothing. Anorexia nervosa and bulimia nervosa are primarily disorders of young women. The prevalence of anorexia is approximately 1% in the United States. The average age at presentation is 17 years, although it can also be first identified in middle age. Anorectics have a distorted body image, believing they are fat even when objectively they are emaciated. They tend to be brought in by concerned family members. Bulimia is a much more common disorder, with a lifetime prevalence of 3–5% in the general population and up to 20% in certain groups of young women. Bulimics, who are often of normal weight, can conceal their disorder more successfully, and generally present with gastrointestinal and other somatic complaints.

B. Diagnostic Criteria

1. Anorexia nervosa. There are two types: the *restricting type,* in which the person has not regularly engaged in binge-eating or purging behavior (i.e., self-induced vomiting or misuse of laxatives or diuretics), and the *binge-eating/purging type,* in which the person has regularly engaged in these behaviors. The *DSM-IV* criteria are:

   a. Refusal to maintain body weight at or above a minimally normal weight for age and height (approximately 85% of expected).
   b. Intense fear of gaining weight or becoming fat, even though underweight.
   c. Disturbance in the way in which one's body weight or shape is experienced, such as "feeling fat" even when emaciated, undue influence of body weight or shape on self-evaluation, or denial of the seriousness of the current low body weight.
   d. In postmenarcheal females, amenorrhea (i.e., absence of at least three consecutive expected menstrual periods).

2. Bulimia nervosa. Bulimia nervosa can be either of the purging type, when there is self-induced vomiting or the misuse of laxatives, diuretics, or enemas, or the nonpurging type, where other inappropriate compensatory behaviors are used, such as fasting or excessive exercise, but not purging. The *DSM-IV* criteria are

   a. Recurrent episodes of binge eating, which includes both (1) eating a definitely larger amount of food than usual over a short time period (e.g., 2 h) and (2) a sense of lack of control over eating during the episode.

   b. Recurrent inappropriate compensatory behavior in order to prevent weight gain, such as self-induced vomiting; misuse of laxatives, diuretics, enemas, or other medications; fasting; or excessive exercise.

   c. The binge-eating and inappropriate compensatory behaviors both occur on average, at least twice a week for 3 months.

   d. Self-evaluation is unduly influenced by body shape and weight.

   e. The disturbance does not occur exclusively during episodes of anorexia nervosa.

3. Compulsive overeating. This can consist of either discrete binging episodes or a generalized loss of control over eating, so that amounts larger than needed for weight maintenance are regularly eaten despite a desire to limit one's food intake. Recurrent episodes of binge eating in the absence of regular use of compensatory behaviors is currently classified in the *DSM-IV* as "eating disorder not otherwise specified (NOS), but is described in the research section as "binge-eating disorder." Addictive features are present as indicated by (a) loss of control over eating behavior, (b) continued overeating despite adverse consequences, and (c) obsession or preoccupation with obtaining, preparing, and consuming food.

C. Physical Manifestations

1. Anorexia nervosa. Malnutrition may be so severe that hospitalization is required. Death may ensue. Malnutrition may result in loss of heart muscle, arrhythmias (bradycardia, atrial flutter, and atrial fibrillation), hypotension, congestive heart failure, and sudden death. Fatigue, weakness, dehydration, constipation, intolerance to cold temperatures, and increased susceptibility to viral and bacterial infection may occur. Prepubertal patients may experience growth delay. In postpubertal patients, menses cease when percent body weight drops below a minimum. Decreased fertility and amenorrhea are associated with lowered levels of luteinizing hormone (LH) and follicle-stimulating hormone (FSH). In the absence of menstrual periods, osteoporosis tends to develop. Laboratory abnormalities can include low white cell count; low glucose, cortisol, and serum zinc levels; as well as hypokalemia, hyponatremia, hypocalcemia, and hypochloremic alkalosis and elevated serum amylase levels of salivary origin.

2. Bulimia nervosa. Although body weight may be normal, unexpected weight fluctuations are often seen. Laboratory abnormalities can include electrolyte disturbances, low serum magnesium, and elevated serum amylase. Symptoms include abdominal pain due to gastric and esophageal irritation, and abdominal distention. Physical signs include erosion of dental enamel caused by stomach acid in a person who vomits, enlargement of the parotid gland, resulting in "chipmunk" facies, esophageal tears, and abrasions of the dorsum of the hand (sustained during repeated thrusting of the finger into the throat). Laxative abuse can cause irritation of the colon. Peripheral muscle weakness and cardiomyopathy can result from recurrent use of ipecac to induce vomiting.

3. Compulsive overeating associated with obesity. Obesity increases the risk of insulin resistance, diabetes mellitus, hyperlipidemia, hypertension, gallbladder disease, sleep apnea, chronic hypoxemia and hypercapnia, and degenerative joint disease (especially of the knees). Upper-body obesity is an independent risk factor for heart disease.

D. Comorbid Mental Disorders. Among patients with anorexia, 50–75% have comorbid major depression and/or dysthymia; 10–13% have obsessive–compulsive disorder (OCD), with symptoms focusing primarily on symmetry and exactness. Recovered anorexics continue to score high on perfectionism scales. Family members have an increased incidence of generalized anxiety, obsessive–compulsive personality disorders, and OCD. Among patients with bulimia, 43% were reported to have anxiety disorders; 12%, bipolar disorder; and 50–75%, personality disorders or significant personality-trait disturbances. Obese binge eaters when compared with obese non–binge eaters exhibit more psychiatric disorders, primarily affective disorders.

1. Commonly associated *DSM-IV* Axis I mental disorders include depressive disorders, posttraumatic stress disorders, dissociative disorders, adjustment disorders, and anxiety disorders.
2. Self-destructive and self-defeating behavior is not unusual, including suicidal ideation or suicide attempts, substance abuse or progression to dependence, attempts at geographic cures, and engagement in other high-risk behaviors.
3. Addictive eating disorders are frequently associated with significant maladaptive personality traits. Food becomes a substitute for love, relationships, and a primary means of coping. A history of significant physical, emotional, or sexual abuse is not uncommon.

E. Comorbidity with Substance-Related Disorders. There are substantial rates of multiple addiction among eating-disordered persons, particularly bulimics. Rates for alcohol and other drug dependence appear to increase with age and range from 13–22% for high-school students and college freshmen to a prevalence of concurrent or prior substance abuse of approximately 50% in several studies completed on women in their 30s and 40s. Among patients with anorexia, alcohol and drug addiction seem to cluster in the bulimic subgroup rather than the restrictor subgroup. The incidence of alcohol and drug-abuse problems is higher in the families of patients with bulimia nervosa than in families of controls (Hudson et al., 1987). Women undergoing chemical-dependence treatment had a 15% lifetime prevalence of anorexia or bulimia, which is significantly higher than expected (Hudson et al., 1992). Some patients tend to binge-eat when intoxicated, while others tend to substitute binge eating for alcohol and drug use. During treatment of one of these disorders, the other commonly worsens. Additionally, in dually diagnosed patients there is a high likelihood that either disorder can precipitate the other.

F. Cultural and Gender Differences. Eating disorders are a contemporary epidemic, limited to societies where food is plentiful and fueled by the Western cultural ideal of slenderness in women. Poverty and lower educational level are associated with increased rates of female obesity. Blacks, Hispanics, and Native Americans have an increased prevalence of obesity. Two-thirds of teenage women think that they are fat. Eating disorders are approximately 10 times as common in females than in males. Among men, they are more common in models, athletes, flight attendants, gymnasts, wrestlers, jockeys, runners, and swimmers—those engaged in activities that require weight control.

Eating disorders may be more common in homosexual than heterosexual men, because of cultural pressures within the gay community to be thin. In both sexes, bulimia and anorexia are often accompanied by compulsive exercising (Yates, 1991).

G. Assessment

1. Diagnostic workup. All patients with eating disorders should undergo a comprehensive history and physical examination, eating and weight history, biopsychosocial history, relationship and family history, growth and development history, and a thorough sexual history, including evaluation for possible childhood sexual and/or physical abuse, which is found in a significant proportion of patients with bulimia and obesity. A family history will often reveal eating disorders in previous generations. Psychometric testing is valuable in some cases. Because of the frequent presence of coexisting affective disorders or chemical dependence, psychiatric and addiction evaluations are mandatory. Initial data gathering may be facilitated by a screening test such as the Eating Disorders Questionnaire, the Diagnostic Survey for Eating Disorders, the Eating Disorders Inventory, or the Stanford Eating Disorders Questionnaire, and by using a semistructured interview instrument such as the Eating Disorders Examination (all referenced in Yager et al., 1993).

2. Differential diagnosis

a. Anorexia nervosa. Other disorders that can mimic anorexia include Addison's disease, Alzheimer's disease, cancer of lung or pancreas, inflammatory bowel disease, hyperthyroidism, atherosclerosis manifested as ischemic heart disease or mesenteric artery syndrome, polyarteritis nodosa, thiamine deficiency, and depression.

b. Bulimia nervosa. This can increase susceptibility to cancer of the GI tract, mechanical obstruction of the pylorus, mesenteric artery syndrome, metabolic alkalosis, opiate withdrawal, postconcussive syndrome, posterior fossa tumor, or psychogenic spontaneous vomiting.

c. Obesity. This is often characterized by low metabolic rate, hypercortisolism polycystic ovaries, hypothyroidism, excess insulin dose in a diabetic, and appetite-regulation abnormalities due to hypothalamic disease. Drugs that can cause weight gain include tricyclic antidepressants, phenothiazines, oral contraceptives, glucocorticoids, and progesterone.

H. Treatment.
Treatment of eating disorders involves a combination of nutritional rehabilitation, psychosocial treatment, and medications. Where concurrent chemical dependence is present, this needs to be addressed first.

1. Initial treatment. Medical indications for hospitalization include emaciation (a decrease in body weight of 25–30% below ideal) in anorexia, significant electrolyte abnormalities, and abnormal cardiac function. Psychiatric indications include severe depression; inability to function in the home, school, or workplace; or failure of outpatient treatment after 3 months. Clearly, treatment of addictive eating disorders is a long-term, primarily outpatient treatment dependent on the patient's dedication to a program of recovery.

2. Nutritional rehabilitation and restoration of normal weight. For anorexic patients, the goal is at least 80% of ideal body weight, by means of a diet that will provide 250–500 calories per day (cal/day) above daily energy requirements; patients are unlikely to accept high-calorie supplementation.

3. Psychotherapy. Structured intensive group psychotherapy yielded greater improvement than did antidepressants alone in outpatients with bulimia nervosa (Mitchell et al., 1990). Cognitive-behavior therapy is the mainstay of treatment of the eating disorders. Individual therapy and family therapy are also useful modalities.

4. Pharmacotherapy. Antidepressants, used primarily for concomitant primary depression, also have specific value in eating disorders. Prozac, 60 mg/day, is superior to placebo in reducing the frequency of binge–purge episodes (Fluoxetine Bulimia, 1992). Fluoxetine also facilitates short-term weight loss in obese individuals, as does a combination of the norepinephrine agonist phentermine (15 mg daily) and the serotonin agonist fenfluramine (20 mg TID). The use of amphetamine-like compounds such as these, whether controlled substances or the over-the-counter (OTC) preparation phenylpropanolamine, are generally contraindicated for patients with an addictive disorder because of the propensity for abuse or addiction and the failure to demonstrate any effectiveness other than short-term weight loss. Anorectic drugs may best be viewed like nicotine patches in the treatment of smoking dependence or naltrexone in alcohol dependence, an adjunct to early treatment. Pharmacotherapy is generally not useful for treatment of anorexia, other than for associated depression.

J. Continuing Recovery. Eating disorders are chronic and tend to relapse. For example, one study showed that 4–12 years after treatment for anorexia, nearly 70% of patients were still preoccupied with weight and dieting, and only about 30% were still eating normally. Most obese patients eventually regain all their lost weight. Bulimic patients, on the other hand, respond well to treatment; bulimia is uncommon after age 40. Continuing care is advisable for eating disorders. Ongoing insight-oriented psychotherapy and group therapy are helpful for all the eating disorders. A mutual support group, Overeaters Anonymous (OA), is based on the 12 steps of AA. Information about this program can be obtained from Overeaters Anonymous World Service Office, Box 92870, Los Angeles, CA 90009, (213) 657-6252.

REFERENCES

Selected References on Addictive Sexual Disorders

American Society of Addiction Medicine. *Patient Placement Criteria for the Treatment of Psychoactive Substance Use Disorders.* Washington, DC: American Society of Addiction Medicine, 1991.

Carnes P: *Contrary to Love: Helping the Sexual Addict.* Minneapolis: CompCare Publishers, 1989.

Carnes P: *Don't Call it Love.* New York: Bantam, 1991a.

Carnes P: Gender differences in normal and sexually addicted populations. *Am J Prevent Psychiatry Neurol* 3(1):16–23. 1991b.

Coleman E: Is your patient suffering from compulsive sexual behavior? *Psychiatric Ann* 22:320–325, 1992.

Earle R, Crow G: *Lonely All the Time.* New York: Pocket Books, 1989.

Earle R, Earle M: *Sex Addiction: Case Studies and Management.* New York: Brunner/Mazel, 1995.

Irons RR: Sexually addicted professionals: Contractual provisions for re-entry. *Am J Preventive Psychiatry Neurol* 3(1):57–59, 1991.

Irons RR, Schneider JP: Addictive sexual disorders. In NS Miller (ed): *Addiction Psychiatry.* New York: Norton, 1996.

Kasl C: *Women, Sex, and Addiction.* New York: Ticknor & Fields, 1989.

Norwood R: *Women Who Love Too Much*. New York, Jeremy Tarcher Publishers, 1985.

Schneider JP: *Back From Betrayal: Recovering From his Affairs*. Center City, MN: Hazelden Educational Materials, 1988.

Schneider JP, Irons RR: Differential diagnosis of addictive sexual disorders using the DSM-IV. *Sexual Addiction Compulsivity* 3(1), 1996.

Schneider JP, Schneider BH: *Sex, Lies and Forgiveness: Couples Speak on Healing From Sex Addiction*. Center City, MN: Hazelden Educational Materials, 1991.

Sealy JR: Psychopharmacologic intervention in addictive sexual behavior. *Sexual Addiction Compulsivity* 2(4):55–74, 1995.

Selected References on Pathologic Gambling

Blume SB: Treatment for the addictions: alcoholism, drug dependence, and compulsive gambling in a psychiatric setting. *J Substance Abuse Treatment* 3:131–133, 1986.

Breo DL: In treating the pathological gambler, MDs must overcome the attitude, "why bother?" *JAMA* 262:2599–2606, 1989.

Gamblers Anonymous: Sharing recovery through Gamblers Anonymous, Los Angeles: Gamblers Anonymous Publishing.

Irons R: The gambling addiction. *Atlanta Medicine* 69:32–35, 1994.

Lesieur HR, Blume SB: The South Oaks Gambling Screen: a new instrument for the identification of pathological gamblers. *Am J Psychiatry* 144:1184–1188, 1987.

Lesieur HR, Blume SB: Characteristics of pathological gamblers identified among patients on a psychiatric admissions service. *Hosp Commun Psychiatry* 41:1009–1012, 1990.

Lesieur HR, Blume SB: Pathological gambling, eating disorders, and the psychoactive substance use disorders. *J Addictive Dis* 12:89–102. 1993.

Lesieur HR, Rosenthal RJ: Pathological gambling: a review of the literature. *J Gambling Stud* 7:5–40, 1991.

Selected References on Eating Disorders

Anderson AE (ed): *Males with Eating Disorders*. New York: Brunner/Mazel, 1990.

Bouchard C, Tremblay A, Despres J-P, Nadeau A, Lupien PJ, Theriault G, Dussault J, Moorjani S, Pinault S, Fournier G: The response to long-term overfeeding in identical twins. *N Engl J Med* 322:1477–1482, 1990.

Fluoxetine Bulimia Nervosa Collaborative Study Group. Fluoxetine in the treatment of bulimia nervosa. *Arch Gen Psychiatry* 49:139–147, 1992.

Hudson JI, Pope HG, Yurgelun-Todd, et al.: Psychiaric disorders in bulimic outpatients. *Amer J Psychiatry* 144:1283–1287, 1987.

Hudson JI, Weiss RD, Pope HG, McElroy SK, Mirin SM: Eating disorders in hospitalized substance abusers. *Amer J Drug Alcohol Abuse* 18(1):75–85, 1992.

Mitchell JE, et al.: A comparison study of antidepressants and structured intensive group psychotherapy in the treatment of bulimia nervosa. *Arch Gen Psychiaty* 47:149–157, 1990.

Orbach S: *Fat is a Feminist Issue*. New York: Berkeley Books, 1978.

Overeaters Anonymous World Services. *Overeaters Anonymous*. Torrance, CA: Overeaters Anonymous, 1980.

Roth G: *When Food is Love*. New York: Penguin Books, 1991.

Roth G: *Breaking Free from Compulsive Overeating*. New York.

Stunkard AJ, Foch TT, Hrubec Z: A twin study of human obesity. *JAMA* 256:51–1 57, 1986.

Stunkard AJ, Harris JR, Pedersen NI, McClearn GE: The body-mass index of twins who have been reared apart. *New Engl J Med* 322:1483–1487, 1990.

Yager J, Anderson A, Devlin M, et al.: Practice guidelines for eating disorders. *Amer J Psychiatry* 150:207–228, 1993. Reprinted by the American Psychiatric Association, 1993.

Yates A: *Compulsive Exercise and the Eating Disorders.* New York: Brunner/Mazel, 1991.

CHAPTER 18

CULTURAL CONSIDERATIONS IN THE MANAGEMENT OF ADDICTIVE DISEASE

Andrea G. Barthwell, M.D.
Encounter Medical Group, P.C.
Chicago, Illinois

I. INTRODUCTION

Addiction can be viewed as a disorder that results from the interaction of multiple causal factors—biophysical, psychological, and sociocultural—over time. This chapter examines the sociocultural factors that influence addiction among groups of individuals.

The ethnicity or cultural background of a patient may profoundly influence that person's alcohol and drug use pattern or health consequences of use, which may be accelerated as a result of preexisting disease states. The degree to which these cultural/ethnic backgrounds influence those patterns (independent of socioeconomic factors such as employment and poverty) is not well understood. Since, as physicians, we are taught pattern recognition (clusters of signs and symptoms) as a basis for formulating a tentative diagnosis, the variance in patterns observed across ethnic and cultural groups may influence our ability to formulate a correct diagnosis. As physicians, we need to know that these variant patterns exist; that is the basis of this chapter. It is beyond the scope of this chapter and this treatise to define those variants in their entirety.

Five tenets underlie this chapter: (1) all patients are not equal—clinically, pathologically, socioculturally, environmentally, or biogenetically; (2) in order to differentiate among diagnoses of early substance use, abuse, and addiction, the physician must have a high index of suspicion that is combined with effective assessment and screening skills and predicated on the use of transcultural communication; (3) across individuals and ethnic or cultural groups (as described elsewhere in this book), substance use along the continuum (incidental use, experimental use, regular use, abuse, or addiction) may be variant; (4) in order to be successful at making a transcultural diagnosis, physicians will have to adapt their usual diagnostic approach or beliefs; and finally (5), while most physicians are taught to identify and treat end-stage disease, physicians must intervene across the full spectrum of alcohol and drug problems and select management strategies according to the severity of substance-use problems. The severity as self-perceived may vary across different cultural contexts.

Manual of Therapeutics for Addictions, Edited by Norman S. Miller, Mark S. Gold, and David E. Smith.
ISBN 0471-56176-2 © 1997 John Wiley & Sons, Inc.

II. RACIAL AND ETHNIC GROUPS OF COLOR: HEALTH STATUS

A. Limitations of the Data

1. It is well established that there are limitations to the information sources about drug use prevalence in various communities. Many of the surveys currently in use (e.g., High School Senior Survey, National Household Survey, etc.) may not represent the true rates of alcohol use or patterns of alcohol consumption in certain communities (i.e., urban-based African-American individuals, where there are high rates of school dropouts). This could lead to a finding of lower rates of alcohol use among those African-American youths who stay in school.

2. The National Household Survey may underrepresent the number of individuals who are in a household if they are being housed temporarily or are not shown on the lease. This may lower the total count in the household survey, thereby leading to an increase in the incidence of alcohol use and abuse in the certain communities with unregistered members as a common occurrence.

B. Report(s) on Health

1. In 1985, the Department of Health and Human Services, Office of Minority Health, issued its landmark document, *Report of the Secretary's Task Force on Black and Minority Health* and suggested that

   > Despite the unprecedented explosion in scientific knowledge and the phenomenal capacity of medicine to diagnose, treat, and cure disease, Blacks, Hispanics, Native Americans, and those of Asian/Pacific Islander heritage have not benefitted fully or equitably from the fruits of science or from those systems responsible for translating and using health sciences technology.

   Included in that comprehensive report was a discussion of the significant disparities in mortality rates between white Americans and ethnic groups of color and between ethnic males of color and white males in particular.

   a. The Task Force concluded that, on the basis of these disparities, in 1979–1981 there were at least 14,500 excess deaths among black males under age 45.

   b. The three leading causes of excess mortality for black males under age 45 were homicide (accounting for 38% of all excess deaths), followed by infant mortality (23%), and cardiovascular disease (13%).

2. In that year, the Pan-American Health Organization issued a report on health status of adolescents in the Americas, including the United States. This report emphasized that "current times offer a unique opportunity to focus on and try to solve or prevent the problems of adolescents and youth. . . . Never before have these problems been so clearly and dramatically defined."

   a. The public health community is now more cognizant of the fact that, while health indicators for black and Hispanic American adolescent males have improved over the long term—concomitant with improvements for the general population—the past 10 years have seen the disparity escalate between white and ethnic groups of color relative to key indicators (e.g., such as life expectancy, infant mortality and death rates from certain causes have deteriorated or remained stable for males from ethnic groups of color, at the same time that they have improved for other populations).

III. RACIAL AND ETHNIC GROUPS: ALCOHOL AND DRUG USE

There is considerable diversity within the groups discussed below. Despite this diversity, these cultural and ethnic groups have collective patterns of use and related problems that are quite different from the population as a whole. Few studies have entailed systematic comparisons across these groups or examined a sufficient number of relevant variables. There may be important cultural differences among various communities of ethnic groups of color in their tolerance for alcohol consumption, their use of alcohol in ritualized behavior, and the social dislocation secondary to alcohol abuse, as well as the excess morbidity and mortality associated with alcohol use and abuse. These differences may be influenced by nutritional status, socioeconomic status, education, employment, income, housing, and the safety in the immediate environment. Community customs, rituals, and shared beliefs may also be important.

A. Cultural Customs. Cultural customs, including alcohol drinking patterns tend to endure migration despite pressures toward assimilation.

1. Drinking patterns of many African-American subpopulations in the United States may represent influences of the European countries that colonized their countries of origin prior to independence or the drinking patterns of African-American descendants of slaves.

2. Culture can be reinforcing of negative and positive drinking and drug-use behaviors.

3. Cultural factors that may affect a person's vulnerability to chemical dependence include life crisis, social inferiority, cognitive distortions, affective distortions (which are based on relationships to others within and outside the group), and life stressors, socioeconomic status, including social class and stigma associated with drinking.

4. Culture, tradition, and rituals set the patterns of use that are normative for a collective and control the rituals to protect the individual from ill effects of the substance and others from an individual who is affected by the mood or mind-altering chemical. When that control is lifted or affected by synergistic interaction of the dominant or other culture, cultural control over alcohol use patterns may or may not only fall apart but may also be unable to reestablish any control.

5. Cultural blends deriving from ethnicity and racial or biogenetic mixing are many.

B. Genetic Contributions. Genetic contributions are substantial in alcoholism, including the transmission of the propensity for alcoholism and the potential to experience consequences.

1. While much of the work that has been done on ethnic groups of color has looked at groups as a homogenous population, there has been a significant transethnic mating within this country among African-Americans, Native Americans, European-Americans, and others.

   a. There are significant numbers of individuals who were the offspring of involuntary transethnic mating emerging from the institution of slavery.

   b. This transethnic mating may give rise to variant genetic traits that either predispose to or protect from becoming alcoholic.

      (1) Few such traits have been discovered, but they do exist (e.g., the flushing reaction among people of Asian ancestry).

    (2) Biological variation may account for some part of observed differences in complications arising from chronic alcohol use (e.g., disparate rates of cirrhosis between Caucasians and African-Americans).

2. The biological influences on susceptibility to alcohol at varying times are equal to, less important than, or more important than environmental factors.

C. Socioeconomic Factors. Socioeconomic factors have been implicated as important determinants of alcoholism, and potentially addiction.

1. Alcoholism and drinking behaviors and norms have been found to vary across social class. In the United States, many historical and social events have combined to create a situation in which large proportions of members of minority populations are found in lower social class or identified with lower social classes, and the outcomes of low social classes. This has resulted in a tendency for the behaviors related to those members of lower social class to be generalized to the entire group.

2. The criteria for social class categories in the majority culture may not apply directly to categories within cultures. Boys and girls are socialized in different ways and are taught to value themselves for different reasons. Some of this value to self and society may be gender-specific, some may be group-bound, and some be both. Boys may be socialized to derive their value from their ability to support their families; girls, for their ability to nurture their families.

IV. AFRICAN-AMERICANS

African-Americans are a culturally distinct population bound together by connective factors and forces that give them unity while preserving the heterogeneity that exists within the group. African-Americans in a broad context encompass descendants of people who originated in Africa and where involuntarily brought to America, people with ties to Africa who had a similar experience in the Caribbean and who have since voluntarily migrated to America and Africans who are voluntary immigrants. Thus, African-Americans are a highly complex and diverse people, characterized along two dimensions—one in terms of interactions and responses to interactions with European Americans and the other in terms of their own internal dynamics, both as individual personalities and as a collective group.

A. Major Themes in a Historical Context

1. While the heterogeneity among blacks is often noted, a quest for identity is the major theme of African-American existence in the Western world. African-Americans have had to contend with transplantation and adjustments, the effects of social, cultural, and environmental contact and changes have been, in many respects, more devastating and intense for African-Americans because of the uniqueness of their journey to the Americas, and their experiences in the American world.

2. The historical record for African-Americans in this society has consisted of sociocultural adaptation and survival processes.

    a. African-Americans' experiences have been profoundly affected by the institutions and processes of slavery, racism, and oppression.

  b. The individual and collective character has developed in an environment antithetical to their character, personality, and behavior.

  c. These cultural disruptions have had a profound effect on African-Americans as a whole and are experienced in different ways by African-Americans across gender, class, and country of origin.

B. African-Americans—Social Ecology

  1. Of the total United States population, 11.5% is African-American; this represents 11.2% of the total U.S. male and 11.8% of the total U.S. female population.

  2. The median age of African-Americans in this country is 24.9 years (vs. 36.1 years for whites), and 15% of African-Americans are under 15 years of age.

  3. The life expectancy of African-Americans in 1983 was 65 years for men and 74 years for women, contrasted to 72 and 79 years for white men and women, respectively. The age-adjusted mortality rate per 1000 population for African-Americans is 7.7; for whites it is 5.3

  4. The percent of African-American households headed by women (37.7%) is more than 3 times higher than that of nonminority households headed by women (10.9%).

  5. One of every three African-Americans (34%) lived below the poverty level in 1981. This rate is consistent with that of Hispanic and Native Americans, but substantially higher than that of nonminorities (11%).

C. African-Americans and Addictions

  1. There may be important cultural differences among various African-American communities in their tolerance for alcohol and drug consumption, their use of alcohol and other drugs in ritualized behavior, and the social dislocation secondary to chemical use, as well as the excess morbidity and mortality associated with alcohol use and abuse. Cultural customs, including alcohol drinking patterns, tend to endure migration despite pressures toward assimilation.

  2. African-Americans and what the data show

  a. The 1990 National Household Survey reported that irrespective of gender, whites consumed alcohol in larger percentages than did African-Americans. The finding of higher abstinence rates among blacks and whites has been observed by various investigators in various settings.

  (1) Whites tend to have their peak years of heavy alcohol consumption between 18 and 25 years of age. Among African-Americans, the ages of 18–29 represent a period of high abstinence rates, with heavy drinking increasing dramatically after 30 years of age.

  (2) Even among age-matched whites and African-Americans, African-Americans reported less daily alcohol consumption than whites.

  (3) African-American women are more likely to abstain than their white counterparts, but when drinking suffer consequences sooner.

  (4) Heavy drinking patterns vary between African-American and white women by age. Heavy drinking among African-American women peaks later than for white women.

V. NATIVE AMERICANS

Native Americans include American Indians, Aleuts, Alaskan Eskimos, and Native Hawaiians. American Indians are the smallest minority group in the United States. Tribal identity is a more useful way of operationally defining cultural identity for Native Americans, who use a self-identifier as membership in or affiliation with a specific tribe or tribes. Following that, membership in a clan or society within a tribe is described.

A. Native Americans—Social Ecology

1. In 1980 Native Americans numbered approximately 1.5 million, less than 1% of the total population, but 2 times that of the 1970 census. These increases are probably due to changes in health care, the high birth rate among American Indians and Alaskan Natives, and an increased reporting of identification in this group.
2. The birth rate among American Indians is nearly twice that of other groups, and the average life expectancy is 6 years less. Native Americans along with African-Americans have the highest rates of injury and death from nondisease causes. The average American Indian family has 4.6 members. The median age of American Indians is 22.4 years.
3. Nearly one out of every four American Indian households is headed by a woman, and approximately half (48%) of American Indian women are employed outside the home.
4. The overall educational attainment of American Indians is the lowest of all ethnic groups of color. The 1980 census revealed that fewer than one out of three (33.3%) have graduated from high school, and that only 7% hold college degrees.
5. One-half of all American Indians live in the western or southwestern United States, 24% on reservations and 8% on historic trust areas in Oklahoma. Most of these reservations have fewer than 1000 residents; one reservation has a population greater than 100,000.
6. Statistically, intermarriage is occurring at a higher rate between American Indian women and white men than between Indian men and women from other ethnic and racial groups.

VI. LESBIANS AND GAY MEN

A. Lesbians and Gay Men and Addictions

1. Lesbian, gay, and bisexual clients are willing to attend treatment programs that deal specifically with lesbian and gay alcoholics.
2. Sexual orientation may not be apparent to an observer, and the patient may be invited to reveal his/her sexual orientation when it is clinically relevant.
   a. Sexual orientation should not affect care.
   b. Sexual orientation should not be ignored.
   c. Professionals should be aware that gay and lesbian identity can play a role in the development of alcoholism and addiction.

3. Social networks are an important component of recovery.
   a. There are many cultural groups within the lesbian and gay community.
      (1) These cultural groups may have value systems different from the ones assumed for the gay and lesbian community.
      (2) There may be groups that do not identify with the gay or lesbian community.

VII. HISPANIC-AMERICANS

Hispanic-Americans in the United States are significantly affected by alcohol and other addictions. Moreover, there is a lack of knowledge and understanding of the close relationship between the sociocultural context and addiction. This lack of knowledge and understanding on the part of healthcare professionals often contributes to treatment of Hispanics that is either irrelevant or of inferior quality.

A. Hispanics—Social Ecology

1. Hispanics account for almost 9% of the United States population.
   a. There are 22.4 million Hispanics.
   b. 63% are of Mexican origin.
   c. 12% are Peurto Rican.
   d. 5% are Cuban.
   e. 20% are from Central and South America.
2. These subgroups are extremely diverse relative to national origin, cultural and ethnic origins of forefathers, generational status in the United States, and socioeconomic status.

B. Hispanics and Addictions

1. The full extent of alcohol and drug use among Hispanics is difficult to assess.
   a. 68% of Hispanic males drink alcohol
   b. 70% of Hispanic females have less than one drink per month or none at all
   c. The link between HIV/AIDS and drug use is significant in the Hispanic population.
      (1) Hispanic infants account for nearly one-quarter of all pediatric AIDS cases; 71% of these are classified as drug-related.
      (2) Nearly 85% of Hispanic children with AIDS contracted it prenatally.
2. Comparisons among different groups of Hispanic-Americans have been made:
   a. Hispanic males with incomes greater than $30,000 per year were twice as likely to be heavy drinkers than those with lower incomes.
   b. Drinking frequency rates were similar for Mexican-Americans, Puerto Ricans, and other Hispanics.
      (1) Mexican-American males were more likely to be both abstainers and heavy drinkers.
      (2) Cuban-Americans were least likely to be abstainers or frequent heavy drinkers.

(3) One-third to two-thirds of the women in each group were abstainers, while 4% or fewer were heavy drinkers.

(4) The overall incidence of nondrinkers is accounted for mostly by Hispanic females who exhibit especially low drinking patterns.

(a) There are strong cultural prohibitions against women who drink excessively, as in many other cultures.

3. Factors that may influence or contribute to the development of drinking problems may include the level of acculturation or recency of immigration, the stress of acculturation, poverty, discrimination, educational attainment and congruency between educational attainment and employment opportunities, family alcohol- and drug-using behaviors, and socioeconomic status.

VIII. CONCLUSION

A substantial body of research explores, in isolation and in interaction, the multiple causal factors of alcoholism and other addictions, including the biophysical, psychological, and sociocultural. Growing evidence indicates that ethnic groups differ in the rates of initiation, consequences of use, maintenance use patterns, and cessation of use.

Close examination of the literature that explores ethnic and cultural differences leads to the conclusion that some groups engage in rates of use higher than in the general population. Often, this is an opinion rigidly held by the general uninformed public that is resistant to evidence to the contrary. These rates may be artifacts of cultural conditioning or have more to do with socioeconomic conditions than with culture and ethnicity.

What is abundantly clear is that physicians must render to their patients competent care based on understanding addiction in its cultural and ethnic context for the patient receiving care. What is also abundantly clear relative to the care that physicians must render to their patients is that understanding addiction in this context of cultural factors can be important in the ultimate success of the intervention.

SELECTED READINGS

Arredondo R, Springer N: *Hispanic-Americans, Principles of Addiction Medicine.* Washington, DC: American Society of Addiction Medicine, 1994.

Attneave C: American Indians and Alaska Native families: immigrants in their own homeland. In M McGoldrick, J Pierce, J Giordano (eds): *Ethnicity and Family Therapy.* New York: Guilford Press, 1982, pp 55–83.

Cetano R: Drinking patterns and alcohol problems among Hispanics in the U.S. A review. *Drug Alcohol Dependence* 12(1):37–59, 1983.

Cetano R: Ethnicity and drinking in Northern California: a comparison among whites, blacks and Hispanics. *Alcohol Alcohol* 1026:31–144, 1984.

Gordon I: *The American Family and Social/Historical Perspective,* 3rd ed. New York: St Martin's, 1983.

Greeley AM, McCready WC, Theisen G: *Ethnic Drinking Subcultures.* New York: Praeger Publishers, 1980.

Harper FD: Research and treatment with black alcoholics. *Alcohol, Health Research World* 1022, 1980.

Heard D: The epidemiology of drinking patterns in alcohol related problems among U.S. blacks. In L Spiegler, DA Tate, S Aitken, M Christin (eds): *Alcohol Use Among U.S. Ethnic Minorities*. 1989.

Hubbard RL, Schlenger WE, Rachal JV, Bray RM, Graddock SG, Cavanaugh ER, et al.: Patterns of alcohol and drug abuse in drug treatment clients from different ethnic backgrounds. In TF Babor (ed): *Alcohol and Culture: Comparative Perspectives from Europe and America*. New York: *Annals of the New York Academy of Sciences*, 1986.

Isrealstam S, Lambert S: Homosexuality as a cause of alcoholism: a historical review. *Internatl J Addictions* 18:1085–1107, 1983.

John R: The Native American family. In CH Mindel, RW Habenstein R Wright Jr (eds): *Ethnic Families in America*. New York: Elsevier, 1988, pp 325–363.

Lex B: Review of alcohol problems in ethnic minority groups. *J Consult Clin Psychol* 55:293–300, 1987.

Lillie-Blanton M, Mackenzie E, Anthony J: Black-white differences in alcohol use by women: Baltimore survey findings. *Public Health Rep* 10:124–133, 1991.

Parrish KM, Higuchi S, Stinson FS, Towle LH, Dufour MC, Harford TC: The association of drinking levels and drinking attitudes among Japanese in Japan and Japanese-Americans in Hawaii and California. *J Substance Abuse* 4:165–177, 1992.

Pohl M: Lesbians and gay men. In *Principles of Addiction Medicine*. American Society of Addiction Medicine, 1994.

Sasaki T: Intercultural research of drinking between Japanese Americans and Mainland Japanese: drinking patterns in problem drinking. *Jpn J Alcohol Drug Dependence* 20(1):28–39, 1985.

Szapocznik J, Kurtines W: Acculturation, biculturalism, and adjustment among Cuban Americans. In AM Padilla (ed): *Acculturation, Theory, Models and Some New Findings*. Boulder, CO: Westview Press, 1980, pp 139–160.

Tremble JE: Stereotypical images, American Indians and prejudice. In PA Katz, DA Taylor (eds): *Eliminating Racism, Profiles in Controversy*. New York: Plenum Press, 1988.

PART  IV

TREATMENT PRACTICES

CHAPTER 19

NONPHARMACOLOGIC TREATMENTS OF ADDICTIVE DISORDERS: GENERAL PRINCIPLES

Gregory B. Collins, M.D.
Section Head, Alcohol and Drug Recovery Center
Department of Psychiatry and Psychology
Cleveland Clinic Foundation
Cleveland, Ohio

I. INTRODUCTION

Nonpharmacologic treatment approaches for addictive disorders have achieved a degree of sophistication and efficacy only in the last 60 years or so, since the founding of Alcoholics Anonymous. So much of what we understand as "rehab" evolved from AA philosophy and methodology, adapted, modernized, and augmented by sophisticated medical and psychological treatment techniques. The union of basic AA principles with psychological treatment techniques gave birth to hospital-based rehab programs and free-standing residential treatment facilities, all supported by halfway houses, outpatient centers, and self-help groups. The unifying philosophical principle remains the 12 steps and 12 "traditions" of AA, bolstered further by the disease model of alcoholism. Contemporary alcoholism treatment is, therefore, an amalgamation of medical, psychological, psychosocial, and spiritual modalities interacting in a quasi-organized framework to assist the individual in achieving and sustaining lasting, contented sobriety. The goals of the rehab experience are as follows: to have patients gain a better understanding of the severity and consequences of their addictions, to have patients become aware of their mental defense mechanisms, to help patients gain awareness that they are alcoholic or addicted, to help patients gain an improved emotional state and healthier outlook, and to develop strategies that will prevent relapse.

II. THE ENTRY PHASE

Often those who are dependent on alcohol and drugs enjoy the substances they use, and find comfort, relief, narcosis, or euphoria in them. Genetic susceptibility probably plays a part in this powerful interaction between susceptible host and poisonous pathogen. The drug "induces its own taking" by controlling the victim's attitudes, thinking, and behavior in ways that foster and maintain access to the substance, which is viewed by the victim as ever

Manual of Therapeutics for Addictions, Edited by Norman S. Miller, Mark S. Gold, and David E. Smith.
ISBN 0471-56176-2 © 1997 John Wiley & Sons, Inc.

more beneficial or needed. Outside positive influences are viewed as meddlesome, intrusive, or interfering, and are resisted with anger, alibis, deceptions, and a host of other defense mechanisms. Treatment starts when a crisis forces an alteration of the sick status quo. The crisis may be an internal one as the addict perceives his/her gradual loss of control and mounting deterioration. Or, the crisis may be an external one, brought about by "concerned others" who may "constructively coerce" the sick person to seek help. A professional evaluation is usually the first step in treatment, and the patient is triaged to any one of a number of specific modalities, depending on the patient's deterioration, level of cooperation, medical, or psychiatric status, and ability to abstain.

III. GROUP THERAPY

A. General Considerations. Group therapy is the hallmark of "Minnesota Model" treatment, and patients in programs based on this model have group therapy meetings several times per week. Some of the groups are educational, providing basic information and indoctrination about the disease concept of addiction, Narcotics Anonymous or Alcoholics Anonymous, and family dynamics. Total abstinence from mood-altering chemicals is emphasized. Counselors, who are themselves recovered, and recovering volunteers also provide inspiration and hope that recovery can be attained. Education cannot benefit a mind that is closed, distracted, or hostile; therefore, group therapy is employed for its effectiveness against the pathologic mental state of the addict. In addiction, there is a preponderance of negative emotions—anger, resentment, guilt, shame, or grandiosity. These negative states are powerful, long-standing phenomena that provide the emotional justifications for continued chemical use. Anger and resentment foster the drug use through inherent spitefulness or entitlement, as well as through the rejection of others' attempts to control the substance use. The user feels no obligation to comply with those who are the hated objects of his/her anger, and those around the user become progressively more helpless, isolated, and impotent in their attempts to provide external controls. Guilt and shame produce a similar result in the acceleration of refuge in the offending chemical. Self-loathing fosters an attitude of hopelessness and despair, which frustrates the possibility of constructive change. Others are given to grandiosity and euphoria, emotions that provide a false and exaggerated sense of self-confidence and self-adulation. The opinions and perspectives of others are discounted and scorned. Addicts begin to believe that they are superior to others, and are entitled to anything they want. These pathologic mood states serve to perpetuate access to the drug, by promoting a sense of personal entitlement and by limiting the power of outside (healthy) influences. In group therapy these pathologic mood states are attacked vigorously by counselors and other peer patients in treatment and are also linked to pathologic thinking states or "defense mechanisms," patterns of cognition that reinforce the negative emotions and perpetuate the chemical use. Sick emotions give rise to sick thinking and vice versa. The defense mechanism of *denial* is the hallmark of addictive cognition, blocking the full appreciation of the extent and severity of the addiction. Loss of control over the substance is not realized, and the gravity of the addictive consequences is denied partially or totally. Chemical excess is seen by the afflicted person as necessary and good through exaggerated *rationalization,* in which incongruous and illogical alibis and excuses are offered for using. *Projection of blame,* taken to an extreme, reinforces a person's self-justification, while mobilizing anger and resentment outwardly. These defense mechanisms foster addictive behaviors including drug overuse, concealment, lying, alibiing, and unresponsiveness to correction. The goal of therapy groups is honesty, self-realization, and mobilization of the need for change. Although the groups promote personal responsibility and ownership for one's actions, they are nonpejorative and nonblaming, and the attitude of the staff is supportive, caring, and nonjudgmental, while at the same time always pushing for improvement.

IV. MULTIDISCIPLINARY TEAM APPROACH

A. General Considerations. At first glance, it would seem that the founders of Alcoholics Anonymous, "Dr. Bob" Smith, and "Bill" Wilson, did not rely on a multidisciplinary team to find their own sobriety and launch the fellowship of AA. Nonetheless, if one studies the roots of the AA movement, it is clear that the multidisciplinary approach was one of the main strengths of the movement as it gathered in the knowledge of physicians, psychiatrists, clergy, nurses, and recovering individuals, all working together to help the alcoholic to obtain the elusive goal of lasting sobriety. This early approach in AA has evolved into a highly specialized, but nonetheless multidisciplinary methodology widely used in chemical dependency treatment programs. With assistance from many disciplines, the chemically dependent person is first detoxified and then is restored to physical, emotional, and spiritual health. The effective accomplishment of this broad restorative goal requires the input of people with different skills—a true multidisciplinary group. Such a group obviously needs to work in a harmonious fashion in order to accomplish its goal of total recovery for the chemically dependent person. Nonetheless, the very diversity of backgrounds and experiences of the team members in many ways works against this harmonious interaction, often resulting in rivalry, resentment, and even therapeutic sabotage. Since the alcoholic can easily "divide and conquer," splitting staff and playing on biases and rivalries to remain entrenched in the addictive cycle, staff coordination and teamwork must be achieved and maintained to facilitate the process of change and recovery.

Treatment for alcoholism must be multidisciplinary. Many different skills are needed to treat cases of chemical dependency, which is a physical, emotional, social, and spiritual disease. Medical treatment is often the necessary first priority, to address all possible physical consequences of the disease, including withdrawal syndromes and types of organ pathology. The emotional and cognitive consequences of the disease are no less important, since the "alcoholic thinking" reinforces the disease process through denial, minimization, and rationalization. Motivation to stop drinking may be weak, and pathologically reinforcing defense mechanisms may be well entrenched, including denial, rationalization, and projection of blame. Intervention at the psychological level requires skills in individual and group therapy, and requires the ability to change or influence attitudes and behaviors of patients. Since brain damage is a frequent concomitant of substance abuse, assessment skills are needed using psychological testing and other forms of psychiatric or psychological evaluation. The psychosocial component of the chemical-dependence disease process also requires special skills. Social stabilization and restructuring are very important, as the patient who has a severely damaged social support system will be at a great disadvantage in developing a new, recovery-oriented support system after leaving the treatment center. For example, the alcoholic salesperson who has to contend with client entertainment may require intensive counseling and nondrinking social skills or may need a vocational change. Likewise, the alcoholic who lives in close proximity to a bar may need social service help in moving to protect sobriety. Last, but certainly not of least importance, are the spiritual skills required to treat the disease process. These spiritual skills involve the treatment team in endorsing the AA 12-step program, which would emphasize certain aspects of healthy spirituality, and deemphasize pathologic aspects of spirituality. This spiritual approach to the disease process places a strong emphasis on examination of spiritual defects and needs, while promoting a process of spiritual revitalization. These widely divergent skills needed to treat the many facets of the addictive disease process illustrate why it is so important for the patient to be treated, not by one individual, but by a team, in order to assure the best chance of recovery.

It is important that there is a team approach to chemical-dependence problems, as these patients are often complex, and potential pitfalls are numerous. If a physician is attempting to treat a chemically dependent patient independently, there may be difficulty and danger in "enabling" the patient by providing continued prescriptions of the drug of abuse or a substitute drug. Endless demands and manipulations for chemicals can sabotage well-intentioned physicians unless the emotional–cognitive or "thinking part" of the disease process is altered at the same time. To treat the symptom of pathologic manipulation, lines of communication must be maintained between all personnel of various disciplines. Coordination and supervision of the treatment team constitutes a major activity of the clinic administrator and psychiatric consultant. Countertransference (feelings or reactions of the therapist toward the patient) may help or hinder the treatment of those difficult people. Many times, if treated in a one-to-one setting, the therapist may "act out" personal issues with the patient, especially since many professionals in this field have had personal experience with some type of chemical-dependence process, either through their own addictions or through addictions in the spouse or family of origin. These past experiences, if not modulated through a team approach, can produce therapeutic "blind spots" and distortions, and might make one-to-one treatment difficult or unsuccessful. For example, the therapist may begin to act out repressed anger at the chemically dependent family members of long ago, through inappropriate irritability with the patient. Or, the therapist may be enabling of the patient's addiction, perhaps by "rescuing" or rationalizing relapses, and may not be aware of this. Therefore, it is important that a team of people be available to support each other in reality testing and in evaluating their own behaviors. This personal emotional energy can be very useful in the treatment of chemically dependent patients if it is recognized for what it is, and if it is then channeled appropriately. It is clear that it is much easier to manipulate a person working in solitary fashion than to manipulate a group of therapists working in unison.

B. Burnout Prevention. A team approach to chemical-dependence treatment is also important because treating these patients on an individual basis can be time-consuming, demanding, and emotionally exhausting. The high frequency of "burnout" for professionals treating these patients is well known. Not being able to share with team members the inevitable feelings of frustration, anger, and confusion can contribute to a more rapid rate of burnout. It is important that the team itself function as a supportive, reality-oriented group, allowing an individual team member to be directed in a gentle, nonthreatening way, should involvement with the patient become unhealthy or dysfunctional. Without this group interaction, an individual therapist could continue with a formulation for treatment that would either ignore or exaggerate aspects of the patient's personality and/or dysfunction to the detriment of recovery. These errors are less likely when there are other professionals involved in the patient's care who also feel a responsibility for the patient's progress and treatment.

C. Clinical Roles. Since the goal of treatment is to allow patients their best chance for recovery, a multidisciplinary team will afford the best opportunity as the contribution of each team member will be different because of specific training. In all cases, physical health, or at least a stable physical condition, is an essential aspect of recovery, necessitating the skills of physicians and nurses. Additionally, a psychiatrist will see subtleties of the patient's emotional state that may need specific treatment that others might miss. Likewise, a social worker may see "slippery areas" in the patient's social network that a psychiatrist might not be attuned to. A psychologist will be able to identify nuances in the patient's cognitive functioning, that might not otherwise be discovered. The 12-step component, provided by counselors and AA volunteers, is also essential after discharge, since the patient cannot take the treatment team home. The 12 steps and peer support are essential in continually reinforcing the changes in attitude and perspective for the maintenance of stable, "quality sobriety." A true multidisciplinary team approach to treatment allows the widest possible range of modalities in helping the person to restore health physically, emotionally, cognitively, socially, and spiritually.

D. Process Issues. The effective interdisciplinary team incorporates a dynamic, interactive, fluid pattern of interrelating to achieve internal and external goals important for the completion of its task. The team must move from an amorphous state of nondefinition of role to one that incorporates a certain amount of role clarity, without inflaming role-based rivalries and "turf battles." The team must also function within the philosophical framework in which the input of all members is valued and important, balancing the strong influence of "core members," while at the same time fostering participation and ownership by supportive and temporary team members as well. All of these issues must be dealt with smoothly and imperceptibly in order for the critical internal goals to be achieved, specifically, fostering the recovery of the chemically dependent patient, while at the same time addressing external pressures. These external pressures may come from governmental funding agencies, hospital administrations, insurance companies, professional reference groups, or even recovered volunteers. Each of these groups may have its own agenda for "who should be doing what and how it should be done." The team must address itself to the needs and wants of these constituencies, and must negotiate an acceptable modus operandi with these external influences on its functioning. The complexity of these interactions is truly astounding and must often, of necessity, give way before task-driven initiatives. Who is best suited for the job by skill, experience, and interest is a decision the group must resolve by its deliberative, decisionmaking process. The team must then support the decision and enthusiastically buy into its implementation with their expertise and energy. Questions about who makes what decisions and how decisions are made, implemented, and evaluated, require serious procedural effort. Teams can choose how to decide from a full range of possibilities, including total unanimity, consensus, majority rule, authority rule, or default. Any form of decisionmaking will be appropriate in certain circumstances, but who defines these circumstances, and what permission is required from team members may give rise to other procedural issues. Finally, questions about how decisions are implemented, what sort of acceptance or "buyin" is expected from the team, and who validates the decisionmaking process in the outcomes may need to be determined.

E. Team Communication. The effective flow of communication is essential to all procedural aspects of team play. Some of the rules governing information flow are found in the decisionmaking procedures. In fact, some of the same questions need to be raised when discussing communication or decisionmaking, such as who, when, how, how often, why, and where. Similarly, many styles of communication patterns may be employed: hierarchical, round-robin (everyone speaks), authoritarian (power speaks), informational, and educational, to name only a few. Each form is appropriate in given situations, however.

Factors influencing team communication patterns need to be addressed frequently. Active participation must be encouraged for all members. Time must be allotted for the free exchange of ideas and feelings. Openness to new ideas and divergent opinions encourages active participation and values the contributions made by each member. The notion of dialog in both directions of the hierarchy across interdisciplinary lines promotes the sense of team spirit and ownership of goals. Style of leadership on a team also determines communication patterns, atmosphere, structure, and expectations. Effective leadership leads to a sense of empowerment of staff, enhancement of learning and competency, team ownership of the shared goal, and added excitement to work. Finally, norms—as the unwritten rules governing behaviors—are developed. Norms are often the unspoken guidelines for socialization into systems. Their existence is most felt when violated. Like feelings, norms are neither good nor bad, "they just *are.*" Their appropriateness should be measured by their usefulness to the team in completing its assigned task. In our experience, these norms pertain to just about every circumstance of team interaction. Our team norms affect where people sit at a conference table, their style of clothing, who speaks first (and last), and the use of "therapeutic language" (e.g., AA, psychiatric, "street," or mix). Other issues such as uniforms, punctuality, degrees on name tags, or even argument styles fall into the category of team norms, all of which must be negotiated and resolved. In summary, the process of developing procedure parallels the formation of the team. All processes of the team are fluid, dynamic, and interactive.

F. Dealing with Conflict. Conflict and interpersonal tension are an expected and inevitable consequence of the multidisciplinary nature of the team. The very backgrounds and personal experiences of the individuals lead to a collision of ideas and priorities, which, when overlaid with role-related personal issues, becomes a major obstacle to the team's accomplishing of its task. Perhaps fundamental in a chemical-dependence treatment setting, is the recognition that the patient's sobriety is the top priority. How that goal can best be achieved is an issue in which it can be argued ardently from every side, but ultimately it is the patient who wins from this discourse, and the entire staff can derive satisfaction from that knowledge. In acting conscientiously toward the goal of helping the patient attain sobriety, self-serving competitive tendencies can be set aside without much "loss of face" and without a sense of "losing the therapeutic argument." This "fervent discourse," especially in treatment planning sessions, should not be viewed as an "argument," but rather as an energized dialog in which everybody puts forth maximum effort. Usually, in our experience, when this happens a consensus gradually or rapidly emerges that "sweeps all before it." The consensus is powerful and palpable and is generally not to be denied even by authoritarian core members. Hearing and heeding this consensus is analogous to searching for the "group conscience of AA," an AA tradition that recognizes that the collective wisdom of the group is generally superior to that of any one individual. The enactment of this tradition in a professional team setting generally works well and can serve as a role model to the patient in heeding this "group conscience" very carefully in the AA program. Even so, at times the energy level and intensity of dialog among team members can become so passionate that conflicts escalate beyond the "comfort zone." At those times, deferring final resolution of the program to another time, seeking new information, or "smoothing ruffled feathers" by verbal or physical expressions of friendly concern may be needed. Carrying a grudge or "getting even" are behaviors that work counter to the spirit of unity and compromise, which must be part of any organizational team's functioning.

G. Decisionmaking. Decisionmaking is often the true test of teamwork in a multidisciplinary setting, as groups will typically struggle over "who decides how to decide" and finally "who decides" enumerable times. As time goes by, members will learn to set aside reference-group loyalties and to become more interactive, interdependent, and less authoritarian. Trust, commitment, and enthusiasm eventually evolve. This high level of interactive trust does not happen "by accident"; rather, it is the end result of struggling, readjusting, negotiating, clarifying, and dialoguing. Individual members start out "programmed for conflict" with their reference-group loyalties, past experiences, and individual agendas that they have already. Only gradually are these diminished with disclosure, negotiation, and compromise. A fine balance point is sought in which each member retains individuality, but is not blinded or motivated solely by that. The group process is always to be supportive. No one "goes away mad." Rather, most often the participants feel electrified and uplifted by the experience of participating, and have the glow of realization that the end result of a deliberation was better by far than the thinking of any one individual present.

H. Self-Help Groups in the Treatment Team

1. General considerations. The involvement of the self-help groups' philosophy and members is both crucial and complicated at the same time. Alcoholics Anonymous (AA) is an independent "fellowship" whose principles, articulated largely in the form of 12 steps and 12 traditions, has provided a philosophical structure for many other self-help groups today, including Narcotics Anonymous, Cocaine Anonymous, Sex Anonymous, and many others. Since its founding by two alcoholics in 1935, AA has provided a philosophy that provides the foundation for many treatment programs. The AA philosophy encompasses mental, emotional, and spiritual aspects, and newcomers look to more senior members as positive role models in the application of program fundamentals. An AA-based recovery program is a spiritual, cognitive, and behavioral way of life that enhances a personal and interpersonal sense of well-being while promoting a value system based on honesty and humility.

Typically, members do not consider AA as a "treatment" per se, which they associate with professionalism and a fee-for-service approach. AA philosophy, although emphasizing psychological restructuring, does not rely on traditional psychiatric methodology. Treatment programs typically put heavy emphasis on participation in AA, both during and after the acute treatment phase.

Most treatment programs emphasize the first five steps of Alcoholics

Anonymous. These steps emphasize surrendering to the loss of control over alcohol, making a decision to accept outside help, turning one's life over to outside help (including a spiritual "higher power"), and the taking and sharing of a moral inventory. Treatment programs operate to facilitate this process in every way possible. Typically, community volunteers or members of AA or NA provide motivational presentations or conduct self-help group meetings for patients. AA materials such as the "Big Book," 12 steps, and 12 traditions, and various pamphlets are available and may be mandatory reading for patients. Workbooks are also available to facilitate "first-step work," which focuses on the recognition and acceptance of powerlessness and unmanageability over alcohol and mood-altering drugs. The importance of this step cannot be overemphasized. The degree and quality of work on this step will determine, to an enormous extent, the subsequent treatment course and the outcome of therapy. Those who "work a good first step," generally have a much smoother progression through the remainder of treatment. Once beyond the initial intensive phase of treatment, patients are strongly encouraged to become lifelong members of AA or similar 12-step support groups. Often patients will be encouraged to attend community AA meetings as part of the initial treatment process, sometimes in the company of temporary "sponsors" who guide and direct newcomers to the program. This "fellowship" serves the purpose of a shame-free introduction to a support system, while at the same time promulgating the message of surrender, help, and hope for the addicted person.

Furthermore, treatment programs may rely heavily or even exclusively on self-help group members to fill their staff positions. Typically, patients receive a strong, comprehensive orientation to the principles of AA, and are given vigorous encouragement to join and become active in the fellowship as a means of sustaining sobriety. Many then return to the treatment center as "AA volunteers," providing additional helping resources to patients and families in the center. Outcome research and clinical experience has proved that meaningful relationships between professionals and self-help groups are extremely valuable. Research on treatment outcomes among alcoholics increasingly finds that participation in AA improves changes for successful rehabilitation. The role that AA assumes is both philosophical and organizational. New patients in a treatment program can be inspired by a recovering volunteer who can expose them to the philosophy and methodology of learning to live sober "one day at a time." Hospitalized patients can actually see others who have recovered from the illness of alcoholism and who have rebuilt their shattered lives and restored themselves to health and sanity. The patients have an opportunity to "tell it like it is" to others who have suffered similarly, and patients who hesitate to discuss their situations with professionals will often confide in other alcoholics. The AA philosophical approach encompasses mental, emotional, and spiritual aspects, and the volunteers who embody these principles act as positive peer supports and role models. Functionally, AA structures patients' rehabilitation through the 12 steps and 12 traditions and outlines "how to work the program." Through shared anecdotal experiences and a "what will work for me will work for you" approach, the therapeutic changes occur.

2. Problems. However, several pitfalls can occur between treatment professionals and members of AA, primarily involving conflict and rivalry. Self-help groups can be extremely sensitive about cooptation by professionals, as the methodology of "self-help" is modified into a professional–client relationship. Boundary disputes and ideologic differences may also create conflict.

The roles and responsibilities of the AA member and professional differ significantly. For example, the helping professional is bound by federally mandated confidentiality laws and operates by a legally regulated medical approach. AA members, however, although respectful of anonymity, are not necessarily governed by as many guidelines when they interact with newly recovering patients. They may feel comfortable breaching anonymity "when it is within the fellowship" or if it is intended to help a patient. Thus, in this way and in many others, professionals and AA members operate under different guidelines. At times, when the two groups vigorously disagree, rivalry rather than cooperation may ensue. Frequent interaction, congruent ideas about treatment, and appropriate linking strategies will mitigate rivalry. Employing staff personnel who are members of AA or other self-help groups will often bridge the gap. Integration of self-help group members into the treatment team may not be easily accomplished or maintained. Staff members who are involved in self-help groups themselves may realize that their dual involvements may evoke conflicting loyalties, and they may have a difficult time separating appropriate behaviors for each circumstance. For many years, it was felt that AA members could not even serve as paid staff in an alcohol treatment setting because of possible violations of AA traditions, especially those regarding anonymity, nonaffiliation, and receiving money for AA work. More significantly, the problems inherent in adapting a self-help approach to a professional setting may be difficult. For example, the AA injunction "let go and let God" may be a reasonable guideline in a self-help group, but in the hospital setting with an expectation of care, such an approach might not be appropriate. Those "two hatters" (staff members in self-help groups) who are too narrowly focused or rigid will find it difficult or impossible to accommodate to the realities of a professional setting with its red tape, bureaucracy, paperwork, accountability, and teamwork emphasis. On the other hand, other "two hatters" will adapt successfully and find the treatment setting to be an opportunity to help others when they are most receptive, even if compromises must be made with external constraints.

Many of the same problems with "reference-group loyalty" in professionals impact on the integration of self-help group members as volunteers or staff. While the achievement of sobriety would be generally an accepted goal, the question of "what is the best way to get there" might be fraught with dissension. The decision of whether the team takes a "whole person" or narrower "alcoholic" approach, or the degree to which AA attendance must be insisted on are examples of potentially controversial subjects. The necessity for team members to buy into "group norms" is somewhat at odds with the AA tradition of "cooperation but not affiliation," and there may be a need on the part of the AA to "hold back" a bit of the self to assure that they have not been coopted by the "professionals." The issue of "degree of membership" is also a confounding problem. Are AA members "core members," or are they supportive or even temporary members? Often there is a wide discrepancy between the staff or administrative view and that of the AA volunteers or staff.

The resolution for such obstacles to teamwork lies, of course, in communication, negotiation, and compromise. A clear understanding of AA philosophy and tradition is of great help to the self-help members (who may not have studied the original traditions carefully) and to professional and administrative staff (who need to understand the sensitivities and needs of self-help group members). Special programs for recruiting and retaining the "special skills" of recovering AA volunteers have worked well in hospital settings. Integration into a professional team does, in fact, require special skills, namely, the ability to be flexible and to adapt to the needs, circumstances, and norms of the team. Not everyone has these skills, and recruitment and selection processes must be undertaken with this limitation in mind. Specialized orientation and training, with clearly defined norms and expectations, may be of great help. Using a nonprofessional staff intermediary may help promote acceptance of accountability by AA members. Such an arrangement avoids the tension generated by AA members feeling accountable to professional staff; and when "corrections" have to be made, there will be much less bitterness between the AA volunteers and the professionals.

V. ANCILLARY THERAPIES

A. Milieu Therapy. Milieu therapy can provide the right balance of objective detachment and loving support that addicts require. Once defensive resistances are down, the learning process can begin. The presence of recovering people as staff or volunteers gives a message of understanding and optimism to the newcomer. Group therapy, with other addicted peers, facilitated by at least one rehabilitation professional, is employed to foster identification with and acceptance of the reality of the disease process, of the need for corrective action, and of program principles. Since all the peers are "in the same boat," there is a high level of mutual acceptance and trust, and entrenched defenses can be confronted and, hopefully, set aside. Often group inventory taking, done in the form of inventory sharing or in other forms of self-disclosure such as shared biographies, reveal individual strengths and weaknesses, document the destructive disease process, and allow access to helpful correction and praise. The result is hopefully a corrective emotional experience in which the addict recognizes his/her own powerlessness over the drug, accepts the need for ongoing help from this supportive treatment network, and resolves to continue on a path toward the rebuilding of a healthier identity.

Treatment plans are individualized and taken to account strengths, weaknesses, and psychosocial realities in building a long-term sobriety program. There is great attention to detail in altering old addictive ways. Staff attempts to bring out the patient's better self, with constant emphasis on good grooming, manners, language, attitude, and conduct. Often a sound preaddictive personality is discovered, and old strengths and talents, long buried by addictive neglect, are allowed to flourish. Often these people rediscover themselves as attractive and competent individuals without the distorting influences of drugs. In other cases, adaptive social skills have never been developed, because of the early onset of the disease process, and rehabilitation must involve the teaching of new social skills and behaviors. A good milieu creates a sense of something dramatic happening—the birth or rebirth of a new person. This intensive process has historically been done in inpatient hospital units or residential isolated settings for the physical stabilization, detoxification, personality transformation, strengthening of social supports, and spiritual renewal. The environment is almost hermetically sealed, and the transformation process is aggressively fostered around the clock, while old addictive patterns are discouraged and corrected. It is a total immersion form of treatment, and few outside distractions are tolerated. Many programs prohibit newspapers, magazines, or television. Contacts with the "outside" are usually severely limited. The power and effectiveness of this treatment approach are impressive. Patients relinquish their well-entrenched addictive defenses, learn the program steps, and conform to the recommended treatment plan for abstinence and continued involvement in a support network, including treatment aftercare and self-help group meetings.

B. Family Therapy. Family therapy is typically an important aspect of Minnesota Model treatment. Typically, family members of the addict are "other victims" of the disease, and are also unwitting accomplices. Victimization occurs to the family members from the addict's self-absorption, entitlement, guilt, rage, and erratic behavior. Family members are frequently the objects of extreme emotional neglect or physical abuse. Their frustration and rage are understandable, especially in view of the addict's persistent denial that such events ever occurred or had any significance.

The family itself plays a part in the propagation of the illness through the family members' own reactions to the addict. Their rage and anger foster in the addict more defensiveness, withdrawal, resentment, shame, and guilt, with the result being worsening of negative emotions, and with the progression of more substance use. The family members may also be caught up in their own denial and rationalization mechanisms, buying into the addict's alibis or excuses, or minimizing the extent and severity of the addictive disease process. Often they resist or sabotage the eventual prescription, the necessity for permanent abstinence, and for ongoing support from the treatment network. These lifestyle changes may be resisted out of habit, stigma, misunderstanding, ignorance, or denial. The persistence of these faulty beliefs by the family can eventually erode the alcoholic's resolve, and can precipitate relapses. In treatment, the family members are typically exposed to educational videos, staff discussions, and other family members who have been through the recovery process. In a very real way, they must recover also, from their own misconceptions, defenses, and rationalizations. The lifestyle changes that are inherent in a continued recovery program must be supported by them in a wholehearted, grateful, and enthusiastic way. Minnesota Model programs exert strong efforts by staff and volunteers to accomplish this transformation.

VI. SUMMARY

A multidisciplinary team approach to the treatment of chemical dependence is a concept that goes well beyond the mere presence of different disciplines. The illness itself requires specialized inputs from medicine, psychiatry, psychology, social work, nursing, self-help programs, and many more. None of these disciplines can carry the whole weight of rehabilitating a recovering patient. All must work together to accomplish this task. Yet the way in which they work together is critically important as well. Team members must overcome their natural reference-group loyalties and competitive biases from past training and experience to work together in a cooperative fashion to facilitate the process of recovery. It is only by setting limits on individual "ownership and entitlement" that real teamwork can emerge. Such "individuality," if left unchecked, probably is destructive to team morale and functioning in the long run. Ultimately, the group process or the "group conscience" (as the AA members put it) will show that its wisdom is superior to that of any one individual.

SELECTED READINGS

Alcoholics Anonymous, 3rd ed. New York: Alcoholics Anonymous World Services, 1976.

Collins GB: Contemporary issues in the treatment of alcohol dependence. *Psychiatric Cln North Am* 16:33–48, 1993.

Collins GB, Barth J, Zrimec GL: Recruiting and retaining volunteers in a hospital alcoholism program. *Hosp Commun Psychiatry* 32(2):130–132, 1981.

Collins GB, Weiss K, Cozzens D, Thrope J, Kotz M, Janesz JW: A multidisciplinary team approach to the treatment of alcohol and drug addiction. In NS Miller (ed): *Comprehensive Handbook of Drug and Alcohol Addiction.* New York: Marcel-Dekker, 1991, pp 981–999.

Fox R: A multidisciplinary approach to the treatment of alcoholism. *Internatl J Psychiatry* 5(1):34–44, 1968.

Mann GA: History and theory of a treatment for a drug and alcohol addiction. In NS Miller (ed): *Comprehensive Handbook of Drug and Alcohol Addiction.* New York: Marcel-Dekker, 1991, pp 1201–1212.

Reuben IM, Beckhard R: Factors influencing the effectiveness of health teams. *Milbank Quart* (July):317–335, 1972.

Twelve Steps and Twelve Traditions. New York: Alcoholics Anonymous World Services, 1953.

CHAPTER 20

TREATMENT MANAGEMENT FOR ACUTE AND CONTINUING CARE

Daniel H. Angres, M.D.
Michael Easton, M.D.
Rush University Medical School
Chicago, Illinois

I. OVERVIEW

At present, the field of addiction medicine is undergoing significant growth in our understanding of substance-related disorders and their treatments. Until recently, the treatments for all addictions were limited and standardized such that most individuals (regardless of the type of severity of their disorders) received the same type of treatment modalities and intensities with little variation. Great progress was made in improved outcomes for chemically dependent individuals with these traditional models. Over the past 10 years we have seen an increasing number of treatment interventions developed to help individuals with drug and alcohol addictions. Increasingly, a wide variety of treatments are being administered in less restrictive settings. These changes are due in part to increasing understanding of treatment outcomes for these disorders and continuing directives to manage the care of these disorders. In light of our increasing treatment options and management of treatment resources, it is becoming ever more important to understand which individuals will differentially benefit from specific treatment types, intensities, and settings. In the following chapter we will review the information used to make contemporary treatment recommendations and try to elucidate some of the information available on treatment matching. Multiple factors need to be considered in order to determine the appropriate type of treatment and level of care.

II. PATIENT FACTORS

A. Severity. Severity of addiction can be determined by a variety of factors. The most common one looks at the type and means of administration and quantity of substance a person is using. Most importantly, one must evaluate the loss of control that leads to the consequences one is suffering from their substance use (legal, social, employment, relationships, monetary, psychiatric, etc.). In general, the greater the number and severity of consequences, the more severe the problem. And the greater the severity of the addiction, the more intense and greater duration the treatment is going to need to be overall.

Manual of Therapeutics for Addictions, Edited by Norman S. Miller, Mark S. Gold, and David E. Smith.
ISBN 0471-56176-2 © 1997 John Wiley & Sons, Inc.

Integration of 12-step concepts in treatment are essential components of any quality program.

B. Type of Addiction. It is increasingly clear that the course and treatment outcomes of various addictions are different. Alcohol and many other drug addictions appear to respond well to available treatments; in particular, the abstinence-based methods of short to intermediate duration, IV drug addictions (narcotics, stimulants, cocaine) appear to require alternative or additional interventions we most commonly use. Individuals with these problems tend to need highly structured, residential, intensive, and longer-term treatments, ranging from months to years.

C. Comorbid Conditions

1. Psychiatric. The presence of psychiatric conditions can have significant ramifications on the setting and type of treatment an individual will receive. It may also affect the overall efficacy of the most commonly used interventions. In general, it appears that individuals with selected psychiatric disorders do not do as well in traditional treatment programs for addiction as do individuals without such conditions.

> *Psychotic Disorders.* Because of the nature of illnesses, such individuals have significant impairments with their ability to think, understand information, and evaluate their own and others' behavior given the particular social context in which they are enmeshed. In addition, they have difficulty benefiting from more insight-oriented approaches and usually have significant impairment in their ability to form interpersonal relationships and participate in normal socialization. These individuals are usually at high risk for decompensation during times of high emotional stress. They tend to respond better to treatment in psychiatric settings within specialized treatment programs, and once stabilized, may be appropriate for a traditional addictions setting. It is important that these individuals get psychiatric treatment (both pharmacologic and psychotherapeutic) as part of their overall program.

> *Mood, Anxiety Disorders.* Except during severe exacerbations, these individuals are frequently treated in traditional addictions settings. Pharmacologic agents are seldom required because these disorders respond to cognitive behavioral techniques in addictions treatment.

> *Personality Disorders.* These individuals are frequently treated in addiction settings. Various settings will see different types of disorders. Sociopathic and borderline personality disorders tend to be the most challenging clinically. Each presents unique treatment challenges. In general, these individuals demonstrate poorer outcomes in traditional programs. They frequently require specialized interventions, more structured programs, and longer, more intensive, treatment.

> *Dementia.* This patient population is a significant challenge and has been underaddressed by treatment programs and research in general. Overall, they require alternative treatments to traditional programs and frequently fall through the cracks of available resources. Because of a variety of cognitive problems present in these individuals, many may have great difficulty developing insight into their condition or making behavioral changes. In general, the focus of treatment frequently ends up being changing the individual's environment as opposed to changing the individual.

Other Addictions. Included in comorbid conditions, consideration should be given to other compulsive behaviors. The coexistence of eating disorders, compulsive sexual behaviors, gambling, and compulsive spending occur quite common with the chemically dependent populations. These problems need to be identified and worked on concurrently with the chemical dependence and any additional treatment.

2. Medical. Significant medical illness can affect a patient's capacity to participate in treatment. Patients who are severely debilitated (e.g., transplant, dialysis, AIDS) may not have the stamina or physical mobility to participate in intensive, structured treatment programs. Specialized treatment interventions frequently need to be individually developed for such situations. Chronic-pain patients are a unique challenge in that some may need narcotic therapy. Their overall management is highly complicated, and generally such treatment can be integrated into traditional pain management programs that include addiction treatment.

D. Gender. Gender influences the prevalence and course of many addictive disorders. In general, women have lower rates of addiction, tend to have later onsets, and a more rapid progression, and frequently are predated by significant psychiatric or medical illness. Commonly, the psychosocial issues addressed by both men and women are different and need to be addressed via various methods of intervention. Women's addiction programs exist, and in certain situations, may be beneficial.

Pregnancy: Pregnant addicts require specialized extended treatment services both pre- and post-partum. Specialized requirements include the health of the mother, the course of the pregnancy, fetal development, and postpartum child development and parenting abilities. Not uncommonly, women with more severe alcohol or drug use during pregnancy are enrolled in high-intensity day, residential, or hospital programs during the course of their pregnancy.

E. Age: The Elderly. Substance-related disorders in this population are prevalent and underrecognized. They represent a major problem in this group. The elderly frequently have a high rate of medical comorbidity and complications with prescription drug abuse as well as alcohol addiction. Although prevalent, they are underserved by present-day addiction treatment services. They frequently have a number of specialized needs or disabilities restricting their ability to participate in or benefit from typical programs.

F. Patient Preference. One of the most important factors that we frequently overlook is whether the patient is motivated to follow our treatment recommendations. One should not make the mistake of assuming that, because a patient may not want to follow one's treatment recommendations, that individual is unmotivated. One should try, within reason, to formulate a treatment plan along with the patient to enhance motivation. Intervention and addiction treatment are intended to motivate the patient.

G. "High-Accountability" Patients. This category would include individuals who are highly accountable in society for the well-being of others; healthcare professionals, including physicians, nurses, dentists, and pharmacists; as well as other highly accountable individuals such as commercial airline pilots, attorneys, and people in other safety sensitive positions. These individuals typically need a milieu that has expertise in working with professionals.

III. NONPATIENT FACTORS

In many instances, factors external to the patient may have the greatest influence on their treatment outcome. It is imperative in evaluating individuals and developing treatment plans that many of these factors be taken into account.

A. Family and Relationship Problems. When "significant others" or family members are involved in their routine life, the effects of the patient's illness on the family system must be addressed. An individual's addiction frequently causes multiple ramifications that do not simply resolve once one's addiction goes into remission. Potential for relapse is far greater if a patient returns to a dysfunctional home environment.

B. Employment Problems. Frequently individuals are referred or mandated to treatment by an employer. It becomes important to include these individuals in the patient's treatment. The employers' attitudes toward addiction and treatment will have a significant impact on the patient's follow-up planning and must be taken into account when developing one's long-term treatment plan. Many companies have a contract with *employee assistant programs* (EAPs) to intervene and manage impaired workers. These programs have varying degrees of involvement—from screening and referring to case management and monitoring individuals' participation with treatment, aftercare, and functioning at work. In many instances, the treating clinician or program will work closely with EAPs.

C. Legal Problems. The judicial system or professional licensing boards that, in effect, refer patients to treatment can have significant effects on the patient's motivation and the degree of stress that the patient may be experiencing during and after treatment (e.g., risk of returning to jail, loss of driver's license, professional license). The judicial or licensing boards may specify the setting, intensity, and lengths of treatment. In addition, the outcome expectations and consequences for some of these individuals may be different (e.g., with impaired physicians, zero tolerance to relapse is frequently enforced). On the other hand, you may have the ability to enforce certain follow-up interventions that may improve long-term aftercare (e.g., random frequent urine toxicology, mandatory participation in aftercare groups). In addition, you may become very involved as an advocate for the individual working closely with their legal representation.

D. Socioeconomic Status and Environment. The environment to which one returns after treatment can have one of the greatest influences on long-term outcome. Frequently, long-term aftercare plans are greatly affected by this. Individuals without supportive environments or severe addictions, those who would return to areas where drug use is high, or those with suboptimal housing options frequently will experience greater difficulties. For these individuals, longer-term placements such as residential settings or halfway houses are frequently indicated.

E. Accessibility to Treatment. Not infrequently, individuals will not have adequate treatment programs in their vicinity and may have to commute great distances to receive appropriate treatment. In such situations, persons who could easily participate in low-intensity outpatient programs may have to go to other locations where they can live in residential treatment settings. This also provides a long-term logistical problem in that aftercare usually needs to be developed in their relative area.

F. Therapist Factors. This may be one of the most salient yet underevaluated and underappreciated factors in influencing treatment outcomes. Regardless of the program or therapist philosophy, frequently their personal qualities (e.g., empathy) will have a substantial effect on whether patients benefit from their services.

G. Reimbursement Status. One's ability to administer treatment is increasingly being determined by managed-care providers or limited coverage. In many situations, this may be the primary determinant of type, setting, and intensity of treatment a person can afford to receive. Those without ability to pay for services will frequently have their treatment determined by the availability of publicly funded programs.

IV. TREATMENT MODALITIES

Treatment settings can be viewed in a number of different ways. Treatment intensity will take into account the degree of restrictiveness of the treatment (e.g., residential, day hospital, low-intensity outpatient program), in that these tend to mandate the hours of treatment provided.

A. Residential Rehabilitation/Inpatient Settings. Most treatment settings tend to follow an AA or 12-step treatment approach administered by addiction counselors and appropriately certified physicians. These programs until recently tended to be freestanding and 21–28 days in duration. The patient populations tend to be different than that seen in a psychiatric setting in that individuals tend to not have psychotic or more severe chronic mental illness. Those with significant comorbid psychiatric illness can do well in these settings if specialized expertise is provided in this patient population. Until recently these types of programs were the mainstay of chemical-dependence treatment. With less financial support, outpatient settings have been emphasized whenever possible.

B. Day or "Partial" Hospital. This usually constitutes the same treatment program that was delivered in a hospital setting but is less restrictive, and patients either live at home or in a residential setting. It generally consists of 40 h/wk of treatment 5 or more days per week. This usually consists of individuals who have supportive living environments and the capacity to remain abstinent for brief periods (evening and weekends) but need daily structure and treatment. Patients may remain in this type of setting for one week or up to months depending on their condition. Living in the community can assist in developing community (e.g., AA) support while the patient is in active treatment.

C. Intensive Outpatient (IOP). The programs tend to be 20 h/wk either in the day or evening and tend to run for 4–8 weeks. They are for individuals who do not need to be completely removed from their environment or work but need a structured and supportive setting. These are individuals who have the capacity to remain abstinent for adequate periods of time such that they can participate in an unrestrictive treatment environment and often appropriate for continuation of work or school while in treatment.

D. Low-Intensity Outpatient (LIO). There is increasing evidence that at least individuals with less severe addictions can respond to low intensity long-term treatment. Increasingly, this type of intervention is being used more frequently by a variety of programs and can also be adapted to an office practice setting. Such treatment usually requires up to 4 h/wk during the initial 2–4 months of treatment and phases down to an hour per week for an extended period of time. It is for individuals who have minimal cooccurring problems complicating their addiction, have supportive environments, and can maintain abstinence in a nonrestrictive treatment environment. This type of treatment may also be used as a long-term aftercare for any of the more intensive treatments mentioned above.

E. Recovery Residence. Recovery residence involves a living setting in the community where the addicted individual is living with other addicts and alcoholics in a monitored environment. This monitoring may come from outside the setting, or there may be individuals living within an apartment or a complex that is internally supervised. This is a very powerful therapeutic modality where individuals learn to bond in what is often referred to as a "recovering family" situation. Here they are able to actually live in the community, develop meaningful relationships with other addicts and alcoholics, and begin to learn to "live sober" with others in a community setting. This particular setting is often combined with a day hospital or evening outpatient program that allows for a full-time "treatment setting" at a significantly lower cost than an inpatient or residential rehabilitation setting. The degree of responsibility by the patient has often been positive if the patient is clinically able to handle this setting. There is less dependence on a highly structured setting and more interdependence among patients in the community, including the 12-step community as a whole.

F. Aftercare. Aftercare typically follows day or IOP and LIO treatment programs and extends to 6–24 months past discharge. The treatment that occurs after a formal outpatient or inpatient program is critical to recovery. Aftercare often takes the form of weekly professionally facilitated monitoring groups and with some individual follow-up. Here, individuals get continued treatment and support and also are monitored for their compliance to the overall treatment plan, which will typically include 12-step meetings and sponsorship.

G. Psychiatric Setting. A significant portion of patients treated in a psychiatric setting suffer with comorbid addiction disorders. Patients treated in these settings tend to have more complicated problems and need specialized care. Psychiatric settings are beginning to recognize the prevalence of this problem and are designing addiction treatments for these individuals. Until recently, these settings tended to view addictions as resulting from psychiatric conditions and underappreciated the fact that they are primary diseases in and of their own right.

H. Office Setting. Many individuals are not seen in clinics or intensive treatment programs, but are treated by a single individual as part of that practitioner's office clientele. A number of treatment models have been developed for this setting. Individuals with primary alcoholism and without other significant cooccurring alcohol-related problems may do well in this type of setting. This treatment can be administered by any health professional doing psychotherapy or by primary-care physicians in addition to patient attendance at 12-step recovery meetings.

V. TREATMENT APPROACHES

Many different treatment approaches have been utilized in the treatment of chemically dependent individuals. These approaches are outlined in the following pages. The predominant form of chemical-dependence treatment in the United States has been based on the disease model of chemical dependence—in other words, recognizing chemical dependency as a biogenetic psychosocial disease that requires total abstinence for complete remission and sustained maturation in recovery. In addition, there has been a strong emphasis in most programs toward a 12-step recovery orientation period where not only is emphasis on Alcoholics Anonymous and similar 12-step groups highly recommended or required as an adjunct to treatment but many of these concepts are approached within the treatment setting itself. In addition to a commitment to complete abstinence from all addicting substances, there is a reliance on the community of other chemically dependent individuals with an emphasis on psychological, social, as well as spiritual repair.

A. "12-Step"–Oriented Treatment. This model emphasizes complete abstinence, psychosocial, and spiritual recovery and involvement in 12-step self-help groups. The Comprehensive Assessment and Treatment Outcome Research study (CATOR) evaluates the outcomes of over 8000 patients (inpatient and outpatient) who participated in these types of programs. It found that 45–65% of individuals remained abstinent for one year after treatment; that participation in these programs resulted in improved quality of life, decreased healthcare utilization, and improved vocational functioning. Abstinence rates were increased to 80% with attendance at 12-step groups and/or aftercare. Finally it indicated that continued long-term aftercare and/or participation in AA improved that outcome.

B. Self-Help Groups. The prevalence of self-help groups is ever-expanding in our society. Most, but not all, follow the AA or 12-step philosophy. Overall, they offer a meaningful support system and a philosophical or spiritual approach to help one deal with their condition. These groups are influenced not only by their empirical orientations but also by the particular group of individuals at any given location. The help one may receive in such programs varies widely from one group to another. They are ubiquitous, are free of charge, and offer significant support to individuals in need. Although they may service in and of themselves for a number of individuals, they are not to be substituted for professional treatment when it is indicated. They make excellent adjuncts to treatment. It is also important that the therapist recommending self-help groups understand their philosophy, language, benefits, and pitfalls. They are essential short-term *and* long-term elements of recovery. Working knowledge of the "12 steps" is essential for the therapists who treat alcoholics and drug addicts.

C. Group Therapies. Group therapies are essential modes for therapy for addiction treatment. They consist of a wide variety of techniques depending on the setting, therapist, and patient population. For those able to benefit from and tolerate a group experience, they can be a very supportive, educational, and therapeutic setting.

D. Individual Supportive Psychotherapy. This form of treatment has been more recently used in a number of research protocols for the treatment of alcoholism. Psychotherapy has always been used as an adjunct to group therapies in addiction treatment. It does not endorse the use of any particular model to help with abstinence but supports individuals with whatever endeavors they make to achieve abstinence. The therapist functions as an empathetic nonjudgmental support system. Counseling is given in some fundamental skills to help with abstinence. Alcoholics Anonymous or other self-help group participation is usually recommended but is not a prerequisite to treatment. This form of treatment is highly adaptable for an office setting by a primary caregiver and may be very effective in treatment of individuals with uncomplicated alcoholism.

E. Cognitive-Behavioral Approaches. These encompass a wide variety of techniques to help individuals achieve abstinence and diminish relapse.

- *Cognitive Therapy.* This was originally developed for the treatment of depression and anxiety. It has been modified to help individuals with addiction disorders.
- *Social Skills (Coping Skills) Training.* This has been recently investigated in a number of alcoholism research protocols. It focuses on helping individuals identify high-risk situations that may lead to drinking and look at alternative behaviors for such situations. It also used techniques to help individuals who do take a drink (a lapse) to avoid relapse.

F. Pharmacotherapy. As our understanding of the biological underpinnings of addiction grows, we are increasingly looking at rational drug development strategies to help with the treatments of these individuals. Treatments may consist of aversive agents, blocking, or "anticraving" agents and drug substitution.

Aversive Agents. These are agents that cause aversive reactions to occur with drug exposure. At present, two such agents exist for the treatment of alcoholism: Antabuse and Calcium Carbamide (not available in the United States). These block the metabolism of alcohol, resulting in increased accumulation of paraldehyde, causing a number of physical distressing symptoms. When used with patients who want to stop drinking and when such use is supervised, these provide effective interventions in preventing alcohol consumption. They have not been proved better than placebo when given to a general population of alcoholics in unsupervised settings.

Agent Substitution. This is when an agent of the same class is substituted for the abused drug. Examples of this are methadone maintenance for heroin addicts and nicotine patches for cigarette smoking. Here the goal is to decrease or eliminate the harmful effects of aspects of the drug use, but not the drug itself (e.g., crime, IV drug use, pulmonary effects of cigarettes). This pharmacotherapeutic treatment approach has been evaluated only for narcotic (on a long-term basis) and nicotine (on a short-term basis) dependence.

Blocking Agents (Anticraving Agents). This consists of using agents that act centrally to intervene in the neuropharmacologic process that leads to the pathologic consumption of addicting substances. A variety of agents have been evaluated in both preclinical and clinical settings such as dopaminergic, serotonergic, GABA, and a variety of other agents. To date the opiate blocking agents have demonstrated the most robust findings in animals.

Other. A variety of pharmacotherapies has been evaluated to help newly abstinent individuals with mood or craving states. Unlike blocking agents, they are not targeted to affect the neurochemical process of addiction, but more to alleviate dysphoric mood states that might lead to relapse. Dopaminergic agents and noradrenergic reuptake blockers have been investigated to decrease cocaine withdrawal dysphoria and craving, but the results of these studies are equivocal. These same agents have also been investigated in newly abstinent alcoholics to alleviate symptoms of depression. A number of other antidepressants have been looked at in such a light. The studies tend to be small and contradictory.

G. Contingency Management. This is based on contracting and setting up predetermined positive or negative consequences to specified events (e.g., abstinence or relapse). The effectiveness of this depends on the consequences and their significance to the patient. This type of behavioral treatment is frequently used when mandated by the courts, parole boards, licensing boards, and at times employers.

H. Cue Exposure. This is based on classic conditioning theory. Unpleasant, aversive stimuli (e.g., electrical shock, nausea) are coupled with either drug or alcohol exposure. The results of controlled trials of this modality are contradictory. This may be helpful in short-term reduction of use but probably is not a good long-term treatment alternative.

I. Individual Psychodynamic Therapy

Psychodynamics-Oriented. This is frequently used as an adjunct to addiction treatment. It is also more frequently needed for individuals with comorbid personality disorders or other psychopathology. This form of treatment may, on its own, be effective for individuals with addictions. It has been realized that the administration of such treatment required novel techniques during the early stages of treatment. It must be more structured and goal-oriented, focusing on reduction and cessation of drug or alcohol use. A number of structured short-term psychodynamic treatments have recently been developed and are presently being evaluated in clinical tails.

Interpersonal Therapy. This therapy uses modified psychodynamic principles to help individuals focus on difficulties in interpersonal functioning. It has been demonstrated as a useful adjunct in mild to moderately dependent cocaine and opiate abusers.

J. Network Therapy. This was designed to be used in an office practice. The fundamental premise is to enlist significant individuals whom patients choose to help them achieve and maintain abstinence. Therapists help individuals form supportive, therapeutic networks and become involved with the individuals in their treatment.

K. Community-Based Model. This model has been used for the chronic mentally ill for many years. Its basic premise is that if you can't change the individual, change the condition, environment, and situation around that person. It focuses on effecting nontreatment factors. This involves interventions on both the individual and social levels. Individual changes consist of developing social supports or placing impaired individuals in controlled environments. Social interventions consist of changes in local ordinances affecting access, initiating monitoring programs in workplaces, and setting up systems that deter use and reward alternative behaviors.

L. Couple or Family. The consequences of one's illness will affect the family or system within which that individual lives. In addition, the family or system will effect the individual and the course and presentation of their illness. Given these phenomena, significant others and family members must be included when evaluating any individual, and appropriate interventions must be made. These can vary from simply educating and advising significant others, involving them in helping with the recovery of the family member, or involving the family or significant others in therapy themselves. The theoretical orientation of such therapy (structural, strategic, psychodynamic behavioral, etc.) will vary depending on the setting, therapist, and clientele.

M. Vocational Training. Although in and of itself, this is not a treatment for substance-abuse disorders, the ability to achieve and maintain employment can be a significant part of an individual's recovery. In certain sociodemographic populations, patients must be trained or helped to seek and obtain treatment. When this is incorporated into treatment, the outcome of certain patient populations will be significantly affected. This has been found effective, for example, with chronic drug addicts who have been unemployable for extended periods of time and individuals who lose their jobs because of drug or alcohol use and need assistance in preparing for and starting new alternative careers.

N. Harm Reduction. From a social and at times individual point of view, the goal of treatment is to reduce the adverse or harmful consequences associated with drug or alcohol use, abuse, and dependence. Harm reduction strategies are used both at an individual and social level to decrease the frequency and intensity of drug or alcohol use and increase the safety of its use. Examples would be decreasing needle sharing to limit the transmission of bloodborne diseases and helping individuals develop strategies to decrease the frequency of their use of and exposure to drugs and alcohol. These types of strategies are usually part of social programs and are not seen in addiction treatment settings (with the exception of education regarding needle cleaning in programs working with IV drug users).

O. Controlled Use. The vast majority of these studies have been conducted in the area of alcohol research with nondependent individuals. In the addiction field, it is widely viewed that controlled drinking is not an adequate treatment strategy for individuals with dependence. Although many alcohol-dependent individuals can control their alcohol consumption at given times, it is generally accepted that, with continued exposure, most will return to pathologic, out-of-control use. These treatment strategies can be successful with nondependent users as part of harm reduction strategies (e.g., college students, individuals who receive their first DUI). In these individuals, "sensible or rational drinking" programs have been shown to be very effective in reducing the frequency and quantity of alcohol consumption.

VI. TREATMENT MATCHING

The art of matching the appropriate treatment with the correct treatment modality and setting is one of the greatest challenges of this field. There are a number of patient placement criteria that are being distributed. One of those is the ASAM Patient Placement Criteria, which have evolved over the recent past as an excellent resource in this area. The ASAM Placement Criteria are concerned primarily with choice of treatment levels, looking particularly at inpatient versus outpatient treatment and length-of-stay issues. Four levels of care are addressed by the ASAM Patient Placement Criteria: Level I—outpatient treatment, Level II—intensive outpatient or partial hospitalization treatment, Level III—medically monitored intensive inpatient treatment, and Level IV—medically managed intensive inpatient treatment.

The placement criteria emphasizes six dimensions: acute intoxication withdrawal potential, biomedical conditions and complications, emotional behavioral conditions and complications, treatment acceptance / resistance, relapse potential, and recovery environment. On the basis of these dimensions, patients can be placed at one of the four levels of care mentioned. So, for example, a severe withdrawal risk would require medically managed intensive inpatient treatment, or as a severe withdrawal risk, but one that can be managed in a monitored intensive inpatient would require a somewhat lesser level of care. Degree of severity of any of the criteria dimensions then would determine level of care at any given time. Also, managed care has placement criteria that often emphasize cost-effectiveness as well as clinical treatment considerations. In general, the chemically dependent individual needs a treatment setting modality and level of intensity that would support the nonuse of mood-altering addicting substances, including reducing the variables that may trigger the use of these chemicals, ensuring that self-harm or harm to others is eliminated as a significant risk, and that the individual has the correct setting in which to develop the skills necessary to maintain long-term abstinence.

We need to emphasize that there rarely is one specific setting modality or intensity, but that the patient's needs and requirements would change over time. Today, for not only cost containment, but optimal clinical impact, "flexibility" is a key term. It is important to provide the appropriate level of care at the specific time that care is needed. For example, an individual who may need intensive inpatient stabilization for purposes of detox and minimizing risk to self or others may be able to move from that level of care after a brief 3-day stabilization to enter a less restrictive setting (such as a day hospital with residence component), which after a few weeks may then be followed by return to work and an evening outpatient setting. This, in turn, can then be followed by a long-term aftercare program as outlined in the next chapter. Or the scenario may necessitate a long-term placement in a halfway house or therapeutic community if that need is required. It then becomes a matter of ongoing evaluation to determine the appropriate level of care for the specific time and needs of any individual patient as that person evolves through the recovery process.

A. Acute Stabilization and Assessment Phase. The acute treatment phase is utilized during periods when an individual's addiction is fully symptomatic. The main goal here is to stabilize individuals, initiate abstinence, educate patients on the treatment of their disorders, and comprehensively assess the patients in order to match them to the appropriate treatment setting. This may include detoxification and can be an intensive inpatient or outpatient treatment or low-intensity outpatient treatment. Depending on the patient's general make-up, treatment history, and illness severity, this phase may be completed quickly or may require an extended assessment for more complicated individuals. In most cases, the assessment is done during the first few days to a week of the individual's treatment. Of increasing frequency, the assessments are being done in specialized services before the individual is matched to a treatment program.

1. Triage. The role of triage is to quickly and comprehensively evaluate whether an individual has an addictive disorder and is in immediate need of medical detoxification, and what type of program may be most appropriate. In many programs, the triage team is separate and independent from the treatment programs; in others it may actually be a part of the initial assessment.

2. Detoxification. In the past, individuals were hospitalized for detoxification and remained for another 21 days for treatment. Today most treatments are ambulatory, resulting in detox being separated from other components of treatment. Although there is a treatment component during detox, the main focus in on the medical management of the individual.

a. Inpatient detox. This should be reserved for individuals who are unable to participate in an outpatient detox, or have histories of serious withdrawal symptoms or complicating psychiatric or medical problems. In general, the length of stay is short (2–4 days) in the uncomplicated patient with follow-up and completion of the detox on an outpatient basis. When more severe psychiatric or medical problems are involved, length of stay generally increases.

b. Outpatient detox. These programs are increasing in number in that most individuals can do well in this less restrictive setting. In general, patients are participating in a structured outpatient program at the same time. Patients need to be compliant with daily visits and generally require a supportive and structured environment to participate in ambulatory detox.

c. Assessment. This is the first and perhaps one of the most important components in giving individuals good comprehensive care. The more quickly one can assess and identify patient needs, the more effective treatment will be. The assessment is a comprehensive detailed evaluation of the type and severity of the individual's addiction and cooccurring problems (financial, social, family, work, medical, psychiatric, legal, etc.). A good comprehensive assessment at the beginning of treatment will help you quickly identify problem areas and allocate specific resources to deal with those problems. This will help increase treatment outcome, efficiency, and cost-effectiveness.

The following chart represents, in a general way, various clinical presentations and recommended placement for those presentations. This chart, as opposed to the dimensions used for the ASAM Criteria, uses inpatient data in a more generalized way to include both monitored and managed settings. Here, however, emphasis is on intensive outpatient services and extended care. There is a great deal of variability, however, in the placement possibilities of any one patient. For example, what may initially appear to necessitate one level of care might actually warrant a trial in a lesser level of care. All the considerations previously mentioned should be factored into this matching process. Again, we emphasize the need to have dynamic process in treatment matching moving patients from various levels of care that currently match their present needs.

Clinical Presentation	Inpatient	Day Hospital[a]	Intensive Outpatient[a]	Halfway House
Medical detox; risk to self or others	—[a]			
Work and/or home environment poses increased risk for noncompliance		—[a]		
Patient able to work without high risk of noncompliance			—[a]	
Patient's living situation poses high risk of noncompliance				—[a]

[a]This can include option of concurrent recovery residence.

Failure to maintain abstinence does not *always* mean involvement in a more restrictive level of care. Adding another modality (e.g., recovery residence) or treatment approach (e.g., blocking agents such as Revia) or other combinations may be more appropriate in the long term.

VII. MAINTENANCE PHASE

The maintenance phase is the long-term management one administers with any chronic illness. At this point, individuals have well-established treatment programs. In general, the patient is abstinent or his/her treatment goals have been achieved. The maintenance phase is used to monitor the individual, manage slips and relapses, and deal with exacerbations of the condition or other cooccurring problems—variables in improving an individual's overall outcome.

A. Self-Help Groups. These recovery groups are viewed by many as the mainstay or backbone of recovery. All individuals should be encouraged to become involved in such programs and utilize them as long-term recovery programs and support systems. Alcoholics Anonymous and other 12-step programs (cocaine, narcotic, overeater, gambler, etc., anonymous organizations) are the ¤oldest and most common self-help groups available. They are a spiritual program founded on 12 steps people should follow to help them cope with their illness and improve the quality of their lives. There are thousands of groups in the United States and worldwide; memberships are in the millions. More recently, other types of self-help groups have developed. Other groups have developed for individuals with comorbid psychiatric disorders. Regardless of their philosophical orientations, these groups and their individual can provide powerful, therapeutic, and cost-effective long-term intervention and support for many individuals.

B. Halfway House. A halfway house is a useful option for individuals who complete an inpatient or outpatient setting and need extended structure and support. Typically, this setting requires working in the community while living with other addicts and alcoholics in a monitored living arrangement. Weekly therapy and support groups and regiments for self-help involvement are typical. Generally 3 months of involvement are required at minimum. A step down "three-quarters house" is a similar setting, but typically less monitoring is required. Less formal settings (e.g., Oxford Houses) involves recovery residents living together for mutual support with little or no formal external monitoring. These living arrangements are excellent options for individuals who have failed in short-term treatments and/or whose environment significantly compromises efforts in recovery. Individuals in these settings need to be stable enough so as to not require strict monitoring (e.g., therapeutic community).

C. Therapeutic Communities. A small percentage of individuals need to be chronically maintained in a highly structured environment to control their illness, particularly intravenous addiction. This tends to be due to the severity of their illness, comorbid psychiatric or medical problems, or the lack of a healthy environment for them to return to. Most such programs tend to have limited stays (rarely >12–18 months). Yet there are those individuals who predictably do poorly when not in such an environment. Such individuals tend to need long-term chronic structured care. The restrictiveness of such facilities may vary from highly structured with little independent time to residential or halfway houses where individuals work during the day and return to a structured therapeutic environment in the evenings and weekends.

D. Extended Structured High-Intensity Outpatient Care. Certain conditions require longer-term, more structured, higher-intensity treatment. This may be a result of particular types of treatments such as methadone maintenance or the complicating factors of comorbid conditions.

E. Dual-Diagnosis Programs. For a number for individuals with more severe chronic psychiatric disorders (e.g., schizophrenia and other psychoses, manic-depressive illness), more intensive, longer-term chronic treatments are usually indicated. In general, these types of programs meet numerous times a week, consist of a variety of psychosocial and medical interventions, and are open-ended. In general, patients may be treated, maintained, and monitored in these programs for years. These programs function as a major support system for such individuals and their families.

F. Weekly Treatment (Group or Individual). The majority of individuals with addiction disorders who seek continued professional services will use these types of treatments as part of the long-term maintenance or aftercare.

1. Group. A wide variety of long-term aftercare groups exist for individuals with addiction disorders. These tend to meet 1–2 h/wk and vary from 12-step professionally run support groups to more psychologically oriented process groups. Which type of group is best suited to which individual is still unclear. It is becoming more evident that given the heterogeneity of individuals, the patient makeup group should be tailored to meet specific needs.

Patients with cognitive or psychiatric impairments may need separate, specialized groups. Also, specific long-term groups may be created to meet the needs of specialized patient populations based on either gender, life events, medical conditions, or other factors (e.g., women's, AIDS, organ transplants, geriatric, war veterans, professionals groups). In general, the individual can also, more effectively and safely, work on interpersonal coping skills in this protected environment.

2. Individual. The majority of individuals seeking long-term treatment for addiction disorders and their consequences participate in this modality of treatment. The therapeutic techniques that are used vary widely from 12-step-oriented, psychodynamic, behavioral, cognitive, to supportive. Which type of therapy is suited for which individual is presently unclear. The advantage of this form of treatment is that individuals receive more specific attention to their needs and more in-depth therapeutic interventions can be administered.

G. Urine Monitoring. Some individuals may require long-term monitoring for use of habit-forming substances. Although this may be therapeutically indicated for a variety of individuals, in general, it is mandated by a legal or licensing body. It is not uncommon that impaired health professionals be linked to a monitoring system for 2–5 years as a condition of their returning to work. It is also being used with increasing frequency by the legal system for individuals mandated to treatment while on parole, following DUIs, and in custody cases where one of the parents has a substance-dependence disorder. Although it is not viewed as a therapy, one should never underestimate the true therapeutic effect such an intervention provides.

H. Methadone, LAAM, or Buprenorphine Maintenance (MM). Generally, narcotic substitution maintenance therapy is a longer-term treatment that may range from a few months to years. In general, it consists of the medical management of narcotic administration, a variety of levels of intensity of psychosocial support, and monitoring for use of other habit forming substances. The variety and quality of services vary greatly among these clinics. In general, individuals begin with daily visits to the clinic. As they progress, the frequency of clinic visits decreases, as does the intensity of their supportive therapies. In general, as long as individuals are being administered narcotic substitution, they are required to attend their clinic programs a few times a week, are monitored for use of other substances, and are expected to meet requirements set by their program.

I. Professionals' Aftercare. Healthcare professionals, attorneys, commercial airline pilots, and other highly accountable individuals typically need a more comprehensive, long-term aftercare setting. In some areas, this has been referred to as a "Caduceus" aftercare. This represents a period of typically 2 years or more of professionally facilitated monitoring aftercare groups on a weekly basis. Also included is a random urine-monitoring requirement for self-help participation and often adjunctive treatment as need (e.g., individual psychotherapy). Very typically for healthcare professionals, licensing boards or other entities may be involved in the process. In addition, the State Medical Society of Physician Assistance Programs has a highly sophisticated network throughout the country that assists in both assessment and the ongoing monitoring process. These programs also participate in the assessment and monitoring of high-accountability groups other than physicians in many states. This form of "contingency contracting" has led to very high recovery rates in this subgroup of patients and has assisted in helping to ensure public safety.

J. Professionals' Treatment. Some high-accountability individuals (e.g., healthcare professionals, airline pilots) may need extended treatment (>6 weeks) in a specialized setting. Some data suggest that this population can have better outcome when treated in a setting that has a milieu composed of many of these "high-risk" professionals. Also, an observation phase following primary treatment (often referred to as "mirror-image placement") can help these patients' transition into their professional roles and still prioritize their recovery.

SELECTED READINGS

Galanter M: *Recent Developments in Alcoholism: Alcoholism and Women*. New York: Plenum Press, 1995.

Harrison PA, Hoffmann NG: Treatment outcome. In NS Miller (ed): *Comprehensive Handbook of Drug and Alcohol Addiction*. New York: Marcel Dekker, 1991, Chapter 63.

Keso L, Salaspuro M: A comparison of two aversion treatment methods of alcoholism. *Alcoholism: Clin Exp Res* 14(4):584–589, 1990.

Miller NS: *Principles of Addiction Medicine*. Washington, DC: American Society of Addicition Medicine, 1994.

Miller NS: *Treatment of the Addictions*. Binghamton, NY: Haworth Press, 1995.

Miller NS, Owley T, Eriksen A: Working with drug/alcohol-addicted patients in crisis. *Psychiatric Ann* 24(11):592–597, 1996.

Roman PM: Inpatient alcohol and drug treatment: a national study of treatment centers. Executive Report. Institute for Behavioral Research, University of Georgia, 1–22 (supported by NIAAA).

Schulz JE: 12-step programs in recovery from drug and alcohol addiction. In NS Miller (ed): *Comprehensive Handbook of Drug and Alcohol Addiction*. New York: Marcel Dekker, 1991.

Vaillant GB: *Natural History of Alcoholism.* Cambridge, MA: Harvard University Press, 1983.

Walsh DC, Hingson RW, Merrigan DM: A randomized trial of treatment options for alcohol-abusing workers. *N Engl J Medicine* 325(11):775–752, 1991.

ALCOHOLICS ANONYMOUS AND NARCOTICS ANONYMOUS IN CLINICAL PRACTICE

John Chappel, M.D.
University of Nevada
Reno, Nevada

AA has been and remains to this day a major influence in the field of alcoholism and its treatment, and there are no signs that its significance is waning.
(*APA Treatments of Psychiatric Disorders*, 1989, p. 115)

I. INTRODUCTION: WHY AA AND NA?

These 12-step programs help to get alcoholics and other drug addicts sober. More importantly, they are the most effective means known to enable alcoholics and drug addicts to remain sober and continue normal adult growth and development. Therefore, every clinician should know how to refer and support their alcoholic and other drug-addicted patients in working a 12-step program of recovery in AA and/or NA.

II. EVIDENCE OF EFFECTIVENESS

A. Twenty-eight (28) of the original group of less than 100 hopeless alcoholics who developed AA's program of recovery recorded their stories in the first edition of AA's Big Book (AA, 1976). Fifteen years later a follow-up of this group revealed that 23 (82%) were still in recovery. Of these, 15 (65%) had no relapses (AA, 1957, p. 220).

B. In a perspective study lasting 35 years, Vaillant found that attendance at AA accounted for 27% of the variance of good clinical outcome such as marriage, a job; and stable socioeconomic status accounted for only 7% of the variance (Valliant, 1983).

C. In a one-year follow-up of over 5000 alcoholic inpatients and outpatients, abstinence rates were strongly associated with attendance at AA meetings. For inpatients who did not attend AA, the abstinence rate was 49%. For regular (weekly) AA attenders the abstinence rate was 76% (Harrison et al., 1991).

D. AA has conducted random sample surveys of its membership every 3 years since 1968. Following the 1989 survey an analysis of the data

Manual of Therapeutics for Addictions, Edited by Norman S. Miller, Mark S. Gold, and David E. Smith.
ISBN 0471-56176-2 © 1997 John Wiley & Sons, Inc.

indicated that dropout rates are highest in the first year with 50% of those starting in AA dropping out in the first 3 months. Of those sober less than a year 41% will continue in AA for another year. Of those sober from 1 to 5 years, 83% will continue in AA for another year. Of those sober over 5 years, 91% will continue in AA for another year.

1. AA membership has been stable over the years in the following ways:
   a. The majority have a sponsor and belong to a homegroup.
   b. Average length of sobriety >4 years.
   c. Average attendance at three AA meetings per week.
   d. Steady growth of membership to over 1 million in the United States and Canada.
2. AA membership has been changing in the following ways:
   a. Increasing number of women, to >33.3% the total membership.
   b. Increasing number of young people, under 30 years of age to >20% of the total.
   c. An increasing number of members who were also addicted to other drugs. Alcoholics with other problems often benefit from working a program of recovery in AA (Chappel, 1993).

III. What AA (NA) *DOES* AND *DOES NOT* DO

A. What AA (NA) *Does* Do

1. AA (NA) is a voluntary organization of recovering alcoholics (drug addicts) who follow the program of recovery developed from 3 years of field research and described in Chapters 5 and 6 of the "Big Book" of AA (1976).
2. AA (NA) members are organized into autonomous groups that hold a variety of meetings (see Section III.C, paragraph 2, below) to which alcoholics (drug addicts) are welcome. Any interested person, including physicians, is welcome at open meetings where practical education about alcoholism (drug addiction) and recovery is available.
3. A good description of AA is included in the preamble, which is read at many meetings:

Alcoholics Anonymous is a fellowship of men and women who share their experience, strength, and hope with each other that they may solve their common problem and help others to recover from alcoholism.

The only requirement for membership is a desire to stop drinking. There are no dues or fees for AA membership; we are self-supporting through our own contributions.

AA is not allied with any sect, denomination, politics, organization or institution; does not wish to engage in any controversy neither endorses nor opposes any causes.

Our primary purpose is to stay sober and to help other alcoholics achieve sobriety.* [The preamble is copyrighted by the AA Grapevine, Inc. Reprinted with permission.]

---

*The AA 12 steps are reprinted with permission of Alcoholics Anonymous World Services, Inc. Permission to reprint this and other copyrighted material does not mean that AA has reviewed or approved the contents of this chapter or that AA agrees with the views expressed herein.

B. What AA (NA) *Does Not* Do

1. AA does *not* run membership drives to try to persuade alcoholics into joining. AA is for alcoholics who want to get sober. (AA is a program of attraction, not promotion.)

2. AA does *not* check up on its members to see that they don't drink. It helps alcoholics to help themselves.

3. AA is *not* a religious organization. All members are free to decide on their own personal ideas about the meaning of life.

4. AA is *not* a medical organization, does *not* give out medicines or psychiatric advice.

5. AA does *not* run any hospitals, wards, or sanitariums or provide nursing services.

6. AA is *not* connected with any other organizations. But AA does cooperate with organizations that fight alcoholism. Some members work for such organizations—but on their own—*not* as representatives of AA.

7. AA does *not* accept money from sources outside AA, either private or government.

8. AA does *not* offer any social services, does *not* provide housing, food, clothing, jobs, or money. It helps alcoholics stay sober, enabling them to earn these things for themselves.

9. AA lives up to the "Anonymous" part of this title. It does *not* want members' names to be told on TV or radio or in the newspapers. Members do *not* tell other members' names to people outside AA.

10. AA does *not* provide letters of reference to parole boards, lawyers, court officials, social agencies, employers, and others.*

C. The Physician's Role

1. Neither AA nor NA claims to have all the answers to alcoholism or other drug addiction. Members of these organizations want to be friendly with their friends. *All* physicians are viewed as friends of AA (NA). Special committees have been set up to work with us. These are usually called "cooperation with the professional community" (CPC), treatment facilities (TFs), or hospitals and institutions (H/I) committees. They can be reached by calling the AA (NA) number in the telephone directory for your community.

2. The physician's role has been well established over decades of treating alcoholics and other drug addicts. The following are covered in depth in other chapters in this book:

   a. Educate the patient about alcoholism and other drug addiction.

   b. Make the diagnosis early.

   c. Communicate the diagnosis to the patient despite the presence of denial or minimization.

   d. Detoxify the patient and reinforce abstinence as the long-term goal of recovery.

   e. Manage associated medical and psychiatric problems in ways that enhance recovery; prescribe controlled (addicting) medications *last* whenever symptom relief is needed.

   f. Introduce patients to AA (NA) and help them make personal contact

---

*This section is reprinted from the pamphlet *A Brief Guide to Alcoholics Anonymous.* Copyright 1972 by AAWS. (Reprinted with permission.)

with someone who will take them to a meeting. This personal contact, accompanied by physician support, has been demonstrated to be much more effective than just recommending AA (NA) (Sisson and Mallams, 1981).

g. Support the patient in working a 12-step program of recovery, recognizing that there will be many temptations to drop out of the program and that 50% do drop out in the first 3 months (Chappel, 1993).

IV. HISTORY

A. By the twentieth century alcoholism and drug addiction were well known to practicing clinicians.

1. The first epidemic of alcoholism occurred after 1750 in Britain after the discovery of distillation led to making gin—the first high-dose delivery system of a drug to the brain.

2. Benjamin Rush, M.D., the "father of American psychiatry," described alcoholism as a disease in 1814 and prescribed abstinence as the treatment. Ever since, physicians have developed increasing skill at withdrawing addicts from their drugs.

3. Epidemics often occur after new discoveries make it possible to develop high doses of addicting drugs to the brain; for example, an epidemic of opioid addiction followed the discoveries of the hypodermic syringe and the extraction of morphine from opium. The "soldier's disease" was the term used to describe continuing self-injection of morphine after the Civil War.

B. In 1935, following many medical alcohol detoxifications, two hopeless drunks, Bill W. and Dr. Bob S., managed to stay sober by talking to each other.

1. They worked with other hopeless alcoholics, most of whom were in hospitals and both medicine and religion had been unable to help them stay sober.

2. Over a 3-year period of empirical field research, almost 100 hopeless drunks were staying sober. This method of maintaining sobriety is described in Chapters 5 and 6 of the book *Alcoholics Anonymous* (1976).

3. Research in the 1980s and 1990s has consistently shown that AA is the most effective way for alcoholics to maintain long-term sobriety (Miller, 1995; Vaillant, 1983) NA probably plays a similarly effective role in long-term recovery from drug addiction.

4. AA and NA are compatible with the treatment of all medical and mental disorders. They should be considered essential in the treatment of all addictive disorders.

V. HOW A 12-STEP PROGRAM OF RECOVERY IN AA/NA WORKS

A. Factors Present in Recovering Alcoholics. Vaillant, in his landmark prospective study of alcoholism, described four factors that were present in recovering alcoholics who achieved stable sobriety (Vaillant, 1983, p. 190):

1. One or more substitute dependencies.

2. Reminders of the medical or behavioral consequences of the person's alcoholism.

3. Some source of hope and self-esteem.
4. Unambivalent social support, especially a love relationship.

All of these can be found in AA (NA), which was the only significant (27% of the variance of good clinical outcome) contributor to stable sobriety in Vaillant's research.

B. One Alcoholic (Addict) Talking to Another. This was the beginning of the discovery of how to establish and maintain stable sobriety. As Dr. Bob, the alcoholic surgeon and cofounder of AA, said,

> I had read a great deal and talked to everyone who knew, or thought they knew, anything about alcoholism. But . . . he was the first living human being with whom I had ever talked, who knew what he was talking about in regard to alcoholism from actual experience. *In other words, he talked my language*
>
> [AA 1976, p. 174, emphasis added]

Dr. Bob went on to treat thousands of alcoholics and was known as the "Prince of the twelve steppers." He stated that talking to another alcoholic helped him stay sober. "Every time I do it I take out a little more insurance for myself against a possible slip" (AA, 1976, p. 175).

C. Attending Meetings

1. This is where the newly recovering alcoholic (addict) becomes part of the Fellowship of AA or NA. The welcome and acceptance of newcomers is warm and genuine.
2. The core at each meeting is a sharing of experience, strength, and hope as all participants work to remember their addiction and maintain their sobriety.
3. If a person does not like a particular meeting, there are many others to choose from. Clinicians should know the characteristics of the following kinds of meetings:
   a. Open
   b. Closed
   c. Beginners
   d. Step study
   e. "Big Book" study
   f. Speaker
   g. Discussion
4. Inform your patients of the acceptance they will experience at a 12-step meeting. The welcome an active alcoholic or drug addict receives at AA or NA meetings is much better than they experience in the healthcare system. The smelly, sick, and shaking person is greeted with a smile, given a cup of coffee, and told to keep coming back. This tolerant acceptance reflects the responsibility motto of AA: "Whenever anyone, anywhere reaches out for help, I want the hand of AA to be there. For that, I am responsible."
5. The newcomer is considered the most important person at a 12-step meeting. This generative principle is the reason you will always be able to find members of the fellowship who will make 12-step (see below) calls on your patients. You will also find it easy to find people in good recovery who will take you to open meetings and help you learn what it means to work a 12-step program of recovery in AA or NA. Ask for someone from the CPC committee.

D. Choosing a Sponsor

1. A majority (85%) of AA members report that they have a sponsor.

2. It is recommended that newly sober alcoholics or addicts look around to find someone of the same sex who has the kind of recovery they would like to have. They must then *act and ask* that person to be their sponsor.

3. Until a sponsor is acquired, it is useful to recommend that your patients ask for a temporary contact who will introduce them to the local fellowship and take them to meetings.

4. The main task of a sponsor is to help the sponsee (your patient) work the steps and develop a personal program of recovery that will make sobriety not only tolerable but also beneficial. It is especially important to find a sponsor before starting to work steps 4 and 5 (see below), which are both difficult and anxiety-producing. If you think back on the good teachers or mentors you have had, it will be easier to understand the importance of a sponsor for your patient.

5. Research has shown that having a sponsor significantly reduces the risk of relapse (Sheeren, 1988). You can also assure your patients that they will be helping the person they ask to be their sponsor. In a 10-year follow-up study, 91% of those who became sponsors had maintained stable sobriety (Cross et al., 1990).

6. A sponsor will help your patients work on being honest, open, and willing (HOW) to change. That change is toward becoming the best human beings they can be. It has been said that the greatest gift anyone receives from working a 12-step program of recovery is oneself as a human being. It should also be noted that AA states that no one in the fellowship is perfect and that they claim progress rather than perfection (AA, 1976, p. 60).

E. Choosing A Homegroup

1. A homegroup is one in which your patient feels comfortable and agrees to attend its meetings regularly.

2. A majority of AA members (85%) report that they have a homegroup.

3. A homegroup can serve as both an extended family and a recovery support system. This makes choosing a homegroup particularly important for alcoholics or other drug addicts who are isolated or whose current support system enables their addiction.

4. A phone list can be of great benefit to the recovering addict. The homegroup provides a number of people who would be willing to be called if a new member were having trouble with remaining sober. Using a phone list has been shown to significantly reduce the risk of relapse (Sheeren, 1988).

5. The homegroup introduces the new member to responsibility and service—both of which diminish or disappear with addiction. Responsibility and service start in small ways with setting up or taking down chairs and helping with coffee. Taking on responsibility and getting involved in service by helping make

AA or NA available to other alcoholics or drug addicts appears to help the addicted brain heal, thus making sobriety not only tolerable but a positive experience.

F. Working the Steps. The 12 steps were originally discovered through empirical research to help hopeless, chronic alcoholics maintain sobriety. Since 1939 the 12 steps have been adapted to over 200 human problems, including behavioral addictions. As you review the steps, think about how they could be useful to problems other than alcohol or drug addiction.

Step 1. *We admitted that we were powerless over alcohol—that our lives had become unmanageable.*

    a. Addresses problem of denial, which usually takes an extreme view of the terms "powerless" and "unmanageable." It can be humorous, but tragic, to hear skid-row drunks describing their abilities to control their intake of alcohol and how they manage life. The issue here is relative. Powerlessness (loss of control) occurs when one drinks or uses more drugs than had been planned, or were used when one had not planned to.

    b. Step 1 promotes honesty and self-examination. Resistance to this honesty can be great. The physician can help by connecting the problems one has been having to one's drinking and/or drug use. Physician warning, based on connecting alcohol use with medical problems, has been shown to have a beneficial long-term effect, even with more severe cases of alcoholism (Walsh et al., 1992).

    c. Step 1 addresses the reality of intermittent impaired control and accepts an identity as an alcoholic or addict. This difficult step has almost immediate benefits in helping the person stay sober. This benefit is summed up in the AA saying: "For many years I was not an alcoholic but I was drunk all the time. When I became an alcoholic, I stopped drinking, and haven't had a drink since."

    d. The principle AA members find in this step is *honesty.*

Step 2. *"Came to believe that a power greater than ourselves could restore us to sanity."*

    a. The power referred to in this step gives atheists and agnostics trouble. The simplest way to deal with this is for people to recognize that they need help. In this context Mowrer's statement can be very helpful: "I alone can do it, but I can't do it alone." Chapter 4 in the Big Book of AA, entitled "We Agnostics," may also be of use to the resistant patient. Reminding the person of the mysteries of life and healing may make it easier to accept that there is a power greater than oneself.

    b. The sanity referred to in step 2 is simply the recognition that continued use of alcohol or other drugs will have continued negative effects on the person's life. The "insanity" of addiction is the enduring belief that the addicting drug can be used "this time" without any adverse consequences. Most addicts have a secret hope that treatment will show them how to drink or use other addicting drugs without any problems!

    c. Working this step helps open the recovering person to new internal experiences. Psychoanalysts have said that this may be a step in the direction of "taming and transforming infantile omnipotence" (Khantzian and Mack, 1989). At the least it helps the person recognize that "I am not God."

    d. The principle that AA members find in this step is *hope*.

Step 3. *Made a decision to turn our will and our lives over to the care of God as we understood Him.*

    a. A difficult step for atheists and agnostics. They can be helped by thinking of an accepting and loving life force within themselves. AA and NA give individuals freedom to understand a loving and caring Higher Power in any way they want to or can.

    b. The great benefit of practicing "letting go" is that it weakens the grip of obsessions, craving, worries, and resentments. It begins a positive internal experience that continues in steps 5, 7, and 11. This experience includes acceptance, which helps relieve shame; forgiveness, which helps relieve guilt; and care, which helps reduce self-destructive behavior.

    c. The principle that AA members find in this step is *faith*.

Step 4. *Made a searching and fearless moral inventory of ourselves.*

    a. This is the easiest step for health professionals to understand. Taking a personal inventory is done by many healthy individuals, and it is a fundamental part of psychotherapy.

    b. The problem for most alcoholic and other drug-addicted persons is that this step arouses guilt, shame, grief, and other powerful negative emotions. The intensity of these feelings may be strong enough to trigger relapse. For this reason it is recommended that the recovering person obtain a sponsor before beginning step 4.

    c. The benefit of working step 4 is that the individual gets prepared for honest sharing in human relationships. It also helps develop an observing ego and a recognition that "I can make mistakes and at times need help."

    d. The principle that AA members find in this step is *courage*.

Step 5. *Admitted to God, to ourselves, and to another human being the exact nature of our wrongs.*

    a. This action step arouses anxiety that it will result in reactions of anger, disgust, and rejection. Fortunately, working steps 2 and 3 have begun thoughts and experience of a loving, accepting, and forgiving "higher power." This experience, combined with the support of a sponsor who has already worked the steps, helps overcome the anxiety.

    b. Note the wisdom of the sequence in step 5. A loving "higher power" is more likely to accept us. We are more likely to accept ourselves than we think others will. When the final difficult admission is made, usually to one's sponsor, a homegroup member or a clergy person, there is usually great relief that their reaction is not rejecting or punitive.

    c. Working step 5 helps develop honesty with oneself and with others. This is an essential part of the capacity to be intimate with other human beings. Social skill and the ability to develop and maintain a social-support system are enhanced.

    d. The principle that AA members find in this step is *integrity*.

Step 6. *Were entirely ready to have God remove all these defects of character.*

    a. A very difficult step that follows logically from step 4. After alcohol and other drug use stops, characterologic and personality problems continue. These are hard for any of us to recognize. Outside help is often necessary. Steps 4 and 5 set the stage, with help from a sponsor and hearing others struggle with these problems at meetings.

    b. Note the wisdom of simply getting ready to have a "higher power," something other than self, remove selfishness, dishonesty, impulsiveness, blaming, and other dysfunctional personal characteristics. The emphasis here is on awareness of aspects of oneself which have a negative effect on others. Working step 6 encourages personal honesty and willingness to change.

    c. The principle that AA members find in this step is *willingness.*

Step 7. *Humbly asked Him (God) to remove our shortcomings.*

    a. The humility which has developed from working the previous steps recognizes the fact that I am a fallible human being who needs help, but is capable of improvement. Those who have trouble with the male pronoun are encouraged to use "Her" or my "higher power."

    b. From a medical and psychiatric point of view steps 6 and 7 are both fascinating and mysterious. We have no medicines that alter personality, and managed care will not allow the lengthy, difficult psychotherapeutic efforts needed to effect these changes. The fact remains that many members of AA and NA describe long-term behaviors descriptive of antisocial, narcissistic, avoidant, and borderline personality disorders that have slowly subsided and even disappeared as they work these steps over the years.

    c. The principle that AA members find in this step is *humility.*

Step 8. *Made a list of all persons we had harmed, and became willing to make amends to them all.*

    a. This combination of awareness and willingness to act builds on to previous preparation, especially the working of step 4. Making the list is painful, but a valuable preparation for repairing damaged relationships.

    b. Barriers to saying we are sorry are common in all of us. It is much easier to blame others, resent what they have done, and justify our own actions. For this reason people who have harmed us are added to the list.

    c. Help from a sponsor is not only useful, but necessary in working this step. The sponsor will often suggest a hierarchy beginning with those it will be easy to make amends to, and ending with those with whom that task may be difficult or even impossible. One of the wise sayings in AA is, "If you have an unresolvable resentment about someone, pray for the son of a bitch!"

    d. Becoming willing to make amends requires thinking about other people. This is an essential part of the capacity for empathy. It also helps develop skill in maintaining relationships, which every person, including physicians, needs.

    e. The principle that AA members find in this step is *brotherly love.*

Step 9. *Made direct amends to such people wherever possible, except when to do so would injure themselves or others.*

  a. This action step arouses anxiety, which may be extreme. When the recovering person considers actually seeing someone to whom an apology is owed, there are often fantasies of rejection, punishment, or even violence.

  b. Support is necessary for working this step. It usually comes from a sponsor, members of the homegroup, and even healthcare professionals. With support, the amends can be made in a safe, sensitive, and caring way.

  c. Working this step helps repair damaged relationships. It also helps in maintaining any relationship. With this step comes an experience of forgiveness and relief from guilt. The most important aspect of this is the ability to forgive oneself, even when the wronged person refuses to forgive you. With these actions, the stage is set for generativity, the passing on to others what one has learned—a characteristic of the mature adult.

  d. The principle that AA members find in this step is *justice.*

Regarding the "promises," the "Big Book" of AA describes the alcoholic as selfish. "Self-centeredness! That, we think, is the root of our troubles. . . . The alcoholic is an extreme example of self—will run riot, though he usually doesn't think so" (AA, 1976, p. 62). Following a lengthy description of steps 8 and 9 in Chapter 6 of the "Big Book," the following paragraph, often referred to as the "promises," appears (AA, 1976, p. 83):*

> If we are painstaking about this phase of our development, we will be amazed before we are half way through.
> We are going to know a new freedom and a *new happiness.*
> We will not regret the past nor wish to shut the door on it.
> We will comprehend the word serenity and we will *know peace.*
> No matter how far down the scale we have gone we will see how our experience can benefit others.
> That feeling of uselessness and self pity will disappear.
> We will lose interest in selfish things and gain interest in our fellows. Self seeking will slip away.
> Our whole attitude and outlook on life will change.
> Fear of people and of economic insecurity will leave us.
> We will intuitively know how to handle situations which used to baffle us.
> We will suddenly realize that God is doing for us what we could not do for ourselves.

These results do not come easily, but I have heard them referred to often by recovering people who have spent years working a 12-step program of recovery.

Step 10. *Continued to take personal inventory and when we were wrong promptly admitted it.*

  a. This would be a great step for every physician to practice regularly. Daily self-observation, associational problem solving, and honesty with oneself and others are characteristics of maturity and are skills learned in psychotherapy and psychoanalysis.

  b. Many AA and NA members view step 10 as a valuable way to maintain sobriety and keep character defects in check. Self-observation and admission of problems are important relation-

---

*Sentences from the original AA (1976) text are listed separately here for emphasis. Reprinted with permission from AAWS.

al skills that set the stage for developing both intimacy and generativity.

c. The principle that AA members find in this step is *perseverance*.

Step 11. *Sought through prayer and meditation to improve our conscious contact with God as we understood Him, praying only for knowledge of His will for us and the power to carry that out.*

a. This longest step poses problems for atheists and agnostics. One agnostic AA member said, "Translation can be used to make step 11 useful, even to me: 'Be still and listen.' If I do that, I might hear something useful—if not from God, then possibly from myself." What is heard at meetings, in the development of a group conscience, and from one's sponsor may also help in this regard.

b. The spiritual part of the 12-step programs is the most controversial and most misunderstood. Despite the references to God in the steps, AA and NA are not religions. Atheists and agnostics are welcome. There is no catechism or creed to learn. The entire emphasis is on participants developing whatever experience they are capable of with the "higher power" that created this universe and us in it. Evidence supporting this fact is that in over 60 years of existence there has not been one fight or other acts of violence between AA members over the issue of God or a "higher power."

c. The absolute freedom AA and NA members have to develop their own spiritual experience leads to tolerance for the experience of others. The 12-step programs may be among the most tolerant organizations in existence, especially for down-and-out drunks who want to change their lives.

d. Working step 11 is a form of spiritual exercise that can lead to spiritual health. The benefits of spiritual health are outlined, in part, in the "promises" (see above). This is an active working step that emphasizes recovering individuals' responsibilities for taking charge of their lives and solving their own problems, asking only for the knowledge and power to do this.

e. The principle that AA members find in this step is *spiritual awareness*.

Step 12. *Having had a spiritual awakening as the result of these steps, we tried to carry this message to alcoholics, and to practice these principles in all our affairs.*

a. The spiritual awakening refers to freedom from the bondage of self-centeredness. There are two sayings in AA that illustrate this fact:

(1) "Spirituality is the ability to get our minds off ourselves."

(2) "AA works for people who believe in God. AA works for people who don't believe in God. AA *never* works for people who believe they *are* God."

b. Action is required in carrying the message of recovery to alcoholics or other drug addicts. This reflects the experience of Bill W. when he discovered that he needed to talk to another alcoholic in order to maintain his sobriety. The message of recovery is not a sermon, or even good advice. It is a personal sharing of the recovering person's experience with his/her problem, the strength that has been found as a result of working the program, and the hope that the currently suffering alcoholic or other drug addict can find similar relief and healing.

c. The principle that AA members find in this step is *service*.

d. Practicing the principles of the 12 steps in one's life leads to the following:

(1) Honesty with oneself and others.

(2) Openness to new experiences.

(3) Acceptance and forgiveness of oneself and others.

(4) Willingness to attempt activities that result in personal change.

(5) Humility with a willingness to ask for help.

(6) Courage to make amends and work for change in oneself and in the world.

(7) Altruism in helping others with no monetary compensation.

e. The terms "spiritual awareness," "God," and "higher power," create difficulties for many professionals. AA, in the "Big Book," explains these as the basis for "the personality change sufficient to bring about recovery from alcoholism." No sudden conversion or religious belief is necessary. "Most of our experiences are what the psychologist William James calls the 'educational variety' because they develop slowly over a period of time." The result is an "unexpected inner resource" that helps alcoholics honestly face their problems with openness and a willingness to change (AA, 1976, p. 569).

A review of this section will provide evidence that working a 12-step program of recovery is compatible with all forms of medical treatment. The only area of potential problems is when we prescribe addicting (controlled) medications for our recovering patients. The other chapters in this book will help you prescribe in ways that present the least likelihood of problems for your patients.

VI. PROBLEMS IN UTILIZING THE 12-STEP PROGRAMS IN MEDICAL PRACTICE

Despite the demonstrated benefits of AA and NA in helping alcoholics and other drug addicts, it is only recently that postgraduate medical education has required residents to learn about them. For example, it was not until 1989 that psychiatry residents were required to have some structured education about "self-help" groups. This fact means that many practicing physicians and medical school faculty have little or no knowledge about 12-step programs and how to use them with their patients. Bissell and Haberman (1984), in a study of 407 health professionals in recovery from alcoholism, found the following mistaken beliefs about the 12-step programs:

1. *They are religious organizations, which may be fanatic or cult-like.*
   AA and NA are spiritual and *not* religious organizations.

   a. The only requirement for membership is a desire to stop drinking or using addicting drugs (AA tradition 3).

   b. Atheists and agnostics are welcome.

    c. There are no membership classes with catechism or creed to be learned, followed by membership ceremonies.

    d. AA/NA members can belong to *any* or *none* of the world's religions.

    e. Neither AA nor NA conflicts with or supports any of the world's religions.

    f. Cults remove their members from family and communities, AA and NA return their members to sober, constructive, responsible lives in their families and communities. They have no opinion regarding outside interests.

    g. While some AA or NA members may be fanatic, neither organization is. Both AA an NA are responsible, not-for-profit organizations that practice democratic principles and do not proselytize or evangelize. They depend on attraction and not promotion.

        The 12-step program visits, which all physicians should know how to help their patients obtain, consist *only* of AA or NA members sharing their experiences, strengths, and hopes with others who may be suffering from alcohol or other drug addiction.

2. *They are a kind of folk medicine with no scientific basis.*

    a. The 12-step program of recovery was developed through empirical field research when medicine, psychiatry, psychology, and religion had all failed to help severe alcoholics to remain sober.

    b. AA has been found to be significantly more effective in helping alcoholics maintain long-term stable sobriety than has any kind of medical treatment (Vaillant, 1983).

    c. AA and NA are compatible with all forms of medical and psychiatric treatment. Psychoanalysts now describe AA as a "sophisticated psychosocial form of treatment" (Khantzian and Mack, 1989). While well-intentioned but ignorant AA or NA members may tell people to stop taking medications, AA has no opinion on this issue. An excellent pamphlet, *The AA Member—Medications and Other Drugs* (AA, 1984), recommends that AA members take the medications their doctors prescribe for them. It also recommends that AA members find physicians who are knowledgeable about alcoholism.

3. *As substitute dependencies, the 12-step programs are equally unhealthy addictions.*

    a. This mistaken belief is probably based on the time and effort needed to effectively work a 12-step program of recovery. Substitute dependencies for alcohol and other addicting drugs are necessary if the recovering person is to attain stable sobriety (Vaillant, 1983). To be effective, any substitute dependence is going to require time and energy.

    b. Working a 12-step program of recovery has been demonstrated time and again to be far more healthy than alcohol or other drug addictions. No one has died prematurely from an addiction to AA or NA. There have been no documented adverse consequences from working a 12-step program of recovery. Most of the problems described by people are adverse responses to other members of AA or NA. If focus is maintained on working the steps, choosing a sponsor with the kind of recovery the person wants, choosing an accepting and loving homegroup, and learning to share in an honest, open, and willing way, the outcome will always be positive for the individual.

    c. Working a 12-step program of recovery can be considered to be a form of self-care. In this respect, the objective is very similar to the mistaken beliefs people have about exercise. While addiction to exercise, with adverse consequences, is possible, the benefits of exercise have been well documented. It is now considered to be an essential part of self-care.

d. The self-care benefits of working a 12-step program of recovery contribute to mental and social health in much the same way that exercise contributes to physical health. Those of us who have personally experienced the benefits of endurance exercise have learned to ignore these fearful, projective objections raised by others. In averaging 20–30 miles per week of running for the past 20 years, I have heard many otherwise knowledgeable physicians warn me about "ruining my knees". A recent x-ray led the orthopedic surgeon to state that my knees, at age 63, resembled those of a 20-year-old. It is my professional opinion that working a 12-step program of recovery has the potential to make a similar contribution to our quality of life.

While these objections are often raised by our medical colleagues, the following are often raised by our patients:

1. *"I'm not like them."*

   a. In the early stages of alcohol and other drug addiction, denial makes it almost impossible for the person to identify with recovering alcoholics and other drug addicts.

   b. Do not argue, but encourage your patients to keep going to meetings. It is useful to remind them of the pain already experienced with their addictions, and the possibility, if not probability, that it will get worse. Second, it helps to remind them that addiction has affected many people like themselves, and if they keep looking, they will eventually find them. In most cities there are many different meetings held each week. If these people keep looking, they will find one they like.

   c. AA and NA meetings provide good *opportunities to both listen and think*. If your patients don't like what is being said, there is a golden opportunity to think and open their minds meditatively. Although I am not an alcoholic or other drug addict, I attend many open AA and NA meetings. I cannot remember one meeting where I could find nothing to identify with in listening to the speaker. Any honest sharing of experience, strength, and hope addresses common areas of human experience. For anyone open to their own human experience, this sharing is often touching and inspiring with regard to our capacity to change.

2. *"They all smoke and drink. It's bad for my health."*

   a. Smoking in AA and NA meetings is a good reason for concern for the health-conscious person. Fortunately, there are increasing numbers of nonsmoking meetings. These are usually listed in the meeting schedules that can be obtained from the central offices of AA and NA.

   b. The accusation that AA or NA members continue to drink or use drugs is occasionally true, but is more often a projection on the part of your patients. They can be encouraged to be tolerant of those AA or NA members who are not clean and sober, since they are especially in need of the program. More importantly, reassure your patients that these programs are the best places to find recovering alcoholics and other drug addicts who know how to stay clean and sober and to enjoy sobriety.

    c. Support your patients' concerns for health. Assure them that sobriety will help their physical health. Use the evidence in this chapter and from our growing experience that working a 12-step program of recovery will eventually help their mental and social health as well.

VII. CONCLUSION

Working the 12-step program is not easy. It requires help from others, especially a sponsor and a homegroup. There is a cost of time and energy. When we refer a patient to a 12-step program two benefits can be expected:

1. *Sobriety.* Abstinence from intoxicating, addicting drugs, which exempts caffeine and nicotine, is a great benefit that sets the stage for improved health, relationships, finances, and learning.
2. *Mature Growth and Development.* The tasks of adult growth and development are *intimacy,* the ability to be genuine and open with others; *generativity,* the ability to pass on what one has learned to others; and *integrity,* a sense of wholeness and acceptance of one's self.

The latter benefit goes beyond the usual goals of medical treatment, but it is one that any physician can support. These potential benefits for our patients make it worthwhile to take the time and effort to refer them to the appropriate 12-step program and support them as they work a 12-step program of recovery.

    AA and NA can be contacted by calling the number listed in your local telephone directory (White Pages) under "Alcoholics Anonymous" and "Narcotics Anonymous." Miller (1995) concluded, after a review of the literature: "Treatment outcome research thus far confirms that there exists a large variety of treatment methods that appear to work in the short run (weeks and months. . . . Only one method of treatment appears to be effective and to consistently work in the long run (years to lifetimes), mainly abstinence based treatment when combined with regular, continuous and indefinite attendance at AA meetings. (NA is probably as effective, but sufficient data are not yet available)."

REFERENCES

Alcoholics Anonymous: *AA Comes of Age: A Brief History of AA.* New York: AAWS, 1957.

Alcoholics Anonymous: *Alcoholics Anonymous: The Story of How Many Thousands of Men and Women Have Recovered from Alcoholism,* 3rd ed. New York: AAWS, 1976.

Alcoholics Anonymous: *The AA Member—Medications and Other Drugs.* New York: AAWS, 1984.

Bissell L, Haberman PW: *Alcoholism in the Professions.* New York: Oxford University Press, 1984.

Chappel JN: Effective use of AA and NA in treating patients. *Psychiatric Ann* 22(8):409–418, 1992.

Chappel JN: Long term recovery from alcoholism. *Psychiatric Clin North Am* 16(1):177–187, 1993.

Cross GM, Morgan CW, Mooney AJ, Martin CA, Rafter JA: Alcoholism treatment: a ten year follow-up study. *Alcohol Clin Exp Res* 14(2):169–173, 1990.

Harrison PA, Hoffman NH, Sneed SG: Drug and alcohol treatment outcome. In NS Miller (ed): *Comprehensive Handbook of Drugs and Alcohol Addiction*. New York: Marcel Dekker, 1991, pp 1163–1200.

Khantzian EJ, Mack JE: Alcoholics Anonymous and contemporary psychodynamic theory. *Recent Devel Alcohol* 7:67–89, 1989.

Miller NS: *Treatment of the Addictions: Applications of Outcome Research for Clinical Management*. New York: Haworth Press, 1995.

Pittman B: *Stepping Stones to Recovery*. Seattle, WA: Colen Abbey Books, 1989.

Schuckit M: *Drug and Alcohol Abuse: A Clinical Guide to Diagnosis and Treatment*, 4th ed. New York: Plenum Medical Book, 1994.

Sheeren M: The relationship between relapse and involvement in Alcoholics Anonymous. *J Stud Alcohol* 49:104–106, 1988.

Sisson RW, Mallams JH: The use of systematic encouragement and community access procedures to increase attendance at AA and Alanon meetings. *Am J Drug Alcohol Abuse* 8(3):371–376, 1981.

Vaillant GE: *The Natural History of Alcoholism*. Cambridge, MA: Harvard University Press, 1983.

Walsh DC, Higson RW, et al.: The impact of a physician's warning in recovery after alcoholism treatment. *JAMA* 267(5):663–667, 1992.

CHAPTER 22

TREATMENT EFFICACY

Norman S. Miller, M.D.
University of Illinois at Chicago
Chicago, Illinois

I. EVALUATION OF ABSTINENCE-BASED TREATMENT

A. Survey. In a national survey of alcohol and drug inpatient treatment centers, data were collected in interviews on site with treatment center administrators, program directors, clinical supervisors, marketing personnel, and other employees. The total sample consisted of 125 private, hospital-based, and freestanding centers. Sampling regions were chosen in such a way that the overall sample would approximate a representative composite of treatment programs across the country.

According to most center administrators (97.6%), treatment center ideology was based on a strong belief in the disease concept of alcoholism. Ninety-five percent (95%) of the administrators reported that their treatment programs were based on the "12-step program" of Alcoholics Anonymous. With regard to beliefs about treatment goals, about 90 percent (90.4%) of the administrators reported that a treatment goal other than complete abstinence was not acceptable for any patient in recovery.

B. Evaluation Study of Abstinence-Based Treatment

1. Demographic characteristics. In Table 22.1, demographically, the inpatient and outpatient populations were relatively similar except for age and work status. The outpatients were much more likely to be in their 20s, with fewer cases over 50 or under 20. The fact that slightly fewer outpatients were married and more had never married may be related in part to the younger age of the outpatients. The inpatients also included more minorities, but educational attainment was essentially identical for the two groups.

More of the outpatients were employed full-time. However, this possible indicator of higher vocational functioning did not yield substantially higher incomes as seen in Table 22.2. Over half of all the patients had personal incomes of $20,000 or less, but only about a third had family incomes in that range. For both inpatients and outpatients, 36% reported family incomes over $30,000. Of all items in the CATOR database, personal income was the most likely to be the one that patients refused to answer. Even questions about being sexually abused or arrested have had lower refusal rates. In the case of family incomes, the patient may have been unable or unwilling to indicate the incomes of others in the family.

In summary, inpatients and outpatients were similar in their demographic

Manual of Therapeutics for Addictions, Edited by Norman S. Miller, Mark S. Gold, and David E. Smith.
ISBN 0471-56176-2 © 1997 John Wiley & Sons, Inc.

TABLE **22.1. Demographics**

	Variable	Inpatients ($N = 6508$) %	Outpatients ($N = 1572$) %
Sex	Male	69	73
	Female	31	27
Age	<20	6	3
	20–29	27	35
	30–39	32	35
	40–49	14	19
	≥50	18	8
Ethnicity	White	87	90
	Black	7	6
	Other	6	4
Marital status	Never married	29	34
	Separated or divorced	22	24
	Widowed	3	1
	Married	46	41
Degree	None	15	12
	High school only	56	56
	Vocational or associate	15	17
	College graduate	14	15
Work status	Full-time	62	71
	Part-time	10	9
	Not working by choice	11	6
	Unemployed	17	14

characteristics. Both populations were composed largely of white males, between the ages of 20 and 40, high-school-educated, employed, and from middle-class to lower-middle-class households.

2. Clinical characteristics. In contrast, substantial differences are noted for the clinical characteristics of the two groups. Although a comparable number of patients in both treatment groups were alcoholics, more than twice as many of the inpatients were dependent on prescription drugs, stimulants, and opiates. Cocaine and marijuana dependence were much higher in the inpatient group (Table 22.3).

Of the inpatients, 15% admitted using at least two drugs other than alcohol on a weekly basis, but only 8% of the outpatients admitted such heavy drug use. Further, 45% of the inpatients had used alcohol or other drugs within 24 h of admission as contrasted to 21% of the outpatients; 14% of inpatients and 4% of outpatients have used multiple drugs within a day of admission. In summary, the inpatients were dependent on more drugs and are much more likely to have ingested such drugs just prior to admission.

A global clinical severity index was developed from the number of symptoms for alcohol and other drug dependence, and the patterns of symptoms for alcohol and other drug dependence, the patterns of symptoms and frequency and recency of use. The results of this index are presented in Table 22.4. While over one-third of the outpatients fall in the lowest ranges of this

TABLE 22.2. Personal and Family Incomes for Inpatients and Outpatients

Income range	Inpatients ($N = 6508$)		Outpatients ($N = 1572$)	
	Personal Income (%)	Family Income (%)	Personal Income (%)	Family Income (%)
<$10,000	29	13	28	14
$10,000–$20,000	25	17	28	18
$20,001–$30,000	19	19	20	20
>$30,000	18	36	19	36
Won't say	9	15	5	12

index, only about one in seven inpatients showed such low indications of severity. In contrast, over 40% of the inpatients scored in the higher ranges as compared to only 20% of the outpatients.

Other differentials can also be noted in subsequent discussion of outcome correlates. Inpatients had higher levels of medical care and vocational functioning problems prior to treatment. These indications suggest a greater scope of involvement or later stage of illness for the inpatients. Therefore, when considering the outcome findings to follow, one must remember that these are not comparable populations. The placement issue is not which type of treatment is superior, but rather which patients require the structured control of an

TABLE 22.3. Clinical Characteristics

Variable		Inpatients ($N = 6508$) (%)	Outpatients ($N = 1572$) (%)
Diagnosis of dependence for	Alcohol	82	80
	Prescription medications	12	5
	Marijuana	23	19
	Stimulants	7	3
	Cocaine	19	15
	Opiates	3	1
Number of drugs used at least weekly (alcohol not included):			
	1	26	22
	2	10	6
	3+	5	2
Number of substances, including alcohol, used within 24 hours of admission:			
	1	32	17
	2	9	3
	3+	4	1

TABLE 22.4. Clinical Severity Index

Clinical Severity Score	Inpatients (%)	Outpatients (%)
0–2	15	36
3–4	24	28
5–6	28	18
7–8	19	10
9–12	14	6

inpatient program to begin the recovery process and which patients can initiate that journey with intensive outpatient services.

3. **Continuum of care.** Previous analyses have revealed that the general observed 1–1year abstinence rates tend to be in the 60–65% range. When the projected outcomes for all cases, including noncontacted individuals, were computed, the results tended to fall within the range of 45–60%. The observed abstinence rates for these samples under discussion were slightly over 60%. In addition, more than 25% report at least 6 months of complete abstinence in the year after treatment. Thus, the current data are in conformity with earlier estimates that treatment afforded improvements for the majority of cases (see also Table 22.5).

4. **Medical care.** The evidence clearly indicates that treatment has the ability to offset much, if not all, of its costs. The data on medical care utilization from Table 22.6 are compatible with earlier work.

The inpatient utilization rates were consistently higher than those of outpatients both before and after treatment. Over one-fourth of the inpatients had been admitted to a hospital for medical, psychiatric, or detoxification admissions within the past year as compared to approximately one-fifth of the outpatients. Almost one in four inpatients had a medical admission compared to one in six of the outpatients. Emergency room and outpatient clinic visits

TABLE 22.5. One-Year Abstinence By Continuum of Care and Self-Help Support

Variable		Inpatients (N = 6508)		Outpatients (N = 1572)	
		% Attending	% Abstinent	% Attending	% Abstinent
Months of continuing care attended in year:	0	42	53	34	48
	1–5	32	55	33	61
	6–11	19	71	18	68
	12	8	88	14	89
AA attendance:	Non-attender	54	47	43	49
	Regular attender	46	74	57	80

TABLE 22.6. Medical Care Utilization One Year Before and After Treatment

Variable		Inpatients (N = 6508)		Outpatients (N = 1572)	
		Before (%)	After (%)	Before (%)	After (%)
Hospitalizations	Medical	23	10	16	7
	Psychiatric	5	2	4	1
	Detoxification	16	4	9	2
	Any admission	28	14	21	9
Emergency-room use	Medical	31	22	29	22
	Psychiatric	3	1	3	1
	Any ER use	30	24	29	23

show no significant differentials. The data suggested that a larger portion of the inpatients had serious medical problems. Some of these may have been related to consequences of addiction (Table 22.6).

Nevertheless, both inpatients and outpatients showed significant decrease in posttreatment medical care utilization for expensive hospital services. Admissions for medical conditions were reduced by over 50%. Previous studies have demonstrated that for recovering patients reductions are stable over a 2-year period. Relapsed patients, however, showed a significant rise in hospitalizations in the second year after treatment. This suggested that medical cost offsets are directly proportional to the recovery rate. Clinic visits show little change before and after treatment suggesting no shift of cost from hospital to ambulatory services.

C. Epidemiologic Study of Alcoholics Anonymous. Since 1968 the membership of AA has been surveyed triennially by systematic statistical procedures according to established epidemiologic techniques. Questionnaires were sent to a stratified random sample of 3% of the AA members from each delegate's area in the United States and Canada or to approximately 10,000 members in the 1989 survey. The survey has revealed consistently over the years a high dropout rate (50%) in the first 3 months with a gradual leveling off to a plateau by 1 year.

1. The results of the survey can be summarized accordingly:
   a. Of those sober less than a year, about 41% will remain in the AA Fellowship for another year.
   b. Of those sober less than 5 years, about 83% will remain in the Fellowship another year.
   c. Of those sober 5 years or more, 91% will remain in the Fellowship another year.
2. The attendance at AA has been very stable; the average number of meetings per week is 3. In the 1989 survey, the number of women members increased to almost one-third the total membership. Those members under 30 years old represent more than one-fifth of the total membership and those over 50 years old represent just under one-fourth the total. An increasing number of members are also addicted to other drugs (46%).

D. Controlled Studies

1. **Abstinence-based studies.** Controlled studies also find significant treatment outcomes for abstinence-based programs, particularly when combined with referral to AA. The first randomized clinical trial of abstinence-based treatment showed significant improvement in drinking behavior as compared to a more traditional form of treatment. One hundred forty-one employed alcoholics were randomized to the abstinence-based program ($N = 74$) or to traditional type treatment ($N = 67$). The abstinence-based treatment was significantly more involving, supportive, encouraging to spontaneity, and oriented to personal problems that the traditional-type treatment. The dropout rate was 7.9% for abstinence and 25.9% at traditional, and participation in outpatient treatment was significantly better after the former. Overall, the abstinence-based treatment obtained better results in 1 year abstinence rate than a more traditional-type treatment.

In a second controlled study, a random assignment of 227 workers newly identified as alcoholics was made to one of three treatment regimens: compulsory inpatient treatment, compulsory attendance at AA meetings, and a choice of options. Inpatient backup was provided if needed. On seven measures of drinking and drug use, the hospital group fared best and that assigned to AA the least well; those allowed to choose a program had intermediate results. The estimated costs of inpatient treatment for the AA and choice groups averaged only 10% less than the costs for the hospital group because of their higher rates of additional treatment. The conclusion was that, although less costly than inpatient care, an initial referral to AA or choice of programs involved more risk than compulsory inpatient treatment. The hospitals for inpatient treatment were abstinence-based with eventual referrals to AA at discharge.

II. OTHER FORMS OF TREATMENT

A. **Overview of Studies.** In a general review of forms of treatment other than the abstinence-based model, it was surprising to note the large volume of studies reported in recent decades. A major source of confusion was that a large number of these studies pertained to the treatment of alcohol problems, and it was not always clear whether they refer to alcoholism or an addiction to alcohol.

Included in these studies was a vast array of methods, studies that included small numbers of subjects without replication or follow-up beyond a few weeks or months. The results appeared consistent when taken as a whole, but given the uncertainty of diagnosis, small numbers per treatment method, and short follow-up, it was unclear what, if any, relevance these studies may have to the ultimate prognosis for the alcoholic.

Another serious omission is the lack of inclusion of other drugs in addition to alcohol. The contemporary alcoholic particularly under the age of 30 was often addicted to other drugs that include marijuana, cocaine, opiates, and benzodiazepines. The relevance of a particular treatment in only alcoholism was questionable given the propensity of other drugs to promote relapse to alcohol in alcoholics, and the reverse, the relapse to drugs after the use of alcohol by a drug addict.

What is perhaps not so surprising was that these methods are very rarely used in the United States despite the claims by the investigators of the effectiveness of the treatment methods. Many of these studies were conducted under controlled conditions with random assignment of patients to comparison interventions. However, rarely in these studies was any comparison made to no interventions or treatment at all. Moreover, the sample assignment was biased because of patients' selection of one treatment over another or the refusal to enter the study. Additionally, the generalizability of the results was limited because of small sample sizes, patient selection biases, lack of replication, and the novelty of treatments (little previous history of the method).

Why these methods are not used despite "scientific proof" is complex but can, therefore, be attributed to their lack of specificity to alcohol addiction, relevance to how an alcoholic or addict eventually sustains long-term recovery, and limitations in employing controlled research in psychosocial phenomena. Also, the refusal of many of these investigators to embrace other forms of research such as epidemiologic and evaluation methodology, and religious adherence to randomization, further questions their ability to show the openness and rigor required in studying addictive behavior.

B. Psychotherapy and Counseling. The studies in general do not examine psychotherapy alone but rather in conjunction with another form of treatment such as inpatient or outpatient treatments. The studies do not reveal consistently positive results despite clinical intuition that individual attention to the alcoholic or addict is valuable. The studies show that adjunctive psychotherapy or counseling resulted in no differences or, contrary to the expectations of the investigators, the trends favored the patients who did not receive the additional therapies.

C. Confrontation. While confrontation is considered a mainstay in the treatment of the alcoholic or drug addict, studies that examine the effectiveness of this particular technique are lacking. The few available studies show that confrontation can have a substantial impact on the eventual treatment response, particularly in regard to drinking behavior. One study regarding subjective states of denial did find a positive benefit from confrontation.

D. Aversion Therapy. The principal goal of aversion therapy is to produce an aversive reaction to alcohol by establishing a conditioned response in an individual. The ingestion of alcohol is paired with a negative stimulus in order to produce an automatic negative response when exposed to alcohol alone. The four major types of aversive stimuli are nausea, apnea, electric shock, and imagery.

There is a large body of research into this modality of therapy. Aversive conditioning strategies appear to show effectiveness for a period of a few months. However, the studies report a reduction in consumption rather than total abstinence, so that the success of these approaches is not as great if continuous abstinence is used as a criterion. Another major confounding variable is that many centers utilizing the aversive methods refer their patients to Alcoholics Anonymous following the aversive treatments. To what extent the attendance at AA meetings independently influences the overall results from aversive therapy remains unknown.

E. Controlled Drinking. The controversy surrounding this form of treatment begins as an oxymoron. The studies that examine "problem drinkers" find improvement in the drinking behavior at 1- and 2-year follow-up. Of interest is that the group that does consistently the best in most studies is the group that abstains the most or has the greatest days of abstinence. In general, because among those who receive training for "controlled" drinking the abstainers do the best, actual controlled drinking is associated with a poorer outcome. Further problems in these studies are that the criteria used for the consequences from alcohol consumption lack sensitivity and specificity. The threshold for what is considered problem drinking determines the effectiveness of outcomes. Given the propensity for rationalization and minimization by active alcoholics for the reasons why they drink, in addition to quantity and frequency, their self-reports must be critically examined.

At the same time, the results from studies on controlled drinking involving actual alcoholics (those with alcoholism and alcohol dependence) indicate that alcoholics cannot drink without loss of control. In large studies involving over 1600 alcoholics, less than 1% of the alcoholics were able to return to "normal" drinking without adverse consequences. It is important to bear in mind that the loss of control experienced by the alcoholic may take more than a few weeks or months, and in some cases years, to manifest itself. Vaillant (1983) and others have shown that the natural history of alcoholism is one of chronic remissions and exacerbations to drinking with attendant, adverse consequences.

In a study of controlled drinking, those alcoholics who appeared to receive benefit at 1 and 2 years later showed severe relapse into fatal alcoholism. In this particular study, these alcoholics had significantly greater numbers of abstinent days than did controls, indicating that abstinence rather than controlled drinking led to better outcomes early on.

Most of the other studies are anecdotal, small numbers (<10), and short duration of follow-up (months). A recent study showed (as have previous studies) that those who abstain continue to do the best in terms of adverse consequences from drinking.

F. Operant Methods. The idea that operant conditioning techniques can alter drinking behavior through behavior modification has been studied extensively. Although there are few controlled studies, the abundance of the studies claim effectiveness of this form of treatment for alcoholism. Overall, as expected, perhaps, reinforcement and punishment contingencies can be used to enhance program compliance, but the ultimate impact on drinking behavior depends on the effectiveness of the program itself.

G. Broad-Spectrum Approaches

1. Social skills training. The studies investigating social skills training are based on the assumption that alcoholics are deficient in social skills. The studies investigate social skills training as an independent and adjunctive method of treatment for alcoholism. The studies tend to contain small numbers of highly selected subjects who are followed for brief periods of time. Also confounding variables such as participation in other aftercare programs such as AA are not well controlled.

2. Stress management. These studies are based on the techniques of relaxation management training. As with social skills training, stress management is frequently combined with other forms of treatment such as aversion therapy. The technique of biofeedback relaxation training is often combined with other forms of alcoholism treatment.

3. Community reinforcement approach. This method has promise but has not been extensively studied. The concept is to change or restructure family, social, and vocational activities for the alcoholics in their habitat iin the community. This is akin to "changing people, places, and things" in its fullest meaning. Studies to date tend to examine smaller components such as job finding or disulfiram compliance.

All three methods focus on coping mechanisms as a treatment for alcoholism. The studies show that the methods are effective for those who are deficient in coping skills. While these approaches may be intuitively appealing, studies also show that many of the difficulties in coping result from the drinking that caused the stress, and they subsequently improve postdrinking during abstinence. However, the basic problem of alcoholism or uncontrolled drinking is left unaddressed or untreated so that any gain from this method is subject to ultimate failure.

4. Relapse prevention. The major proponent for this method of treatment has been Marlatt (1973). The principal ingredient is a behavior approach to relapse prevention. The emphasis is on the outside influences of the alcoholic or addict. The goal is to reduce the "triggers" that are viewed as precipitants in the relapse to alcohol and drugs. Abstinence or reduced consumptions are seen as the measures for positive behavioral changes.

The major drawback is the lack of attention to the root causes of addictive behavior in regard to alcohol and drugs, namely, the mind and brain. Ultimately, chemical experience strongly suggests that without changing the "inside," the rearranging of the exterior, specifically, geographic cures, will result in relapse to alcohol or drugs. The variance between the relapse prevention model and the disease approach is clearly seen in these opposing strategies. Increasingly, the disease model would recommend changing "people, places, and things" in addition to making fundamental changes in attitudes and behaviors.

III. LENGTH OF TREATMENT AND SETTING

These studies are basically flawed by the lack of inclusion of the form of treatment employed by the vast majority in the United States, namely, abstinence-based treatment. The results indicate that a greater length of stay does not translate into a better treatment outcome. The level of intensity of treatment does not correlate with success in treatment in some methods. Moreover, in these studies the methods are diverse and the levels of treatment varied, so that comparisons from one treatment setting to another are difficult.

A recent study of multicenters of similar modalities and settings for treatment of addiction found that the greater the number of services, the better the treatment outcome. In this study it appeared that the level of intensity correlated with better outcome when units of service of comparable forms of treatment are examined.

IV. CONCLUSIONS REGARDING TREATMENT EFFICACY FOR ALCOHOL AND DRUG DISORDERS (ADDICTION)

1. Treatment outcome research thus far confirms that there exists a large variety of treatment methods that appear to work in the short run (weeks and months).
2. Treatment outcome research confirms that only one method of treatment appears to be effective and to consistently work in the long run (years to lifetimes), namely, abstinence-based treatment when combined with regular, continuous, and indefinite attendance at Alcoholics Anonymous meetings (Narcotics Anonymous is probably as effective, but sufficient data are not yet available).

REFERENCES

Alden L: Evaluation of a preventative self-management programme for problem drinkers. *Can J Behav Sci* 10:258–263, 1978.

Azrin NH: Improvements in the community-reinforcement approach to alcoholism. *Behav Res Ther* 14:339–348, 1976.

Azrin NH, Sisson RW, Meyers R, Godley M: Alcoholism treatment by disulfiram and community reinforcement therapy. *J Behav Ther Exp Psychiatry* 13:105–112, 1982.

Blake BG: A follow-up of alcoholics treated by behaviour therapy. *Behav Res Ther* 5:89–94, 1967.

Boland FJ, Mellor CS, Revusky S: Chemical aversion treatment of alcoholism: lithium as the aversive agent. *Behav Res Ther* 16:401–409, 1978.

Cannon DS, Baker TB, Wehl CK: Emetic and electric shock alcohol aversion therapy: six- and twelve-month follow-up. *J Consult Clin Psychol* 49:360–368, 1981.

Chaney EF, O'Leary MR, Marlatt GA: Skill training with alcoholics. *J Consult Clin Psychol* 46:1092–1104, 1978.

Chappel J: Long term recovery from alcoholism. In NS Miller (ed): *Psychiatric Clinics of North America*. Philadelphia: Saunders, 1993, pp 177–189.

Edwards G, Guthrie S: A comparison of inpatient and outpatient treatment of alcohol dependence. *Lancet* 1:467–468, 1966.

Edwards G, Guthrie S: A controlled trail of inipatient and outpatient treatment of alcohol dependence. *Lancet* 1:555–559, 1967.

Ends EJ, Page CW: A study of three types of group psychotherapy with hospitalized inebriates. *Quart J Stud Alcohol* 18:263–277, 1957.

Faia C, Shean G: Using videotapes and group discussion in the treatment of male chronic alcoholics. *Hosp Commun Psychiatry* 27:847–851, 1976.

Glover JH, McCue PA: Electrical aversion therapy with alcoholics: a comparative follow-up study. *Br J Psychiatry* 130:279–286, 1977.

Goodwin DW: Alcoholism: who gets better and who does not. In R Rose, J Barrett (eds): *Alcoholism: Origins and Outcome*. New York: Raven Press, 1988, pp 281–1292.

Gorelick DA: Overview of pharmacological treatment approach for alcohol and other drug addictions: intoxication, withdrawal, and relapse prevention. In NS Miller (ed): *Psychiatric Clinics of North America*. Philadelphia: Saunders, 1993, pp 141–156.

Harrison PA, Hoffman NH, Sneed SG: Drug and alcohol treatment outcome. In NS Miller (ed): *Comprehensive Handbook of Drug and Alcohol Addiction*. New York: Marcel Dekker, 1991, pp 1163–1200.

Helzer TE, Robins LN, Taylor JR: The extent of long-term moderate drinking among alcoholics discharged from medical and psychiatric treatment facilities. *N Engl J Med* 312:1679–1682, 1985.

Hoffmann NG, DeHart SS, Fulkerson JA: Medical care utilization as a function of recovery status following chemical addictions treatment. *J Addictive Dis* 12:97–108, 1993.

Hoffmann NG, Harrison PA, Belile CA: Alcoholics Anonymous after treatment: attendance and abstinence. *J Addictions* 218:311–1318, 1986.

Hoffmann NG, Miller NS: Treatment outcomes for abstinence-based programs. *Psychiatric Ann* 22(8):402–408, 1992.

Jackson TR, Smith JW: A comparison of two aversion treatment methods of alcoholism. *J Stud Alcohol* 39:187–191, 1978.

Keso L, Salaspuro M: Inpatient treatment of employed alcoholics: a randomized clinical trial on Hazelden-type and traditional treatment. *Alcohol Clin Exp Res* 14(4):584–589, 1990.

Laundergan JC: *Easy Does It: Alcoholism Treatment Outcomes, Hazelden and the Minnesota Model.* Center City, MN: Hazelden Foundation, 1982.

Levinson T, Sereny G: An experimental evaluation of "insight therapy" for the chronic alcoholic. *Can Psychiatric Assoc J* 14:143–146, 1969.

Lieberman MA, Yalom ID, Miles MB: *Encounter Groups: First Facts.* New York: Basic Books, 1973.

Liskow BI, Goodwin DW: Pharmacological treatment of alcohol intoxication, withdrawal and dependence: a critical review. *J Stud Alcohol* 8:356–370, 1987.

Litten RZ, Allen JP: Pharmacotherapies for alcoholism: promising agents and clinical issues. *Alcohol Clin Exp Res* 15(4):620–633, 1991.

Longabaugh R: Longitudinal outcome studies. In R Rose, J Barrett (eds): *Alcoholism: Origins and Outcome.* New York: Raven Press, 1988, pp 267–280.

Marlatt GA: A comparison of aversive conditioning procedures in the treatment of alcoholism. Paper presented at the annual meeting of the Western Psychological Association, Anaheim, CA, April 1973.

McCance C, McCance PF: Alcoholism in North-East Scotland: its treatment and outcome. *Br J Psychiatry* 115:189–198, 1969.

McClelland T: Unpublished data.

Miller NS: History and review of contemporary addiction treatment. Co-published simultaneously in the *Alcoholism Treatment Quarterly* 12(2):1–22, 1995; and in NS Miller (ed): *Treatment of the Addictions: Applications of Outcome Research for Clinical Management.* New York: Haworth Press, 1995, pp 1–122.

Miller NS, Belkin BM, Gold MS: Cosynchronous use of alcohol and drugs. *NY State J Med* 90(12):596–600, 1990.

Miller NS, Chappel J: History of the disease concept. *Psychiatric Ann* 21(1):1–8, 1991.

Miller WR, Hedrick KA, Taylor CA: Addictive behaviors and life problems before and after behavioral treatment of problem drinkers. *Addictive Behav* 8:403–412, 1983.

Miller WR, Hester RK: The effectiveness of alcoholism treatment methods: what research reveals. In WR Miller, N Heather (eds): *Treating Addictive Behaviors: Processes of Change.* New York: Plenum Press, 1989.

Miller NS, Hoffmann NG: Addictions treatment outcomes. Co-published simultaneously in the *Alcoholism Treatment Quarterly* (Haworth Press) 12(2):41–155, 1995; and in NS Miller (ed): *Treatment of the Addictions: Applications of Outcome Research for Clinical Management.* New York: Haworth Press, 1995, pp 41–55.

Nowinski J, Baker S: *The Twelve-Step Facilitation Handbook.* New York: Lexington Books, 1992.

Oei TPS, Jackson P: Long-term effects of group and individual social skills training with alcoholics. *Addictive Behav* 5:129–136, 1980.

Ogborne AC, Wilmot R: Evaluation of an experimental counseling service for male Skid Row alcoholics. *J Stud Alcohol* 40:129–132, 1979.

Pendery ML, Maltzman TM, West LJ: Controlled drinking by alcoholics? New findings and a re-evaluation of a major affirmative study. *Science* 217:169–175, 1982.

Rosenberg SD: Relaxation training and a differential assessment of alcoholism.

Unpublished doctoral dissertation, California School of Professional Psychology, San Diego, CA (University Microfilms 8004362), 1979.

Schaefer HH, Sobell MB, Mills KC: Some sobering data on the use of self-confrontation with alcoholics. *Behav Ther* 2:28–39, 1971.

Sisson RW: The effect of three relaxation procedures on tension reduction and subsequent drinking of inpatient alcoholics. Unpublished doctoral dissertation, Southern Illinois University at Carbondale, Carbondale, IL (University Microfilms 8122668), 1981.

Smart RG: Employed alcoholics treated voluntarily and under constructive coercion: a follow-up study. *Quart J Stud Alcohol* 35:196–209, 1974.

Sobell MB, Sobell LC: Individualized behavior therapy for alcoholics. *Behav Ther* 4:49–72, 1973.

Tomsovic M: A follow-up study of discharged alcoholics. *Hosp Commun Psychiatry* 21:94–97, 1970.

Vaillant GB: *Natural History of Alcoholism.* Cambridge, MA: Harvard University Press, 1983.

Vogler RE, Lunde SE, Martin PL: Electrical aversion conditioning with chronic alcoholics: follow-up and suggestions for research. *J Consult Clin Psychol* 36:450, 1971.

Walsh DC, Hingson RW, Merrigan DM: A randomized trial of treatment options for alcohol-abusing workers *N Engl J Med* 325(11):775, 1991.

Weddington WW: Use of pharmacologic agents in the treatment of addiction. *Psychiatric Ann* 22(8):425–429, 1992.

Zimberg S: Evaluation of alcoholism treatment in Harlem. *Quart J Stud Alcohol* 35:550–557, 1974.

PART V

SPECIAL TOPICS

CHAPTER 23

A GUIDE TO MANAGED CARE, SOCIAL WELFARE, AND MEDICAL BENEFITS

Kathleen Kim, M.D., M.P.H. and Joseph A. Flaherty, M.D.
Department of Psychiatry
University of Illinois at Chicago
Chicago, Illinois

I. INTRODUCTION

This chapter provides a guide to private and public-sector benefits. Since there are regional differences in percentage of patients insured by managed-care companies, as well as differences in state policies for social welfare and medical benefits, this chapter should be considered a general overview.

II. BACKGROUND

A. 1980s. In the 1980s there was an unprecedented growth in mental health and addiction services. In particular, profit-making inpatient addiction treatment programs expanded dramatically. This increase was fostered by the decline of certificate-of-need legislation as well as the inclusion of addiction treatment benefits into the standard package provided by employers and government insurance. Between 1980 and 1986, admissions to private psychiatric hospitals for treatments of addictive disorders increased by 64% (Wilson, 1993). The increased numbers of admissions reflected both high rates of addictive disorders, and an opportunistic use of addiction treatment benefits.

B. 1990s

1. Managed care. To better manage the quality and cost of addiction treatment, managed care limited the intensity of addiction services, and specifically inpatient acute care. From 1991 to 1993, inpatient treatment for anything but immediate detoxification was phased out by most payers (Flaherty and Kim, in press). Even the standards for admission to detoxification prior to outpatient treatment were evaluated and revised. To compensate for the "loss" of inpatient treatment, standardized outpatient addiction treatment models were quickly developed.

2. Pros and cons. Supporters of managed care claim that by managing services better, more people will have access to medical and mental health / addiction services. They contend that in medical and mental health / addiction

Manual of Therapeutics for Addictions, Edited by Norman S. Miller, Mark S. Gold, and David E. Smith.
ISBN 0471-56176-2 © 1997 John Wiley & Sons, Inc.

services, some services are unnecessary, are provided inefficiently, or have marginal benefits (Boyle and Callahan, 1995). They believe that managed care is better than fee-for-service care because it expands access to care, uses dwindling healthcare resources more responsibly, and reduces the use of unneeded services (Boyle and Callahan, 1995). Skeptics believe that the trend toward managed care will limit patients' choice of providers and treatments, reduce quality of and access to care, and disrupt the provider–patient relationship.

III. MANAGED CARE

A. Definition of Managed Care. Managed mental healthcare has been operationally defined by Goodman et al. (1992) as "any patient care that's not determined solely by the provider." *Managed care* is a generic term that is associated with organizations such as group and staff model health maintenance organizations (HMOs), individual practice associations (IPAs), and preferred-provider organizations (PPOs). (A glossary of terms is in Section III.A.5.) Other organizations are often characterized as managed care because they use the techniques of managed care. These techniques include assuring cost and quality of care, assuming risk, and offering comprehensive services within a budget (Boyle and Callahan, 1995). Some Medicaid programs and state mental health departments are in the process of adopting managed care techniques to control costs and quality of care (see Section III.B.3.).

1. Background. Historically, mental health and addiction services have not had the same public sector or private support as have the medical services. Discrimination and the belief that persons with psychiatric and addictive disorders are responsible for their own problems lead to the concept that these persons are less entitled to benefits. Private and public funding often limit mental health and addiction coverage; they provide fewer benefits than those allowed for medical illnesses of the same range and severity. Traditional insurance plans and HMOs restrict mental health and addiction benefits more stringently than they do medical care benefits, by setting caps on numbers of hospital days or outpatient visits, or by imposing annual or lifetime dollar limits (Boyle and Callahan, 1995).

2. Quality and access to care. Critics claim that managed care could adversely affect the quality of and access to care. Managed care does use less costly providers and treatments, and a lower quantity of services. However, there is no consensus on type, level, or quantity of care. Preliminary research suggests that quality of care in managed mental healthcare is comparable to that in fee-for-service mental healthcare (Boyle and Callahan, 1995). Boyle and Callahan write that "quality of care is often mistakenly connected with the quantity of care" (Boyle and Callahan, 1995). More services do not always mean better outcomes. They suggest a "continuum of obligations"; there is a greater obligation to provide more services if an illness is comparatively severe and if an absence of service might jeopardize the state of a person's mental health. With regard to access to care, Boyle and Callahan suggest a similar continuum, and for the same reason: "not to further disadvantage the already disadvantaged" (Boyle and Callahan, 1995). The persons with severe and persistent addictive disorders would receive more services than those with less severe illnesses.

3. Positive changes. Several positive features have emerged from the trend toward managed care (Flaherty and Kim, in press). The proportion of mental health and addiction treatment spent on patients with major psychiatric and addictive disorders increased as the percentage provided to relatively healthier people decreased. The mental health field has now adopted the concept of differential therapeutics and the practice of making quick and efficient decisions about the type and level of intensity of care when the patient is first seen by a mental health professional. Long waiting lists and complicated intake processes have been eliminated and replaced by telephone triage and efficient placement of patients into treatment programs.

4. Issue of confidentiality. Critics complain that managed care requires health professionals to disclose an increasing amount of confidential information to obtain certification for treatment. There are valid reasons for clinical reviewers to have privileged information: "to protect patients from treatment that might have iatrogenic effects, to be good stewards of limited resources, and to seek treatment that is guided by the patient's condition rather than by arbitrary entitlements" (Boyle and Callahan, 1995). In order to manage care, clinical reviewers have to make decisions based on confidential information about the patient. Boyle and Callahan (1995) contend that the most important concern is how the managed-care company will use and protect this privileged information.

5. Glossary

a. Benefit. This is the amount payable by the benefit plan for services used by the covered person.

b. Capitation model. This is a model of service delivery in which providers receive a standard payment for each covered person regardless of services delivered. According to Swift (1995), in the capitation model, "the economic incentives for the provider are to minimize service utilization, which maximizes income."

c. Consolidated omnibus budget reconciliation act (COBRA). This is a federal law requiring that in specific circumstances when an employee loses insurance coverage (e.g., termination of employment), employers must provide the employee the option to continue their insurance for a specified period (usually 18 months).

d. Copayment. This is a specified dollar amount that the covered person pays for hospital and/or outpatient expenses; the remainder is paid by the insurance company.

e. Deductible. This is the amount of eligible charges the covered person must pay before his/her benefits begin.

f. Eligible charges. These are charges for covered services that are medically necessary and based on reasonable and customary charges.

g. Fee for service. This is a model of service delivery in which providers receive payment based on services delivered. According to Swift (1995), in the fee-for-service model, "the economic incentives for the providers are to maximize service utilization, which maximizes income."

h. Health maintenance organization (HMO). This is a managed-care plan that provides comprehensive benefits on a prepaid basis; there are no insurance claim forms and no waits for reimbursement. HMO members must choose a primary-care physician from physicians participating in the HMO provider network. The primary-care physician coordinates routine medical and mental health/addiction care as well as referrals for specialty care. In addition to having the primary-care physician coordinate all types of treatment, HMO members can only use hospitals affiliated with their HMO.

i. Individual practice associations (IPAs). These constitute a network of physicians who offer services at discounted rates to plan participants.

j. Out-of-pocket maximum. This is the maximum dollar amount that the covered person pays for healthcare expenses in any given year. Once the person pays this amount, the insurance plan begins paying 100% for eligible expenses.

k. Point-of-service plans. These are plans that combine traditional health coverage with HMO-type benefits. At each "point of service" (whenever a participant receives medical care), the participant may choose in-network services or go outside the network for treatment. By going to an in-network physician, the participant will receive a higher level of benefits.

l. Preexisting condition. This is any disease, injury, or condition for which the person was diagnosed, received treatment, or took prescription medication for a specified period (usually 3–6 months) preceding their effective date of coverage under the health plan.

m. Preferred-provider organization (PPO). This is a network of hospitals that offer services at discounted rates to plan participants.

n. Reasonable and customary charge. This is the charge for a medical service that reflects the local geographic area; the training and experience of the provider, and any usual circumstances or medical complications.

B. Future Trends. Although it is always difficult to predict future changes in a rapidly changing environment, a few things do seem reasonably certain.

1. Cost savings. There is no question that managed care for mental health and addiction services is here to stay for the foreseeable future. The impetus is coming from employers who are increasingly being recognized as the payers and from employees as well. Business has achieved actual savings under managed care, and employees selecting managed-care services have saved money by paying for reduced premiums.

2. Consolidations. There will likely be further consolidations of both payers and providers (physicians and hospitals). Small businesses are already banding together to create larger organizations that increase their bargaining power with managed-care companies. Their success is leading to larger organizations. Similarly, providers, eager to regain control of service delivery and to eliminate the "middle man" (i.e., managed-care companies), are forming networks to obtain larger contracts for both primary and specialty care. With increasing capitation, the risk of carrying for large groups of people will be pooled across disciplines (Swift, 1995). For example, if an addictive disorder increases medical or surgical costs, it is more likely to be addressed (Swift, 1995). Providers are either forming their own companies or using managed care companies to provide administrative and technical services such as registration and enrollment, authorization for services, electronic billing, and information systems. Companies that provide these services are referred to as *administrative service organizations* (ASOs).

3. Government insurance. Medicare and Medicaid will follow the managed care route in most states as this appears to be the best way for the government to control, if not actually reduce, costs. However, to make the transition to managed care, the government will have to improve its current information systems and utilization review processes. At the present time, the Medicare and Medicaid information systems are designed for the traditional fee-for-service delivery model, that is, to process claims for services provided. These systems are not designed to assure quality of care or measure treatment outcomes.

4. "Carve out" versus "Carve in." Several key decisions will be made on a state-by-state basis and by individual companies and provider groups and will markedly affect mental health and addiction services. The first decision is whether to "carve out" or "carve in" mental health and addiction services as well as the related question of subcapitation. Most managed-care mental health and addiction services are currently carved out; a separate entity (managed-care company or ASO) receives a capitated contract for these services separate from the general medical services and, in turn, manages their own network of providers who work on either a capitated or reduced fee-for-service basis. It is highly likely that carve-in contracting will grow in market share in the next 2 years. Under a carve-in system, a provider group contracts for all medical and mental health / addiction services. This group develops an internal system for referring to psychiatry, usually going through a "gate-keeper" in the form of primary-care physicians. As more experience is gained with managed-care mental health and addiction services, companies are likely to subcapitate by offering a set amount per member per month for these services, regardless of the number of referrals or amount of treatment provided. In this manner, mental health / addiction provider groups will become mini-managed-care companies and will need to establish excellent information and case management systems in order to provide quality care. It is very likely that carve-in / carve-out variations with numerous reorganizations of both providers, ASOs, and payer groups will continue over the next 5 years. By the year 2000, there will be enough reliable data to determine the best ways to deliver managed mental health and addiction services.

5. Public-sector implications. One major unanswered question will be the role of the existing public services for mental health and addictions in each state. Historically, public services have been provided to the poor, those without private insurance, and those with limited government insurance. Since increasing numbers of Medicaid and Medicare patients will be enrolled in managed-care plans, the demand for public services will decrease. We will witness a number of experiments where states eliminate these programs and put the money into the managed-care system, where the state agencies become the umbrella or ASO for mental health and addiction services, and other models where the state agencies provide the "safety net"; that is, these agencies will deliver services after other sources of payment have been exhausted (e.g., catastrophic care). For example, public services will be provided to indigent patients with chronic addictive disorders who have exhausted their Medicaid coverage.

6. Changes in addiction treatment. Under any of these scenarios, we can predict the types of new addiction treatment offerings that are likely to evolve. In fact, addiction psychiatry is likely to be the first benefactor of the managed-care era because of direct association with reducing the costs of the treatment of other medical (and psychiatric) disorders. Increased patient volume and demand for services will cause these systems to look at less expensive but equally efficacious ways to treat addictions and maintain sobriety. We can expect new innovations that will focus on briefer treatments and closer affiliations with community resources. There are several high-risk and highly treatable groups of patients with addictive disorders, the successful treatment of which will save costs by reducing morbidity and mortality, and decreasing use of other health resources. Pregnant addicts cost the system considerably because both they and their infants have increased lengths of hospital stay and increased short- and long-term healthcare needs. Cocaine addicts are often kept in the hospital an extra day because of withdrawal, and their infants' withdrawal symptoms often prompt physicians to keep them under observation an extra day or two. These infants are also more likely to suffer from birth anomalies (e.g., urinary-tract defects) that further add to the costs. When these problems are added to suspected child neglect in cocaine-addicted mothers, additional services, including rehospitalization, are likely. With the capitation model, the costs for these services are going to come out of the provider groups rather than the government or an insurance company. Therefore, we are going to see increased use of screening instruments for alcohol, nicotine, and other substances early in the pregnancy, and increased efforts to engage these women in addiction programs and aftercare. Similar efforts will be made with candidates for elective surgery, cardiac defects, and a variety of chronic illnesses.

   7. Changes in information to consumers. Finally, managed mental health and addiction services will improve the information that they provide to consumers. These services will disclose physician incentives so that payers and consumers will know whether the plan's physicians are rewarded financially for offering preventive services (e.g., screening exams) as opposed to keeping patients out of the hospital. They will also base financial incentives on quality of care, not reduction of services (Boyle and Callahan, 1995).

C. How to Work with Managed Care. To work with managed care successfully, clinicians must be aware of certain principles:

   1. *Be patient-oriented.* Make sure your services are user-friendly and patient-oriented. Review how a patient accessed treatment with you, the entire process from the patient's initial phone call through to the follow-up. In addition to being important clinically, big business and insurance companies will use patients' satisfaction surveys in selecting addiction treatment programs.

   2. *Remember the "gatekeeper."* The gatekeeper is the primary-care physician, employee assistance program, or triage worker who referred the patient to your addiction services. Since gatekeepers are also our customers, their satisfaction is critical. We have to understand their perspective and rectify whatever problems they have with our services. We need to see what type of patients the gatekeepers have difficulty treating, and we need to educate them about the benefits that can be derived from early interventions and treatment.

   3. *Remember your other "customers."* Although the patient is your most important customer, and the gatekeeper is critical, they are not your only customers. Peers, managed-care companies, employers, and the government are also your customers, and they also have important interests in costs and posttreatment productivity.

   4. *Have the data.* Treatment outcome evaluation research has shown that addiction treatment is successful and cost-effective (Swift, 1995). With accurate data (e.g., demographics, diagnostic, symptom, treatments and outcomes measures), we will be able to predict what works well for a particular type of patient. There-

fore, a good information system is critical to the success of addiction programs. Even though we will all be informed by national data, we need to know how well those models generalize to the patients that we see.

5. *Be part of a strong network.* Join a network with quality providers. Few addiction services can deliver treatment to all types of patients. Each service will be lacking in certain kinds of programming (e.g., residential treatment, specialized programs for women). In part, services will be judged by the quality of affiliated services and the ease of patient flow among these services.

IV. CASE MANAGEMENT

A. Definition. *Case management* is a generic term which describes the coordination and supervision of patient care. In the United States, case management was first used for coordinating treatment of the chronically mentally ill. Various studies have shown that case management reduces hospital recidivism and improves the quality of patients' lives (Solomon, 1992). The goal of case management is to appropriately link patients to services and provide a continuing, therapeutic relationship. Initially, case managers were master's prepared social workers or counselors who were employed by public and private agencies delivering mental health and addiction services. In the past 10 years, bachelor's prepared persons have become case managers. The term *case manager* is also applied to clinician reviewers of managed-care benefits.

1. Addiction treatment. The latest trend in addiction treatment is to develop a number of different tracks, with varying levels of intensity, and to some extent, to employ a menu of services (Goodman et al., 1992). Soon, addiction treatment will not follow standardized protocols with regard to discharge criteria rather than time. Outpatient settings may have programs that vary from 3 to 5 days per week in the intensive phase and may decrease to one day or less in the transition phase. The type of treatment that a patient requires, such as number of inpatient days, or numbers of outpatient hours, will be dependent on that person's clinical condition, previous treatment, concurrent treatment in other psychiatric services, and severity of addiction disorder, as well as careful assessment of support, coping skills, and environmental issues relevant to the possibility of relapse (Flaherty and Kim, in press).

2. Role of case managers. As a consequence, case managers will play a critical role in monitoring the patient's progress through these different levels of care and for a much longer outpatient surveillance (Flaherty and Kim, in press). Much of this case management activity had been initiated by employee assistance programs (EAPs) that took responsibility for the ongoing monitoring of the patient in the workplace after they had completed a treatment program.

3. Training of case managers. Case managers will require a variety of psychological, social, and medical evaluation skills. They will maintain contact with the patient as he/she moves throughout the treatment programs, and they will make community liaison and home visits. The skills of the case manager will have to match the severity of the patients' addictions as well as other characteristics. For example, case managers working with dually diagnosed patients (those with addictive and psychiatric disorders) will need both addictions and mental health training.

4. Working with case managers. Clinicians should work closely with case managers in order to ensure high-quality care of their patients. Remember the following principles:

    a. Maintain high-quality services even though quality is not currently considered a priority when all case managers choose a treatment program. However, over time, quality will become an issue as outcome data become more standardized and available for comparison.

    b. Maintain a collegial relationship with the case managers. Case managers appreciate clinicians who understand that addiction treatment is guided by the patient's condition rather than by a set of entitlements.

    c. Individualize your treatment plans. We have to move away from a standardized, or "one size fits all" model, into treatment plans (and programming) that are tailored for the particular needs of each patient.

V. SOCIAL WELFARE AND MEDICAL BENEFITS

There are a variety of social welfare and medical benefits in the United States. Few clinicians know much about these benefits or the eligibility criteria for them. The 1995–1996 Congress will likely change some of these benefits and eligibility criteria. This section summarizes a 1993 paper by Pike Cain (1993).

A. Social Welfare Benefits

1. Social security. This is a federal insurance program that provides monthly retirement checks to the elderly, to blind and disabled persons, and to the widowed spouse or children of the deceased person who was covered by the Social Security plan. To qualify for Social Security, a person must have worked and paid into the program. The amount of the retirement benefit is determined by a formula that takes into account the individual's age, number of years worked in covered employment, and amount paid into the program.

2. Social security disability insurance (SSDI). This term is often confused with Supplemental Security Income (SSI). Both programs are administered by the Social Security Administration and provide monthly checks to disabled persons unable to work. Eligibility for SSDI is based solely on disability, and eligibility for SSI on both disability and financial need.

Anyone who would otherwise qualify for Social Security and has sufficient work credits (years of covered employment) may be eligible for SSDI if a severe physical or mental disability prevents that person from working. The disability should last at least 12 months. Adults whose illness began before adulthood may be eligible for SSDI on the basis of their parent's work history and vestment in Social Security. SSDI has no "means" test; that is, there is no eligibility requirement based on the person's financial status. After receiving SSDI for 2 years, the person is also eligible for Medicare health benefits. Applications for SSDI are made at the local Social Security office.

3. Supplemental security income (SSI). This is a financial assistance program available to the elderly, blind, and physically or mentally disabled persons. Eligibility for SSI is based on financial need. Anyone receiving SSI is automatically eligible for Medicaid health insurance. In addition, people with SSI are eligible for fuel assistance, property tax abatement, food stamps, and surplus food programs. Applications for SSI are made at the local Social Security office. A person who meets requirements can receive both SSDI and SSI monthly checks, and can be covered by Medicare and Medicaid.

4. Aid to families with dependent children (AFDC). This is a federally authorized, state-administered income support program. It was started in 1935 as part of the Social Security Act. Eligibility is based on financial need and the absence of one or both parents from the home. In addition to monthly income, benefits include Medicaid health insurance and in some states, work-training programs. Applications for AFDC are made at the local welfare office.

5. Unemployment compensation insurance. This is a federal–state program that provides financial benefits to those who lose their jobs "through no fault of their own" (Pike Cain, 1993). Eligibility rests on the number of hours that an applicant was employed during the previous year. The amount of the unemployment insurance benefit depends on the employee's earning during the covered time period. Application for unemployment benefits is filed with the local employment office.

B. Medical Benefits

1. Medicare. This is a federal health insurance program that is administered by the Social Security Administration. To receive Medicare, a person must have earned sufficient work credits in employment covered by Social Security and must be either 65 or older or have been on SSDI for at least 2 years. Medicare Part A covers hospitalization. Medicare Part B, for which an individual pays a monthly premium, covers physicians' fees and other health-care costs. Since Medicare does not pay for the total costs of medical bills or medications, most Medicare recipients supplement the program with other insurance. Medicare has no means test. Applications for Medicare are made at the local Social Security office.

2. Medicaid. This is a federally reimbursed, state program that provides health insurance to the poor. Although state programs vary, individuals receiving AFDC or SSI automatically receive Medicaid; those receiving general welfare assistance may receive more restrictive Medicaid benefits. Depending on the state, one may receive a Medicaid card when one is declared eligible for AFDC or SSI, or when applications for Medicaid are made at the local welfare office. A person with a low income receiving SSI or AFDC who has earned enough work credits under Social Security can receive both Medicaid and Medicare.

3. Emergency health benefits. In most states, persons who are homicidal, suicidal, or gravely disabled because of serious mental illness can receive acute inpatient care through the state department of mental health. Also in most states, persons with severe addictive disorders can receive detoxification through the state department of alcohol and drug addiction. Many states also fund outpatient addiction treatment programs for public-sector patients. For more information, contact your state department of alcohol and drug addiction.

C. Other Services

1. Food programs. The federal food stamp program, which is administered by state welfare agencies, is designed to provide adequate nutrition for low-income households. Applications for food stamps are made at the local welfare office. The Women, Infants, and Children (WIC) Supplemental Food program is a federal program designed to improve the health status of pregnant women and infants. It provides supplemental food, vitamins, counseling, and referrals for healthcare. Each state sets its own income eligibility criteria.

2. Rehabilitative services. Each state has a vocational rehabilitation agency; eligibility for services is set by the federal government but interpreted by states. Services include evaluations, counseling, and training for persons with physical or mental disabilities that are significant obstacles to employment. Means tests are not as stringent as for welfare programs.

REFERENCES

Boyle PJ, Callahan D: Managed care in mental health: the ethical issues. *Health Affairs* 14:7–22, 1995.

Flaherty J, Kim K: Addiction treatment in the managed care era. In NS Miller (ed): *Addiction Psychiatry: Comprehensive Textbook.* Philadelphia: Saunders, in press.

Goodman M, Brow J, Deitz P: *Managing Managed Care,* Washington, DC: APA Press, 1992.

Pike Cain, L: Obtaining social welfare benefits for persons with serious mental illness. *Hosp Commun Psychiatry* 44:977–980, 1993.

Solomon P: The efficacy of case management services for severely mentally disabled clients. *Commun Ment Health J* 28:163–180, 1992.

Swift RM: Health care economics for alcohol treatment clinicians. Recent advances in the treatment of alcoholism (syllabus pp 1–6). Paper presented at Rush-Presbyterian-St. Luke's Medical Center, June 1995.

Wilson CV: Substance abuse and managed-care. *New Directions Ment Health Serv* 59:99–105, 1993.

CHAPTER 24

FORENSIC AND ETHICAL ISSUES

Amin N. Daghestani, M.D.
Department of Psychiatry
Loyola University Medical Center
Maywood, Illinois

Substance abuse stands as one condition that probably leads to more behavioral problems than any other psychiatric disorder. It is no wonder that social attitudes toward alcohol and drug use have been ambivalent, and usually polarized between permissiveness on one hand and prohibition on the other. The "moral theory" in the etiology of alcoholism has always had its supporters at various times. The relationship between the loss of individual responsibility and addiction has been the center of many forensic cases and medical–legal arguments. The extent of legal and ethical questions relating to drug abuse treatment has expanded over the years. This chapter outlines those main forensic and ethical issues usually encountered by substance abuse treatment professionals or programs working in the field of addictions (Table 24.1).

I. PROFESSION-RELATED ISSUES

These are generally issues that are encountered in the course of medical practice. They may relate to both the diagnostic or treatment process, or may arise as a result of an impairment of the practitioner personally, as in the case of the addicted physician.

A. Confidentiality

1. Rules against disclosure of information. Federal laws protecting the confidentiality of alcohol and drug abuse patients were first established by the Congress in 1975, and later amended in 1987 under the "Confidentiality of Alcohol and Drug Abuse Patients Records." This law states that the disclosure of records or other information concerning any patient in a federally assisted alcohol or drug-abuse program is prohibited. Any state provision that requires a disclosure that is prohibited by this federal rule from a federally assisted alcohol or drug-abuse program is invalid. A psychiatrist working in these facilities who releases information without authorization may be subjected to a lawsuit or penalties. The main purpose of confidentiality is to encourage addicted patients to seek treatment while their privacy is assured. If patient confidentiality is not maintained, an invasion of privacy is considered.

Manual of Therapeutics for Addictions, Edited by Norman S. Miller, Mark S. Gold, and David E. Smith.
ISBN 0471-56176-2 © 1997 John Wiley & Sons, Inc.

TABLE 24.1. Forensic and Ethical Issues in Substance Abuse

Profession-Related Issues	Assessment Issues	Treatment Issues	Research Issues
Confidentiality	High-risk patients	Patient intervention	Consent
Commitment	Urine toxicology	Prescribing practices	Controlled drinking
Documentation	Child abuse and reporting duties	Countertransference	
Addicted physicians		Pregnancy and breast feeding	
		Managed care	
		Liver transplant	

2. Exceptions to confidentiality rules. Exceptions are bound by federal and state laws, the latter of which vary from state to state. All information released must be accompanied by a statement describing the confidential nature of the information and prohibiting redisclosure of the information. Disclosure of information may be made under the following circumstances:

    a. With patient consent (all consent forms should contain the information listed in Table 24.2).

    b. Disclosure to other staff of the treatment program.

    c. Disclosure that does not reveal the identity of the person or identify that this person is or was an alcohol or drug-abuse patient.

    d. Communications relating to medical emergencies.

    e. Communication that is authorized by a valid court order.

    f. Disclosures that concern a crime on the premises of a treatment program or against program personnel.

    g. General disclosures for the purpose of research or as part of an audit or examination of the program.

    h. Disclosures that involve reporting of child abuse or neglect.

    i. Communications made pursuant to a qualified service organization agreement. An example is when a program enters into a written agreement with an outside agency to perform services such as urine screens, accounting, or legal or vocational counseling as long as those organizations agree to comply with the confidentiality regulations.

TABLE 24.2. Patient Consent

Conditions of the consent

  Written

  Informed

  Intentional

  Voluntary

Contents of the consent

  The name of the program making the disclosure

  The name of the program, individual, or agency receiving the information

The name of the patient subject to disclosure

  The need for or the purpose of the disclosure

  How much and what kind of information is to be released; only information relevant to the purpose should be released

  A statement that patient may revoke the consent at any time; revocation of consent should be submitted in writing

  The date on which the consent expires if not previously revoked

  Signature of patient (for patients under 18, it is up to state regulations)

  The date the consent is signed

3. Confidentiality of a deceased patient. Information may be released by the executor or other representatives who are appointed under state laws.

4. Disclosures to third-party payers. This could be done after a valid patient consent is made. The disclosure should be limited to only that minimum amount of information needed to accomplish the disclosure's purpose.

5. Disclosures to employers. This could be done after a valid consent is signed. Despite this, the program should exercise judgment and limit information to what is necessary or to only verify treatment status.

6. Criminal justice system referrals. An individual whose probation or parole is conditioned on treatment may not revoke his or her consent. This is the only situation in which the regulations permit a program to require irrevocable consent.

7. Confidentiality in group and family therapy
   a. Information obtained from the family about the patient are included under privileged information.
   b. Explain to group therapy members about confidentiality rules.

8. Confidentiality and new technology
   a. *Examples:* using voice mail, E-mail (electronic mail), computerized records, or fax machines.
   b. Don't leave detailed messages; rather, leave only name, telephone number, and time you may be reached.

9. Confidentiality and debt collections
   a. Try to communicate with patients about debts first.
   b. In the case of a legal suit for debt collection, reveal only information needed for the collection; for instance, for itemized bills, write only "office visit."
   c. Suits for debt collection often result in a counterclaim for malpractice.

10. Confidentiality and patient criminal activities. It is advisable to seek a legal opinion in circumstances involving patient criminal activities, when the patient reports past crimes, or in regard to search and arrest warrants.

11. Duty to warn. Psychiatrists must take reasonable steps to protect an intended victim of a threat made by a patient. Sometimes the physician is able to make a report about such threats without revealing patient-identifying information.

12. Confidentiality and requests for subpoenas. Subpoenas should be distinguished from the type of court order exempted by federal law. The subpoena compels the psychiatrist only to appear and it should not be ignored. The program may not release information even if the subpoena is signed by a judge. It has the right to object to the subpoena and not to provide the records.

B. Commitment. Most drug-abuse treatment programs don't accept patients who require commitment. Patients who are dangerous to self or others are usually admitted to general closed psychiatric units. The term of the commitment varies from 72 h in California to 15 days in New York. The basis for emergency civil commitment is
   1. That the patient is mentally ill.
   2. That the patient presents a rather imminent danger to self or

others. Courts may issue a warrant for taking to the hospital an individual who meets the criteria for emergency hospitalization. To avoid liability for wrongful commitment, the psychiatrist should ensure that a decision to commit has been made only after an adequate examination of the patient has been done. Requests coming from third parties to commit a patient should be approached in a circumspect manner.

C. Documentation

Keeping detailed records of patients is an important part of their ongoing assessment and care. Medical record documentation is also considered "a legal document" that could be subpoenaed or used in court in malpractice suits. Records should be accurate, legible, and timely. Some use word processors or phone dictations for documenting reports or progress notes.

1. What records should contain. Records should reflect the interaction each time the patient was seen, for what purpose, and for how long. Instructions given over the phones should also be recorded. Table 24.3 outlines what records should contain.

2. How long the record should be kept. The length of time records need to be kept varies, and it should not be for less than 6 years for the adult patient. The statute of limitations varies for different situations, for example

    a. For malpractice: 2–3 years.

    b. For breach of contract: 6 years from the date the last treatment was provided.

    c. For minors: records should be kept until the patient reaches the age of 21 years.

    d. For ethical cases: the timeframe could be indefinite.

3. Altering records. Records should not be altered. Altering records could be very damaging to the defense of a malpractice suit.

4. Format of the records. The accuracy and manner in which the records are kept indicate the thoroughness and attentiveness of the patient. Each entry

TABLE 24.3. What Records Should Contain

How the patient was referred and by who.

History, psychiatric, and physical examination.

Laboratory workup, including urine toxicology screen.

Progress notes to reflect changes in the patient's mental or physical condition—what warnings were given, what alterations were considered.

Medications: names, doses, frequency, amount prescribed; name and telephone number of the pharmacy if the prescription was made over the phone.

All consents and authorization forms.

Communication and correspondence concerning the care of the patient.

Personal impression or speculation of the psychiatrist can be kept in a separate record.

should be dated and the time noted. It should also be signed, especially if multiple providers use the same records. It is suggested that after each patient visit, the physician should record his/her subjective and objective data and assessment and treatment plan for the patient.

5. Who can access the record. Under various circumstances and usually with the patient's written consent, the following can access a patient's record:

  a. Under some state laws, patients have the right to see their records.
  b. Utilization review at a managed-care company.
  c. Personal representative of a deceased patient.
  d. Parents of a minor child.
  e. A governmental agency for security clearance.
  f. Plaintiff's attorney in a malpractice action.

D. Addicted Physician. The problem of the addicted physician is increasingly recognized by the profession and has been more visibly highlighted by the media.

1. Impact. Substance abuse by the physician will likely impair his/her clinical judgment. This obviously could have detrimental effects on the care of patients.

2. Reporting of an impaired colleague. It is often the colleague of an impaired physician who is first to suspect a drug abuse problem by the physician. The physician who suspects a colleague of having a practice impairment has an ethical responsibility to peers and to the general community to report any suspected impairment. Often, the physician assistance committee in the hospital or the medical society where the physician is practicing is contacted. The licensing agencies have a state-mandated power to protect the public from potentially harmful practitioners.

3. Physician assistance committees. Most states have established special physician assistance committees, usually in connection with their medical societies. With proper assessment, empathic intervention, careful monitoring, and diligent case management, most addicted physicians maintain an excellent rate of recovery and are able to return to a fully productive and rewarding medical practice.

II. ASSESSMENT ISSUES

These are issues that are encountered during the assessment or diagnostic phase. They include dealing with high-risk patients and issues surrounding urine toxicology and child abuse.

A. High-Risk Patients

1. The suicidal patient. Suicide and suicidal attempts account for a large percentage of all psychiatric malpractice and litigation. It is generally agreed on that the prediction of dangerousness is highly uncertain. The psychiatrist, nevertheless, has two responsibilities in relation to the potentially suicidal patient: duty to assess and duty to protect. In all instances the physician should keep adequate and thorough medical records.

  a. Duty to assess. The psychiatrist should perform a comprehensive evaluation of patients who carry suicidal potentials. This mainly implies the assessment of the dynamic interplay of various risk factors that increase the likelihood for suicidal behavior in patients. Failure to conduct a thorough examination of the patient could be viewed as breach of duty. Records of past treatment should be obtained. Important risk factors to be assessed should include history of substance abuse, past suicidal attempts, lack of social support, and the presence of major recent losses.

b. Duty to protect. If a patient is deemed to be suicidal or potentially suicidal, adequate precautions should be instituted immediately. In most situations admission to a closed psychiatric unit for suicidal precautions should be considered. Communication from other staff such as nurses and family members should be responded to and not ignored. Plans for adequate discharge follow-up should be made. Patients should not be prescribed large amounts of medications that could be used in attempting suicide.

2. The homicidal patient. Potentials for violence and danger to others should be assessed in every substance-abusing patient.

a. Duty to assess. Poor impulse control coupled with the disinhibiting pharmacologic effects abused substances will have on the brain make the assessment of dangerousness in addicted patients extremely important. History of violence or legal problems in the past should be elicited.

b. Duty to warn and protect. Psychiatrists have responsibility to protect the intended victims of a patient who is making violent or homicidal threats. The landmark case of *Tarasoff v. Regents of the University of California* has been used in other states for similar cases. It permits the victims of a violent patient to recover damages against the patient's psychiatrist. It has been argued that this duty to protect extends to a duty to also protect the society. Recently, other potential Tarasoff-type duties have been identified, such as in the context of AIDS. One limitation for Tarasoff is that when the victim is clearly aware of the potential danger against him / herself. In dealing with potentially violent patients, issues of confidentiality and adequate recordkeeping should not be ignored. Signs for potential violence should be assessed. Appropriate warning to potential victims and clear discharge plans for violent patients should be made.

3. The comorbid patient. Patients who present with a history of both mental illness and substance abuse are considered another high-risk group of complex pathology and behavioral problems. Often the dually diagnosed patient presents with more frequent rate of hospitalizations, polydrug addiction, more associated psychopathology, and positive family history and genetic loading. With fewer available psychosocial resources, the dually diagnosed patient often experiences more legal trouble than the average substance abuse patient would.

B. Urine Toxicology. Requiring urine testing for employment could be perceived as a coercive measure or intrusion on individual privacy or freedom. Other potentially legal issues related to urine testing center around issues of public safety and discrimination against special groups. The question is to what extent should the result of urine screen determine the job or legal status of an individual. Urine specimens in forensic cases should be collected utilizing the "chain of custody" procedure to ensure accurate collection and better handling of the specimen. In addition to screening tests, the results should be confirmed by more specific and sensitive methods such as gas chromatography–mass spectrometry (GC / MS).

C. Child Abuse and Reporting Duties. History of child abuse and neglect is reported by or observed in some substance-abusing parents. The rationale for reporting child abuse to state authorities is the protection of minors. Reporters are granted immunity from civil liability for reports made in good faith. Physicians have mandatory reporting duties in every state. The definition of *child abuse* extends to physical, emotional, and sexual abuse of children. The source of abuse for the purpose of definition must be the parent or the legal guardian of the child. Abuse of children by others is handled by ordinary law-enforcement channels. The physician encountering a potential child-abuse situation should follow a two-step process of issues to be addressed: (1) whether the alleged conduct constitutes child abuse and (2) whether there is a duty to report.

In addition to child abuse, some states have two other reporting duties by physicians:

1. *Reporting Disorders that Impair Driving.* Many addicted patients report history of DUI problems and convictions. Six states require the reporting of conditions that are likely to impair the ability to control and safely operate a motor vehicle such as episodes of loss of attention or awareness "blackouts," chronic alcoholism, or drug abuse.

2. *Reporting Elderly Abuse.* Some states require the reporting of elderly abuse or the abuse of a dependent adult.

III. TREATMENT ISSUES

A. Patient Intervention. Confrontation of addicts in denial has been helpful in bringing many patients to treatment. A more organized form of confrontation is called "intervention," where employers or family members facilitate the involvement of patients in therapy. Some patients have, nevertheless, perceived this as coercion, or even as impingement on their right of privacy. Of interest is that some legally mandated addiction therapy or treatments that followed interventions have a better outcome than voluntary "control" groups where no such positive coercive measures were taken.

B. Prescribing Practices. Using manipulative techniques some addicts have been able to go "doctor shopping." Unfortunately, some, although few, of these physicians do prescribe addictive drugs "for profit" and are subject to prosecution by law enforcement authorities. Physicians should receive a particular education in the field of substance abuse starting in medical school. Enabling behavior by healthcare providers needs to be understood as a destructive behavior to treating substance abuse patients.

C. HIV Infection. Intravenous drug abusers are vulnerable to contracting HIV infections. Following are some legally related issues drug addicts use as a means for obtaining money to purchase drugs such as cocaine and crack:

1. *Prostitution.* This has been used by some drug addicts as a means for obtaining money to purchase drugs such as cocaine and crack.

2. *HIV Testing.* Testing for HIV should not be performed on patients without securing the patient's informed consent specific for HIV testing.

3. *HIV and Duty to Warn.* HIV patients often want to prevent information about their condition from reaching others. Some states have adopted laws protecting HIV and AIDS information. At the same time there is a duty to warn third parties who might be

involved with the patient. Courts in many states have held that healthcare providers have a duty to warn their parties of potentially dangerous behavior of persons under their care. These statutes sometimes forbid disclosure of the infected person's identity, while allowing the at-risk third party to be informed of any potential exposure or risk. Programs should consult the attorney for the state agency that funds them about their legal obligations.

D. Countertransference. Psychotherapy with addicted patients could prove to be the one area that causes the most concern in treatment. Countertransference phenomena in treating addicted patients could create a variety of situations that could pose serious ethical or legal problems as outlined in Table 24.4.

E. Addiction, Pregnancy, and Breast Feeding. Psychoactive substances cross the placental barrier as well as the mammary glands in breast feeding, making the fetus or the infant a passive, innocent, and unconsenting recipient of drugs used by the mother. Some states have attempted to prosecute addicted mothers in an attempt to protect the infant or the unborn. For the long run, public educational programs and availability of treatment facilities should prove to be more beneficial than punitive measures.

F. Managed Care. The concept of managed care has assumed increased importance in healthcare economics. Addictionologists have to deal with various groups such as local utilization review, HMOs (health maintenance organizations), PPOs (preferred-provider organizations), and IPAs (independent practice associations). When dealing with these groups, the physician should obtain patient consent to provide information to the managed-care company. Only pertinent information is to be released. The physicians should appeal denial decisions by the company if they feel that the patient is in need of a

TABLE 24.4. Countertransference in Treating Addicted Patients

Countertransference Reactions	Therapeutic, Ethical, or Legal Questions
Identification with patients	Inability to set therapeutic limits
Denial of drug abuse	Misdiagnosis
Rationalization of drug abuse	The goal of abstinence not established
Undertreatment	Severe withdrawal symptoms not anticipated
Overtreatment	Perpetuating the cycle of drug abuse
Withholding reaction	Empathic failure
Rejection of patients	Treatment dropout
Enabling behavior	Therapeutic boundaries not established
Acting out	Therapeutic boundaries not established
Sexualization	Destruction of the trusting physician–patient relationship

particular treatment in question. The physicians should avoid abandonment of the patient.

G. Liver Transplantation. The scarcity of livers available for transplants in patients with liver failure calls for a system of priority allocation. In the case of alcoholics, the question of distributing scarce resources could pose a true ethical dilemma. It would be helpful in these situations for physicians to consult with the treatment team and ethical specialists after a thorough assessment of the patient's prognosis is made.

IV. RESEARCH ISSUES

A. Consent by Subjects. All patients participating in research projects should sign an informed consent voluntarily. They should be informed that their receiving of treatment is not contingent on their participation in research.

B. Controlled Drinking. Ethical questions concerning research that involve drinking procedures have been raised. Such research may give the participating patients the false assumption that they could drink in a controlled "social" environment, thus ignoring the basic tenets of addiction pathology and its treatment principles.

SELECTED READINGS

American Medical Association: *Council on Ethical and Judicial Affairs, American Medical Association Code of Medical Ethics: Current Opinions with Annotations.* American Medical Association, 1992.

American Psychiatric Association: *The Principles of Medical Ethics with Annotations Especially Applicable to Psychiatry.* Washington, DC: American Psychiatric Association, 1989.

Bissel L, Royce J: *Ethics for Addiction Professionals.* Center City, MN: Hazeldon, 1987.

Brooks MK: Ethical and legal aspects of confidentiality. In JH Lowinson, P Ruiz, RB Millman, JG Langrad (eds): *Substance Abuse, a Comprehensive Textbook,* 2nd ed. Baltimore: Williams & Wilkins, 1992.

Brown-Miller A: Ethical dilemmas in the drug free workplace. *Addiction Recovery* 12(4):12–14, 1992.

Chankin W, Walker NA, Paone D: Drug using families and child protection: results of a study and implications for change. *Univ Pittsburgh Law Rev* 54(1):295–324, 1993.

Cohen C, Benjamin M: Alcoholics and liver transplantation: the ethics and social impcat committee of the transplant and health policy center. *JAMA* 265(10):1299–1301, 1991.

Cohen S: Drugs for pleasure: ethical issues. *Drug Abuse Alcohol Newsl* (Vista Hill Foundation) VIII(7), September 1979.

Fingarette H: Alcoholism: can honest mistakes about one's capacity for self-control be an excuse? *Internatl J Law Psychiatry* 13(102):77–93, 1990.

Imhof JE: Countertransference issues in alcoholism and drug addiction. *Psychiatric Ann* 21(5):292–306, 1991.

Landwirth J: Fetal abuse and neglect: an emerging controversy. *Pediatrics* 79:508–514, 1987.

Loewy EH: Drunks, livers, and values. Should social value judgments enter into liver transplant decisions? *J Clin Gastroenterol* 9(4):436–441, 1987.

Lundberg GD: Mandatory unindicated urine drug screening: still chemical McCarthyism. *JAMA* (21):3003–3005, 1986.

Macbeth JE, Wheller AM(N), Sitber JW, Onek JN: *Legal and Risk Management Issues in the Practice of Psychiatry*. Washington, DC: Psychiatrists Group (PPG), 1994.

Nadelson CC: Ethics, empathy, and gender in health care. *Am J Psychiatry* 150:1309–1314, 1993.

Oberman M: Sex, drugs and pregnant addicts: ethical and legal critiques of societal responses to pregnant addicts. *J Clin Ethics* 1(2):145–152, 1990.

Popivits RM: Confidentiality vs. the courts: your legal obligations. *Addiction Recovery* 12(7,9–10), November–December 1992.

Willms J, Schneiderman H: The ethics of impaired physicians. In DH Brock, RM Ratzan (eds): *Literature and Bioethics*. Baltimore: Johns Hopkins University Press, 1988, pp 123–131.

INDEX